THE EARL OF CLARENDON

George. 4th Earl of Clarendon.
after a painting by Sir Francis Grant.

LONDON: EDWARD ARNOLD

THE LIFE AND LETTERS OF
GEORGE WILLIAM FREDERICK
FOURTH EARL OF CLARENDON

K.G., G.C.B.

BY

THE RIGHT HON. SIR HERBERT MAXWELL

BART., F.R.S., D.C.L., LL.D.

IN TWO VOLUMES

VOLUME II

Stat sua cuique dies, breve et irrevocabile tempus
Omnibus est vitae.

WITH PORTRAITS

LONDON
EDWARD ARNOLD
1913

CONTENTS OF VOL. II

CHAPTER XIII. THE FOREIGN OFFICE

CHAPTER XIV. WAR WITH RUSSIA

CHAPTER XV. THE CRIMEAN WAR

CHAPTER XVI. THE PARIS CONFERENCE

CHAPTER XVII. ENGLAND DURING THE MUTINY

CHAPTER XVIII. OUT OF OFFICE

CONTENTS

CHAPTER XIX. GLADSTONE'S BUDGET

CHAPTER XX. THE MISSION TO BERLIN

CHAPTER XXI. THE DUCHY OF LANCASTER

CHAPTER XXII. THE FOREIGN OFFICE ONCE MORE

CHAPTER XXIII. FOREIGN TRAVEL

CHAPTER XXIV. LAST DAYS

LIST OF PLATES IN VOL. II

THE EARL OF CLARENDON

CHAPTER XIII

THE FOREIGN OFFICE

'Government is a contrivance of human wisdom to provide
for human wants.'   BURKE.

IN each of the successive stages of Lord Clarendon's public
service it was his lot to take over the control of the affairs
committed to him when they were on the brink of
convulsion.   As in 1833, when he arrived at Madrid
simultaneously with the outbreak of the Carlist war—as
in 1847, when he assumed the government of Ireland and
had to grapple with famine and rebellion—so now in 1853
he took the seals of the Foreign Office at the moment when
the storm in the Orient, so long pent up, was rising at last
to wreck the peace of Western nations.   So long pent up !
to trace the brewing of that storm one has to go
back three hundred years—to the treaty whereby Suleymân
the Great committed the Holy Places in Jerusalem and
Bethlehem to the care of Latin monks under protection
of the French crown, then worn by François I.   The Greek
Church, indignantly resenting this, from time to time
obtained firmans from the Porte conflicting with the rights
of the Church of Rome.   The Latin monks were expelled
in 1757 and the Greeks installed as custodians by imperial
ordinance ; but the Latins found their way back, and
there ensued a joint occupation of a most uneasy character.
In 1850 the French government demanded of the Porte
that, in virtue of Sultan Suleymân's grant, the Latin
monks should keep the key of the main door of the Church
of Bethlehem and one of the two keys of the Sacred Manger,

besides placing in the Sanctuary of the Nativity a silver star embossed with the arms of France. To these conditions the Porte promised compliance in a note to the French Minister at Constantinople dated 9th February 1853. By a later note these terms were modified, being considered unduly favourable to the Latins, and keys were given to the Greek monks also. The French government accepted the modified terms, and such an arrangement might have been expected to satisfy nineteenth-century statesmen.

The Emperor of Russia, Sovereign of the Greek Christians, and charged under the treaty of Kainardji (1774) with the duty of maintaining their rights and defending their interests, took a reasonable course. Believing that the Ottoman Empire was on the point of falling to pieces, he made frank overtures to Sir Hamilton Seymour, British Ambassador at St. Petersburg, proposing that the Danubian principalities should be incorporated in the Russian Empire, Egypt and Crete in the British. This proposal was not entertained, and matters passed into the hands of diplomats. During Lord John Russell's brief sojourn at the Foreign Office he took a step which had a very important influence upon subsequent events : he sent Lord Stratford de Redcliffe as ambassador to Constantinople.

Lord Aberdeen to Lord John Russell.

15th February 1853.—I think it will be necessary to be very careful in preparing instructions for Lord Stratford, if, as I presume, we must consider his memorandum as giving an outline of what he would desire. ' The assurances of prompt and effective aid on the approach of danger ' given by us to the Porte would in all probability produce war. . . . It may be necessary to give them moral support and to endeavour to prolong their existence ; but we ought to regard as the greatest misfortune any engagement which compelled us to take up arms for the Turks. . . . Above all, we ought not to trust the disposal of the Mediterranean fleet (which is peace or war) to the discretion of any man.

Now Lord Stratford shared Lord Palmerston's distrust (to use no stronger expression) of Russia's emperor and Russian diplomacy. He had, besides, a personal *grief* against Nicholas, who in 1833 had positively refused to receive him as ambassador at St. Petersburg, although he had been gazetted as such. When, therefore, he arrived at Constantinople in April and found Prince Menschikoff established there with a large military suite, his suspicions about Russian designs were confirmed, and he prepared to resist them. Russian troops were already massed upon the Moldavian frontier, and on 8th March, a month before Stratford's arrival, Colonel Rose,[1] acting as *chargé d'affaires*, applied to Admiral Dundas, commanding the Mediterranean fleet, to send a squadron to Besika Bay for the protection of Constantinople. Dundas had the sense not to move without instructions from home ; late on the night of 19th March Sir James Graham rang up the household in Grosvenor Crescent, bringing to Clarendon Dundas's despatch. Next morning a meeting was held at the Admiralty to settle what was to be done—Aberdeen, Russell, Graham and Clarendon. At Clarendon's suggestion Palmerston also was invited ; 'never was so good a hit,' said Graham afterwards ; for it disarmed Palmerston, who, had he been left out, would have been sure to work mischief.

These five ministers thus assembled had, for the first time, to face the probability of war with Russia. Lord John Russell, Palmerston, and, with somewhat less decision, Graham, were for prompt action. Graham had already put ships in commission to reinforce the Mediterranean fleet, and Russell called for the immediate despatch of a fleet to the Baltic ; but Aberdeen and Clarendon persuaded the others that, as yet, there was no *casus belli*, and that action should be suspended for the nonce.

Lord Cowley, who had succeeded Lord Normanby in 1852 as ambassador to France, enjoyed Lord Clarendon's complete confidence from first to last, and more direct

---

[1] Created Lord Strathnairn in 1866.

understanding of the course of events can be had from his private letters, which were almost daily, than from official despatches.

Lord Cowley to Lord Clarendon.

PARIS, *9th March* 1853.—I have just had a long chat with Bourqueney, whom I know very intimately, during which he gave me some details of his conversation with the Emperor, the most salient points of which I think it will interest you to know. I can only communicate them in a private letter, because they were confided to me too confidentially to enable me to put them into a despatch. I will begin with Eastern affairs.

B. asked H.M. whether he had read Lord John's speech on Eastern affairs.

The Emperor.—' No : but I mean to read it to-night.'

B.—' But your Majesty must have heard the contents, and you must among other things have heard the opinion therein expressed that no *peaceful* solution of the Eastern question is possible, whenever the Ottoman Empire is dissolved.'

The E.—' Why could not a Congress settle it ? '

B.—' Your Majesty might try it ; but what chance would there be of an agreement among the Powers ? '

The E.—' I will be frank with you. The idea of establishing Christianity where Infidelity now exists has always had a charm for me. I could not regret such a change.'

B.—' But that, sir, is your *pensée humanitaire* : I want to know your *pensée politique.*'

The E.—' Well, I have told it you, as I have told it to Europe. It is—peace : an honourable peace. But since you question me as to my thoughts, let me hear yours.'

B.—' Why are we not to try and keep the patient alive ? We may do this with the help of England. A good understanding with England has always been the principle of my political creed, as I believe your Majesty knows.'

The E.—' It is knowing that, that I have chosen you for your present post.'

. . . I asked Bourqueney whether he meant me to understand that the Emperor was philanthropist enough to stand by and see Russia take possession of Constantinople, under the plea that she was conferring a benefit on Christendom. ' By no means,' he replied. ' The philanthropy of the Emperor extends to France as well as to Russia.' . . . Nothing, Bourqueney said, could be more cordial than the expressions of the Emperor with regard to England throughout the conversation.[1]

Friendly feelings towards England such as these did not prevail in the other courts of Europe at this time. On the contrary, great was the irritation against her by reason of the ready asylum she afforded to political refugees and revolutionaries, notably Kossuth and Mazzini. The latter, especially, was believed to have been concerned in the grave attempt on the Emperor of Austria's life at Vienna on 18th February.

Lord Cowley to Lord Clarendon.

PARIS, 27*th February* 1853.—MY DEAR CLARENDON,—The question of the refugees will, I fear, become a very serious one. I have heard but one opinion since I have been at Paris, and that is, that we cannot refuse to do something in the matter.   People seem to think that if the renewal of the Alien Bill is impossible, the government may and ought to obtain powers which will enable them to get rid of . . . . Mazzini and Kossuth. I have been very careful, but no less positive, in my language, basing it upon the impossibility of condemning a man in England without proofs of his guilt, but I should not do my duty by you or by the government if I did not tell you that nobody can or will admit this argument.   Dr. de Lhuys has avoided the subject with me altogether, which I do not like ; and I know that attempts have been made already to induce the Emperor to join in some declaration in conjunction with the Northern Powers against the abuses by refugees of the asylum afforded them in England.

I dined at the Tuileries last night ; but the Empress was unwell, and the Emperor in such a fuss about her that I had no satisfactory conversation with him.   He asked about our armaments, and whether we still persisted in thinking he meditated an invasion of England.   I answered, as I always do, that we trusted to his pacific intentions, but that neither he nor any one else could answer for what events might produce.

Hatzfeldt mentioned to me yesterday that Dr. de Lhuys had let fall in the course of conversation with him on Eastern affairs,

[1] Cf. Lord Stratford de Redcliffe's report of an interview with the Emperor of the French on the following day (*Life,* ii. 236-9.)

that if Austria entered Turkey, France would consider herself justified in crossing the Rhine. He—Dr. de Lhuys—has not made use of any expression of this nature to me; but he is evidently *très préoccupé* as to the line which France should take in case either Austria or Russia should assume a hostile attitude towards Turkey.

Henry Reeve wrote on 2nd March about the refugees that he had seen a letter from Metternich saying that they were crazy at Vienna about the harbour afforded by Great Britain to political desperadoes. Cowley, however, was able to send satisfactory assurance next day that Louis Napoleon had too lively a recollection of the asylum which *he* had found in England during adversity to allow him to think of joining the Northern Powers in their contemplated menace on the subject. Moreover, he had not forgotten that Great Britain had separated herself from these Powers in the matter of recognising him as Emperor, and had taken a line of her own. 'I wish,' adds Cowley, 'that you could get a line put into the *Times*, acknowledging the fair dealing of the Emperor in this matter. It would, I think, do good. Of course they must give it on *on dit* authority.'

Cowley, however, was unable to dissuade the emperor from compromising the prospects of peace by sending the French fleet into the Eastern Mediterranean.

'My whole day,' wrote Cowley on 22nd March, 'has been spent in endeavouring to persuade the French government to stop their fleet, if only for a few days, at Naples, in order to give time to receive further explanations and intelligence from Constantinople. I have failed entirely. . . . Dr. de Lhuys' obstinacy and false reasoning exceed all belief. I have not yet succeeded in seeing the Emperor himself, who evidently fights shy of me.'

Lord Clarendon to Lord Stratford de Redcliffe.

F.O., *23rd March* 1853.— . . . Rose acted hastily in sending for the fleet, and Admiral Dundas very discreetly in not quitting Malta without orders from home. The French government have come to a precipitate decision in ordering their fleet to sail, but it will not go further than Salamis.   Why it goes at all they are rather puzzled to say.   After all the solemn and personal assurances given to us by the Emperor of Russia, it would have been utterly unjustifiable on our part to doubt his word, and we do therefore believe that the independence and integrity of the Turkish Empire are not endangered by the mission of Prince Menschikoff.

When Cowley did obtain audience with the Emperor, he found some change in his feelings towards the English government.   ' How is it possible for me to rely upon an ally who is governed by parliament ?   Where will England be after the next Reform Bill?   How am I to interpret the hostile insolence of the English press towards France ? ' and so on.   The French fleet sailed : M. Drouyn de Lhuys declaring that France could no longer put up with British hesitancy.

24th March.—Dans notre mouvement vers les eaux de la Grèce il n'y a ni défiance, ni arrière pensée.   Vingt fois nous avons proposé à Londres de concerter à deux quelque chose en vue des événements plus que probables ; on disait alors que c'était trop tôt : on dit aujourd'hui qu'il est peut-être trop tard, et on nous demande de nous arrêter !

Clarendon was neither blind nor indifferent to the gross misgovernment which made it so difficult for a Christian state to defend the Porte in its difficulties with Russia. His instructions to Stratford de Redcliffe were explicit on that score.   ' Nor will you disguise from the Sultan and his ministers that perseverance in his present course must end in alienating the sympathies of the British nation, and making it impossible for Her Majesty's government to shelter them from the impending danger, or to overlook the exigencies of Christendom, exposed to the natural consequences of their unwise policy and reckless administration.[1]   But, little as Clarendon had intended it when he urged that Palmerston should be invited to the meeting at the Admiralty on 20th March, the presence of that master-

[1] *Despatch*, 26th February 1853.

ful spirit told unfavourably to a peaceful solution of the embroglio. Clarendon's purpose was to preserve unity in the Cabinet, believing that to be vitally essential to the public safety ; for he knew how easily Palmerston could, and how willingly he would, upset the Coalition coach if he were excluded from the innermost counsels of his colleagues. He succeeded in conciliating Palmerston, who wrote to his brother on 3rd April—' We may have some difficulty next year about parliamentary reform, but enough for the year are the troubles thereof. As yet, nothing can be more harmonious than our Coalition Cabinet.' Nevertheless the Cabinet was divided on the Eastern question from the first—between those who considered that the best means of averting war was to take a firm stand against Russian demands, and those who shrank from using any language or taking any action that might precipitate the hostilities. All were of one mind that peace should be preserved if possible, but they were sadly at variance as to the surest means of securing it. Hence clouded counsel and temporising measures, which, coupled with the peace-at-any-price speeches of Bright, Cobden and Milner-Gibson, gave the Czar's Cabinet to believe that England would never go to war for the Turk. Looking back over these months of indecision, Clarendon wrote to Aberdeen on 4th November that the situation had reached a point of danger which might have been avoided by firm language and decided action at the outset. ' Russia would then, as she is now, have been ready to come to terms, and we should have exercised a control over the Turks that is now not to be obtained.'

On 5th May Prince Menschikoff presented to the Porte a draft convention, not only securing the claims of the Greek Church in respect to the Holy Places, but establishing the Czar's protectorate over the Christian subjects of the Sultan. He demanded an immediate reply to this draft as an ultimatum, and when Reschid Pasha, who had just taken over the Turkish Foreign Office, asked for five or six days to deliberate upon such a momentous document, Menschikoff peremptorily refused the request ; whereupon the Ottoman Council declined to entertain the convention at all. Whatever may have been the Czar's intention, and he has been credited with a strong aversion for war, the purpose of his emissary had been accomplished; Menschikoff had established a pretext for rupture with the Porte, and returned to St. Petersburg, while more Russian troops were hurried to the frontier.

Clarendon, on behalf of Queen Victoria's government, expressed approval of the action of the Sultan's ministers. ' No sovereign,' he wrote to Lord Stratford, ' having a proper regard for his own dignity and independence, could admit proposals which conferred upon another and more powerful sovereign a right of protection over his own subjects. . . . Fourteen millions of Greeks would henceforward regard the Emperor as their supreme protector, and their allegiance to the Sultan would be little more than nominal while his own independence would dwindle into vassalage.' [1]

There can be no doubt that Menschikoff purposely forced the pace at Constantinople, and that he exceeded his instructions by extending his demands far beyond the reasonable claims of the Greek Church in respect of the Holy Places. All this time the Russian ambassador in Paris, M. Kisseloff, was assuring Lord Cowley, in perfect good faith, that the Czar wanted nothing beyond what it was known the Sultan was ready to grant. The Russian Foreign Minister, Count Nesselrode, was probably kept in ignorance of the terms upon which Menschikoff had based his ultimatum; but after that ultimatum had been delivered and rejected, he wrote on 31st May to Reschid Pasha declaring that if the Porte refused to comply with the terms demanded by Prince Menschikoff, the Russian troops would be ordered across the frontier in order to secure guarantees for their performance.

Meantime parliament was applying itself to colonial and domestic matters. Mr. Gladstone brought in his budget of ' long views,' re-imposing the income-tax for seven years, abolishing or lowering the duties upon nearly three hundred

[1] Lord Clarendon to Lord Stratford, 31st May.

articles, repealing the tax on soap (£1,111,000), etc.—in all, a gross remission of taxation amounting to £2,568,000, to be recouped by the extension of legacy duty to real property and the extension of the income-tax to Ireland. But for that Ireland was to receive compensation by the cancelling of a debt of four or five millions due by the Irish to the British Exchequer.

A note in Lord Carlisle's journal at this time shows that Peelite leaven had not yet dissolved the ties that bound the true Whigs together.

5th March 1853.—Dined with R. Grosvenor. It was his annual political dinner, and consisted of his brother Westminster, Lord John, Clarendon, G. Grey, V. Smith, Lord Enfield, Lord Bessborough, Marcus Hill, Lord Overstone, Tufnell, William Cowper, Granville. We reckoned ourselves a collection of pure Whigs. It went off well, though I do not think we were in such uproarious spirits as at the last dinner, which was immediately after the breaking up of Lord John's government.

From Lady Clarendon's Journal.

13th April 1853.— . . . Things are looking rather serious for the government as regards Gladstone's budget, which in itself is a good plan, but it is feared will unite so many parties in opposition to it that it will have great difficulty in passing.

Last night there were two small defeats in the Commons, showing that the Tories make a compact phalanx under d'Israeli, and that, combined with the Irish brigade, they can put the government in a minority. Then there is another difficulty in the fact that Sir C. Wood has been pledged against extending the Income Tax to Ireland, which he seems to have done when opposing d'Israeli's budget, and he seems to think that, if Gladstone extends the Income Tax to Ireland, he (Sir C. Wood) cannot remain in the government. Sir James Graham, of course, is very much alarmed ; Lord Aberdeen thinks it serious, tho' not so much as Graham, and Prince Albert is anxious.

21st May.—A short time ago George found out that Lord John Russell was much, and naturally, annoyed at never having received one line from the Queen, tho' as leader of the House of Commons he wrote to her constantly about the debates. Now, considering what his position had been with her as Prime Minister for so many years, the constant correspondence which then naturally took place between them, and the personal sacrifice which Lord John made in taking office under Lord Aberdeen, it really was most discourteous in her to stick so closely to the sort of etiquette which she establishes of corresponding almost exclusively with the Prime Minister. I say *almost*, because she does often write to George.

Upon finding all this out, George spoke about it to Lord Aberdeen that he might mention it to the Queen. Lord A., who, I must say, seems always eager to do what is right, did speak to the Queen ; the result was a beautiful letter from the Queen to Lord John, which enraptured him, and produced a most loyal reply. What good George does by his tact and good feeling, and how he smoothes rough edges !

19th July.—We dined at the Cravens. Lord Malmesbury sat near me, and, in talking about the amount of work in the Foreign Office, he said that people were apt to talk of Mr. Canning taking such pains about his despatches, and writing them over two or three times. Lord Malmesbury, feeling curious about the amount of work done at the F.O. in those days, had the despatches counted for the year 1828, and found that in that one year the despatches sent from the F.O. amounted to 5000, whereas in Lord M.'s year of office they were 33,000.[1]

27th.—We gave a dinner and a 'tail.' . . . In consequence of Mr. Henry Fitzroy's bill there has been a strike amongst the cabmen, and to-night not a cab was to be got in London. Some of our guests came on foot ; some were prevented coming.

28th.—London presented really a curious sight, entirely clear of cabs. . . .

29th.—The cab strike goes on. It is reported that 4000 policemen have struck for better remuneration.

30th.— . . . The cabs began to ply again to-day. What put an end to the strike was a deputation from the cabmen to Hayter[2] last night, when he told them that nothing could be done for them while the strike lasted, that an end must be put to it, and then they should have a committee of the House of Commons to inquire into their grievances. The omnibus

---

[1] In 1852, 32,043 despatches were received and sent out ; 35,113 in 1853, the year that Clarendon took the Foreign Office, and 48,850 in 1854.

[2] William G. Hayter (1792-1878) was Liberal Whip at this time. Created a baronet in 1858 : father of the present Lord Haversham.

drivers were invited by the cabmen to strike too, but declined. They raised the price of their fares, and then handed over the additional gain to form a fund to pay for the feed of the cab horses—the sum, William Cowper told me, amounting to £1600.

Prince Menschikoff's mission—the manner thereof as much as the matter—strengthened Lord Stratford in his conviction that the ultimate aim of Russia was a war of aggression and the break-up of the Ottoman Empire in Europe. That being so, he resolved that the crisis should be brought about at the time most favourable for Turkey and her guarantors—not delayed to suit the convenience of Russia. The impression has very generally prevailed that upon Lord Stratford must be laid a large share of responsibility for the war when it did come. Into the tangled discussion which has arisen over that question it is no part of the present writer's duty to enter. Lord Stratford's conduct of the negotiations, and the spirit in which he carried out the instructions of the Cabinet, have been very ably vindicated by his biographer, Mr. Lane Poole. Nevertheless it is clear from Lord Clarendon's private correspondence that neither he nor his colleagues were able to maintain confidence in Lord Stratford during these exceedingly difficult and complex negotiations. They knew him to be without a rival in experience of Turkish affairs and Turkish ways ; but they suspected him of undue prejudice against Russia, and, while complying officially with his instructions, allowing his personal opinions and sympathies to be known to the Sultan and his ministers. Moreover, in dealing with the French Ambassador at Constantinople and with Admiral Dundas, Stratford's tone was peremptory and overbearing, leading to continual friction. 'I hope,' wrote Sir James Graham on 9th May, 'that our Ambassador of *Peace* will maintain more amicable relations with the Corps Diplomatique at Constantinople than appears to subsist between him and his fellow-countrymen in the Navy. He is a Bashaw—too long accustomed to rule alone. Such temper and such manners are not the pledges or emblems of peace. . . .

I have directed Admiral Dundas to prevent, if possible, all unseemly and open misunderstanding with our Ambassador.'

Clarendon defended Stratford's actions as long as he could, perhaps because he had in fresh remembrance his own feelings of indignation when, as 'the man on the spot' in Ireland, he could not induce the Cabinet to share his view of the gravity of the situation and agree to the measures which he had seen to be necessary. On 6th June he wrote to Reeve : 'A letter of 2nd inst. from Westmorland, who had just seen young Nesselrode, and it is clear that the whole onus of Russian failure is to be laid upon us alone, or rather upon Stratford, who no more deserves it than you do, and it is an unworthy dodge.' Anyhow he told Lord Stratford on 26th May that it was indispensable—a strong word—'indispensable to take measures for the protection of the Sultan, and to aid his Highness in repelling any attack that might be made upon his territory.' Stratford himself neither advised nor expected more than this. Admiral Dundas received orders to sail from Malta to join the French fleet in Besika Bay, and to take his further orders from Lord Stratford.

In his excellent and generally well-balanced narrative of the events of this summer Mr. Herbert Paul seems to have misinterpreted the motives and attitude of what has been called the war party in the Cabinet.

The war party (he says) at first consisted of Lord Palmerston, Lord Lansdowne and the Duke of Newcastle, who were afterwards joined by Lord John Russell, Lord Clarendon and Sir James Graham. . . . Lord Palmerston used to vent his sarcasm, which was not of a very high order, upon ' peace-at-any-price men.' War at any price was his object in 1853.[1]

Such an estimate of Palmerston's policy at this time is very wide of the mark. So long as Russia abstained from violating Turkish territory, and so long as Constantinople was not threatened with attack, he and Clarendon wished

[1] *History of Modern England*, i. 311, 314.

and worked for peace as heartily as did Lord Aberdeen himself. Aberdeen was all for ' moral influence.' Cowley, he wrote to Clarendon on 21st March, ' seems to have spoken very prudently. We desire the preservation of Turkey, but we must take special care to avoid entering into any engagement with France, either positive or conditional, upon this subject. We have a general treaty, to which all the Great Powers are parties. This is enough for the present.'

Neither Palmerston nor Clarendon believed in ' moral influence ' as a check upon Russia or a support to Turkey, unless it was exerted by a Power that was ready, and known to be ready, to enforce it by arms. To advise Turkey and to remonstrate with Russia, and then to stand aside when the advice had been acted on and the remonstrance brushed aside, seemed to them as insincere as it was un-dignified. Moreover, when France showed herself ready to discharge her obligations under the joint treaty and invited Great Britain to co-operate with her, it seemed a paltry excuse to evade these obligations on the plea that Austria and Russia were hanging back.

When, therefore, Count Nesselrode informed the Ottoman Council that, if they persisted in their rejection of Men-schikoff's ultimatum, Moldavia and Wallachia would be occupied by Russian troops, the British and French govern-ments agreed that, although this might not in itself be considered *casus belli*, preparation must be made to resist further aggression.

Divided counsels in Queen Victoria's Cabinet had no counterpart in those of the Czar's. When it became certain that the frontier would be violated, the Four Great Powers were forced to decide upon a line of action, and a con-ference was hurriedly held in Vienna for that purpose. Clarendon submitted a project of convention to be put forward by Lord Westmorland, British Ambassador at Vienna, who was to act as plenipotentiary. Lord Aberdeen still shrank from the consequences if Russia were to reject the terms of that or any other convention that might be agreed to at the conference.

Lord Aberdeen to Lord Clarendon.

ARGYLL HOUSE, *7th June* 1853.—As we are drifting fast towards war, I should think the Cabinet ought to see where they are going. . . . I do not object to proposed draft, provided it it understood that no actual engagement to make war is adopted, and that we are still free to take the last step or not, as we may think proper.

The independence and integrity of the Turkish Empire may be a great object of European policy, and, under certain circumstances, may call for the most vigorous exercise of warlike measures. But we are under no obligation or guarantee, and ought to look at this matter with perfect freedom.

29th.— . . . As the result of a Turkish war is matter of opinion and cannot be foreseen, I have no desire that you should adopt my views. I feel pretty confident, however, that any war, whether successful or unsuccessful, will speedily lead to the dissolution of the [Turkish] Empire as at present existing, although perhaps we may continue for some time to talk with grave faces of its ' integrity and independence.'

On 2nd July Prince Gortschakoff (who had borne arms in a worthier cause against the great Napoleon) crossed the Pruth with 60,000 men and occupied Moldavia and Wallachia.[1] The Vienna conference drew up a Note embodying terms for the peaceful settlement of the dispute, and presented it to the Russian and Turkish governments.

Unluckily, in their haste the plenipotentiaries expressed themselves in terms so ambiguous in parts that, although that was very far from the intention of the signatories, these might be interpreted as giving away the whole case against Turkey. They were so interpreted by the Russian government, which accepted the Note at once. Not so the Porte, which proposed certain modifications. Ministers suspected that Lord Stratford, while carrying out his official instructions to urge the Sultan to accept the Note, had privately encouraged him to insist upon the modifications. His immediate recall was contemplated ; but Lord Cowley

---

[1] These two Danubian principalities were under the suzerainty of the Sultan, and were united in 1859 under the name of Roumania, still under the Sultan's suzerainty. The independence of Roumania was declared in 1878 and secured by the treaties of Berlin and San Stefano.

was the only diplomat considered capable of replacing him, and he could not be spared from Paris. The course of events in England, within and without the Cabinet, may be gleaned from Clarendon's private correspondence.

Lord Palmerston to Lord Clarendon.

31*st July* 1853.— . . . I admired greatly your [*illegible*] letter to Seymour,[1] but I did not like to say too much in its praise at the Cabinet, for fear that by doing so I might lead others to think it was too strong.   I can assure you that it is a great comfort and satisfaction to me to know that the conduct of our foreign relations is in such able hands as yours, and your administration of your important department is attended with this advantage to the country that, from a variety of circumstances, you can say and do things which could not so easily have been said or done by me. . . .

Sir James Graham, M.P., to the same.

ADMIRALTY, 16*th August.*—I always foreboded mischief from a H. of Commons discussion on foreign affairs at this critical juncture.   We have a stand-up fight between Cobden and Palmerston—the former the champion of Russia and Christianity — the latter the sworn ally of Turkey and Mahometanism.   Both made very able speeches in opposite senses ; but both pushed their doctrines to an extreme.   Cobden, in the long run, will have England with him ; but the Derbyites were enchanted with Palmerston and cheered him to the echo. So did young India, who were most offensive in their language towards Aberdeen.   Fortunately it is the last night of the session ; and before we meet again the Turkish affair, at least for the present, will probably be adjusted ; otherwise the breach on our side of the House would soon spread into an open rupture. . . .

18*th August.*— . . . Stratford is hardening himself to resist the proposed Note from Vienna. . . . Notwithstanding the peremptory order to the contrary, he is quite capable of advising the Turk to be refractory.   In this case you should be ready to supersede him without loss of a day, and to send either Bulwer or Howden to give effect on the spot to the fixed purpose of the

[1] Sir H. Seymour, British Ambassador at St. Petersburg.

Allies. We shall now be able to act without interrogatories administered in parliament and without speeches calculated to mislead the Turk into false confidence that he will be supported in resistance to reasonable demands. This delusion may lead him into a pitfall.

Lord Aberdeen to Lord Clarendon.

OSBORNE, 19*th August* 1853.—In consequence of your intelligence this morning, I thought it better to alter an expression in the Speech, and instead of making the Queen say that she had 'a confident expectation,' I proposed 'good reason to hope.'[1] The Queen made some resistance, as I had sent her a copy of the Speech yesterday, which she preferred, and would not now have any misgivings.

I fear Stratford intends to give us some trouble, otherwise he might have acted on the telegraphic despatch, as the other ministers were ready to do. I hope the arrival of the *Caradoc* may bring him to his senses. We must at last be plain with him, as well as his friend Reschid.

20*th.*— . . . I have prepared the Queen for the possibility of Stratford's resignation, which I agree with you in thinking by no means improbable, and which she will not at all regret. . . . In fact, I think his delay in obeying your instructions conveyed to him by telegraphic despatch would justify his recall.

26*th August.*— . . . The Turkish modifications, although not absolutely altering the sense of the Note, are not insignificant. I cannot say what the Emperor [of Russia] may be disposed to do for the sake of peace ; but I am sure that we have no right to ask him to agree to further alterations, after what he has already done. He accepted our first proposal in its full extent, without the least hesitation. He agreed as promptly to an alteration proposed by the English government in the interest of the Porte. I should not think it probable that he would submit to have the work of the Four Powers altered by the Porte. Indeed, he made an express stipulation to this effect.

The conduct of the Porte is suicidal, and some fatal influence

[1] The Queen's Speech on the prorogation was delivered by commission. The passage referred to, as amended, ran, ' Acting in concert with her Allies, and relying on the exertions of the Conference now assembled at Vienna, Her Majesty *has good reason to hope* that an honourable arrangement will speedily be accomplished.'

must be at work. It can only be explained by a desire that the affair should end in war.

Lord Clarendon to Lord John Russell (at Roseneath).

F.O., *25th August* 1853.—MY DEAR LORD JOHN,—I enclose a copy of the telegraphic despatch just received from Constantinople, which realises our fears that the difficulty now would be more Turkish than Russian. . . . I have all along felt that Stratford would allow of no plan of settlement that did not originate with himself. Musurus[1] has just been here, and was in despair when I told him that the Note had not been accepted. He thinks his government has committed a great mistake.

Lord Palmerston to Lord Clarendon.

26th August.— . . . You have had the most difficult part assigned to you that any man ever had to play. You have been put into the position of a general who, having taken the command of an army one day, should be called upon to go into action the next, before he had made himself acquainted with the qualities, habits and dispositions of his officers, and before he had had time to sound the tactics of his opponents ;[2] and who, moreover, should find himself fettered by a council of war some of whose members were of the slow-march school. But you will only get the more credit for that successful result which, in spite of momentary obstacles, you will ultimately attain.

Lord Cowley to Lord Clarendon.

PARIS, *29th August* 1853.—You must not show me up, but De la Cour[3] in the despatches which Thouvenel showed me says that he has no doubt that Lord Stratford's strange conduct, as he calls it, has had much to do with the attitude taken by the Porte. Publicly and officially, he adds, Lord Stratford has obeyed his instructions, and called upon the Ottoman government to accept the Vienna Note ; but he lets it be seen at the same time that his private opinion is at variance with his official language, and he does not bring that personal influence to bear which would have been so useful at the present moment. De la Cour asserts

---

[1] Turkish Ambassador at St. James's.
[2] Like Maréchal Ney at Quatre Bras.
[3] French Ambassador at Constantinople.

further that, to his *intimes*, Lord Stratford uses the most violent language, that he disapproves all the proceedings at Vienna, declares war preferable to such a solution, that the position of Turkey was excellent, etc. etc. Then he goes on to say that they shall know that his name is Canning, that he will resign, that he knows the government of England is not united on this question, and that a change must take place there which will bring into power the friends and supporters of his policy in Turkey. I think it is fair that you should know this. I wish I could feel that it was quite as fair in me telling it. Upon the whole, however, I feel that I am performing a painful duty, and that you will receive this communication in the sense in which I make it.

Lord John Russell had now become more warlike in his utterances than even Palmerston dared to be.

Lord John Russell to Lord Clarendon.

ROSENEATH, 1*st September* 1853.— . . . I am glad you have advised the French to delay the decision about the fleet ; but I think only one decision can be made. If the Russians have not begun to evacuate the principalities when our despatch arrives, the Sultan should be told that if he wishes to have the fleets in the Sea of Marmora, and will give us and the French possession of the forts of the Dardanelles, they shall go there. A retreat to Salamis (' unconquered Salamis ') would leave a stain upon our honour, not easily effaced.

Sir James Graham, on the other hand, had become more anxious for peace.

3*rd September.*— . . . I hope you will not allow Europe to be involved in war because Canning [1] thinks that he can write better than anybody else, and because he is resolved to embroil matters at home and abroad, in the hope of obtaining a triumph for his own morbid vanity and implacable antipathies.

It was only to his colleagues in the Cabinet and to Lord Cowley that Clarendon allowed his doubts and dissatisfaction with Lord Stratford's proceedings to be known. Even to Henry Reeve, with whom he corresponded so confidentially, he would not admit that the failure of the negotiations was

---

[1] Lord Stratford de Redcliffe.

due in any measure to the British ambassador. ' There
are letters,' he wrote to Reeve on 9th September, ' and
despatches from Stratford of the 25th—very warlike, and
rejoicing in the state of *preparedness* to which the Porte
has brought itself.   He has evidently caught some of the
martial ardour with which his friends are inspired.   Nevertheless I believe he honourably endeavoured to get the
Note accepted, and that we have no reason to complain
about that.   He is again riled about the *Times* not being
complimentary.'

Lord Clarendon to G. C. Lewis, M.P.

G. C., 12*th September* 1853.—Your view of the present state
of the Eastern question, and of the change in our position
consequent upon the Turkish refusal of the Note, is the natural
one ; yet such are the peculiar circs. of the case that we cannot
act upon it, and it is impossible at this moment even to guess
how we shall get out of the most curious, and at the same time
embarrassing, entanglement that six great nations ever found
themselves in.

The modifications of the Turks are, to a certain extent,
amendments ; but they neither are of vital importance nor give
the additional security that counterbalances the risk of delay
and danger of war ; but, on the other hand, it cannot be denied
that the Turks who are about to contract an engagement have
a right to look closely at its terms, and we should not be justified
in cramming down their throats what they declare they can't
digest. . . .

Stratford, moreover, the real Sultan . . . although he
ostensibly and officially obeys his instructions, lets his dissent
from them be known, and upon that the Turks act.   We can't
press the Turks too hard about the Note—1st, because public
opinion at home would be against it, and 2nd, because, if we
did, they would certainly refuse and say they would fight it out
single-handed.   We should still have to help them, because
otherwise Russia would be established at Constantinople in a
twelvemonth.   On the other hand, if they yielded and took the
unmodified Note, there would be a revolution which would cost
the Sultan his life and his throne.   His brother, who is already
intriguing against him, would succeed to the throne and bring
into office the most fanatical, ignorant war party that has been

known in Turkey for many years. So you see it is difficult steering. . . . Moreover, my position does not improve, for Aberdeen is more Russian and Palmerston more Turkish than ever.

When Lord Aberdeen formed his ministry in 1852, it was understood between him and Lord John Russell that, after holding the premiership for a while, he should retire in Russell's favour. More than a year having passed without any change being made, Lord John became very restive and caused much trouble to his colleagues.

From Lady Clarendon's Journal.

12*th September* 1853.— . . . Lord John is dissatisfied with his present position and anxious to be again Prime Minister ; indeed he does not apparently mean to go on as things are now. He told Lord Aberdeen, however, that he should *support* his government.

'Ah,' said Lord A., 'I know what that means ; you would not turn us out till you had an *opportunity* ! '

Lord Aberdeen then asked Lord John whether the reasons were removed which had made him say that he could not form an administration at the time Lord A. formed his ; to which Lord J. replied that his friends were very kind, and seemed to think the difficulties not insuperable—thought there might be some opposition got up against him on the question of Reform—in short, appears quite in the dark about his own position in the estimation of his usual supporters. . . . Lord Aberdeen goes to George at the F.O. almost every day, and has long conversations—very interesting, of course, but they do not facilitate the writing of despatches and letters. . . . George thinks that this plan of Lord John taking Lord A.'s place will be very injurious to his own fame and will break up the ministry, besides exposing Lord John to great mortifications. Sir James Graham *would* remain, Lord Palmerston hardly *could* : the others, I believe, have not been sounded, and the plan is so little matured as yet that Lord Aberdeen has not proposed it to the Queen, though she and Prince Albert must have some suspicion about it, for the Prince talked upon the subject to George when he was at Osborne.

Lord Palmerston is to go to Balmoral on Thursday : this is

one of the triumphs of George's good advice. Lord Aberdeen
also followed another piece of good advice given him by George—
not to speak to Lord P. about the Queen's feelings with regard
to him, which Lord A. had been inclined to do. . . . Lord A.
said that when he announced to Lord P. that he was to go to the
Queen, he thought that Lord P. looked rather sheepish, but
said that he was of course at the Queen's orders.

The Queen had written to Lord Aberdeen rather a snubby
letter about it, saying that her feelings about Lord Palmerston
were quite unchanged, and Lord A. told George that he had
asked to see Lord Palmerston before he started for Balmoral,
as he thought it might be right to warn him of the Queen's
feelings. George begged Lord A. to do no such thing : that it
was for the Queen and Lord P. to settle that matter. He told
Lord A. that he thought he ought to write the Queen rather a
savonnade for what she had said about Lord Palmerston ; that
as it was an object to get Lord P. in the government that she
herself professed to desire to be in power, in order that he might
not be in opposition to that government, it was desirable that he
should be kept in good humour—that a public slight should
not be put upon him by excluding him from going where, as
Home Secretary, he was particularly the fit person to go, and
perhaps the slight would be the very thing which, in his heart,
he would like best.[1]

While most of his colleagues were enjoying their holidays,
Clarendon remained at the Foreign Office, claiming but one
free day in the week to spend with his family at the Grove.
The prospects of a peaceful settlement were dwindling, but
he would not give up hope so long as there was no actual
rupture. Accordingly he assented to the decision of the
Vienna conference to put pressure on the Porte to withdraw
its modifications of the Note. This brought a fiery remonstrance from Lord John Russell, who wrote from Roseneath
on 17th September expressing his displeasure. ' It is
degrading Turkey—not to reject her modifications, but
to reject them after submitting them to the Emperor of
Russia . . . and you must not be surprised if I were to
decline any responsibility for it.' This was, in effect,

---

[1] Lord Aberdeen's *savonnade* is printed in the *Letters of Queen Victoria*,
11th September 1853.

another threat of resignation. Lord John wrote still more strongly on the 22nd, after seeing the details of the Russian government's refusal to accept the modifications: 'The fatal facility of the electric telegraph led you and Lord Aberdeen and Lord Palmerston to take a step of which the best that can be said is that it has done no harm. I am not sorry the Czar has thrown off the mask.'

Before receiving Lord John's letter of the 22nd Clarendon replied with some warmth to that of the 17th: 'When you have done things I disapproved my first thought has always been how best to fight your battles and share your responsibility. Your first thought seems to have been declining to share responsibility with me.' Back came a rejoinder from this most difficult of colleagues showing how, in his Highland solitude, he was brooding over the fancied indignity of occupying any other than the first place in the government.

ROSENEATH, 23rd September.—On more than one occasion I have had to summon all my patience to my aid; but you have made me feel my degradation more than I ever felt it before. You assumed that I was to be the chief organ for defending in the House of Commons that which I had no share in deciding, and of which I had previously recorded my disapproval. It was impossible that I would so lower myself, or that I should not feel the blow you had inflicted upon me more than all the other humiliations I have endured.

Lord John's subsequent letters during the autumn recess are of a very warlike tone. 'As to the question of war for us,' he wrote to Clarendon on 27th September, 'I had already considered all the evils you mention, and they are only to be encountered *if our honour is at stake*. I know something of the English people, and I feel sure that they would fight to the stumps for the honour of England. To have held out such encouragement to the Turks as we have done and afterwards to desert them, would be felt as deep disgrace and humiliation by the whole country.' To Lord Aberdeen he wrote in even more forcible terms, declaring that he would resign office rather than consent to forcing the unmodified Note upon the Porte. And now something happened to justify the Turkish government in insisting upon the modifications. While the Powers, through their representatives at the conference, were endeavouring to persuade the Sultan's council that these modifications were really little if anything more than verbal, Count Nesselrode wrote confidentially to the Russian minister at Berlin, pointing out that the Turkish modifications undoubtedly did deprive Russia of the right of protectorate over the Christian subjects of the Sultan which the original draft had conferred. When this letter of Nesselrode's was accidentally published, it altered the whole nature of the case.

Lord Clarendon to the King of the Belgians.

F.O., 1st October 1853.—. . . If the Emperor had adhered to his own conditions and not given reasons for rejecting the modifications, they might have been pressed upon the Porte ; but when it was made clear by Count Nesselrode's despatch to Baron Meyendorff that inferences were to be drawn from the Note, and claims established that never were intended by the conference, it became impossible, because it would have been dishonourable, to ask the Porte to adopt one interpretation of the Note when we had been fully warned that another, and totally different, meaning was attached to it by the party to whom it was to be addressed.

Lord Clarendon by this time had made up his mind that war was inevitable ; but Lord Aberdeen still shrank from any act that might precipitate a rupture. After the French fleet had sailed for Salamis, and the Cabinet had resolved upon sending the British fleet to the Dardanelles, he wrote a strong remonstrance to Clarendon.

. . . If you expect a *coup de main* it is not at the Dardanelles that you can prevent it. . . . If we have good reason to expect an attack on Constantinople, and are disposed to quarrel with Russia for the protection of the Turks, we ought to approach the capital, or rather to enter the Black Sea, by which means any naval movement on the part of Russia could be effectually stopped. The only effect of such half measures as are recommended would be to release the Emperor of Russia from the obligations which he has voluntarily contracted towards us, without accomplishing our own object.

It is not probable that, had the proposal to enter the Black Sea been laid before the Cabinet, it would have received any support from Lord Aberdeen. Anyhow, Clarendon had no wish to press matters so far. He was satisfied with the purely defensive measure to which he considered the government were pledged by their obligations to the Porte. ' I recommend,' he replied to the Prime Minister, ' this as the last measure that will satisfy public opinion and save the government from shame hereafter, if, as I firmly believe, the Russian hordes pour into Turkey from every side. It may do some good to ourselves, which should not be our last consideration.'

Lord Clarendon to Lord John Russell.

1st October 1853.— . . . If we had such a man as Cowley at Constantinople, I have little doubt that matters would long ago have been arranged ; but I quite agreed with you at the time that Stratford's experience and influence rendered him the fittest man for the emergency ; but then we were not prepared for such an amount of Russian deceit, and that called forth all his Russian antipathies, and made him from the first look to war as the best thing for Turkey. In fact, no settlement would have been satisfactory to him that did not humiliate Russia. He has never entered sincerely into the views of the government, and has been making political capital for himself. However, there he is and we must make the best of him. . . . The project of a Note from Vienna will be a total failure for its object, I am certain, but if it gives some assurance of the Emperor's [Nicholas] non-desire for *ingérence*, it may furnish a peg for future negotiation. I verily believe that, if two or three sensible people, meaning honestly, and having real power to treat, were to meet together for an hour, the whole thing might be settled.

Lord Clarendon to Sir H. Seymour.

5th October— . . . Brunnow has done a very unwise thing off his own bat by inquiring in a semi-hostile, $\frac{3}{4}$ insolent tone, what we meant by sending steamers through the Dardanelles. The answer I have given him may not be palatable to his Court, but he has brought it on himself. I don't see that matters are made much worse by a declaration of war (Nesselrode & Co. had no idea that such an event was probable !), and as that annuls all treaties, we may perhaps come to some arrangement, though I own I have not the least expectation of it. I send you Nesselrode's objections. How an old diplomatic fox like him could have committed such a *niaiserie* as writing that despatch passes my comprehension ; but with our view of it, and the intentions it discloses, even Nesselrode himself would admit that we could no longer recommend the Vienna Note to the Porte.

Lord Clarendon to G. C. Lewis, M.P.

GROSVENOR CRESCENT.—*Sunday 9th October* 1853.—The Cabinet was harmonious yesterday—Palmerston less cocky and Aberdeen less timid than on Friday, and all my drafts of despatches succeeded pretty well. The fleets are not to assume an aggressive attitude, but are to defend Turkish territory against attack. . . . With reference to public feeling in England, we could not well do less, and if any Russian attack were made upon Turkey that our fleets might have prevented, we never should have heard the end of it. I see little chance of averting war, which, even in the most sacred cause, is a horrible calamity ; but for such a cause as two sets of Barbarians quarrelling over a form of words, it is not only shocking but incredible.

From Lady Clarendon's Journal.

14*th October*.— . . . Never saw George so much worried about this Eastern question as he has been to-day. He said that no man's *mind* could stand it : he had been occupied with interview after interview, harassing and unsatisfactory. Musurus, the Turkish minister, had found objections and difficulties in everything proposed ; so much so that George said he would have discovered some danger in an invitation to dinner. At last George seems to have lost patience and told him that he was *digne représentant de son pays*,

Then Lord Aberdeen, who is going to Windsor to-morrow, had been with George as usual ; when various people were waiting for audiences of George, he would go over old blue-books, finding out mistakes and dangers in everything ; till George quite lost patience with him too, and said that he *must* see the people who were waiting for him.

Still the British Cabinet laboured for peace. A fresh Note was drawn up, omitting the objectionable passages, and Lord Aberdeen, who was ready to pay almost any price for peace, tried to persuade his colleagues to accompany this Note with a declaration that the Four Powers would not ' permit themselves, in consequence of unfounded objections or by the declaration of war, which they have already condemned, to be drawn into a policy inconsistent with the peace of Europe, as well as with the true interests of Turkey itself.' This meant that the Powers, in putting pressure on the two parties to the dispute, confined their action to moral influence, which they would decline to enforce by arms ; just one of those half measures—barking without meaning to bite—whereof Clarendon had learnt the futility in Spain.

The Prime Minister having failed to get his colleagues to agree to such a flaccid declaration, next proposed that the Turks should bind themselves not to undertake hostilities during negotiations that were to be conducted on the basis of the new Note. This was accepted by the Cabinet, with the addition of the words ' for a reasonable time ' added on Lord John's motion. Meanwhile the Russians remained in possession of the principalities ; the Sultan's ministers interpreted ' reasonable time ' as fulfilled by a fortnight, and on 18th October they formally declared war against Russia.

' These telegraphic despatches,' wrote Lord John to Clarendon, ' are the very devil. Formerly Cabinets used to deliberate on a fact and a proposition from foreign governments ; now, we have only a fact. To be sure it is a great fact. . . . It shows the Turks have some spirit left.'

The Duke of Argyll has left a note describing the proceedings within the Cabinet.[1]

[1] ' At every Cabinet meeting the time was now mainly taken up by hearing all the important despatches read to us. There is in all such documents a great amount of repetition, and the phrases of diplomacy are to a large extent so artificial and conventional that the work did sometimes seem wearisome beyond endurance. But we had two great

Lord Clarendon to Sir C. Wood.

- *20th October* 1853.— . . . When you come to town you shall
see my private letters to Stratford, and I think you will admit
that your own views as to not giving unnecessary offence to
Russia cannot be more strongly put. I agree in every word
you say, and can honestly affirm that peace has been my only
object. I won't say *à tout prix*, because the abandonment of
the Turks would be dishonourable, and a departure from our
British and European policy in the East would be utterly indefensible—but to maintain our principle and protect our ally by
a peaceful, and not a warlike, solution has been the aim I have
kept steadily in view. The only *atom* of success yet obtained
is that active hostilities have been warded off till the winter,
when they will be comparatively harmless. I don't disguise
from myself, however, that things look as ill as possible for us
peacemongers. But unless it is absolutely necessary, I should
think the calling together of parliament before Christmas an unmixed disaster : the speeches and newspapers would then render
all arrangement impossible. Lord John is in favour of it, and
Aberdeen is not much against it. The first Cabinet must decide,
and a very important decision it will be.

From Lady Clarendon's Journal.

8th November.— . . . George believes that Lord Stratford
and Lord Palmerston are in communication together.[1] It is a
curious fact that, some time ago, Lord Palmerston broached
a proposition to the Cabinet almost in the words of that now
come from Turkey for an offensive and defensive alliance against

alleviations. The first was the constant recollection that, on the apparently most trivial points in discussion before us, the issues of peace or of
a bloody war depended. The second source of relief was the liveliness
and humour which characterised the reading of our Foreign Secretary,
Lord Clarendon. His running comments were inimitable. His readings
of the character of each diplomatist were often as good as a play, and
were a real help in enabling us to judge how far we could trust each
separate estimate of the situation at the separate courts ' (*Autobiography*,
i. 450, 451).

[1] ' It has been suggested on the authority of the Russian Foreign Office,
with reference to the supposed understanding between Lords Stratford
and Palmerston, that " if the private correspondence of these two statesmen could be known, it is probable that in it would be found the secret
of all this Oriental crisis." The insinuation belongs to a long series of a
similar character in the Russian official " history " : it is wholly false.
Lord Stratford wrote twice to Lord Palmerston in 1853, on insignificant
subjects, such as about a traveller who brought an introduction from the
Home Secretary. There was no political correspondence between them '
(Lane Poole's *Life of Lord Stratford de Redcliffe*, ii. 231).

Russia. George saw Lady Stratford this morning . . . and did not disguise from her his opinion that Lord Stratford was forwarding the cause of war and not that of peace.

Lord Clarendon to Lord Cowley.

F.O., 10*th November* 1853.— . . . It is a misfortune and complication that we cannot feel sure of Stratford acting with us for a peaceful solution. He pretends to do so, and writes notes and gets promises and appears to carry out his instructions ; but it is impossible to believe, if he put his heart into it and set about the work *as he knows how to do there,* that everything in our view should fail as it does. It is painful to arrive at such a conviction ; but it is difficult to come to any other. He is *bent on war,* and on playing the first part in settling the great Eastern question, as Lady S. de R. admitted to me two days ago he now considered it to be——that the time was come and *the man was there* for curbing the insolence of Russia and resettling the balance of power in Europe. In short, he seems just as wild as the Turks themselves, and together they may, and will, defeat every combination coming from the West, however well devised it may be.

Full allowance ought in justice to be made for the difficulties Lord Stratford had to contend with, which were real and manifold, although no doubt his peculiar temperament and masterful character tended to increase them. On 25th November C. Alison wrote to him :

The great embarrassment is the number of peace-makers. Lord Clarendon sends a very reasonable project ; and before we have half beaten it into the heads of the Turks, the Frenchman abandons us to advocate an Austrian project newly arrived. With the greatest respect for Cabinets, all this is very foolish and playing into the hands of the Turks. When every one else is dead, I intend to write an Oriental romance to be called *Les Mille et Une Notes* ! [1]

Notwithstanding the excessive labour thrown upon Clarendon during these critical weeks, he seldom allowed a day to pass without writing to his wife. A few extracts may serve to show that she was never long absent from his thoughts.

[1] Lane Poole's *Life of Lord Stratford de Redcliffe,* ii. 316.

GROSVENOR CRESCENT, 26th *September.*—MY OWN DEAR K.,— Aberdeen was worse than ever this evening, for he stayed quite as late and came much earlier. . . . Everything seems drifting towards war. . . . Lord John quite approves of the fleet going up to Constantinople, because it is a war measure, whereas it was only agreed to by Aberdeen for the preservation of peace. . . .

F.O., 27th.—Aberdeen walks out of the room and the clock has struck 7 as usual. . . . No particular news to-day, but the *Herald* has our instructions about the fleet, of course giving a false version of the motives in sending it. There cannot be the least doubt of its having come from the Admiralty, or that we have now, as on previous occasions, been regularly betrayed by that department. The newspapers now, however, render the business of the government almost impossible, and this particular case is a most unnecessary addition to these annoyances. In short, nothing goes right. . . .

F.O., 3rd *October.* — Things get worser and worser. The beastly Turks have actually declared war ; so there is an end of the Olmütz arrangement, out of which something might possibly have been made ; but it 's all over now.

GROSVENOR CRESCENT, *Sunday,* 9th *October.*— . . . Things went off more harmoniously yesterday in the Cabinet than I expected. Palmerston was less cocky and Aberdeen less timid than on Friday, and my drafts of despatches suited the general taste pretty well ; but the discussion lasted till ½ past 5 ; the despatches had to be copied after certain additions which I engaged to make ; I had long palavers with Walewski and Colleredo,[1] and did not leave that blessed building till 9.20. . . . I was dead beat when I went to bed, and slept 8 hours slap right away, which I am not at all the worse for. . . . I asked Lord John if he would like a *tête-à-tête* mutton chop with me, and he comes. . . .

Sunday, 16th.— . . . Aberdeen did not get back from the Queen yesterday till nearly 7, and you may imagine that his talk with me afterwards was *not* short. . . . H.M. appears to be not only anxious but alarmed, and I have no doubt that he did not allay her apprehensions. He wants a menacing announcement to be made to the Porte that, if it does not agree to the new Note, it shall be left to its fate. He was rather elated at finding that this was Albert's notion also, but I know that Palmerston is ready (probably desirous) to resign, rather

---

[1] The French and Austrian Ambassadors.

than consent to such a course, so I suppose a Cabinet shindy is
in petto.

Mine is a charming existence just now, I don't think! I
dined at 9 last night and had *eighteen* full boxes to amuse myself
with afterwards. . . . God bless you, my own dearest. Tell all
our darlings how vexed I am to be so separated from them, and
that they are just now my only pleasant thoughts.

23rd.— . . . Walewski had told me that Stratford and La
Cour [1] were at variance about calling up the fleets, so I was in
the agreeable expectation of the French fleet going up alone,
which really would have been a scrape, and just the sort of
niche that Stratford would have liked to play us; but a telegraphic despatch from him last night set this to rest, for the
Sultan had asked for the fleets, and they were both called up.
Hostilities were to commence in 8 or 10 days or sooner, so I look
upon all hope of peaceful solution as gone. What a horrible
mess! . . .

6th November.— . . . The only news of importance is Reeve's
arrival hot from Vienna, and tolerably fresh from Athens and
Constantinople. I was not able to have much talk with him;
but quite enough to confirm all my worst fears about Stratford's
determination to have a grand general war in which England—
i.e. Stratford—is to play *no secondary part.* He was wonderfully
civil to Reeve, whose description of the isolation in which he
lives, and the utter impossibility of any truth arriving at him,
was amusing, but by no means reassuring.

18th.— . . . The Cabinet lasted till 6, and you may suppose
what a scramble I had to get off the Constantinople and Paris
messengers. I did not leave the F.O. till 9.15. . . . Cabinet
harmonious—regretting P.'s resignation, but not appearing much
alarmed at it.[2] His absence seemed to make J. R. more reasonable upon Eastern affairs. . . .

F.O., *22nd.*—Our Cabinet lasted till 7.30. . . . Things went
pretty smoothly as to the French proposal, the great opponent
being Gladstone,[3] but I believe I have settled it tolerably well
with Walewski. Then came the Palmerston affair, and that is
also pretty well in train. J. R. and Aberdeen both behaved
well, but Graham was most *tankankerous* and ill-disposed, tho'
of course affecting great candour and great regard for P. The

---

[1] The British and French Ambassadors at Constantinople.

[2] Palmerston resigned on 16th December in displeasure with Russell's
proposed Reform Bill; but he resumed office ten days later.

[3] The French proposal was that the allied fleets should occupy the Black
Sea. See Morley's *Gladstone,* i. 491.

matter ended by its being put into Newcastle's hands. The
difficulty is about the first step, which ought to be made by
Palmerston, as he says he was taken too literally at his word,
that he did not wish to resign, and shall be glad to return.

TRAVELLERS', 30th December.—As I gave old Aberdeen an hour
and a half of my company as I came into London this morning,
I thought he would have spared me this evening; but not a
bit of it! He came at 7 and staid till 8. . . . I came here for
dinner, as being more sociable; but as I arrived at 9, I had
the room to myself, and might as well have dined at home. . . .
Walewski showed me the Note that the Porte is believed to have
adopted, and I think it much the best document that has yet
been produced. Even Aberdeen says the Emperor ought to be
hung if he doesn't agree to it. . . . So many things have
happened between cup and lip in this infernal business, and we
have so often been farthest from settlement when we thought
ourselves nearest to it, that I am determined not to believe in
any *fait* until some weeks after it is *accompli*.

Diplomatists, who had spent the summer and autumn
preparing Notes as a basis for averting war, were now busy
devising terms upon which peace might be restored. One
occupation proved as fruitless as the other. On 30th
November the Russian Admiral Nachimoff attacked the
Turkish fleet at anchor off Sinope, battered it into match-
wood, and killed some 4000 Turkish seamen. When the
news came to England it heightened the strong feelings
already prevailing against Russia; the action at Sinope
was denounced as a treacherous massacre, and the popular
voice called loudly upon England to avenge this outrage
upon her ally. Now Turkey was in no sense the ally of
England; the British government had strongly dissuaded
her from declaring war, and had been drawn into an undertaking to prevent the Russians seizing Constantinople.
The affair of Sinope was no more treacherous than that
of Navarino, for the Turks had declared war and sent their
squadron out in sheer bravado.

Lord John Russell to Lord Clarendon.

OSBORNE, 8th December 1853.—MY DEAR CLARENDON,—I have
read your letter of the 4th over and over again, and the more I

read it the more I think it requires explanation. You talk of Turkey making a war of aggression on Russia, the first object of the war on her part being the acquisition of her own provinces unjustly seized. What if she asks the Crimea ? Of course it will not be granted to her ; but are we on that account to allow Russia to cross the Danube and march on Constantinople, and is the only move on our parts to be a retreat of the English and French fleets at the demand of a Russian prince ? . . . As Russia is the aggressor, the only way of protecting Turkey is to say—' If you cross the Danube, the English and French fleets will be ordered to intercept your communications in the Black Sea, and to take all measures which the Admirals may think necessary for that purpose. . . . Another point which it is time to look to is the satisfaction of the Christian subjects of the Porte. When I submitted to you the heads of a scheme for this purpose, and for that of securing peace, you told me that you quite agreed with me ; but that one of our colleagues would dissent from one part of my plan and another from another [part]—one part as being too warlike and the other as being hard on the Turks. Surely it is time to act on your own views, and not to bend the twig a little one way and a little another, so as to have a crooked staff to lean on. Before parliament meets we must have a policy to avow and to stand upon. Since March last we have been carrying messages to and fro to see how much injustice would satisfy the Czar and would be swallowed by the Sultan. I think we should act on settled principles—with ♃ if we can, if not with ♄.[1] If that likewise is impossible—alone.

' Since trifles make the sum of human things,' the following note may be made from Francis Cavendish's journal :

31st December 1853.—A few mornings ago, on reaching the office, I found on Lord Clarendon's table a large parcel which he directed me to open. The contents proved to be four and a half yards of best black cloth, sent, according to an ancient custom, by the Aldermen of London as a gift to the Foreign Secretary, other high functionaries receiving similar gifts. On seeing it Lord Clarendon laughed, and said, ' Ah ! it will do nicely to make me a new pair of evening trousers which I want.' [2]

[1] These ciphers seem to stand for France and Austria.
[2] Society, Politics, and Diplomacy, p. 258.

CHAPTER XIV

WAR WITH RUSSIA

'Every minute now
Should be the father of some stratagem.
The times are wild : contention, like a horse
Full of high feeding, madly hath broke loose
And bears down all before him.'

2 *King Henry IV.*, i. 1.

THE British Parliament is omnivorous, its appetite for legislation insatiable, and, being more *gourmand* than *gourmet*, it is as indiscriminate in the order, as it is indifferent to the materials, of its repast. Yet there arrive moments when it should seem imperative for the rulers of a great empire to concentrate all their faculties and sagacity upon the external affairs of the state. Such a moment, one should say, had arrived in the autumn of 1853, when the hushed apprehension of Europe was loudly broken by the outburst of hostilities on the Danube and the Pruth. It was a moment when it was imperative that the nation should remain calm and the Queen's ministers maintain a united front ; yet it was at this precise juncture that Lord John Russell insisted upon the Cabinet considering his darling project of parliamentary reform—a question tending almost more than any other to unsettle men's minds and divide their opinions.

Nor did it fail to have that effect. Russell made the acceptance of his bill the price of his remaining in the government, and so gravely did his colleagues feel the necessity of avoiding a crisis, that, when he laid the measure before them on 22nd November, 'upon the whole the Cabinet was harmonious.' Strange to say, it was the Peelite Prime Minister, Lord Aberdeen, who declared that the bill did not lower the franchise enough to please him. He said he was never afraid of the people. Clarendon's head was too full of foreign complications to pay much attention to the question : he thought that Russell was doing the right thing at the wrong time. Palmerston criticised the bill temperately, but reflection brought him to another mind. ' When I joined the government last year,' wrote Palmerston to Clarendon on 15th December, ' I told Aberdeen and Lansdowne that I feared the Reform Measure, whenever it came on, would be a difficulty in my way, and so it has proved. I am sorry to go, but I cannot help it. You have a hard task before you. . . . I wish more power to your honor ! '

Lord Clarendon to Lord Cowley.

16*th December* 1853.— . . . You will have heard before this of Palmerston's resignation. It is a great addition to the catalogue of ' untoward events ' that now come pouring in upon us ; but it has nothing to do with the Eastern Question, though we may swear that till we are black in the face and nobody will believe either at home or abroad, particularly as it follows so close upon the disaster at Sinope.

Here follows a long explanation of Palmerston's objection to Russell's Reform Bill as the cause of his resignation.

I am sorely grieved at the event, not alone because it will be a great blow to the government and that I have a sincere friendship for Palmerston, but upon the Eastern Question he was to me an invaluable colleague, and I am afraid our difficulties abroad will be increased by the notion that there will now be a change in our policy, and that we shall be more disposed than hitherto to tolerate Russian encroachment on Turkey or Russian insolence to England. This shall not be the case, however, so long as I am a member of the government, and you may assure Drouyn of it in the strongest terms. . . . Princess Lieven will, of course, be very full of the event and, I suppose, very glad of it. I wish you would call upon her and prevent her writing to St. Petersburg that Palmerston's resignation is a letter of licence to the Czar, or that there will be any change of policy here or less union with France. . . .

From Lady Clarendon's Journal.

20th December 1853.—I called upon Lady Palmerston to express
our great regret at Lord P.'s resigning . . . and told her how
sorry George was—what an assistance Lord P.'s courage, experience and ability were to him in the Cabinet—how the *Times*
articles against Lord P. had annoyed him, etc. Upon this she
immediately entered upon the whole subject—gave me an
account of how, upon the receipt of Lord Aberdeen's letter
saying that Sir James Graham and Lord J. Russell did not
think any modifications could be made in the projected Reform
measure (in which opinion Lord Aberdeen concurred), that Lord
Palmerston had expressed to her his notion that Lord Aberdeen
wished him to resign and had probably made some other arrangement about his place. In short, he felt the letter was so abrupt,
and worded in such a manner, that he thought it best to resign.
Lady Palmerston said that she had urged him not to be in such
a hurry ; but Lord P. said that, having made up his mind,
he thought it would be better to resign at once, and thus to
leave time to arrange for his successor before the meeting of
parliament.

Howbeit, Christmas had not long gone by before
Palmerston was back at the Home Office, having consented
to withdraw his resignation on the assurance that the details
of the obnoxious bill should remain open for discussion,
and ministers soon had enough on their hands to prevent
any attention being given to Lord John and his precious
bill. The British and French fleets entered the Black Sea
on 4th January 1854, and the Czar immediately demanded
an explanation of such an unfriendly act.

Lord Clarendon to Lady Clarendon.

F. O., 2nd January 1854.— . . . The *Caradoc* has arrived at
Marseilles with despatches of the 25th from Stratford, which are
on their way. Important they will be, but unsatisfactory of
course. I don't believe he could bring himself to write us anything pleasant. I have a bellicose letter from Lord John, assuming that the terms of the Porte are what we know them to be,
and proposing that the Emperor should only have seven days for
accepting or refusing them. J. R. secretes something of this

kind daily now ; however, for my part, I am getting in *favor of war*. Of course a patch up would be the least troublesome thing now ; but I believe it would only be playing the Emperor's game and allowing him to make monster preparations for monster objects.

All this time public feeling in England was mounting high and ever higher : low and ever lower were sinking the hopes of those who sighed for peace. Charles Greville has recorded how, at the opening of Parliament on 31st January, while the Queen and Prince Albert were well received in the streets, the crowd reserved all their enthusiasm for the Turkish ambassador. In fact, Prince Albert was the object at this time of considerable unpopularity. The Radical press complained of the share he had in the business of the nation ; Conservative newspapers encouraged the belief that he was secretly acting in the interest of Russia, and incessantly attacked him and Lord Aberdeen. The murmurs grew to an outcry ; the foolish story was actually circulated that the Prince had been arrested on a charge of high treason and committed to the Tower. Clarendon's faith in the Prince's judgment and discretion never wavered : his feelings towards him are clearly reflected from many entries in Lady Clarendon's journal.

From Lady Clarendon's Journal.

12th January 1854.— . . . The attacks upon Prince Albert from a portion of the press continue in a way that is quite dreadful, and must make the Queen very unhappy. Indeed Lord Aberdeen told George that she was so. In talking to him she had said that the Prince's position was considered anomalous ; but what was *her* position ? was it not anomalous that she, the mother of eight children, was not to be allowed the advice and support of her own husband ? The reports are too ridiculous and *too widely believed* for such a civilised country as ours. People talk of sending Prince Albert to the Tower—of sending him out of the country—and all for what ? that he is present when the Queen sees her ministers ! he—a Privy Councillor and her husband ! . . . Lord Granville told Theresa Lewis and me last night that he thought Lord Hardinge had done a good deal of harm by constantly saying he would refer things to the Prince.[1]

Hitherto Sir James Graham had to be reckoned with the peace party in the Cabinet, though he communicated freely and frequently with Lord Clarendon, who held the balance between the two sections. But as the Eastern horizon continued to darken, Graham showed determination that, if war it was to be, the fleet for which he was responsible should not be found wanting. ' I do not think that peace is any longer possible,' he wrote to Clarendon on 15th January. ' The Emperor must fight ; and if he pockets our hostile message to Sebastopol, we must send our ultimatum to St. Petersburg.'

The British army was of the same material, quality and spirit as that which fought its victorious course from Vimeiro to Waterloo : pity that there was so little of it ! Being wholly without reserves, it would savour of irony to describe as mobilisation the measures taken in January by the War and Colonial Office (they were one and the same in those days). There were no men to recall to the colours ; the newly resuscitated militia was called out, but many battalions thereof were destitute of both arms and clothing. However, the Duke of Newcastle and his department bestirred themselves, doing what could be done with the materials at hand. Lord Raglan, trusted of Wellington in the old campaigning days, was chosen for chief command of the field force, and off went Sir John Burgoyne, another Peninsular veteran, to lay out defences round Constantinople. Raglan was sixty-six, Burgoyne seventy-two ; let us show the world how far Napoleon was wrong when he set forty years as the limit of a general's effective age !

For the fleet we need have no qualms ; wooden walls still, you see, but, as Prince Albert observed with just pride, after a review at Spithead, no fewer than sixteen of our battleships are fitted with steam-power and screws ; among them, as he wrote, ' the *Duke of Wellington* with 131 guns (a greater number than was ever assembled before in one

---

[1] Viscount Hardinge had been appointed Commander-in-Chief on the death of the Duke of Wellington in 1852.

vessel) went, without sails and propelled only by the screw, *eleven miles an hour,* and this against wind and tide ! ' In effect, Great Britain then possessed a navy stronger than the combined fleets of any three other Powers.

From Lady Clarendon's Journal.

Sunday, 22nd January.—As George and I were sitting quietly together to-night, a telegraphic despatch came from Berlin saying that a messenger from St. Petersburgh had passed through, bearing instructions to Brunnow, the Russian Minister here, to ask some explanations about the entry of the combined French and English fleets into the Black Sea, and, if those explanations were not satisfactory, he was to ask for his passports. Sidney Herbert, to whom George communicated this news, dropped in shortly after. . . . He said that he was deep in figures with the Duke of Newcastle (Sidney Herbert being Secretary-at-War and the Duke being Secretary-of-State for War and the Colonies). Sidney Herbert said he thought the Duke agreed with him that, *if* we are to go to war with such a country as Russia, which makes nothing of raising a hundred thousand men (and its Emperor boasts that he will have a million of men in the spring), it would be ridiculous for us to propose raising 10,000 men, and that the effect upon our neighbours the French would be much better if we proposed raising 30,000 or 35,000.

Saturday, 4th February.—At 6 o'clock this evening Baron Brunnow took his final leave of George at the Foreign Office— in official language, asked for his passports. Brunnow was much affected, particularly when he read the private note which was to be communicated to the Queen, of whom he cannot ask an audience to take leave, because of the occasion of his departure ! Poor man ! he has ardently desired peace, and is wretched.

7th.—Sir G. Hamilton Seymour, our minister at St. Petersburgh, writes an account of the offer once made to him in private conversation by the Emperor of Russia—to divide Turkey, and for the English share to be Egypt and Candia ! The thing was rejected as it deserved to be—' unceremoniously put aside ' by Sir H. Seymour. The Emperor seems to have felt that he had committed an indiscretion, and Sir Hamilton thinks he has ever since owed him a grudge.

10th.—In the House of Lords Lord Grey asked whether Reform was to come on. Lord Aberdeen replied that it was, but talked about peace in such a manner that George told him he was humbugging the country by giving it hopes of peace for which there was so little real hope, and that if Lord A. did not modify what he had said by informing the House that negociations were now over, he would get up and say so himself; to which Lord A. said 'No, no; I will do it'; which he did. The appearance of vacillation produced an unpleasant laugh in the House.

Four days later Lord Clanricarde pressed for more information as to the relations of Great Britain with Russia, since the rupture of diplomatic relations. 'If we are at peace,' said he, 'what is the peace? and what is the peace that is the object of the war?' In reply, Lord Clarendon used an expression that has become historic :—

The question has been asked whether we are at peace or war. It is one that is very difficult to answer distinctly. We are not at war, because war is not declared : we are not strictly at peace with Russia (a laugh). My noble friend may laugh; but he must know perfectly well that I am correct in saying that we are not at war with Russia, although diplomatic relations with that country are suspended. . . . I consider that we are in the intermediate state ; that our desire for peace is just as sincere as ever ; but then I must say that our hopes of maintaining it are gradually dwindling away, and that we are *drifting towards war*.

Still Lord Aberdeen drew round him such shreds as remained of his tattered mantle of hope. 'I still say,' he wrote to Clarendon on 12th February, 'that war is *not* inevitable ; unless, indeed, we are determined to have it ; which perhaps, for all I know, may be the case.'

Next day, Lord John introduced his Reform Bill in the Commons. 'Lord John has just sat down,' Graham reported to Clarendon at 7 P.M. ; 'much astonishment and no enthusiasm ; but on the whole I should say that the country gentlemen expected something worse and the Radicals something more.' Graham's head was full of more pressing matters. He had to find an admiral for the fleet that had been ordered to the Baltic. 'I return Sir Charles Napier's letter,' he wrote to Clarendon. 'If he would puff himself less and quietly rely on his real merits more, I should place greater confidence in his fitness for the command which he seeks, and be better able to answer the taunts of his enemies, who are to be found among the ablest officers of his own profession.'

Graham's anxiety was not confined to the Baltic fleet. In the Mediterranean the friction between Lord Stratford and Admiral Dundas had become very acute, Dundas declaring that he must resign his command unless he were given entire control of his fleet ; but on 23rd February Sir James Graham wrote to Clarendon that ' war is probably so near at hand that the conflict of rival authorities is almost at an end, and I see no advantage in discussing the merits of the past quarrel. If it proceed further, either Dundas or Lord Stratford must be recalled.'

Misunderstanding was rife in the mists of uncertainty and suspense, but these were soon to be dispersed. On 27th February Lord Clarendon wrote direct to Count Nesselrode (the usual channel of communication having been closed) demanding the evacuation of the Principalities by 30th April, and M. Drouyn de Lhuys made a simultaneous demand on the part of France. The Czar deigned not to make any reply. It was not until the last days of March that these two Powers—allies for the first time in history—made formal declaration of war against Russia ; but long before that British troops had been speeding towards the Orient, and Napier was under orders for the Baltic with a noble fleet. Graham had cast aside all uncertainty of purpose. ' *The* operation,' he wrote to Clarendon on 1st March, ' which will be ever memorable and decisive, is the capture and destruction of Sevastopol. On this my heart is set : the eye-tooth of the Bear must be drawn ; and till his fleet and naval arsenal in the Black Sea are destroyed, there is no safety for Constantinople—no security for the peace of Europe.'

From Lady Clarendon's Journal.

6th March.—Mr. Gladstone brought forward his budget to-day. News came to the House at 11 P.M. that his plan was approved in Liverpool ! ! ! What wonderful things do happen in these electric telegraph days !

11th.—The Baltic fleet sailed to-day—30 sail and more than 1000 guns. The Queen saw it off : her reception was enthusiastic.

15th.—We gave a dinner to the Duke of Cambridge. We had Lord Raglan and Lord Cardigan—rather a military sort of farewell dinner. The people were the Duke of Cambridge, the Walewskis, Duchess of Sutherland, the Bessboroughs, the Raglans, Lady Newburgh, the Hamilton Seymours,[1] Lord Cardigan, Lord Brougham, Lord Burghersh, Major Macdonald and Norman Macdonald.

It may easily be imagined that, finding themselves on the threshold of a European war at the length and issues whereof no man could hazard a guess, neither the Cabinet nor Parliament felt in a mood for Reform. But Lord John Russell was insensible to fitness of time and circumstance. He consented, indeed, to postpone the second reading of his bill till 27th April ; but when he found the majority of his colleagues resolute against taking up the question during that session, he wrote to Lord Aberdeen on 8th April resigning his seat in the Cabinet. However, he was coaxed into withdrawing his resignation, contenting himself with whining to the Queen about the proceedings at the Cabinet, where, he told her, 'Lord Aberdeen was the only person who behaved with a due regard to the honour of the administration.'

From Lady Clarendon's Journal.

8th April.—Lord John Russell has actually written to Lord Aberdeen to resign. Lord A. begged him to postpone his determination till after the cabinet to-day, when, if he changed his mind, his letter might be considered *non avenue*. At the cabinet Palmerston expressed his readiness to resign ; but the matter was patched up by postponing a decision on the Reform Bill.

11th.—Lord John came round, persuaded by the Duke of Bedford. He made his statement in the House of Commons

---

[1] Sir G. Hamilton Seymour had been withdrawn from the Embassy at St. Petersburg.

to-day, putting off his Reform Bill.   They say his emotion was most evident and produced much effect, it seemed such genuine grief at giving the measure up.

War having been declared, the stress had now to be borne mainly by the Admiralty and War Office ; but the labours of the Foreign Office were by no means lightened. Clarendon saw urgent need for riveting the alliance with France by special attention to the personal feelings of her sensitive Emperor.   Great Britain had led the way in officially recognising his imperial standing ; but more was wanted to confirm his status among the hereditary sovereigns of Europe.   He had set his heart upon his nephew Prince Jerome being received as a guest at Queen Victoria's court, and Clarendon strongly urged that his wish should be fulfilled.   It was the one thing wanting to make cordial the newly-formed *entente*.   The Queen, however, received with considerable displeasure a proposal to which she was to become perfectly reconciled within a few months.

Lord Clarendon to Lord Aberdeen.

2nd March 1854.—MY DEAR ABERDEEN,—I am deeply concerned at having in any way annoyed the Queen, and I need not say that it was the furthest from my intention ; but as long as I have the honour of serving Her Majesty, I consider it is my duty to state what I believe to be the truth.   It is for Her Majesty to adopt or reject my opinions.   This country is about to engage in a contest of which it is impossible to foresee the extent or duration.   Our success depends mainly upon our alliance with France, or rather with the Emperor of the French, who is a *parvenu*, and, like all other *parvenus*, bitterly feels his position and seeks to ameliorate it.   His *amour propre* is excessive ; he is always endeavouring to gratify it ; but hitherto has met with nothing but rebuffs, and is all the more sensitive on that account.

I have kept this in view thro' all the troubles and anxieties of the past year, knowing what mischief might have been produced by a want of caution or courtesy in my communications with Walewski or through Lord Cowley, and I have no reason to be dissatisfied with the result.   Unless the Duke of Cambridge had gone the whole way by sea to Constantinople, he could not avoid passing by Paris. . . . The Emperor would have been wanting in civility if he had not invited the Duke to the Tuileries, and the question then seemed to me, not whether it was the habit of H.R.H. to accept such civilities, and not whether royal personages were usually invited to reside at Buckingham Palace, but whether the refusal would be regarded as a personal offence by the Emperor. I am assured that he made a great point of its being accepted, which I can understand, for the invitation is publicly known at Paris, and the refusal will doubtless injure him in public estimation. I thought it was not worth while to mortify a vain man for such a cause, or to run the risk of weakening our relations with France (which depend solely upon him) at a moment when our greatest national interests require that they should be strengthened and confirmed. I state this frankly, and I am sincerely grieved that it should have caused annoyance to the Queen. Will you have the goodness to express my regret to Her Majesty, and at the same time assure her that she shall never again hear a word from me upon the subject of civilities to the Emperor.

Fresh trouble was now threatened from that quarter whence so much had come already. Lord John Russell, to whom, at his own request and despite the scruples of strict constitutionalists, had been assigned the leadership of the House of Commons without specific office, had waited two years for Lord Aberdeen to fulfil his announced intention of resigning the premiership in favour of Lord John. To have done so would have been to break up the Cabinet, for half the ministers would have declined to put themselves under Lord John's lead. On 5th May, therefore, Lord John wrote to Lord Aberdeen: ' I think the time is arrived when I ought either to take office or cease to be a member of your government.' A few days later (10th) he wrote to Clarendon: ' The great want of all is a head of the English Cabinet. If a head could be found, all might be well ; but I cannot imagine how we can go on any longer without any head at all.' The suggestion was obvious ; but it was one that did not commend itself to Clarendon or any other minister. It fell perfectly flat, and Lord John applied himself to pressing for a much needed readjustment of departments.

The War Office and Colonial Office had been combined up to this time under one head. Lord John insisted that they should be separated; rightly enough, though the moment—the beginning of a great war—could hardly be considered propitious for so organic a change. Howbeit, it was undertaken and effected; the Duke of Newcastle taking the War Office, leaving all his old staff behind him at the Colonial Office, and starting with a totally new set of heads and hands to provide men, material and management for the campaign. The natural course to be taken in order to gratify Lord John's desire for a department would have been for him to take the Colonial Office, which was offered to him; but he declined it on the plea of ill-health.

Now Lord Aberdeen felt no relish for having Lord John as a freelance on the flank of the government, which he would certainly be if he did not get exactly what he wanted. He proceeded, therefore, to show extraordinary consideration for a colleague who never showed any for others. Lord Granville was induced to resign the Presidency of the Council to Lord John; to provide for Lord Granville, Mr. Strutt was removed from the Duchy of Lancaster and made a peer, and Sir George Grey was brought in to supply a Colonial Secretary.[1] Still Lord John was not satisfied; for he found himself no nearer the coveted premiership. Incredible as it may seem, he wrote to Lord Aberdeen yet again on 13th July desiring to be relieved of office. 'The weakness of the government lies in the House of Commons, and a change of leader may remedy the defect.' Aberdeen's patience was inexhaustible, and once more Lord John was flattered into withdrawing the fourth resignation he had made within twelve months. The end of the session was at hand, and Lord John went off to Scotland to brood over his thwarted ambition.

All eyes were now turned to the Orient, whence the first decisive news came to encourage hopes of a brief and brilliant campaign.

---

[1] 'Why,' asked some feeble punster, 'is the government like a worn-out dandy?'—'Because it has lost its *strut* and got *grey*.'

23rd November.—When Lord Clarendon came out from the cabinet council this afternoon, his lordship went up to the card showing the mails to go out to-morrow, and reading ' Brussels, Lisbon, Egypt, Syria,' exclaimed ' Confound ! ' then Sweden— ' Murder ! ' Then he asked me, ' Is the lamplighter here a guardsman, that he wears moustachios ? ' I told him that the reason was that the chief clerk, Lennox Conyngham, had offered the man five shillings to grow them, so as to shame the young gentlemen in the office who wore moustachios. Upon this Lord Clarendon laughed and said, ' To shame the young men ! It will rather encourage them, for the man is a very good-looking fellow.' The prejudice against wearing hair on the upper lip was a long time in dying out amongst those in civil life.[1]

It is clear from Palmerston's memorandum to the Cabinet that neither he nor Clarendon could entertain any overtures for a peace that should leave Russia mistress of the Black Sea.

Memorandum by Lord Palmerston.

10th December 1854.—I quite agree with Lord Clarendon and Lord John Russell in the view which they take of this matter. It seems to me that the present moment is most inappropriate for negociation with Russia. We are, in fact, in the middle of a battle upon the issue of which the conditions of peace must depend ; and until that battle is over, each party may be entitled to assume that victory will be on its side. We must wait for the result before we can know how the two parties stand. It is only out of deference to Austria that we can take any step towards negociation at present, without appearing either to truckle to Russia by lowering our terms to what she would now consent to accept, or to insult her by asking new concessions which we have not yet by the success of our arms entitled ourselves to demand ; and yet these concessions must be exacted, and the successes which will entitle them to exact them must be obtained.

It seems to me, therefore, that the offer to negociate ought to come from Russia, and that when it comes, or if it can justly be said ever to have been made, the Sultan ought to be a party to any—even the most preliminary—conference, and that

---

[1] *Society, Politics and Diplomacy* (1820-64), by F. W. H. Cavendish, p. 274.

England, France and Turkey, whether Austria concurs or not, should in such first meeting state fully to Russia all that they demand.

It may, no doubt, be useful that, before such preliminary conference takes place, England, France, Austria and Turkey should ascertain whether they are all agreed as to the conditions to be required, and this might be done by interchange of despatches or of notes. . . . I think we ought to say to the French government that we do not think any note necessary in addition to the despatches which already have been communicated ; but that if we do send a note, it must contain a full and frank statement of the demands which we intend to make with a view to reducing the Russian power in the Black Sea ; and moreover, that we cannot enter into any negociations without the presence of a Turkish plenipotentiary.

The Emperor's timely offer of reinforcements led to some friction in the cabinet, where it came within an ace of being declined. The Duke of Newcastle considered that it was insincere and to be disregarded accordingly. Clarendon took a very different view, and wrote to him that the country was in no position to reject assistance from the French, that England was on the verge of disaster, and that it was no moment for balancing the respective burdens of the Allies or for analysing French character and motives. Next day, 11th November, somewhat high words passed in the cabinet between Clarendon and Newcastle—Clarendon insisting that transports *must* be provided at all costs. Upon this Sir James Graham declared that he could not perform impossibilities—that he had not got the ships to carry the troops. Clarendon took him aside and asked him privately whether he had applied to the mercantile marine, or the great steamship companies. Graham was obliged to own that he had not, and the cabinet separated after coming to a decision that the French government should be informed that transports could not be provided for their troops.

The Queen wrote urgently to Lord Clarendon :

‘ No consideration on earth ought to stand in the way of our sending what ships we can lay hold of to transport French reinforcements to the Crimea, as the safety of our Army and the honour of our Country are at stake. The Queen is ready to give her own yacht for a transport, which could carry 1000 men. Every account received convinces the Queen more and more that numbers alone can ensure success in this instance, and that without them we are running *serious* risks.'

Fortunately Sir James Graham, though he had given no encouragement to his anxious colleague, had not been too proud to act upon his suggestion. The cabinet sat almost daily at this critical time, and at the next meeting (on the 13th) Graham announced that he was in a position to provide immediate transport for eight thousand men through the assistance of the mercantile companies. Mr. Cunard had said that, at such a moment, he would name no remuneration to his company for their services, but would leave it to subsequent arbitration. 'What is Mr. Cunard's Christian name?' asked Lord Palmerston.— ' Samuel,' replied Graham.—' *Sir* Samuel,' said Palmerston with emphasis.[1]

Lord Clarendon to Lady Clarendon.

15*th November.*—No further news to-day, but everybody is miserable about the so-called victory.[2] The reports from Vienna are that we have lost 5000 men (I don't know whether that includes the French). It is too horrible, and makes one sick to think of the anxieties that fathers and mothers and wives are enduring at this moment. The general impression seems to be that the attacks will be renewed, and that one or more will do for us. Then will come the monster catastrophe that you know I have been contemplating so long, which will be a horrible compound of Afghanistan and Coruña. However, I won't go on any more with this, and will only thank God that we are spared the misery that so many are now suffering. Think if Hyde and George[3] were out there now !

From Lady Clarendon's Journal.

18*th November.* — The reports in London are horrid. It is useless to record what is dreadful and may turn out not

---

[1] Palmerston was as good as his word. On 9th March 1859 the Queen created Mr. Cunard a baronet on the Prime Minister's recommendation, in recognition of his services during the war.

[2] Inkerman.   [3] Their two elder sons.

true, as it is not known officially, so I will not record these rumours. . . .

23rd.— . . . The state of the public mind seems agitated and anxious beyond anything I can remember, except *perhaps the personal fright* which prevailed in Dublin in 1848. But now, everybody one meets has some death to deplore or some young or veteran soldier to be anxious about. . . .

The difficulties of the government were immensely increased, the public disquiet intensified, by the line taken by the *Times*, whereof the editor, founding upon the highly coloured letters from his war correspondent, W. H. Russell, chose to include in one common denunciation both ministers at home and officers at the seat of war.

The case for the government is well set out in an article by Cornewall Lewis in the *Edinburgh Review* for January 1855, which the author submitted to Clarendon before sending it to press.

I like it much, wrote Clarendon. . . . The fault is too great brevity and not bringing out certain salient facts prominently enough—the *earnest* entreaties of Omar Pasha to St. Arnaud and Lord Raglan to come with the large portion of their forces, his declaration that the *moral* of his troops required this support, even if it was not given more effectively, the intense anxiety felt here about Silistria, and the utter disgrace that would have awaited the Allies if they had been deaf to the prayer of O. Pasha and the place had in consequence fallen.

Then enough is not made of the cholera—its ravages so much greater than any we know of in England—the impossibility of active exertion under its demoralising influence. . . . The expedition is not done justice to. Let any one bear in mind the numbers at Chobham Camp and think that nearly six times that number had to be conveyed across the sea at the same moment.[1] Let him bear in mind the space occupied by the ships at the Portsmouth naval review and think that more than 600 vessels of different descriptions all were laden and proceeding to their destination at the same moment, while the British men-of-

---

[1] In June 1853 a force of between 8000 and 10,000 men went into camp at Chobham, 'a spectacle,' remarked the *Annual Register*, 'novel to the present generation of Englishmen.' The camp broke up on 20th August.

war were still in fighting trim and ready to engage the whole
Russian fleet if it had ventured to come out. Let him also bear
in mind that embarkation and disembarkation of these troops,
horses, guns, ammunition, stores, etc., was effected without a
casualty, and that the armies were ready in a few hours afterwards to fight and win the battle of Alma, and any impartial
man will admit that the operation was quite without parallel in
ancient or modern history. . . . I think the latter part of the
article tame, and hardly up to public opinion mark. . . . The
explanation of the Four Bases in the last paragraph is much
below the mark and might cause dissatisfaction. I should put
something of this kind.—There is no question at present of curtailing the territory of Russia ; there is no question of humiliating
her, unless she chooses to regard as humiliation the intention of
Europe to be safe from her aggression. England, Austria and
France are agreed about the guarantees upon which that safety
will depend : they consider that Russia must no longer have
the right which she now possesses by treaties to enter the
principalities and to deal with that portion of the Sultan's
territory as her own. They consider that the navigation of the
Danube must be secured, not only by treaty as now (which
only secures the accumulation of obstacles to it), but by an
independent authority at the mouths of that stream. They
consider that Russian preponderance in the Black Sea is incompatible with the maintenance of the Ottoman Empire, and,
consequently, with the equilibrium of Europe. They consider
that it would be monstrous to renew that part of the treaty of
Kainadji by the misinterpretation of which the Emperor of
Russia claims to interfere between the Sultan and 12 millions
of his subjects, and virtually to obtain on land the preponderance he has acquired in the Black Sea—in fact, to displace the
Sultan and become the virtual, until he constituted himself the
actual and inexpugnable, possessor of the Ottoman Dominions.

Is there anything unreasonable in these conditions ? In
demanding them, do England, Austria and France exhibit
ambition or selfishness ? Can they, on behalf of Europe, be
content with less ? Will England and France, after pouring
out their best blood and expending vast treasure, leave things
as they were, and thus expose, not themselves alone, but all
Europe to a recurrence of the same dangers within a few years,
but under circumstances far less favourable for guarding against
them ?

The new session opened on 12th December 1854. Never, in living memory, had parliament met under such depressing conditions—a nation angry and distrustful—a press vociferously invective, the *Times* raging against Raglan and raking up complaints from the private correspondence of discontented officers at the front—all the old mischief over again which had roused Wellington's just ire during the Peninsular War, but aggravated tenfold by an enterprising war correspondent and electric telegraphy. The one bright point in the Queen's Speech was the announcement that Austria had at last concluded a treaty of alliance with Great Britain and France ; this, too, to be dimmed of its radiance when it came to be explained that Austria had no intention of giving active aid in the Crimea—would, in effect, undertake no more than to occupy Moldavia and Wallachia and resist any attempt the Russians might make to re-enter those provinces.

'Johnny is preparing another breeze,' was Clarendon's laconic warning to his wife before the opening of the session. Lord John was clamouring for the removal of the Duke of Newcastle from the War Office, and the substitution of Lord Palmerston, who was far too wide awake to fancy a department which, above all others, had to bear the brunt of the nation's displeasure.

From Lady Clarendon's Journal.

December 1854.—In any changes that may take place, George's own position will be most difficult, placed between his old friends and colleagues of whose conduct (Lord John's certainly and *perhaps* Lord Palmerston's) he will not approve, and the Duke of Newcastle, Sidney Herbert (the Peelite part of the Cabinet), with whom he feels and whose conduct he considers right. Then—how could he be a party to a slur of the most outrageous kind being put upon the Duke of Newcastle ? He is also profoundly disgusted with Lord John's selfish and unpatriotic conduct.

At the cabinet on 6th December Lord John had all but come to open rupture with Lord Aberdeen, laying upon him the blame for the ill conduct of the war and announcing his intention of resigning after Christmas. Aberdeen afterwards told Clarendon that there were certain things his personal honour made it impossible for him to bear, and that he could not go on with the leader of the House of Commons telling him daily that he was incapable. Things were even worse at a cabinet dinner on the 8th, when Lord John repeated his intention of resigning, and created a scene of which Clarendon has left this memorandum :

John Russell was wrong in his facts, insolent in his assertions, and most ill-tempered in his replies. No spoilt child could be more perverse or inaccessible either to kind or firm words, and his look was as if he had plied himself with wine in order to get courage for doing what he felt was wrong, for he several times compared himself to the juryman who complained of the eleven obstinate fellows in the box with him. Everybody was dead against him, though some said nothing. . . . Aberdeen's conduct was a most remarkable contrast, and there the matter rests.

Lord Lansdowne, who had hitherto managed to maintain what measure of concord was possible between the leaders of the two Houses, wrote despairingly to Clarendon, ' it is wearisome to strive continually against the recurrence of the same causes and effects. . . . I will go up to attend a Cabinet if I see a chance of doing any good, but I despond more [of events] at home than at Sebastopol.'

Lord Clarendon to Lady Clarendon.

F.O., *8th January* 1855. — On arriving here I found a telegraphic despatch from Westmorland saying that Gortschakoff had received instructions to enter upon negotiations and that our terms are accepted. So they have had a conference, and I feel sure we shall be entangled in a hollow negotiation which can only tend to an unsound peace or to carrying on the war with Austria alienated. Of course I feel that poor old Westmorland is more likely to be bamboozled than not.

10th.— . . . We all think that this Russian acceptance is only a clever dodge to produce dissension between the Western Powers, and I dare say it will succeed. It is terrible to have such a feeble old woman as Westmorland at Vienna just now ; for this phase in the question is the most critical and important we have yet had. . . . I wish for peace ; but not such a peace as will cover us with shame and land us in another war in two or three years.

11th.—All more gloomy than ever from the East. Raglan's letters to-day are enough to drive one mad. He writes just as if he was Military Secretary at the Horse Guards—about promotions, changes, etc.—but not the most distant allusion to what he is doing or intending. Newcastle is awfully slow, and his department seems to be in as much confusion as the Head Quarters at Balaklava.

Unhappy Newcastle ! his department had not existed independently of the Colonial Office for six months. He could not realise that all that Raglan was able ' to do or intend ' was to keep his army alive during the winter. ' I fear,' he wrote to Clarendon, ' that Raglan *is* but seldom seen. I wish he would devote less time to his desk and more to his saddle ; but long use at the Horse Guards has made his fingers stiff and his b—— tender.'

On 23rd January parliament reassembled after the gloomiest Christmas holidays of the century, and Mr. Roebuck, Radical member for Sheffield, gave notice that he would move for an inquiry into the conduct of the war. This brought matters to a crisis, both within the cabinet and without. When the ship is in danger is the moment for officers to stand by their captain, but the chief officer of the Coalition ship chose this moment to desert his post. At the cabinet next day Lord Aberdeen announced that Lord John Russell had resigned on the ground that he could not resist Roebuck's motion, and submitted to them the question whether the government should resign also. The Duke of Newcastle spoke next, saying that he was quite aware that the public were dissatisfied with the administration of his department and had set their hearts on Palmerston. He was quite ready to resign, if that would avert a break-up of the ministry, and would do all in his power to help his successor to take up the duties. Palmerston expressed himself ready to do what in him lay for the public service. Clarendon next suggested that Lord John might be induced to withdraw his resignation in consequence of Newcastle's generous offer to vacate the

War Office ; but this Lord Aberdeen firmly set aside, saying that although they might consent to sacrifice Newcastle
to the feeling of the country, he certainly would not do so
to propitiate Lord John. In the end they paid Lord John
the compliment of unanimously deciding to resign, a compliment which the Queen declined to ratify, not considering
Lord John indispensable to her council. Lord Aberdeen,
therefore, resumed office, but only for a few days, for on
29th January Roebuck's motion was carried against
ministers by the immense majority of 157—305 to 148.
The announcement of these numbers was received in a
manner befitting the extreme gravity of the occasion. ' The
Conservative party,' wrote Lord Palmerston to the Queen,
' abstained, by order from their chiefs, from giving the cheer
of triumph which usually issues from a majority after a
vote upon an important occasion.' [1]

Lord Clarendon to G. C. Lewis.

F.O., 30*th January* 1855.— . . . The immensity of the
majority was unexpected : 85 or 86 of our own side voted against
us—some of the Tories with us ; but I am glad there can be no
mistake. The worst thing for the country and for ourselves
would have been a majority of 25 or 30. That might have
created a doubt as to whether we should or should not go stagger-
ing on. Lord Aberdeen went down at 2 o'clock with our resignations. I don't know what advice he will give the Queen ;
but his opinion is that Derby is inevitable, because he is the only
man who has a party. I have strongly recommended that the

---

[1] In defending Lord John's action during this crisis, his biographer, the
late Sir Spencer Walpole, found its parallel in that of Moses in Egypt.
' Lord John was constantly asking to resign because Lord Aberdeen would
never accept his resignation. Throughout 1853 and 1854 the leader of
the House of Commons was playing the part of Moses to the Prime
Minister's Pharaoh. The King of Egypt probably thought the Israelite
a very troublesome and unreasonable suitor for constantly asking leave
to retire from the fleshpots of Goshen ; he very likely omitted to remark
that Moses only applied again and again for permission to march because,
again and again, Pharaoh refused " to let the people go." '   If Sir Spencer
had not been briefed for the defence he must surely have detected that the
two cases present no analogy, inasmuch as Pharaoh had the power to
prevent the Israelites leaving him, whereas it was always in Lord John's
power to carry out his reiterated threat of retiring.

Queen should not send for him too hastily, but first consult
Lansdowne or Palmerston as to whether any reconstruction is
possible, in order that the country may be convinced that Derby
was *a necessity*. People may then become better reconciled to
his administration, which I am sure will otherwise be received
with disgust. . . . PRAY get back to parliament if possible.

The coalition cabinet having resigned, the Queen laid her
commands on Lord Derby as head of the most numerous
party in the House of Commons ; for the Whigs had no more
bitter opponents than the Radicals. Derby undertook to
form a ministry, provided he could get help from without, failing which he declared it would be a desperate
attempt. He went straight from Buckingham Palace to
Palmerston, whom he found quite ready to join him and
to take the leadership of the Commons, to which Disraeli
had handsomely agreed to waive his claim ; but Palmerston
made it a condition that Clarendon should remain at the
Foreign Office. Palmerston, failing to find Clarendon, who
was closeted with Lord Aberdeen, went on to sound Gladstone, who was willing enough, but stipulated that, if the
Peelites agreed to serve under Lord Derby, they must join
him in force, and that neither Aberdeen nor Graham should
be left out.

Returning to the Foreign Office, Palmerston found
Clarendon of a mind that brought the negotiations to a full
stop. He told Palmerston that he would make any sacrifice
(and he assured him that remaining in office *would* be a
personal sacrifice)—any sacrifice for the public good, short
of loss of character ; but, so profoundly did he detest Lord
Derby's want of principle, that he felt he could not join
him without compromising his own character. Hearing
this, Palmerston went home and wrote to Lord Derby to
say that, on further consideration, he found that he could
render no useful service by joining his administration.

Thus the project of a second coalition was wrecked.
The Queen sent for Lord Lansdowne on 1st February, who
excused himself on the ground of age and ill health, but
suggested that Lord Clarendon might form a ministry,
Lord John go to the House of Lords and take the Foreign

Office, and Lord Palmerston lead the House of Commons.[1] This advice, which was not approved of by the Queen, was made entirely without previous knowledge on the part of Lord Clarendon, who, when he heard of it, earnestly begged that Lansdowne would not renew it, for he felt conscious that he had not debating power to qualify him for Prime Minister. Moreover, if he were to remain in office, he felt that it should be in his present department, where he held the strings of very numerous and complex negotiations. In this dilemma the Queen felt compelled to consult the author of all the trouble. She asked Lord John whether he thought he could form a government. He said he thought he could, but that it would be difficult without the Peelites, next to impossible without Palmerston, and he ' considered Lord Clarendon's co-operation in the task absolutely essential.'

Such co-operation Clarendon declined to give; neither would the Peelites consent to serve under a minister who had treated Aberdeen and Newcastle so badly.

Lady Clarendon to Mrs. George Villiers.

3rd February 1855.— . . . Lord John told George this morning that he had accepted forming a ministry *if* George would join him. Imagine the very painful predicament, which we *most* deprecated ! No Peelites will join ; Lord Palmerston *will*, to lead the House of Commons, just what he is least fit for. Lord John to go to the House of Lords. Labouchere thought of for the Exchequer ! ! ! Lord Panmure for the War Office—a pure Whig ministry. Yet if George declines it may throw it into Lord Derby's hands. What a fix !

Lord John now wrote to the Queen saying that he thought Lord Clarendon might be reconciled if she expressed to him her wishes on the matter. The Queen accordingly sent for Lord Clarendon on 3rd February.

Memorandum by Queen Victoria.

Lord Clarendon, whom we saw at four o'clock, complained very much of the unfairness of Lord John in making him personally

---

[1] Memorandum by Queen Victoria, 2nd February 1855, and Lord John Russell to the Queen, same day.

answerable for impeding the progress of Lord John's government. The fact was that his opinion was only that of every other member of the late government and of the public at large, which could be heard and seen by anybody who chose to listen and read. So impossible had it appeared to the public that Lord John should be blind enough to consider his being able to form a government feasible, that it was generally supposed that he had been urged to do so by the Queen in order to escape the necessity of Lord Palmerston. He acknowledged that the Queen's decision in that respect had been the perfectly correct and constitutional one, and perhaps necessary to clear the way ; but he hoped that for her own sake, and to prevent false impressions taking root in the public mind, the Queen would afterwards give Lord Palmerston his fair turn also, though he could not say that he would be able to form an administration. The Queen said that this was her intention ; that she never had expected that Lord John would be able to form one, but that it was necessary his eyes should be opened.

Lord Clarendon only regretted the precious time that was lost. He must really say that he thought he could do no good in joining Lord John ; his government would be a ' stillborn government ' which ' the country would tread underfoot the first day,' composed as it would be of the same men who had been bankrupt in 1852, minus the two best men in it, viz. Lord Lansdowne and Lord Grey, and the head of it ruined in public opinion. If he were even to stay at the Foreign Office, his language to foreign countries would lose all its weight from being known not to rest upon the public opinion of England, and all this would become much worse when it became known that, from the first day of Lord John's entering into Lord Aberdeen's government, he had only one idea, viz. that of tripping him up, expel the Peelites, and place himself at the head of an exclusive Whig ministry. Besides he [Clarendon] felt that the conduct of all his colleagues had been most straightforward and honourable towards him, and he was not prepared to ' step over their dead bodies to the man who had killed them.' The attempt of Lord John ought *not* to succeed if public morality were to be upheld in this country. He had avoided Lord John ever since his retirement, but he would now have to speak out to him, as, when he was asked to embark his honour, he had a right to count the cost.[1]

In the course of this interview the Queen remarked somewhat pathetically to Clarendon : ' Lord John Russell may resign and Lord Aberdeen may resign, but I *can't* resign. I sometimes wish I could ! '

Clarendon lost no time in fulfilling his intention of ' speaking out ' to Lord John, with whom and Lord Palmerston he had a meeting at Lord John's house that evening. He told Lord John plainly that he considered he was trifling with the gravest interests of the country by proposing to assume the government at the head of an administration that could not possibly stand, so deep was the resentment and distrust in him caused by his recent conduct towards Aberdeen. Russell in reply declared that he thought, and always should think, that what he had done was ' one of the wisest and most useful acts of his life.' He asked Clarendon whether he might submit his name to the Queen as Foreign Secretary. ' Certainly not ! ' was the reply. During this conversation Palmerston sat silent, screening his face from the fire with a newspaper. When Clarendon appealed to him in support of his opinion that no government that Lord John would be able to form could stand, ' he hummed and haw'd in his usual way,' and said to Lord John, ' I told you that you would meet with some trouble.' That evening, however, Palmerston wrote to Lord John to say that, as he understood from what had passed at their meeting that Lord Clarendon did not intend to join his government, neither would he.

Lord John having requested Clarendon to put his refusal in writing, he did so in the following terms :

GROSVENOR CRESCENT, *3rd February* 1855.—MY DEAR LORD JOHN,—The more I reflect upon the subject, the more I feel convinced that such a government as you propose to form would not satisfy the public expectation nor command the confidence of the country.

To yourself personally, I am sure it would be most injurious if you attempted to carry on the government with inadequate means at this moment of national danger. On public and private grounds, therefore, I should wish to take no part in an administration that cannot, in my opinion, be either strong or permanent. Yours truly,   CLARENDON.

[1] *Queen Victoria's Letters,* 3rd February 1855.

Lord John replied :

CHESHAM PLACE, 4*th February* 1855.—MY DEAR CLARENDON, —Many thanks for your note. I must say I believe you are right. Yours truly,　　　　　　　　　　J. RUSSELL.

I have written to the Queen to resign my task.

By a process of exhaustion, therefore, the Queen's choice of a minister had been reduced to one—to Palmerston, whom three years earlier she had dismissed from her service.

Lord Palmerston to Lord Clarendon.

PICCADILLY, 4*th February* 1855.—MY DEAR CLARENDON,—I have just received an authority from the Queen to endeavour to form a government, and I hasten to say that I must say to yourself that which I said to Derby and to John Russell—that I could not belong to any government in the present state of affairs in which the conduct of our foreign relations was not placed in your hands. I hope and trust that you will enable me to go on by saying that you will do so too. Yours sincerely,
　　　　　　　　　　　　　　PALMERSTON.

I am going off to Lansdowne and then to Aberdeen. I will take my chance of finding you at home during the evening.

It was about half-past eleven that night before the new Prime Minister, a fresh young man of seventy-one, walked in upon Lord and Lady Clarendon as they sat together, to report progress. He had met with no success, so far, with the Peelites, who felt bound by a spirit of loyalty to retire with their old chief. Newcastle, of course, accepted the vote on Roebuck's motion as sentence of his own dismissal ; but he showed a fine spirit in supporting Aberdeen's earnest appeal to the other Peelites to give their support to Palmerston.[1] In the end they yielded, but, as was soon to be seen, in a half-hearted way. Gladstone took the Exchequer, Sidney Herbert the Colonies, his former office of Secretary at War being abolished. For the War Office Palmerston chose Lord Panmure, who had long experience of the House of Commons and had served six years in Lord John Russell's ministry as Secretary at War.

[1] See Newcastle's letter to Gladstone, 5th February 1855 (Martineau's *Life of Newcastle*, p. 254).

Lord Clarendon to Lord Cowley.

WINDSOR CASTLE, *7th February* 1855.—*Having nothing particular to do,* I was made to come down here this morning for an investiture of the Garter, and my whole day has been lost. However, I don't grudge time spent in assisting at an honour conferred on Aberdeen, who is really one of the most honourable, upright, generous-minded men I ever knew. No one who did not know, as I do, would believe how he has been working to form Palmerston's government, and how at last he made his own friends ashamed of the cowardly, unpatriotic, inexplicable part they had determined to take. It is most lucky for them that they have changed, for they would have been like lightning-conductors for Lord John, by attracting to themselves all the popular wrath that has fallen upon him.

However, we must let bygones be bygones and try and make the best of things as they are. The government may do well for a short time, because Palmerston has a prestige in the country, and people believe the war will be conducted with more vigour : but this won't last very long. P. is not a good man for general business : he is apt to mistake popular applause for real opinion, and I doubt his having the particular talent or the vigorous health necessary for leading the House of Commons.

During that never-to-be-forgotten winter of 1854-5, while the allied armies were realising in their frozen trenches and tempest-torn tents that sudden death is to be reckoned one of the milder horrors of war, negotiations had been carried on for a meeting of the Powers to devise terms upon which hostilities might be brought to an end. It was agreed at last that a conference should be held at Vienna, and on 7th February, Lord Clarendon being in attendance at Windsor for an installation of Knights of the Garter, Prince Albert strongly pressed him to go in person as plenipotentiary to the said conference. Clarendon, who was determined not to go, opposed what he described as ' a passive resistance ' to the Prince's arguments ; but so soon as he got back to the quiet of his own room, it occurred to him what an excellent thing it would be if Lord John Russell could be persuaded to go. It would not only keep him out of mischief in the House of Commons, but it would tend to reassure those Continental governments which viewed with considerable disfavour Lord Palmerston coming into power ; for Palmerston had made himself many enemies in Europe, and only one friend—the Emperor Louis Napoleon. So, having obtained the approval of the Queen and the Prime Minister, Clarendon made his proposal to Lord John, who accepted it, conditionally upon two points—the admission of Prussia to the conference, and obtaining the assent of Austria to such terms as would secure reasonable hopes of permanent peace. He felt some misgiving that Austria might incline to accept almost any terms rather than be involved in the war.[1]

Lord Palmerston to Lord Clarendon.

8th February.—I quite agree with you that we cannot possibly evade the negotiation with Russia at Vienna. We are bound in honour to go into it *bona fide*, come of it what may. But Drouyn need not be alarmed : it is scarcely probable that Nicholas will as yet accede to our terms. He will say—take Sebastopol before you ask me to agree that its works shall be destroyed, and capture or destroy my fleet before you seek to impose upon me a limitation as to my ships of war. I told the Queen and Prince that you could not possibly be spared to go to Vienna, and that Castlereagh's going to the Congresses in 1814 and '15 was quite a different thing. All the diplomacy of Europe was then concentrated at that seat of negotiation.

Your idea of John Russell deserves consideration. It seems in many respects plausible.

10th.—There is a great deal in what you say about John Russell for Vienna. The reasons against are his habit of acting upon sudden impulse, his rather dry and stiff habits, his aptitude to be swayed by others, and the circumstance that, if he came back with success, he would be more inconvenient to the government than he would otherwise be ; while equal success, accomplished by anybody else, would be an equal public advantage without the drawback. Nevertheless, I have no objection ; and if he would go to the H. of Lords on his return, with an olive branch round his temples, that would be a good arrangement.

[1] Lord John Russell to Lord Clarendon, 11th February 1855.

Clarendon continued to correspond with Lord Aberdeen, and to invite his opinion as confidentially as if they had still been colleagues. Lord John having suggested to Clarendon the expediency of trying to induce Prussia to join the conference of the Powers, both he and Palmerston approved cordially, whereupon Aberdeen wrote to Clarendon on 12th February:

. . . If Palmerston thought that Lord John's words were words of wisdom, you cannot expect me to think otherwise, seeing that they are my own! You may recollect that I have always had some misgiving about the exclusion of Prussia, and certainly never wished that Austria should be pressed too hard. The visit of Lord John to Berlin is likely to be very useful. . . . Lord John's wisdom is incontestable ; but he has acquired it since he left the Cabinet !

Meanwhile neither Palmerston nor Panmure had been proof against the slanderous complaints about Lord Raglan's inaction and alleged mismanagement. 'It is quite clear,' wrote Palmerston on 4th January, 'that in many essential points Raglan is unequal to the task . . . but it is impossible to remove him.' Panmure's despatch to Raglan on 12th February was one long censure and detailed complaint, to which he made dignified rejoinder, from which I cannot refrain from quoting a couple of sentences :

My lord, I have passed a life of honour. I have served the Crown for above fifty years. . . . I am charged with every species of neglect, and the opinion which it was my solemn duty to give of the merits of officers, and the assertions I have made in support of it, are set at naught, and your lordship is satisfied that your irresponsible informants are more worthy of credit than I am.[1]

'Lord Raglan is not recalled,' wrote Clarendon to his wife on 15th February. 'With all his defects, I believe he is the best man out there. One thing he has done which no one else could have done, he has kept us on perfectly good terms with the French under circumstances more trying than the public have the least notion of.'

[1] The correspondence is printed in the *Panmure Papers*, ii. 521-33, and will repay perusal.

The commander of an army on active service is not free, as a civilian official is free, to divest himself of office when he feels, as Raglan had been made to feel, that he has forfeited the confidence of those who appointed him. Lord Raglan continued to serve with extraordinary patience, until death relieved him from duty a few months later, not before General Simpson, whom Panmure sent out, nominally as chief of the staff, but really to report upon Raglan's supposed shortcomings, had completely vindicated, not only Raglan as commander-in-chief, but the staff and regimental officers under him.[1]

The diplomatic machine was working at this time as uneasily as the military one. In August 1854 General Fenwick Williams had been appointed her Majesty's commissioner at Kars, the headquarters of the Turkish army in Asia. Finding that army in general, and the garrison of Kars in particular, deplorably disorganised, he set to work to restore discipline, to repair and create defences, and repeatedly applied for the necessary stores and munitions to enable him to hold the place in case of attack. His demands were ignored; when compliance with them was promised, it was never fulfilled, nor did Lord Stratford de Redcliffe pay much attention to direct appeals from Williams or reiterated instructions from Lord Clarendon; both Williams and Clarendon being well aware that Stratford could compel the Turkish government to do anything he desired. Months went by: Williams's despatches became ever more urgent; nothing was done to supply his wants, and Clarendon became exceedingly anxious for the safety of Kars.[2] His despatch to Lord Stratford on 11th January was peremptory; Williams *must* be relieved, and Stratford will

[1] That I have not misrepresented the real purpose with which General Simpson was sent out may be seen by referring to his remarkable despatch of 16th April 1855 (*Panmure Papers*, i. 150-3). Such a despatch could not have been written unless he had received private instructions besides the formal ones printed on pp. 71-2 of the same volume.

[2] Subsequent events at Kars—the six months' siege, the capitulation on 28th November 1855 after repeated assaults had been repulsed and half the garrison had died of famine—have furnished matter for one of the most stirring narratives of heroism to be found in military history. Colonel Lake, C.B., who was on General Williams's staff throughout the campaign of Kars, has told the story well and simply in *The Defence of Kars* (Bentley, 1857).

be held responsible for the necessary succour and supplies being sent. This brought nothing but an angry retort from Stratford, somewhat trying to the minister who had all along done what in him lay to screen the ambassador from blame.

Lord Clarendon to Lord Stratford de Redcliffe.

F.O., 12*th February* 1855.—MY DEAR LORD STRATFORD,— Your last sheet of note-paper was, as you say, devoted to a burst of ill-humour against me, and I have been so much pressed for time at the departure of the last two mails that I was unable to send a counter-burst. I am unwilling to do so now, for it is not a style of correspondence that I like or indulge in, and I have never yet known any business, public or private, advanced by ill-humour.

I must, however, say that no man in Europe has so little ground of complaint against me as you have. I have acted with entire confidence towards you, and kept you informed of everything that could be useful or interesting for you to know. I have deferred in all things to your eminent position and great local experience. I have marked, but not noticed, your general disregard of whatever had the appearance of instructions, and your general silence upon matters referred to in my private letters. . . . Last, though by no means least, hardly a week passes without my fighting some battle somewhere for you—more particularly at Paris. The Emperor has told me that he has no ambassador now at Constantinople, because he thought his *chargé d'affaires* would be beneath your notice ; but that things were not improved, and the message I received two days ago was—'Ici et à Londres nous sommes les meilleurs amis du monde : à Constantinople nous sommes en guerre. . . .'

With respect to your particular cause of complaint, you may suppose it was far from agreeable to me to write to you *in re* Williams as I did ; but regard for my own responsibility, and the unanimous feeling of the Cabinet, left me no option.[1]   That

[1] On 1st January Lord Clarendon had written : 'I cannot agree with you about the donkeyism of General Williams. He is an able and energetic man in a position of desperate difficulty, and he deserves comfort and support. . . . The whole affair of his army at Kars is very serious, and, to me, one of unceasing annoyance.' Again, on 8th January : 'I will not disguise from you that General Williams's despatches have produced a most painful impression on the government. The Queen as

army at Kars has interested me more than any other ; we have
been hoping for our own interests that an effective force might
be ready in that country to resist Russian aggression, which, if
successful, would operate immediately on Persia *and elsewhere* ;
and for a year and a half I had represented to you our wish that
it should not be commanded by the greatest cowards and robbers
in the Ottoman dominions ; but no improvement took place.
The government then sent Williams, who certainly was the fittest
of all British officers for the work he had to do ; but when he got
no assistance, or even countenance, from you, I could not, with
any regard to my duty in the responsible office I fill, disguise
from you the impression made upon the minds of my colleagues
and myself, and I must add, of the Queen, though I ought not,
perhaps, to refer to H.M.'s name.

I have written more upon these painful topics than I intended ;
but I assure you it is no burst of ill-humour, or anything but a
desire to keep things straight, if possible.   They may not always
go as you wish ; business may be done at Vienna that you think
should only be transacted at Constantinople ; but the government cannot abdicate its authority, and must judge of how the
public service can best be carried on. . . . I think Lord John's
mission a capital hit : it will help to set us up on the Continent,
where of late we have been going down with awful velocity.   But
I foresee we shall have as much trouble with the Turks as with the
Russians, if not more, and I hope you will keep them in order.
The eyes of Europe will be quite as much upon you as upon Lord
John, and you cannot but be aware that you are generally believed to be *anti-pacific*. . . .

Lord Clarendon to Lord Cowley.

F.O., *9th March.*— . . . Stratford hopes the negotiations will
fail ; which of course means that he won't allow the Porte to
accept any terms of peace.   He appears to think that John Bull
has not yet bled either in purse or person as he ought to have done,

well as her ministers have taken the greatest interest in the army at
Kars, and the manner in which H.M., as well as the government, have
been treated by the Turkish government on the subject, is little short of
insult : for there has been a studied contempt of all I have so repeatedly
written.   Not a single thing has been done ; and if General Williams had
not been sent, I don't believe that a single Turkish soldier would have
been alive there next spring.   Yet the Turkish officers all treat him with
insult, and nothing is done to secure him even decent respect, even in his
capacity of Queen's Commissioner.   The whole thing has annoyed me
more than I can express, and in more ways than one.'

and that he must now come forward *like a man* and make some sacrifices. Musurus, in great confidence, communicated to me the laments of the Porte at the horrible tyranny of Stratford, and the earnest entreaties of Sultan and government to be relieved from an oppressor who prevents them doing what is right because he will have all the merit of it exclusively, and thereby lowers them in the eyes of their people. Of course I could not listen to this ; but I believe it, and sympathise with the sufferers. . . . What a pest that man is ! If I recalled him, however, he would make peace impossible.

From Lady Clarendon's Journal.

17th February.— . . . We dined at the Palace, and met there Mr. and Mrs. Gladstone, Mr. Buchanan the American minister and his pretty niece Miss Lane, Lord Hardinge and General Simpson, the officer who is to go out directly to the Crimea as chief of the staff. He looks *old* for it, but is only 64—younger than Lord Raglan. He seems to have gained a reputation in India.

CHAPTER XV

THE CRIMEAN WAR

'Cheer, boys, cheer! our Queen shall hear our story;
  Courage, true hearts, shall bear us on our way;
Those gone before now beckon us to follow,
  To share in their ranks the glory of the fray.'

Popular Song, 1855.

LORD JOHN RUSSELL had got no further than Paris on his way to Vienna when the Cabinet, though not a fortnight old, had to undergo another crisis. Palmerston had told the House of Commons on 16th February that the government could not assent to the appointment of Roebuck's committee; but he found it impossible to resist the pressure of opinion which demanded that effect should be given to a resolution of the House carried by such a great majority. So he gave way, whereof the consequence was that when the cabinet met on the 21st the three Peelite ministers announced their resignation, because they looked upon the appointment of the committee as a reflection upon Lord Aberdeen. Clarendon declared impatiently that Gladstone acted upon a quirk, Sidney Herbert from sentiment, and Graham from fear. Lord Aberdeen wrote a kindly farewell to Clarendon.

9th February 1855.— . . . I shall always look back to the two years we have passed together, and to the character of our intercourse, with the greatest pleasure. The entire absence of all reserve on my part during that time is a sufficient proof of what I have thought of you and how I have felt towards you.

Sir James Graham expressed himself at greater length.

ADMIRALTY, *22nd February* 1855.— . . . I am touched by the kindness of your expressions of regret at our impending separation. I had feared that anger on the part of my colleagues might predominate over every other feeling at this moment,

69

and I had ventured to look to time only for the mitigation of present displeasure. I never took any decision from a sense of public duty with more pain. I ought to have taken precautions with respect to the appointment of this committee when I consented to join Palmerston's government ; but I was too ill at the time to exercise all the forethought which was necessary, and I was confidently persuaded that the appointment of the committee had served its turn when Aberdeen and the D. of Newcastle were dismissed and when Palmerston was placed at the head of affairs. I fully expected that the committee would have been got rid of and that its flank would have been turned. I still think that, with a little moderation and a little more discretion and skill, the latter operation might have been successfully performed ; but this chance was thrown away on Friday. . . . You truly say that we have worked together for two years and in very trying times, without an angry word or a shade of difference, and the impression left on my mind towards you is indelible. I respect your abilities, and my friendship is warm and sincere. It is not probable that we shall meet again in a Cabinet : my course is run ; but I hope that you will sometimes remember me with esteem.

A ministry, new-born after such protracted throes as those which had attended the birth of Palmerston's, might easily have collapsed under so severe a shock as the Peelite secession ; but Palmerston met it with his own inimitable *sang-froid*, and Lord John came to the rescue by accepting an invitation telegraphed to him in Paris to take the Colonial Office. Clarendon wrote to Lord John : ' I shall say nothing except repeating what I have often said before, that no government calling itself Liberal has a chance of standing without you.'

Clarendon's brother-in-law, George Cornewall Lewis, had just succeeded to the baronetcy on the death of his father Sir Thomas, and in succession to him was elected member for the Radnor boroughs.

Lord Clarendon to Sir G. C. Lewis, M.P.

F.O., 24*th February* 1855.—I send this that you may have more time to prepare yourself for an offer that you will receive from Palmerston to be Chancellor of the Exchequer. Nothing could be more kind and friendly than the spirit in which you have been discussed by the Cabinet, and everybody admitted your knowledge, sagacity and industry. The only doubt seemed to be whether your speaking was quite of a character to suit an excited House in troublous times, and whether you have experience enough in the art to enable you to gild the bitter pills you may have to force down people's throats. I think it better you should know exactly what was thought, in order that you should well consider what you will do.

I did not press you on the Cabinet—1st, because it would have been improper by yourself as well as for me ; 2nd, there was no necessity because all were well disposed ; and 3rd, there was such an honest desire to come to a right decision that all personal sympathies were quite out of the question. Nor did I give them any reason to think that you would accept. I confined myself to saying that no man would be more ready than yourself to assist the government or the country at this difficult crisis, and that no man would give so honest an opinion about your own qualifications for the office. I need not say how delighted I should be to have you as a colleague, but I don't venture to advise, because an Atlas is required for our finances at this moment, and you must be the best judge of what your shoulders can support. Upon the whole I believe that Theresa's will be the best opinion upon the subject.

Lady Theresa seems to have hesitated. Lewis had enjoyed since 1852 the thoroughly congenial occupation of editing the *Edinburgh Review*; should he exchange that post, with all its rich literary association, for the restless uncertainty of official life ? He would take further counsel with his brother-in-law.

'Go off and see Gladstone at once,' was Clarendon's reply. 'Don't wait till you have accepted and then go to him ; but go now and ask him whether he recommends you to accept. That will disarm his criticism hereafter if you *do* accept ; and very likely he will be ready to give you assistance.'

The result fully justified this counsel. Gladstone received him cordially, declined to advise him about accepting the office, but told him that, in the matter of assistance, ' he might command me precisely as if, instead of resigning, I had only removed to another department.' [1]

Lewis ended by accepting the chancellorship, and, having to face a deficit of twenty-three millions, his first budget marked the highest point hitherto reached in the bill for Ways and Means, namely, £86,339,000.[2]

And now came a most embarrassing proposal from the Emperor of the French. Impressed with the disadvantage of dual command in the field and with the incessant risk of divided counsel, he wrote to Palmerston to say that he had determined to go to the Crimea himself and assume personal command of the allied forces. This, he considered, was ' the only way to bring to a rapid conclusion an expedition which otherwise must result in disaster to England as well as to France.' Now the Emperor had been, from first to last, a frank and loyal ally in the war ; how was he to be dissuaded from a project so undesirable without wounding his self-esteem ? It was decided that nobody was so likely to succeed in this as Lord Clarendon, who was a personal friend of the Emperor, and had the gift of putting disagreeable matters in an agreeable way. Accordingly he started on 3rd March for Boulogne, where the Emperor had a camp ; he was back in London on the 5th, and was received to audience at Buckingham Palace, when he was able to report hopefully of the result of his mission. Prince Albert kept a detailed memorandum of the interview,[3] whence we learn that Lord Clarendon was met on landing at Boulogne by Colonel Fleury, the Emperor's most confidential officer, who said that he was anxious to warn him that the Emperor was entirely mistaken in believing that the army approved of his proposal to go to the Crimea. While French soldiers were perfectly loyal to Louis Napoleon as Emperor, they would feel no confidence whatever in being under command in the field of one whom they regarded as a civilian.

[1] Morley's *Gladstone* i. 542.

[2] Sixteen millions were raised by a war loan ; the remaining seven millions by increasing the income-tax from 14d. to 16d., by the issue of Exchequer bills, and by raising the duties on sugar, tea, coffee and spirits.

[3] Printed in Martin's *Life of the Prince Consort*, iii. 231-4.

Forearmed with this piece of information (which was fully confirmed afterwards in conversation with the Emperor's own aides-de-camp and other officers) Clarendon was received to audience with the Emperor, who greeted him with much cordiality. After discussing the probable effects of the death of Nicholas I. upon the policy of Prussia and Austria respectively, the Emperor proceeded to explain his plan of bringing the war to a close by a *coup de main*. As set forth in his letter to Palmerston of 26th February, he undertook to bring up the French strength at the front to 62,000 men, provided the British government would supply ships to carry them. ' Strike quickly,' he had written, ' and Sebastopol will be ours before the 1st of May ! ' He now asked Clarendon whether the British Admiralty could provide transports for the troops. Clarendon at once went into details, which somewhat staggered the Emperor. He reminded him that there were already one hundred and two large British steamships fully employed in the Black Sea ; that a voyage from Sebastopol to Marseilles, involving coaling, loading and unloading stores, embarkation and landing of troops, etc., could not be accomplished in less than a month ; that the Admiralty were already engaged to convey fifteen thousand Sardinian troops to the Crimea, and that the utmost they could do in addition would be to carry ten thousand French, and that not within less than six or eight weeks from the day the order was given.

While thus putting the physical difficulties of the scheme plainly before the Emperor, Clarendon was careful to express the utmost admiration for it if these difficulties could only be overcome. But the difficulties were there, and he proceeded to discuss the Emperor's position should he carry out his intention of taking supreme command at the front immediately. Would he not be condemned to many weeks of inactivity, complaining of the slowness with which the British government were bringing forward his troops and supplies ?

' I think,' said Clarendon, ' your Majesty should not move until everything is ready, when you may give the *dernier coup de main*.' ' C'est le mot ! ' exclaimed the Emperor, ' le dernier coup de main.'

Next, the question of time deserved consideration. Clarendon startled the Emperor by submitting that, even if everything were ready and the men on the ground, four months was the shortest time that would suffice for the most successful campaign. The Emperor could not leave the army in the middle of operations ; and if the campaign should be unsuccessful—what then ? This consideration seemed not to have occurred to the Emperor before. He said he could not possibly be absent from Paris for four months ; *coûte que coûte*, he must be back there by the beginning of May.

Perceiving that his arguments had not failed to make an impression, Clarendon ventured upon more delicate ground —the effect upon the feelings of the British army and public of the Emperor of the French assuming the supreme command of the allied forces. French troops would greatly outnumber the British, who would be reduced to the status of carriers, while the honours of a new campaign would be reaped by the French army. Clarendon assured the Emperor that such a state of things would create a feeling so intense as to make it impossible to maintain the alliance.

The Emperor protested that nothing should induce him to such action as should diminish or interfere with the glory of British arms, that he would submit all his plans to Lord Raglan, leaving it to him to take what part in the operations he deemed right, and so forth.

Next morning Clarendon had another interview, at which the Emperor dwelt chiefly on this matter of national feeling. He expressed no determination upon the main question one way or another, but directed Clarendon to convey to the Queen his solemn assurance that, if he did go to the seat of war, the honour of the British flag would be his first consideration, even beyond that of his own.

Lord Clarendon to Lord Cowley.

F.O., *5th March* 1855.—Walewski before I began breakfast : then the Cabinet : then the Queen for 2½ hours : then the House of Lords, and then P. Rothschild—have pretty well consumed my day, and now I must be off to a large dinner at home. What a scramble one's life is now, and now one is always going by the express train.

I wish you would let the Emperor know that the Queen *would* have the minutest detail of my conversation with him. I don't remember ever to have seen her so anxious and interested as she is about this journey to the Crimea. Of course I could only give her the Emperor's reasons for going, and I could not say that the expedition was abandoned; but the Queen was delighted at learning that the Emperor would not go till everything was ready for him to carry his own plan into execution. She was also greatly pleased with the Emperor's assurance that, if he did go, he would be as careful of the honour of the British flag as Her Majesty herself could be. . . .

I find that, just as I predicted to the Emperor, Nicholas, who died in the full possession of his senses, left a fine valedictory address to Prussia, expressing full reliance on his brother-in-law, who, of course, will henceforward quote these words as his evangile, and become more Russian than ever. . . .

No indication of the Emperor's intentions reached Downing Street for nearly a fortnight. Then came an inquiry from Lord Cowley whether a visit from the Emperor and Empress would be acceptable to Queen Victoria about the middle of April, which made it clear that Clarendon's arguments had prevailed. In Paris the abandonment of the project seems to have been attributed to a different agency.

3rd April 1855.—There was a moment's talk of the Emperor starting for the Crimea. Napoleon III. would prefer, like Napoleon I., to be with his army and share its perils. It was his opinion that the presence of the sovereign on the theatre of war would cement the understanding between the Allies. There had been a hint of friction between Lord Raglan and Saint-Arnaud, which might arise again with Canrobert. The Emperor, by taking over the supreme command himself, would have put an end to such possibilities. His mind was made up : but the Empress set her face against it. She was apprehensive, and her fears were encouraged, I hear, by a fortune-teller, whose cards she secretly consulted. She brought her influence to bear on the Cabinet, and ministers represented to the Emperor that his departure was undesirable. Might not the absence of the head of the state mean a fresh outbreak of audacity among the mischief-makers ?   Besides, the death of Nicholas I. promised a speedy conclusion of peace. The Emperor allowed himself to be over-persuaded : he did not go to the Crimea : he went to England instead.[1]

When Palmerston invited Lord John Russell to come to his aid by taking the Colonial Office, he besought him not to let it interfere with his mission to Vienna. On his way thither, Lord John turned aside to Berlin, in the hope of persuading the Prussian government to send a representative to the Vienna conference. But the government of Prussia was the King of Prussia, who was resolutely determined to keep out of the mess into which the Western Powers had been drawn. Nothing to be done in that quarter therefore ; so Russell hastened on to Vienna, where the plenipotentiaries proceeded to discuss the protocol submitted. It consisted of four points : (1) the Russian protectorate of the Principalities to be replaced by a collective guarantee ; (2) the navigation of the mouths of the Danube to be free ; (3) the naval preponderance of Russia in the Black Sea to cease, and (4) the renunciation by Russia of any protectorate over the Sultan's subjects of whatever religion.

These four points or bases were clearly set forth by the Austrian plenipotentiary, Count Buol, when the conference opened on 15th March. Russell's first difficulty arose from the absence of any accredited representative of the Porte. For this, both he and Clarendon blamed Lord Stratford de Redcliffe, who had been instructed to see that the Porte was adequately represented.

It is too bad of Stratford, wrote Clarendon to Lord John on 28th March, not to have written to you and not to have sent you a proper Turk, for I begged him to do both. . . . But it's just like him. He never will help anybody else, and will always thwart any business which is not carried on at Constantinople, where he can have the principal finger in the pie.

[1] *Intimate Memoirs of Napoleon III.*, by Baron d'Ambes, trans. by A. R. Allinson., ii. 67, 68.

Whether Lord Stratford's motives were of the personal nature imputed to them by Clarendon or proceeded from a conception of policy different from that which he was instructed to pursue, his *insouciance* was so exasperating, and he showed so little anxiety to promote the attainment of peace, that Lord John wrote to Clarendon, ' If you will recall him you will do the public great service.'

The first two points in the protocol having been agreed to by Prince Gortschakoff, difficulties arose over the third and crucial one.

Lord John Russell to Lord Clarendon.

VIENNA, 20*th March* 1855.— . . . During an interval in the conference, while some of its members were smoking their cigars, I took an opportunity to say to Gortschakoff that I hoped he would write to Nesselrode to be very cautious in his instructions on the third point. Gortschakoff took me up at once. He said his instructions had never varied : that they were such as, if a Russian, I should have given myself. Russia could not consent to limit the number of her ships : if she did so, she forfeited honour—she would be no more Russia. I might ask why she wanted a force in the Black Sea—he would tell me plainly, they did not want Turkey—they would be glad to maintain the Sultan ; but they knew that was impossible : he must perish. They were resolved not to let any other Power have Constantinople : they must not have that door to their dominions in the Black Sea shut against them.

Here is an avowal—not only that they mean to maintain a fleet in the B. Sea, but a strong fleet. . . . He was very anxious that we should keep together in our proposals. With this view he suggested that we might propose that Russia should not maintain a greater naval force in the Black Sea than she has at the present time. Altho' this is short of our proposal, yet if Buol will stand by it, I strongly advise your lordship and H.M. government to accept and support it.

Now the British and French plenipotentiaries had been instructed to secure the cessation of Russian preponderance in the Black Sea by strictly limiting the number of Russian warships to three or four for the protection of commerce.

The British Cabinet could not therefore entertain the proposal of Prince Gortschakoff so strongly recommended by Lord John, because, as Lord Clarendon pointed out to him, this would leave Turkey at the mercy of a far stronger fleet than she could afford to maintain. M. Bourqueney, the French plenipotentiary, advocated the complete neutralisation of the Black Sea; and at the end of March, when the French foreign minister, M. Drouyn de Lhuys, and the Turkish plenipotentiary, Ali Pasha, arrived in Vienna to take part in the deliberations, this and the original plan of strict limitation, were the only alternatives before the conference.

Lord Granville went to Paris about the beginning of April, charged to use any opportunity that presented itself of discouraging the Emperor in his intention of going to the seat of war. He kept Clarendon informed of the drift of opinion in Paris, where there was a growing agitation for peace at any cost.

Lord Granville to Lord Clarendon.

Paris, 10*th April* 1855.— . . . Thiers is for peace, but says that a victory must be first obtained. He says that the mass of the people are apathetic; that the Orleanists and Legitimists are for peace, as disadvantageous to the Emperor; that he and 19 other enlightened people alone hold really national opinions on this subject. He says the French government have frightfully mismanaged the war. . . . He considers the deficiency of sea transport to have been the ruin of the Allies in this campaign . . . that in the Peninsular War the French lost 50 per cent—we 3 or 4 per cent—in getting a regiment to the seat of war. He thinks Sebastopol is to be taken; but it must be done in a month, or we shall have the plague. He says that the Minister of Marine is a fool: Vaillant [1] a great officer of Engineers and an honest man, but no administrator. The double command has been hurtful. Napoleon I. was of opinion that one bad general was much better than two good ones. A month ago **he** would have advised the Emperor not to go to the Crimea; now he thinks it is necessary: but he must not come back without success. The English newspapers have not done half the harm the thousands of letters from

---

[1] Minister for War.

the French camp have done. We have free parliamentary discussion to put things right : here, no one believes anything the government or its organs say. . . . In the course of conversation I spoke of the straightforward manner of the Emperor towards England. He said, ' I do not say that he is a sincere man, but he is a perfectly sincere man *with you*. . . .'

I received to-day from Princesse Lieven a green summons—colour emblematic not of the summoner but of the summoned. She talked much of the impossibility of persuading her young Emperor to acquiesce in the humiliation of a great Empire of which he had so lately become the head. I told her that, as a lover of peace, she must hope for a successful issue of the present negotiations ; that as far as regarded England, Lord Palmerston and Lord J. Russell were in a better position than any other two men would be for years to conclude an honourable peace : that they were both pacifically inclined, but that nothing would induce them to go beyond a certain point. They could not do so without loss of character and loss of all influence in their country : that it was whispered that the Russians were determined not to limit their power in the Black Sea, and therefore the continuance of the war was certain.

I stuck to this text with slight variations. She had begun by telling me that she loved her enemies better than before the war : she ended by saying that I was *parfaitement* unsatisfactory—*on a beau tirer, tirer, on n'obtient rien*. . . . On going away she asked whether what I had said about our firmness was *irrevocable*. I replied *irrevocable*. ' Eh bien, vous verrez ; nous aussi nous sommes entêtés ! . . .'

12*th*.—. . . We dined at the Tuileries last night : the whole thing magnificent and well done. . . . The Emperor was very civil to me, much more talkative than when I had before seen him, probably because we had a subject in common last night. . . . He said, with great appearance of sincerity, that his only wish was success : that he could not conceal from himself the effect of peace, unaccompanied by victory, upon the governments of France and England : that, for himself, he would not do anything to disturb the negotiations at Vienna ; but he should be delighted if the news came of a rupture. . . . He ended by saying : ' This is my bill of fare for this year—a visit to London, a victory over the Russians in the Crimea, and a reception of the Queen of England in Paris before the end of summer.' I did not add—' Excusez du peu ! '

Prince Gortschakoff having flatly refused assent to any proposal either for limitation of the Russian naval force or for neutralisation of the Black Sea, Count Buol, on behalf of Austria, brought forward an amended plan for equipoise, providing that, in the event of the Russian fleet in the Black Sea being increased, Turkey should have power to maintain a force equal to it, while Great Britain and France should each have a force equal to half that of Russia. Drouyn de Lhuys and Lord John both approved of this proposal, and agreed to recommend it strongly for acceptance by their respective governments. Lord John, however, returning to London on 29th April, found Palmerston and Clarendon both opposed to the Austrian scheme. The Emperor of the French had inclined at first to approve of it, but he yielded to the objections of the British government, and ended by refusing to accept it. Thereupon Drouyn de Lhuys resigned office and the Emperor telegraphed to Clarendon to send over Count Walewski, ambassador at St. James's, to take up the Presidency of the Council and the Ministry of Foreign Affairs. Walewski was replaced at St. James's by M. de Persigny, of whom Clarendon formed a far higher opinion than he had of the other.

Lord John Russell to Lord Clarendon.

PEMBROKE LODGE, 6*th May* 1855.— . . . I am very much concerned at the removal or resignation of Drouyn. I cannot separate myself from him ; and, having taken at Vienna the same view which he did, his resignation entails mine. I am very sorry for this, and wished to avoid it ; but I have in some measure got Drouyn into this scrape, for at first he was disposed to advise the Emperor to insist on a limitation of ships, and I induced him not to give any advice at all to the Emperor. Afterwards we agreed very much ; and, if he had stayed in office there, I might have gulped, though with difficulty, the rejection of my advice here. . . . It is painful to me to leave a second Cabinet,[1] and will injure my reputation—perhaps irretrievably ; but I see no other course. Do as you please about communicating to Palmerston what I have written . . . but I hope you will

[1] Within six months !

not tie your hands or those of the government by giving arguments against what the nation may ultimately accept. I hold that a simple provision by which the Sultan would reserve the power to admit the vessels of Powers, not having establishments in the Black Sea, through the Straits at his own pleasure at all times . . . and a general treaty of European alliance to defend Turkey against Russia, would be a good security for peace. . . .

Lord Clarendon to Lord John Russell.

GROSVENOR CRESCENT, 7th May 1855.— . . . I am very sorry you did not come in just now, as I wanted most particularly to see you. I now write this *earnestly to entreat* that you will say nothing to anybody at present about your intended resignation; the public interests and your own position are so involved in the question, and so much harm of every kind may be done by a hasty decision, however high-minded and honorable the motives may be, that I do beg of you well to weigh *all* the points of the case ; and let me add that you will not act with fairness, and as I am sure you must wish to act, towards your colleagues, if you do not hear what some of them may have to say. . . .

Throughout these proceedings Clarendon and Palmerston were in constant communication. Palmerston's calm confidence seems to have its reflection in his fine, clear handwriting.

Lord Palmerston to Lord Clarendon.

15th March 1855.—What Cowley says of John Russell is true— he has never been accustomed to deal personally with artful negotiators, and he has an unlucky habit of suddenly giving way on matters in regard to which he had previously taken an apparently irrevocable stand. Horace Walpole, I think, says of the Duke of Bedford of his day that he was never immovable upon any opinion unless it was one which had been instilled into him by somebody else, in direct opposition to his own previous convictions.

26th April.—This is disagreeable, but you may positively and distinctly say that Her Majesty's *present* government cannot and will not accept Drouyn's proposals. If it is to be adopted, it must be by a government under another head.

6th May.— ... As to John Russell's intention, all one can say is that I should think it was the first instance in which a plenipotentiary, having undertaken a negotiation on instructions founded on principles of which he approved, turned round upon his government, and, after the plan he had been instructed to press had failed, should turn round upon his employers and endeavour to force upon them a plan totally different from that which he had undertaken to propose.

7th.— ... If John Russell goes out, he *must* state in parliament *why* he goes out ; if he states his views and those of Drouyn, I must state strongly my reasons for differing from him ; and such a discussion in parliament must evidently and unavoidably throw enormous obstacles in the way of all future negotiations.

23rd.— ... As to offering Russia lower conditions than those which, in concert with France, we settled to offer her, I never will be a party to such a proceeding. ... I am ready to give up the government or to break up the government, whichever may be the course best suited to the circumstances of the moment, but I will not be a party to our national disgrace.

27th.— ... I saw Persigny after he had been with you to-day. He acknowledged that it is the Bourse and other speculations which create a desire for peace ; but I observed to him that a good success would raise all shares and credits quite as much as a bad peace would do. ' Oh,' he exclaimed, ' do not for a moment suppose that the Emperor wants peace, or would make it on any terms till he has obtained a military success. All he wants is to prolong negotiation in order to satisfy people's minds in France and to keep Austria from breaking with us.' ' But,' said I, ' the best and only way of having Austria on our side is to take Sebastopol or win a battle. She will join us if we are strong, and hold aloof from us if we are weak.' He admitted this. He said that as often as the Emperor received our answers differing from his pacific proposals, he always smiled and said, ' After all, the English are right ! ' ... Knowing that the Emperor agrees with us, and having held in the two Houses of Parliament the language which we held on Friday, we cannot give way to a small knot of gamblers and intriguers at Paris, who want for their own dirty objects to sacrifice the honour of two great countries and the future interests of Europe. We must decline firmly, but as civilly as possible.

On 2nd June Palmerston discussed with Clarendon the expediency of recalling Lord Stratford de Redcliffe, who, being intensely jealous of the French acquiring influence at the Porte, treated the French ambassador at Constantinople in a manner very hurtful to his dignity. It was decided that the evils of withdrawing Stratford would outweigh the good, for, if he had great faults, he had also great ability and merit. 'If he were recalled,' said Palmerston, 'and come home angry, as he would do, he would furnish his friend and leader Derby with materials for attacking our Vienna policy, the concessions made by John Russell, etc., and we might find him as inconvenient at home as he is at Constantinople.'

Lord John Russell, expert by this time in resignations and withdrawals of resignation, resisted all appeals from his colleagues during several days; but after a third interview with Palmerston he yielded and resumed. The argument that prevailed with him was—supposing Great Britain had accepted the Austrian compromise and that Russia had accepted it also, France alone declining it as affording insufficient security, how could the British army be withdrawn from the field, forcing the French army to retire also, without any tangible fruits of their bloody and costly campaign?

'I am not a politician,' said Maréchal Vaillant, the French Minister of War, to the Emperor in Lord Cowley's presence, 'but I know the feelings of the army. I am sure that if, after having spent months in the siege of Sebastopol, we return unsuccessful, the army will not be satisfied.' A paltry reason, one might think, for carrying on the war, unless it be remembered that Louis Napoleon could not hope to keep his crown save by the goodwill of his army and the activity of his police; but this was a reason that it was quite impossible to put forward in the House of Commons. So when Lord John had to defend the government against a vote of censure moved by Disraeli on 24th May, reflecting specially on the conduct of the Vienna negotiations, he could not disclose the Austrian proposals with which he had strongly urged his own government to agree. Not a word, therefore, upon that subject : only expressions of resolute purpose to carry on the war until the power of Russia should be curbed. This speech was well received by the House, and helped to increase the majority against Disraeli ; but it had a very different effect in Vienna. Count Buol considered Lord John had committed a direct breach of faith ; had he not undertaken to recommend his government to accept the Austrian proposals, which were not even referred to in this speech ? Count Buol, therefore, to set himself right with the Powers, sent round a circular containing the terms which he had submitted to the conference and which had been approved by the British and French plenipotentiaries. The publication of this circular had a painful effect in England. It seemed as if Lord John had spoken with one voice in Vienna and another at Westminster. Why had he not urged his colleagues to adopt the Austrian scheme of pacification ? If he had done so and failed to persuade them, how could he with honour remain a member of the government ? These and other reflections and innuendoes were poured upon Lord John through the press ; but his tongue was tied through loyalty to the French alliance, and he could not explain that he *had* strongly pressed the Austrian proposals upon his colleagues, and *had* tendered his resignation when they declined to accept them. Lord John was between the horns of a very awkward and unmerited dilemma, which he did not improve by retaliating on what he termed ' the ribald press ' for its attacks on Lord Raglan. Lord John had but a single tongue, the press had a thousand ; the clamour grew so loud that when Sir E. Lytton Bulwer gave notice of a motion of censure on the conduct of the British plenipotentiary at Vienna, it was evident that ministers, standing loyally in defence of their colleague, but equally unable to explain the true reason of the trouble, would be beaten on a division.

Sir George Lewis tried to persuade Clarendon to explain the real state of the case, and so set Lord John right with the House and the nation.

Sir G. C. Lewis to Lord Clarendon.

HOUSE OF COMMONS, *Thursday,* 12*th July,* 7¼ *o'clock.—* . . .
No explanation of a single point in the history of the negotiation
has taken place to-night, and the whole field is open to you
to-morrow if, upon consultation with Palmerston and Lord John,
you should think fit to give a narrative of what has passed.
You might, I think, properly do this upon the first presentation
of the papers, if you confined yourself to a narrative and did not
invite debate.   My impression is that a clear narrative and
exposition of facts made to-morrow and circulated in all the
newspapers of Saturday, might exercise a very material influence
upon the H. of C. debate on Monday.

9.30 P.M.—Hayter,[1] with whom I have just had a conversation,
thinks the case of the government hopeless unless Lord John
resigns.   He says that friends of peace regard him as a traitor
to their cause, and the friends of war look upon him as a faint-
hearted supporter ; while a third class of persons say that they
have no confidence in a government of which a leading member
is so vacillating and mutable in his conduct.   Bethell[2] says that
if Lord J. will not act the part of Curtius, his colleagues must
force him to perform the part of Jonah.

Wilson[3] has just been with me and says the talk of some of the
Tories is that they do not wish to turn out the government ;
but they must have an excuse for not voting.   The nature of
that excuse you will readily apprehend.   I mention all this as
a guide for your decision.   I still think that a clear statement
of facts would have a considerable effect, but I strongly suspect
that the case of the government is past redemption.   I am told
that Gladstone, Seymour and Francis Baring are to support
Bulwer's motion.   The practical alternative is shortly this—a
voluntary resignation to-morrow or the day after, or the adoption
of Bulwer's notion by a large majority on Thursday night.

Clarendon could not adopt the course recommended.
Deeply as he deplored the sacrifice of an innocent colleague,
he felt it to be impossible to adopt the only course that
would save him, which was to get up in his place in the
Lords and explain that the government were unable to

---

[1] Chief Liberal Whip.
[2] Sir Richard Bethell (1800-1873), Solicitor-General ; became Attorney-
General in 1856 and Lord Chancellor (Westbury) in 1861.
[3] James Wilson, M.P. (1805-1860), founder of *The Economist,* Financial
Secretary to the Treasury.

agree in the proposal made by Austria, because to do so would cause disaffection in the French army, thereby endangering the Imperial dynasty of France. Lord John saved the existence of the Cabinet by resigning office, carrying with him this time the sincere regret and sympathy of his colleagues.

Lord Clarendon to Lord Cowley.

F. O., 14*th July.*— . . . I informed you yesterday by telegraph that Lord John had resigned. He offered to do so as soon as Lytton gave notice of his motion ; but it was unanimously declined by his colleagues, who knew that he yielded his own opinions to theirs and to the force of circs. on his return from Vienna. . . . He has acted with his colleagues most cordially : indeed, I never remember so little shade of difference of opinion in the Cabinet as there has been since the first week of May. On Friday night, however, the manifestation of personal ill-will towards him in the House of Commons was so strong, and people were so little inclined to hear reason, that he determined of his own free-will, and independently of the advice of others, to resign. I think he did quite right, though I should much have preferred the whole government going out in consequence of a vote of no confidence.

I cannot bear the thought of throwing over a colleague, particularly when I feel that that colleague has done nothing, except make a bad case for himself when he had a good one. The government, as I told Lord John yesterday when he informed me of the step he had taken, will not fail to be accused of meanness in letting him go, after having secretly connived at his treason. However, if Palmerston had gone out, there would of course have been a great cry against him for bringing in Derby and Dizzy, in whom the country have no confidence. There is only one thing to be sure of, namely, that until Sevastopol is taken, the public will continue to run a-muck, and all classes seem to be animated by the same spirit as the mob in Belgrave Square, and all have their pockets full of stones [1] . . .

Lord John did not long remain in the angelic mood described above. On 7th August he seized the opportunity

[1] On Sunday 24th June, and on several successive Sundays, riotous meetings were held in Hyde Park, ostensibly to protest against a Sunday Closing Bill. On 8th July the mob invaded Belgravia, smashing windows and hustling persons in the streets.

of the Appropriation Bill to make a long discursive speech, reproaching ministers for not accepting the Austrian proposals as a basis for negotiating peace, criticising their conduct of the war, and, lastly, urging them to take action for settling the sorrows of Italy. He seemed determined to increase the difficulties of the harassed Foreign Secretary, having conceived the notion that he—Clarendon—had acted insincerely towards him, a suspicion which that minister's private correspondence shows to have been utterly groundless.[1]

Lord Clarendon to Lord Cowley.

11*th August.*— . . . I fear that the state of things in the Crimea will throw a gloom over the visit [2] that is very undesirable on every account. . . . But bad as things are out there, I feel more downcast at all that has passed at home and the disgraceful exposure of our institutions and our public men. The more I think of Lord John's speech, the more disgusted I feel. He filled up the measure of mischief, and with malice prepense did all the harm in his power to every English interest. It has been with some difficulty and after much reflection that I have refrained from answering him in the H. of L. ; but it appears to me that whatever partakes of personality and recrimination can only now tend to lower us still more in the eyes of the world, and I cannot, for my own satisfaction, do harm to the *res publica*. . . .

13*th.*— . . . I can't get over Lord John's speech at all. Having lived for so many years on terms of such intimate friendship with him, I have felt his misconduct more than I should any other man's. I have lamented many acts of rashness, and some of selfishness, on his part, but I never knew him before to be wilfully malevolent, nor did I believe him capable of anything unworthy, not only of a statesman, but of a gentleman. . . .

Lord Clarendon to Lord Stratford de Redcliffe.

F. O., 11*th August.*— . . . In all my political experience I remember nothing so bad as Lord John's speech on Tuesday last. I can only say that, if I had been called upon for an opinion I should have been ready to take my oath that he *could* not have so spoken. The introduction of that apple of discord Italy (about which he never said a word while he was in the

---

[1] See the *Greville Memoirs*, 3rd series, i. 284.
[2] The Queen's visit to Paris.

government) could be for no other purpose than to set us ill with France and Austria, and to encourage the revolutionary feelings in that country. But the worst of all was proclaiming to the country that Aali Pasha [1] was satisfied with the Austrian terms of peace, and that as Turkey was now fighting the battles of England and France, we ought not to guarantee loans, but provide the whole expense of the war ! I believe that personal recrimination would only make our position worse in the eyes of the world, but it is on that account alone that I have forborne from answering Lord John as he deserves in the H. of Lords. . . .

Among the side issues arising out of the French alliance may be reckoned M. de Lesseps's project of cutting a canal through the Isthmus of Suez. Having been asked by the French government to give it his consideration, Clarendon discussed it with Lord Palmerston, whose objections to the scheme are vigorously set forth in a memorandum dated 17th June 1855, and supply pertinent illustration of the limited range of forecast of which the most experienced statesmen are capable. ' We know,' wrote Palmerston among other objections, ' that, whatever may be said by speculators to the contrary, it is physically impossible except at a cost which must put out of all question its being profitable as a commercial speculation.' [2] The Duke of Argyll has left a note upon this matter showing that Clarendon had conceived, or had been persuaded by Palmerston to adopt, a deep distrust of the project :—

Palmerston surprised me and others by the most vehement opposition. It would, he said, cut off Egypt from Turkey, stop the advance of the troops of the Suzerain Power and place British interests in Egypt and in India at the mercy of France. Clarendon was at that time completely under the sway of Palmerston, and took the same line. I don't think they were supported in it by one single other member of the Cabinet.

Two years later Clarendon was still opposing the scheme from a Foreign Office point of view.

[1] Turkish plenipotentiary at the Vienna conference.
[2] The canal cost £24,000,000 to make and enlarge : the transit receipts rose from £206,273 in 1870 (the year after it was opened for traffic) to £5,217,462 in 1910. The dividend on the ordinary 500 fr. shares in 1910 was 157 fr., and the amount of £4,000,000 invested by Mr. Disraeli on behalf of Great Britain in 1875 is now valued at £37,600,000, and returned a dividend of £1,129,260 in 1911.

Lord Clarendon to Lord Cowley.

8th May 1857.— . . . As to the Suez Canal, I think our language must always be that the scheme has manifestly for its object, and inevitably for its effect, to enable the Pasha of Egypt to cut the painter and declare himself independent whenever it may suit him to do so, and that when an attempt is made we shall all fall back into the relative positions we occupied in 1840-41. France, in spite of her treaty engagements to maintain the integrity of the Turkish Empire, will take part with Egypt ; England *must* side with the Sultan, and it is needless to point out what the consequences of such a state of things must be. . . .

In the following year, however, Clarendon had begun to be impressed by the grandeur of the project, and reopened the matter in corresponding with Palmerston ; but Palmerston was as strongly convinced as ever that the thing was impracticable :—

PICCADILLY, 14*th February* 1858.— . . . What you say about the various interests which have been artfully made favorable to the scheme is quite true ; but the scheme is physically impossible as a paying plan, it would be injurious to Turkey, not really beneficial to Egypt, hurtful to England and ruinous to the persons who might be gulled into becoming subscribers.

In August 1855 Lord Clarendon had to tear himself away from Downing Street to accompany the Queen and Prince Albert on their visit to the Emperor of the French.

Lord Clarendon to Lady Clarendon.

SAINT-CLOUD, 19*th August* 1855.— . . . Hitherto all has been successful. The Emperor was on the quay at Boulogne to receive the Queen and rode by the side of her carriage to the station, the road being lined with soldiers as well as the heights. The best feeling towards the Queen was exhibited there and along the road to Paris. At Paris I expected that the reception would be magnificent and that nothing the Emperor could do would be omitted ; but I was not prepared for such enormous masses of people and spontaneous enthusiasm. . . . The whole road from the station to this place—7½ miles—was lined with troops, 90,000 including National Guards. . . . It is clear to me already that I shall not have one moment to myself the whole time I am here. I am continually sent for, and shall have to assist at every presentation and other ceremonial nuisance ; but I will write at every spare moment. . . . At least seven hours' work is arrived from the Foreign Office.

21*st*.— . . . We dine in full uniform at 6.15, and then go to the Grand Opera, so that the scramble is greater and the time for doing anything less even than I thought for. The accumulation of business undone is frightful. I have not been in bed above five hours any night yet, so you may suppose that I am getting a little tired. . . . The whole concern goes on better and better ; hitherto, there never was so complete a success. . . . I would fain give up some of these gaieties and sights in order to do some work and see the people who are asking to see me ; but I find it would not be well taken, and that both Emperor and Queen expect me to make part of the *cortége*, so go I must. It is all doing immense good to the Emperor, of which one is so glad. . . . How I wish every hour that you were here, my own dear K., and yet there is nothing I have done in which you would have shared, except the play last night. . . .

22*nd*.— . . . I hear from various quarters that no foreigner —royal or other—has ever had the same success with this fastidious people of Paris. The unaccountable dignity, with the short stature, the *bienveillance* of manner and the gracious *sourire* seem to have walked into their hearts. . . . I have been compelled to devote this morning to work, and thought I should have had a little time to write to you ; when lo ! the Emperor sent for me, and I have been two hours with him, till the carriages are all at the door for Paris, the Louvre and all manner of things, so I must be gone.

23*rd*.— . . . I will scribble a line, of course, in haste, for the life of perpetual scramble and insufficient time for a tithe of what is to be done far exceeds my expectation. As for the Queen, no royal person ever yet known or to be known in history comes up to her in indefatigability. Conceive her walking in the heat here for an hour in the morning, then going over the Tuileries, and then for 3½ hours perambulating the Louvre, knowing that she had the ball in prospect at the Hôtel-de-Ville, the weather being the sort of scirocco we had at Mola di Gaeta—do you remember ? She knocked up everybody ;

the Emperor went in great distress for the last league. One of his suite, a very fat man, was so knocked up that he gasped— ' Je donnerais tout—tout—la Vénus de Milo y incluse, pour un verre de limonade !' . . . The Queen has had the most complete *personal* success. Everybody raves of her grace and dignity, and some go so far as to think her very pretty. The constant smile takes the fancy of people. . . .

25th.— . . . Conceive the Queen being led by the Emperor by torch light to visit the tomb of Napoleon—the organ of the Invalides playing *God save the Queen* ! It has made a great impression upon the French people, as well it might : but what a page in history !

Lord Clarendon paid a visit to Mme. de Montijo, the Empress Eugénie's mother, with whom he had been well acquainted when he was minister at Madrid ; indeed, the gossips would have it in those days that their friendship was something more than platonic. With singular frankness she reminded him of how people had talked, and told him that, after her daughter's engagement to the Emperor had been announced, he had shown her—Mme. de Montijo— a letter from some busybody stating that the real father of Mlle. Eugénie was Milor Clarendon ! ' Mais, sire,' she had naïvely exclaimed, ' les dates ne correspondent pas ! '

The next great event was the fall of Sebastopol on 9th September. The Queen was then at Balmoral, and Lord Granville, being minister in attendance, graphically described the scene when the news arrived.

Lord Granville to Lord Clarendon.

BALMORAL, 11*th September* 1855.—Phipps and I had a long walk after grouse yesterday and not much sport. We had copiously dined, and I was trying to keep myself awake by arguing with Her Majesty that it was better to receive commonplace messages by telegraph, which I could read, than to receive important ones in cypher which H.M. could not understand, when the page came in with a message for each announcing the great news. You may imagine the sensation : the Queen rather upset : the Prince in the most extravagant spirits. Poor jaded Phipps and I had to rush up a precipitous hill after him over some very rough ground (Phipps in his tights !) to light a bonfire, drink whiskey and say ' ŭrrāy ' as like a Scotchman as we could.

15th.—The fact is, they [1] are in a great fuss about Pam. They are determined to behave well and with confidence to him, but the old mistrust haunts them, and they suspect him as likely to make a sudden splash before they know where they are, and on ground on which it is difficult for them or for you to [*illegible*] him. There is no doubt that success makes him dangerous in these respects. As Sidney Herbert said—' He always wishes to play double or quits.' We must do our best to keep both sides quiet. I have done my best here ; but if a sore is established either here or in Piccadilly, it will be a nasty one to heal. . . .

The Prince of Prussia (the young one) arrived yesterday : a full-grown, not bad-looking youth. . . . He afforded the Queen endless amusement by never understanding the simplest rules of vingt-et-un, explained to him on philosophic principles by Prince Albert. The little Princess Royal dined with us and looked all dinner most lovingly at him. I fancied, however, that now and then the thought flashed across her very intelligent face that he was a shade slow. I am bound to say that all the remarks I heard from him were sensible and in excellent English,

> ' And as for what's incomprehensible,
> I 'll dare be sworn 'twas full as sensible.'

. . . For God's sake, insist on Simpson being brought away ! We have missed one perfect opportunity : do not let us miss another. I could see Mars [2] spouting the geography which he gets at second hand from Ch. Wood, as if I were in the room with you. Do not give up making suggestions. My experience of the captor of Sebastopol is that, after six persons have made the same remark six several times, he begins to consider the idea contained in it as his own.

To the remarks in the early part of this letter as to the Queen's misgivings about Lord Palmerston, Clarendon replied at once defending his chief :—

THE GROVE, *16th September* 1855.—MY DEAR GRANVILLE,— think they are unfair about Palmerston, and are always ready to let their old rancour against him boil up and boil over, tho' he

---

[1] The Queen and Prince Albert.   [2] Lord Panmure.

has done nothing to justify this since he has been in office, and I have given them abundant reasons to be satisfied that he is moderate and amenable. Like everybody else, he requires to be dealt with after his own fashion, and he won't bear to be *brusqué*, or put down by *authority*. They don't bear in mind the total change that has taken place in P.'s position. He has no colleagues to fear or to upset ; he has attained the object of his ambition ; he can't act upon his impulses at the F. O. ; he is more immediately responsible to Parliament than he ever was before, and he is proud of having, as he thinks, overcome the repugnance of the Court. The Queen, therefore, must not persist in thinking him the Palmerston of old. He has put off the old man and has become a babe of grace with his altered position. He cannot wish to get into trouble ; *but* he requires to be delicately handled.

He was so bent upon the disoccupation of the Principalities that I saw at once it was not a question to be settled between himself and me. I was determined in my own mind that it should not go forward, at least in his shape ; but I made no wrangle about it, and wrote the draft in his own words. I brought it, however, before the Cabinet, and gave my own opinion on the subject. They agreed that we must wait to know the opinion of the Queen and the French government, and I was sure that both would be dead against it.

To show you how strong his own feeling was, I send the letter he wrote me last night. I sent him yours, and wrote him a long one myself, pointing out the various eventualities which might arise from the adoption of his scheme, and the far greater liability to attack in parliament. This evening I got a letter from him which pray show the Queen, as I trust it will convince H.M. that Palmerston is open to reason and is not violently addicted to his own opinion.   The Q. will also, I think, be satisfied with what he says about Naples.

There is a fresh hare started, however, tho' not by P., which may give us trouble.   This evening I got a letter from Cowley, sent by a French courier who was to return immediately with the answer, which Persigny was to get from us.   The Emperor wants us to engage not to make peace until the conditions respecting Poland agreed to in 1815 are recognised and fulfilled by Russia ! There's a dainty dish for Gladstone and Co., who, Palmerston writes word, have just signed a treaty with Dizzy and Co. upon the peace principle !   I had only time to write a few reasons against this ill-advised and inopportune proposal ; but I am not sure that it will be distasteful to Palmerston at first, tho' he will not eventually get into such a *galère*.

Upon the whole I like your account of young Prussia, and hope this quiet bit of Highland cooking will succeed.[1] It would be a good position for our young lady, who would make him a capital Queen : it would be good for Prussia and for us to be so connected, and the idea of it is such poison to the Russian party there that one feels additionally anxious for the event to come off. . . . I am afraid that the fall of Sebastopol, with which Simpson had little to do, will make it still more difficult to remove that elderly gentlewoman from the position she ought never to have occupied. I had words with Mars about her yesterday, but he said that if I had known Simpson as long as he had I should be more alive to her many fine qualities. I said I could only boast of having seen Simpson once, when I was struck by his shiney forehead, his red button of a nose, his *ailes de pigeon*, his circular abdomen and his general appearance of a major of militia or a stockbroker *en retraite*, and I thought to myself that that little old fellow never would do for Chief of the Staff ; so Mars must excuse me if I was unable now to picture to myself Simpson Commander-in-Chief as anything but a round man in a square hole. To which the God of War answering said—' Aye, aye ; all that 's very well ; but you 'll see ! '

Lord Granville to Lord Clarendon.

17th.— . . . I had suspected as much. I explained to the Prince that you did not approve of this plan, which was Palmerston's. He says he hopes you will always let him know when that is the case, as it puts the Queen in a difficulty. I believe you will always be able to keep Pam. straight on these points.

In the office they used to say that Pam. always gave way in a standing fight. If Mars can always, when he is in the wrong, resist Pam when he is in the right, it will be hard if you, with the conditions reversed (and being the only single member, excepting perhaps G. Grey, whom Pam. cannot do without) are not able to do the same. You are in great favour here. . . .

18th.— . . . It 's all very well running down Mars's ability,

---

[1] The Crown Prince of Prussia was paying addresses to the Princess Royal at Balmoral.

but there is no other single member of the Cabinet who can defy the Prime Minister, all his colleagues (excepting perhaps Charles Wood) and the Court itself. You will see that he will retain Simpson in command in spite of us all. It appears that while we were losing our time discussing R[aglan]'s merits, Mars was sending him messages that he would take care and protect him. Are we sure that he is not doing the same with Simpson ? Is the *Daily News* right in saying that Simpson is a connection of Mars—perhaps brother to Venus ? . . . The Prince doubts, but I quite believe, the new limited liability company—Gladstone, Dizzy and Co. S. Herbert told me that they would support Dizzy if he went for peace.

Lord Clarendon to Lord Granville.

F. O., 19*th September.*—I had a long talk with Mars to-day *in re* Simpson, and he showed symptoms of yielding. I put the case on the ground of friendship, not war. I suggested that it would be a kind act not to leave so much gout exposed to so much cold for six months, and that if S. was to wrap himself up in his two unexpected and wholly undeserved ribbons, and come home, people would be a trifle more disposed to believe he had earned them, than if he staid to prove the impossibility of that hypothesis.

This ' old codger ' view of the public interests seemed to make more impression on the God than the arguments and facts hitherto brought to bear on him ; and we at last settled, or as good as, that S[impson] should not stay beyond December, but that till then he might be usefully employed in making the army snug for the winter . . . and we must now try to dock three months off the appointed time.

Lord Granville to Lord Clarendon.

22*nd.*— . . . Your descriptions of Mars are much too amusing. But everything is fair in love and war, and Mars, who is a much more wily creature than he used to be when he was so easily caught by a brother God,[1] will slip through all our nets and keep Simpson in command till we have a great disaster or an honorable peace.

[1] Lord Panmure was clandestinely known among his colleagues as Mars, Lord Palmerston as Cupid.

It will always be the case that civilians at home, poring over maps, are impatient with commanders in the field who may appear slow to take advantage of success ; yet it is only a trained soldier, and that soldier himself at the front, who can weigh rightly the condition of his troops, the problems of transport, supply and communications,[1] and the position of the enemy, before renewing the attack or undertaking pursuit.   Lord Panmure had full confidence in General Simpson ; but he had to defend him from first to last against the distrust in him expressed by other ministers—distrust which was now deepened by letters written by the Duke of Newcastle who, being relieved from office, had gone out to the Crimea to see for himself. But he saw with civilian eyes.   What he saw he could not comprehend, and the accounts he sent home were very disparaging to the British commander-in-chief.

Lord Clarendon to Sir G. C. Lewis.

THE GROVE, 16*th September* 1855.— . . . Simpson says (14th September) ' A council was held yesterday of general officers and admirals, when it was deemed prudent to wait awhile before commencing further operations.'   It is certain that those gentlemen on the spot ought to know more than we do in England ; but their decision is a great disappointment, and I fear that, in the same way as after the Alma last year, long inaction will follow victory and no advantage will be taken of the demoralisation of the enemy. . . . Pray thank Theresa for her delightful joyous letter upon the fall of Sebastopol.   The relief that the event has brought is indescribable.   It will change the aspect of things all over the world, for our inability to take the place was injuring our name and fame everywhere and inviting impertinence even from the smallest states.

Wisely wrote Prince Albert to Clarendon as follows, cautioning him against hasty judgment founded upon imperfect information :—

---

[1] ' The most unpractised general feels this [the maintenance of supply] at once on taking command in a district where his troops are no longer supplied by routine ; or if he does not, the loss of a single meal to his army would sufficiently impress it on him ' (Sir E. Hamley's *Operations of War*, p. 60).

17th September 1855.— . . . I am sorry that the Duke [of New-castle] ever wrote this letter. It is at all times hazardous for a civilian, going into a camp and picking up information from this or that person and listening to the stories flying about there, to give an opinion upon plans of operation, military system, the merit of the different men in command ; but it was particularly so for the Duke, who fell quite into the ways of ' our correspondent.' [1] This siege has been an anomalous one in many ways, and my astonishment is that the troops have borne the 350 days' incessant hard fighting, with every possible discomfort and deaths at the rate of 18,000 to 19,000 men during that period, without grumbling at their commanders, and the government much more. When the Duke speaks of a want of plan (at the time he wrote) it is nonsense, and the result has shown it. The only plan ever gone upon since May was to work up to the Malakoff and take it, which would cause the fall of the town ; but that could not be done without the Redan being equally attacked, and the batteries on the Sapouné being pushed sufficiently low to reach the shipping. This was an operation of the greatest difficulty, costing the French 200 and us 60 men a night ! Yet it was nobly persevered in.

Now you may say that was done by the troops and is no merit of the commanders. Quite true : but it had to be done, and the commanders could not get into the town in any other way. . . . I think the Duke's judgment upon General Simpson hasty and harsh. . . .

The fall of Sebastopol brought immediate relief from racking suspense and apprehension ; but anxiety was far from being at an end. The French army had reaped the laurels necessary for the security of the imperial dynasty ; would the Emperor now yield to the strong feeling in his capital demanding peace on terms short of those for which the war was undertaken ? To that the British Cabinet would never consent : would England then be left to carry on the war without her principal ally ? To avert such a misfortune all the energy and tact of the Foreign Office were called into play, and Clarendon was dismayed by Lord Cowley, most trusted of all his official correspondents,

---

[1] W. H. Russell, the pioneer of newspaper war correspondents, who furnished the *Times* with incessant diatribes upon Lord Raglan's conduct of the siege.

announcing that his private means would no longer stand
the drain upon them entailed by his position as ambassador
at the Tuileries.

Lord Clarendon to Lady Clarendon.

F.O., *9th October* 1855.— . . . To my immense annoyance
and regret Cowley insists on resigning on account of being unable
to meet the expenses. I must somehow try to prevent it, but
the Cabinet did not see how his income could be increased, nor,
in fact, do I. He lately affronted such swarms of M.P.'s that
some of them—Sir F. Kelly for instance—mean to vote for a
reduction of his salary. Pleasant addition to other pleasant
things !

12th.—Robert Grosvenor is going to Paris, and I have charged
him to work on Cowley not to resign. The Queen says ' every
nerve must be strained to retain Lord Cowley. He is worth an
army and fleet to us.'

Lord Cowley was persuaded to remain at his post, which,
in fact, he continued to hold until 1867. The uppermost
question in the deliberations of the allied governments
was what to do with Sebastopol now they had got it.

Lord Clarendon to Lord Cowley.

THE GROVE, *3rd October* 1855.— . . . Immediate demolition
would be public announcement that Sebastopol, and with it the
Crimea, will be ultimately restored to Russia, and whatever the
future determination may be, such an announcement at the
present moment would be highly impolitic. We have come into a
property ; and, having paid very dearly for it, it would be unwise
to order its destruction before we even know of what it consists
or to what uses it may be turned. Demolition, moreover, would
not be consistent with occupation ; and nowhere can the allied
armies and fleets pass the winter more conveniently and economically than at Sebastopol. . . . In short, there are abundant
reasons for not leaving the Crimea at present. It is our *gage*
matériel, and may be made useful in a variety of ways. . . . I
think the public may wait for the details of possession before
disposal is decided upon, and that it will be sufficient to assume
that what has been so hardly gained will not be lightly parted
with.

It is painful to be reminded through the perusal of letters in these years of the want of confidence which the government and the public felt in the generals at the front. The brilliant action on the heights of Alma, indeed, had been in accord with what was expected of them ; but there was no understanding in the Cabinet, still less in the nation at large, of the prodigious difficulties imposed upon the Allies in attempting the invasion of the Crimea. Yet the Cabinet had been fully apprised of the unfavourable opinions expressed about the enterprise not only by Lord Raglan and Admiral Dundas, but by Maréchal Saint-Arnaud, and by such experienced veterans as Sir George Brown and Sir John Burgoyne. The last-named had written just before the landing in the Crimea : ' After much discussion, I think the proposition affording the best chance of success is likely to be adopted ; but it is a desperate enterprise, forced, I believe, on Lord Raglan and the French general by taunts from home.' [1]

Lord Clarendon to Sir G. C. Lewis.

THE GROVE, 4th October 1855.— . . . The most urgent question at this moment is the Commandership-in-chief. Our pet Codrington was found wanting on the 8th ; his seniors we believe to be quite unfit. Panmure inclines to him still ; the Prince, and therefore the Queen, prefer Sir Colin Campbell. I would stand the shot of Windham, but neither of the Lords P.[2] will. That is how the matter rested at the last Cabinet. It is a terrible problem.

The same distrust of those appointed to conduct the war had found expression during the visit of the Queen and Prince Albert to Paris earlier in the year. Her Majesty notes in her diary that the French Emperor ' lamented bitterly the want of invention and energy in both our commanders from the first, and the absence of any great genius. He then spoke very openly and frankly of the defects of *our* generals, and we told him equally frankly what we objected to in *his*.' [3]

[1] *Life of Sir John Burgoyne*, ii. 83.   [2] Palmerston and Panmure.
[3] Martin's *Prince Consort*, iii. 338.

The British ambassador at Constantinople kept adding to the perplexity of the government by disregarding instructions and quarrelling with the French ambassador. 'Stratford,' wrote Clarendon on 6th October, 'is an enormous embarrassment. I don't like recalling him, but I should be heartily glad if he would resign. The chief mischief he could do here would be when the time for real negotiations arrived. Nothing will be more easy than to pick holes in *any* peace that can be made, and S. will be looked upon with reverence in his natural capacity of censor.'

But the direst embarrassment of all to those charged with conducting the war arose from the persistent invective of the *Times*. This culminated on 3rd October 1855 in an attack upon the Prince of Prussia, whose betrothal to the Princess Royal of England was then pending. Clarendon wrote a vigorous remonstrance to his friend Reeve, unaware that Reeve had already decided to sever his connection of fifteen years' standing with Printing House Square in consequence of the tone adopted by the leading journal.

Lord Clarendon to Henry Reeve.

3rd October 1855.— . . . I am really in despair at the doings of the *Times*. Three pitched battles gained would not repair the mischief done by Mr. Russell and the articles upon his letters. He has tried to make his reputation as an author by colouring his picture, and throwing into deep and dismal shade everything that should be sacred to British honour. I have seen many French private accounts of our failure, and they are all more just and generous than the *Times*. They all advert to the fact that the attack on the Malakoff *alone* succeeded, and that was by surprise, while the French masses elsewhere failed. What a French general said on Monday to a friend of mine is perfectly true—that no army in the world can maintain its discipline under such daily incitement to mutiny. All our best soldiers in the course of the year have been put *hors de combat*; the *Times* has succeeded but too well in persuading foreigners not to enter our service; we are obliged to send out recruits, and then, instead of encouraging them and throwing

a veil over our shortcomings, we are exposed to the world as a
cowardly rabble. . . . I am utterly at a loss to understand
what the object can be, but of this I feel sure, that every condition of treason is fulfilled by some of the recent articles in the
Times. I know nothing about the young Prussian Prince and
the Princess Royal ; but if they are to be married some of these
days, as the *Times* assumes, the article of this morning will be a
dagger in the Queen's heart.

5th.—MY DEAR REEVE,—I am not only not surprised at the
decision you have come to, but, as your sincere friend, I should
have been very sorry if you had not taken it ; for no man who
has the honour and interests of his country at heart, or who has
the views of a statesman and the feelings of a gentleman, would
now like to be identified, however indirectly, with such a journal
as the *Times* has become. Its conductors are either so ignorant
that they don't foresee the consequences of their own acts, or
are so wicked that they are indifferent to them, or, for some
objects of their own, they are determined to degrade England
in the eyes of the world and to render all government impossible.
Great irresponsible power was never more abused : it is despotism
committing high treason every day with impunity. . . . I hope,
rather than expect, that the eyes of Mr. Walter or Delane will
be opened, and that they will perceive that there must be something very wrong in a state of things which has imposed upon
you the necessity of dissolving the connection, and has deprived
them of your valuable assistance. . . .

To myself personally, your wise and proper determination
is a matter of much regret, and I must take this opportunity
of thanking you for the many good turns you have done
me by giving a right direction to opinion upon foreign
affairs. . . . I don't know whether the Queen and the Prince
were aware that you had anything to do of late with the
Times ; but of this I am sure, that neither of them could for
a moment have attributed to you even a knowledge of the
article on the Prince of Prussia, which must have given them
so much pain ; but I will take care that you stand completely
right in that quarter.[1]

---

[1] Reeve himself deals very briefly in his journal with the circumstances
of his resignation. ' The moment an attempt was made to interfere with
me and garble my articles, I resigned, and fell back on the *Edinburgh
Review*, which is a sort of peerage as compared with the tumult of the lower
House' (Laughton's *Life of H. Reeve*, i. 339). Lord Clarendon's letters
above quoted put the matter in a clearer light.

Lord Clarendon to Lady Clarendon.

WINDSOR CASTLE, 23rd October.— . . . I am always on good
terms with the people of the house, but I don't remember ever
being so thoroughly friendly and familiar as on this occasion.
I sat next Eliza at dinner yesterday ; we talked politics and
cut jokes at a great rate. Then I had a turn with Joseph ; [1]
afterwards, the whole evening with Eliza, while Frau Kent
was fast asleep, dreaming that she was playing at patience.
Then this morning I got a message not to hurry myself, but as
soon as I had done breakfast the Prince would be glad to see
me. I staid just an hour and a half. Then after luncheon I
was kept for ¾ hour for a private talk, and was ordered to drive
—why, I don't know, for I went airing in a Scotch mist and open
carriage with the Duchess of Athol and Miss Bulteel. Upon
coming in the Queen said : ' Will you come up with us only for
five minutes ? ' and I staid exactly an hour. . . . Thus the
good day's work and absence of interviews which I had proposed
to myself has been an utter failure.

I had a regular argument with both the Queen and the Prince
about dear Sir Robert [Peel]. As I contended, he must either
have been wanting in foresight not to have adopted free trade
principles sooner, or in honesty if, knowing what was for the
public good, he sacrificed it to party as long as he dared. I
routed them both and gave them some new notions, tho' of
course they did not admit it. . . .

Cowley's letter of to-day is very unsatisfactory. The Emperor
is becoming very peaceful—frightened at high prices and the
financial crisis. In short, we shall have great trouble to save
ourselves from being hustled into a shameful peace, I can see
that.

25th.— . . . The Queen was much pleased with a letter I
wrote to Cowley about not withdrawing the armies from the
Crimea. She says it must convince the Emperor. . . .

F.O., 6th November. — Here I am at 7.20 and not a word
written yet to Cowley, Stratford and others ! The Cabinet
began late and lasted long ; and then I had poor old Westmorland squatting upon me till now.[2] As it was a leave-taking

---

[1] Cryptonyms for exalted personages are convenient in private correspondence, and the Queen and Prince Albert are often referred to as
' Eliza ' and ' Joseph.'

[2] John, eleventh Earl of Westmorland, 1786-1859, Peninsular veteran
and experienced diplomat, but being now in his seventy-second year,
had just resigned the embassy at Vienna.

interview, I did not like to cut his twaddle short; but I was obliged at last to request he would make himself scarce. . . .

Palmerston read a very long and rather able letter from Stanley [1] giving a variety of reasons for declining [the Colonial Office], some of which were evidently supplied by Derby; but the tone was cordial; and he expressed gratitude to Palmerston for having by his offer given him a political *status* to which he could not have aspired. . . .

13th.— . . . The Emperor, it appears, is angry with Cowley for having *misunderstood* him about withdrawing troops from the Crimea, whereas he only understood him too well! Perhaps the Emperor now perceives the military and political evils of his project, and is vexed that he should have been taken *au pied de la lettre.*

Delane was here for an immense time—rather *mou* and humble. I did not spare his infernal paper, and I must say he did not attempt to defend anything that was done during his absence, which was the time when it ran a-muck at all men and things. He said that with the slightest management Reeve might have avoided a rupture with the *Times*, but that both parties got angry. Among my complaints was the article in abuse of Simpson.[2] This, he told me, was Reeve's, so I think he is as well out of the *Times* as in it!

F.O., 16*th November.*— . . . A telegram from Cowley says that Bourqueney announces the departure of his messenger from Vienna with *most satisfactory* intelligence. This, I own, alarms me much; not that I fear our being hustled into an inglorious Austrian peace, but I am afraid that the Buol-Bourqueney concoction will try the Anglo-French alliance highly, for all the government and all the entourage of the Emperor will be urging and menacing him to agree to *anything* which will put an end to the war; nor must we disguise from ourselves that a termination *quelconque* to the war would be as popular in France as it would be unpopular here, that L. Napoleon would be applauded for it, and that we should be stoned with stones that we died. So I look for some radical, and perhaps irreconcilable, difference on this matter; which is a bore.

23*rd November* 1855.—I had not been here ten minutes this morning before the French ambassador wished to see me, and

[1] Lord Stanley, afterwards 15th Earl of Derby.
[2] Commander-in-chief at the seat of war.

I was surprised that he walked in with his usual *gaillard*, good-humored look. He began, however, by saying—' J'ai eu une lettre de Lord Palmerston qui m'a beaucoup émotionné, pas tant par la substance que par la forme, qui est bien dure.' He then pulled out the letter, which, of course, I made as if I had not seen,[1] and I managed, partly by agreeing in what P. said, and by saying at the last paragraph : ' Oh, that 's a form of expression used by a man who feels strongly, and Palmerston is in a position that makes him feel strongly.' And so I calmed the little man and made him perfectly reasonable. I must own, too, that I was in better humor with P.'s letter from having just read one from Cowley giving an account of Walewski's insolence and his surprise at our having ventured to suggest any modifications. I was boiling with rage, and therefore defended Palmerston *con amore* ; nor could I deny, when Palmerston asked me this morning whether, in view of Cowley's letter, I now thought his too strong, I really could not say I did. We mean to adhere to our modifications, and I convinced Persigny they were right. I have written a very strong letter to Cowley, and told him to make Walewski understand that we are not a diplomatic and political *contingent*.

24th.— . . . Cowley's letter was again most unsatisfactory to-day. Those French are mad with fear and roguery, and I am afraid that the Emperor is almost as much demoralised as his government. I am sure that if we rejected the terms, the French would make peace on their own hook, and our position would then be a miserable one. The French have been screaming so loudly for peace that I expect Austria will be frightened at the hard conditions she has offered to impose on Russia, and may want to back out of them. In short, it is a very nervous moment.

27th.— . . . Granville, who sees everybody, says that all the people coming home *from different parts of France* are unanimous in saying that, if we mean to go on with the war, we must do it single-handed, for France will have no more of it. . . .

28th.— . . . I have been to Windsor, which *only* cost five hours out of my day ! But these things are unavoidable, and it certainly would not be fair to require that the Queen and her children should be in London at this unhealthy season for the chance of being wanted every now and then. . . . The

---

[1] Lord Palmerston had sent Lord Clarendon a copy of his letter *after* it had gone to M. de Persigny.

Queen, of course, was most gracious ; but awfully fashed at Palmerston's letter to Persigny, of which Palmerston had sent her a copy. She said it was like his worst ebullitions in the olden time. The Emperor is still much annoyed about it, and has spoken to Cowley, who dined on Sunday at the Tuileries, and had a long and, on the whole, satisfactory talk with the Emperor, who was calm and reasonable, and desirous only that the whole truth should be told him always. The alliance, therefore, is much less sick to-day than it was yesterday. . . .

28th November.— . . . Cowley says the King of Sardinia [1] has not made a good impression in Paris. His way of shaking hands with everybody and saying, ' Comment allez-vous, mon cher ? ' when they are presented to him, is not much approved.

This morning came a card to me for Windsor *from Friday to Thursday next*, which is what I call realising one's worst expectations ! It really is a horrible nuisance. The Queen said nothing about it, but she does not *envisager* Victor Emmanuel's visit with much pleasure. They are going to take him to Woolwich, Portsmouth and Aldershot, which he won't like, and not to shoot and beagle, which he would care for. However, it has all been cooked with Azeglio, and if he gets too much bored he won't come again.

From Lady Clarendon's Journal.

1st December.— . . . We dined in St. George's Hall, which is always a magnificent sight. The Queen presented me and several other ladies to the King of Sardinia. He has not much *lady talk*, and he was heard to say afterwards that the Queen *lui avait joué un tour* in having presented these ladies to him and then left him alone to talk to them. With me, weather and theatres were the only subjects talked of, the first of which I think I began—the second he began. To Lady Granville he began—' Et bien, madame, qu'avez vous fait de beau ? ' She could not make out exactly what he meant, so she answered— ' Pas grand'chose, sire.'

He is very soldierlike and powerful in his appearance, not good-looking, and has the most curious eyes. When quite still I do not think they are particularly prominent ; but, when excited, they roll about and look as if they were going to start from his head. He has never lived in society at all and always dines quite alone, as he said rather touchingly to the Queen—

[1] Vittore Emmanuele II.

seul avec mes chagrins. This is the first time he has ever been
out of his country. . . . He told the Queen that he only slept
two hours, habitually going to bed at 12 and getting up at two.
The Queen remonstrated, and told him that he would kill himself if he did that, and he does look in a state of nervous excitement. His usual dinner hour is about 11 A.M., and upon being
asked whether he took nothing more before going to bed, he said
sometimes he drank a glass of cold water. . . . He is plain-
spoken, and said of Lord Palmerston—'Il parle comme les
Lombards : il me fait peur—il me fait peur.' Of Lord John
Russell he said—' Je ne le comprends pas ; il parle de la paix
à un tel point que je ne le comprends pas. Quand on fait la
guerre, on ne la fait pas comme cela ! ' . . . The Queen has
inspired him with great admiration for her character. He said
that he was aware of her virtues, but that he did not expect to
find such *profondeur* in her knowledge. . . . The Prince of
Wales [1] seemed much occupied with the King of Sardinia, and
told me that he could cut off an ox's head at one stroke of his
sword.

Lord Clarendon to Lady Clarendon.

WINDSOR CASTLE, *6th December.*— . . . My conversation with
the King [of Sardinia] was, upon the whole, satisfactory, tho' he
did not much like my shrug of the shoulder when he asked me
what he was going to *gagner* by all this, and whether we could
not manage for him *une petite extension de territoire.* He is
shrewd and, I am sure, thoroughly truthful and honorable. The
Queen seems to have made a most favorable impression upon
him. He told me that he had no idea of finding such a woman.
He knew all about her virtues ; but her knowledge—her
principles in politics and religion—the judicious advice she had
given him—had perfectly astounded him. . . . Only fancy the
Queen being up at 5 this morning to see him off. . . . It has
been a hard day, and I am rather tired at this present writing,
and have still my letters to do for Paris and Vienna. Walewski
has been playing more tricks, and I fear we have not yet come
to an understanding about the Austrian ultimatum. . . .
Palmerston told us to-day that Newcastle was in bad humor
and said everybody out there was to blame, from the general to
the drummer-boy. Do take care of yourself, and then I will
love you always.

[1] Aged fourteen.

13th.—We don't quite agree to the Austrian amendments of *our* amendments, so there must go a rejoinder ; which is rather a bore, as it will exasperate both Austrians and French.   I shall not be surprised now if the whole thing is broken off, which will be another bore.   Palmerston is very rabid, and his feelings about Austria are so savage that he almost compels me to take her part. . . . Walewski is in a furious rage with Persigny, and has demanded officially an explanation from him for having said that the whole Cabinet here thinks him in collusion with Austria, and that there was unfair dealing towards us.

19th.— . . . The feeling about Kars is very strong, and there will be the devil to pay when parliament meets.   I can't reconcile myself to the catastrophe, which may have awfully bad results, and influence the whole of the operations next year. Williams, and his officers of course, won't be exchanged ; they will probably *promène* them all thro' Russia to St. Petersburg. Only think of the Russian loan being levied here ! in the ordinary way of business, too, so I don't see how it can be interfered with ! £200,000 left London yesterday, and the pressure on the money market will be great.   G. Lewis is very low about it and the sinking revenue.   Altogether things are gloomy to-day, and that ass Murray seems to have got up a quarrel with Persia.[1]

22nd.— . . . We have had a long Cabinet—the last before Christmas.   The mails from different parts of the habitable globe did not arrive till 5 this evening, and I have messengers going to Paris, Madrid, Naples, Athens, Constantinople and the United States, to each of which places I send a private letter. Who says my life is not one of uninterrupted enjoyment ?

[1] In justice to Sir Charles Murray it should be stated that, however excusable this slighting reference to him by an overworked Foreign Secretary may be considered, the Persian embroglio was none of Murray's making.   The Shah, a drunken debauchee, was a mere puppet in the hands of his minister, Sadr Azim.   When Murray arrived in Tehran at the end of 1854, Persia was bound under treaty with Great Britain not to occupy any part of Afghan territory.   Early in 1855 an insurrection took place in Herat ; the reigning prince, Syud Mahommed, was killed.   The advance of Dost Mahommed, ruler of Cabul, against Candahar, was made a pretext by Sadr Azim for laying siege to Herat.   In order to get rid of the inconvenient presence of a British minister in Tehran, Sadr Azim got up false charges against Sir Charles Murray and Mr. Thompson, Secretary to the British Mission, accusing them of improper relations with Meerza Hashem's wife, who was related to the Shah, but was in disgrace at Court. This lady was seized and imprisoned.   As her husband was British agent at Shiroz, Murray demanded her release, and an apology for the slander promulgated against him and Thompson.   The Shah thereupon refused to receive Murray until Queen Victoria (to whom he applied the exceedingly objectionable term ' Malikeh ') ' makes us a suitable apology for the insolence of her Envoy.'

Walewski has been at fresh tricks. What do you think of the absurd Russian proposal for peace not having come by telegraph to Baron Seebach (the Saxon minister) as Walewski stated it had, but by a Russian officer sent for the express purpose, who was concealed in Seebach's house, and whom Walewski *saw* and sent back to St. Petersburg ? He has also sent off Seebach himself, nominally to Dresden but in reality to St. Petersburg. It is too bad that we must be acting the part of policemen ; but when one has to do with a man whose moral sense is so misty as Walewski's, and whose duties are subordinate to his vanity or interests, underhand tricks must be expected. Persigny has gone to Paris, where I suppose he will have a regular tussle with Walewski ; but he will probably do a sight of mischief, for he is very indiscreet, and I am afraid when he abuses Walewski to people, he thinks, and accordingly says, that they have abused Walewski to him. . . .

The anticipated ' tussle ' took place. Persigny, returning to London in January, described to Dr. Robert Ferguson the interview with his chief.

From Dr. Ferguson's Journal.

' I have been bothered,' said he, ' hence my illness, doctor.'

Dr. F.—' No wonder. You must have much on your mind. Is peace certain ? '

M. de P.—' Quite certain. The only difficulty will be about Bomarsund and the undertaking not to re-fortify that stronghold. Conceive the folly of Walewski, who would never specify the particulars insisted on by the English Cabinet in the construction of the fifth clause, viz. the non-fortification of the Aland Isles, etc. He and M. de Morny are looking sharper after their private interests than after the public. Walewski has been crying out for peace because he would be ruined by his speculations without it. He has been saying everywhere that the British Cabinet has been throwing every difficulty in the way of adjustment. I went over to Paris and met Walewski, and, in the presence of the Emperor, supported the English alliance and the English views. Words arose so high that the Emperor interposed and reconciled us on the spot. Finding, however, that M. Walewski had been giving false hopes to Russia by permitting his views to be known, and that, as a consequence of such conduct, M. de Nesselrode had sent his son-in-law, M. de Seebach, to foment the discord between the Cabinets, the Emperor sent for the latter and said : " Oh, de Seebach, I wish for peace very, very, very much. Perhaps I should not ask as much of Russia as the British Cabinet does ; but don't deceive yourself ! if you imagine I prefer Russia or peace to the British alliance, you will find out your egregious error. If Great Britain chooses to carry on the war, I will continue it for the next twenty years." On this M. de Seebach said : " This communication, sire, cannot be made by letter. I will start for St. Petersburg myself." He left that day, and immediately returned, with acceptance by Russia of the Austrian ultimatum *pur et simple.*'

Dr. F.—' The conduct of the Emperor is so loyal to his ally that Lord Clarendon should mention it in the House of Lords.'

M. de P.—' That would do good.'

I saw Lord Clarendon on the 19th [January] and gave him my opinion on the above as a topic for his speech.

Lord C.—' That would be difficult.'

Dr. F.—' I differ from you, for you have only to repeat what the Emperor said without explaining the occasion which produced it.'

Lord C.—' M. de Persigny is a straightforward, good little fellow, but he is indiscreet in talking as he does with every member of the Corps Diplomatique against his chief Walewski.'

Dr. F.—' There must be some personal pique between them. Does Walewski desire to return to London ? '

Lord C.—' Oh no ; he is not in accord with any one here.'

Dr. F.—' Persigny told me that the peace which is now all but certain was due to the resolute tone maintained by yourself and Lord Palmerston.'

Lord C.—' If we had not insisted, the result would have been very different, which neither we nor the Emperor could have faced. A petty peace would have shaken him on his throne by giving power to his enemies in France. M. Walewski and the rest are on the verge of ruin—gamblers that would throw their country on the cast of the die.'

Dr. F.—' In a word, they are indirectly bribed by Russia ? '

Lord C.—' Just so.' [1]

The Queen's natural anxiety about affairs was apt to cause her to tax the equanimity of her Foreign Secretary by a telegraphic summons such as the following on 28th

---

[1] From Dr. Ferguson's journal, condensed.

December: 'The Queen, hearing that Lord Clarendon is at the Foreign Office, hopes that he will come down to dine and sleep at Windsor to-day, and hopes that he will come down in time for the Queen to see him before dinner.'

'You may suppose,' runs Clarendon's note to his wife on receiving this summons, 'that I am slightly put out by receiving now—*at* 4 *o'clock*—the enclosed telegram from H.M.[1] I have had interviews all the morning, and none of my letters are done for the various messengers ; but, of course, I can't help myself, and must go.'

[1] Perhaps this is the earliest occurrence (in literature) of the term 'telegram.'

CHAPTER XVI

THE PARIS CONFERENCE

'England! thou hast not sav'd one drop of blood
In this hot trial, more than we of France;
Rather, lost more.'   *King John* ii. 2.

WRITING to Lord Campbell about the objection he had raised on constitutional grounds to the bestowal of a life peerage on Mr. Baron Parke, J. W. Croker referred to certain anomalies in peerage practice, and cited as an instance the position of Lord Clarendon's mother.

Lord Clarendon succeeded his uncle; his mother was Mrs., and his brothers and sisters Misters and Mistresses, Villiers.[1] Well, a notice in the *Gazette* gave the brothers and sisters the rank of earl's children, and we had my Lady Theresa and the Honourable Charles and the Honourable Henry,[2] and a very proper exercise of a decent and reasonable prerogative; but was it decent or reasonable . . . that the mother of these lords, ladies and honourable gentlemen, should have lived and died plain Mrs. George Villiers?[3]

In all Mrs. Villiers's abundant correspondence there is no evidence that she shared Mr. Croker's dissatisfaction with her standing as the mother of a peer. Had she felt it, she would have been sure to have expressed it, for she was a woman of vigorous views and fearlessly outspoken.

From Lady Clarendon's Journal.

22nd September 1855.—Dear Mrs. G. is 80 to-day—a wonderful and admirable woman she is—such a clear intellect—such warm affections—such untiring energy of character—every sense un-

---

[1] He had but one sister.   [2] He meant the Hon. Edward.
[3] *Croker Papers*, iii. 357.

impaired, or nearly so ; for tho' she says her eyesight is not quite as good as it was, it is better than that of many people at 30 ; and one may say the same of hearing and memory. Then her enjoyment and zest for everything surpass those of almost any one—young or old.

Dr. Robert Ferguson, who shared with Sir C. Locock the office of physician-accoucheur to Queen Victoria, and who numbered among his patients half the political, literary and fashionable personages in London, was a very old friend of the Villiers family, left a note about them in his diary for this year, which, as the observation of a shrewd man of the world, may serve to mitigate the biographer's proneness to panegyric.

Mrs. Villiers is one of the cleverest women I ever knew on all that concerns worldly wisdom ; but singularly deficient in higher views and motives. Most of her children are models of manners and of indifference to all higher tribunals than that of the world ; yet their nature leans to nobility of thought. Lord Clarendon is more *actively* kind than a hundred parsons put together, always hunting up opportunities of doing favours in the sweetest way. If his will had been strengthened and motived by high principles strongly felt, he would have been the brightest of examples of a British nobleman. He is weak because he acts on expediency only.

Lord Clarendon to Lady Clarendon.

1st *January* 1856.—Many happy new years to you, my own dearest Katty. We ought to be very thankful for all the blessings we enjoy, and the very few drawbacks to our happiness that we have met with. I am sure it is a great addition to our happiness to see my mother quite as well, if not better, than she was at this time last year, and to think of dear Theresa's state now when compared with her misery twelve months ago. Ainsi tout est pour le mieux dans le meilleur des mondes possibles, and if I was but out of office !—why, I suppose it would be too much happiness, and I should be wishing myself back again.

Within a fortnight of the date of this letter Mrs. George Villiers was no more. She breathed her last on 12th January 1856—the fifty-sixth anniversary of the birth of that son in whose career she had felt so much pride, and whose affection had never failed her.

Peace negotiations, or rather negotiations for devising terms which might form a basis for the preliminaries of peace, were now afoot. Clarendon dreaded that the French government, yielding to rising popular impatience with the war, would throw over their allies and yield almost any terms for a settlement.

Lord Clarendon to Lady Clarendon.

F.O., *7th January* 1856.— . . . Such a day of it! I am quite knocked up. At half-past 11 the Devils began for to come, and they did not cease till 6—the Royal Boy for an hour and a half and Sir E. Lyons for as long. Buol seems to be very firm and unflinching about modifications, and generally to be behaving well. He thinks that the answer from St. Petersburg may arrive to-day. Gortschakoff is, or pretends to be, packing up and preparing to leave Vienna. Brunnow thinks that the Bessarabian clause will never go down in Vienna.

The G. D. Constantine is moving heaven and earth to prevent his brother yielding, and he will probably succeed. I cannot yet bring myself to hope he may fail, which I dare say is wrong ; but we shall leave off so much damaged that I want a little repair, tho' with such men as Panmure to direct the war it is possible that another campaign might still further tarnish our reputation.

On 15th January the Emperor Alexander agreed to fresh terms proposed by Austria and delivered by her in the form of ultimatum. They consisted of three out of the four points at the Vienna conference, substituting for the fourth and most difficult one the neutralisation of the Black Sea instead of the former alternatives of limitation or counterpoise. There was no proposal for such indemnity as the Allies might reasonably have demanded and Russia as reasonably have refused. Palmerston gulped the terms of negotiation, much against his inclination, well knowing that the state of feeling in Paris made it certain that, if England were to insist upon something to compensate her

H

for the blood and treasure spent in the war, she would have to fight for it single-handed.

A congress of the Five Powers was appointed to meet at Paris. Palmerston was inclined to appoint Sir Edmund Lyons as British plenipotentiary. Lyons had succeeded Dundas in January 1855 in command of the fleet in the Black Sea, but he had previously held various diplomatic appointments. However, as he spoke French very imperfectly, Clarendon could not endorse Palmerston's recommendation.

Lord Clarendon to Lord Granville.

F.O., 17*th January* 1856.—Palmerston has written to propose Lyons as our negotiator, assigning to him a great number of qualities that he doesn't possess. He is utterly ignorant of all the main questions that will be under discussion ; and, tho' he may have some ability and some firmness, he is irritable, vain, and more deficient in judgment than any elderly gent. I am acquainted with. I am sure he would be a great failure, and I have written accordingly to P[n].

Finally it was decided that Clarendon should attend the congress himself. He found himself in a very difficult situation, for, while the war spirit was running high as ever in England, and English journals were protesting in advance against any settlement that should not inflict enough humiliation upon Russia, the Emperor Napoleon was ready to accept any terms rather than continue the war. Writing to the Queen on 18th January Clarendon warned her Majesty that, in the present state of public feeling in England, no terms of peace that could be made would give satisfaction, and he felt that his mission to Paris led to the grave of his political reputation, but that he willingly incurred the sacrifice out of a sense of public duty.

Lord Clarendon to Henry Reeve.

The Grove, 26*th January* 1856.— . . . I never consented to do anything with greater reluctance in my life ; but I felt I ought not to shrink from it, having of course gained some experience about the different questions that must come under discussion. But I make no illusion to myself as to what will be my fate. No peace that is within attainable limits can satisfy the excited people of this country. John Bull will be glad enough to put an end to the war ; but he will be without mercy for the terms on which peace is made ; so that the negotiations must be the grave of the negotiators' reputation !

Madame de Lieven having written to inquire of Charles Greville what he thought about the coming peace conference, Clarendon persuaded him to write fully to her (which he was rather unwilling to do), because anything he told her would go straight to the Emperor of Russia. Greville accordingly wrote to assure her that the English government had not the faintest wish to impose humiliating terms on Russia, but only to restrain her from aggression and to secure the peace of Europe.

In the debate on the address when parliament met on 31st January, Lord Derby made a sarcastic speech, expressing his belief, *inter alia*, that the government had humiliated the country by making overtures of peace through the mediation of Austria, and that grave doubts existed as to their sincerity in accepting the terms that had been put forward as a basis of negotiation.

In reply Lord Clarendon explained that Austria had not offered to mediate, but simply to ascertain and make known at St. Petersburg the terms upon which the Allies were prepared to accept overtures for peace. It was impossible, he said, for her Majesty's government, according to their sense of duty, to refuse to accept these good offices. He then addressed himself with some warmth to the charge of insincerity.

My lords, our sincerity in these negotiations has been called in question. Throughout the continent of Europe we are accused of insincerity in accepting these conditions. It has been said that, though we have accepted them, we mean to continue the war, simply because we want war, not for any definite end, but in the expectation that another campaign would be productive of more military glory, which would serve to compensate us for the sacrifices we have made. I mention these reports because they have been so widely circulated, and pretty generally believed, and also because I desire on the part of her Majesty's government to give them the most unqualified denial. However much we may be aware of the spirit which animates our country, however much it may be regretted that the preparations we have made—preparations such as there has been no instance of before in the history of this country—should not be turned to account, and should not be made to redound to the military and naval fame of England, yet I am convinced that the number of persons who put faith in these reports will be very rapidly diminished when it is seen that, notwithstanding all the efforts we have made and all the sacrifices we have undergone, we hold faithfully to the conditions which we have once accepted. But should any attempt be made to deprive us of the conditions which we have a right to demand, and to which we have already agreed, then I believe the people of this country would be as one man. They would not consider any sacrifices too great to carry on the war, and we might then expect conditions of a very different nature from those which her Majesty's government have now accepted, and to which they frankly and honourably adhere.

The conference was formally opened on 25th February, under the presidency of Count Colonna Walewski. The plenipotentiaries were—for France, Count Walewski and Baron de Bourqueney ; for Russia, Count Orloff and Baron de Brunnow ; for Austria, Count de Buol and Baron Hübner ; for Great Britain, the Earl of Clarendon and Lord Cowley ; for Sardinia, Count de Cavour and the Marquis de Villamarina ; and for Turkey, Ali Pasha and Mehemmed Djemel Bey.

Lord Clarendon to Lord Palmerston.

Paris, 29th February 1855.—I am not faint-hearted, and I think I may without exaggeration say that since I came here the language has been firmer and the alliance has been strengthened ; but on your side you don't make sufficient allowance for the totally different state of things which exists here and in England. When you talk of ' we ' and of ' our ' going on with the war if the Russians are intractable, you are probably thinking of the France of two years ago, whereas it is no such thing.

Except the Emperor and Walewski, who does not dare to act contrary to the Emperor's orders, we have nobody here who is not prepared to make *any* peace.   But the Emperor's anxiety not to recommence hostilities is very different from ours, and all his ministers play him tricks.   While we are sending out ships to the Baltic, the Minister of Marine is stopping all preparations at Cherbourg. . . . I agree with you that we shall get everything we want if France and England hold together ; but if France fails us, matters will assume a very different aspect, and it is that state of things that I want the Cabinet to consider and to be prepared for. . . .

3rd March.— . . . I have no hesitation in saying that the alliance, such as it has hitherto existed, is *en jeu* now quite as much as the conditions of peace for which we are contending. . . . I have never yet seen the Emperor so excited as last night, and his manner was *âpre* when he said : ' Permettez-moi de vous dire, milord, que je suis complètement d'un avis contraire.'   My language had certainly not been what he desired to hear, for I had put the position of England and France, with reference to the peace he wished to conclude, in the worst possible light, and endeavoured to show him how, with more firmness and better management, it might have been most satisfactory, and how it was not too late to retrieve it.   His irritation subsided before the talk was over ; but nothing would be so easy as a quarrel at this moment, and some good steering will be required to prevent it ; for the Emperor either thinks, or has been made to think, that we are in the wrong, and he fears a constant increase of our *exigeances* under the pressure of the war spirits in England.   I feel sure that he has not intended to play us false ; but his error has been want of firmness in dealing with Orloff, which led him to receive the Russian negative as conclusive, instead of imposing upon Orloff our affirmatives as the ultimatum of England and France.

. . . There is one thing of which the Cabinet may feel certain, viz. that I have never *on any occasion nor on any point yielded anything*. . . . Of course this has become known, as well as the tone I have adopted in the conferences, and the savage opposition to the Russian lambs and the delay in making peace, are laid exclusively upon me.   I understand that I am not considered to be by nature a wild beast, but that I am the slave of the English newspapers and the representative of your anti-Russian feelings ; and that as peace would be fatal to your government, I am here for the purpose of making it impossible. . . . If we give up certain things, I strongly recommend that it should be done with good grace, and that we should neither be sulky about it, nor let it be thought that we are worsted ; for that would leave sore places, and we should neither get the peace we want nor maintain the alliance intact.

Lord Clarendon to Lord Granville.

PARIS, 8*th March* 1856.— . . . The life here is quite intolerable, for every minister and high functionary has been ordered by the Emperor to give great dinners, which it is impossible to decline, and then one must go to certain soirées and receptions, etc. In short, as you know, social duties at Paris are political obligations, particularly at such a moment ; but when I tell you that I have not yet been able to get ¼ of an hour to take a walk, you will believe that I am nearly knocked up. Nothing can exceed the civility we meet with. . . . I suppose that matters here will soon draw to a close, and, as peace seems unavoidable, I shall just make a great point of its being settled before the armistice expires. We shall not get all we want ; but I think it will be a peace of which we need not be ashamed, tho' a very different one from what we should have got if we could have had another campaign. It is quite clear, however, that that other campaign must have been made without the French, and I need not tell you all the consequences that would have entailed. . . . It has been very nice steering with the Emperor between the necessity of keeping him up to anything like the mark, and yet not pressing him till he run restive. I am on the best of terms with him, and never fail to say all I think ; but the manner of doing this when he happens to think the other way, requires care. I will put modesty aside and own, both that it was right for me to come here, and that it has been attended with the results you predicted. . . . I was rather provoked by some of Pam.'s first despatches and telegrams, as I didn't want to know what Russia was to be told, or what she had accepted and must consequently do ; but as luckily I am old enough to walk alone, you may suppose they did not embarrass me much.

12*th*.— . . . I worked hard enough in England, but at Paris I never have a moment to myself, and much time is consumed in most distasteful work—going to great official dinners of 60 *couverts* and receptions at ministerial houses, which are *de rigueur*. . . . The negotiations are a year too soon, and I have no doubt that another campaign would have enabled us to impose very different conditions on Russia ; but France was determined on peace ; and whatever Palmerston in his jaunty mood may say, we could not have made war alone, for we should have had all Europe against us at once, and the United States would soon have followed in the train. . . .

I need not tell you, therefore, that I have never used any such threat here ; indeed, if I did not abhor swagger and barking when there is to be no biting, I should have abstained from it with the Emperor, who, to this day, has not got over Palmerston's letter to Persigny saying we were quite able to carry on the war alone with the aid of Sardinia and Turkey.

It has been difficult steering, however, with H.M., who under the Russian influence of Walewski, was in a most yielding mood, and wanted the application of the spur to keep him straight ; but if it had been used too much, he would have run restive or bolted. . . . I think the peace will be as good as, under the circs., we have a right to expect. Altho' not what John Bull would call glorious—*i.e.* disgraceful to Russia—it is not one that we need be ashamed of.

I thought that some of Palmerston's early telegrams and despatches had not been seen by the Cabinet, and I was glad to learn from you that they had not, for it was nonsense to write to me what Russia ought to do. However, as you may suppose, they made no impression upon me beyond a little momentary irritation, and I have taken no notice of any of them in my public despatches. . . .

On 22nd March there occurred somewhat of a crisis in the proceedings of the conference, arising out of Walewski's evident partiality for the Russian side of the question at the expense of the British. Walewski was a heavy financial speculator, and was known to have interested motives in bringing the negotiations to a speedy conclusion. On that day, then, when the British plenipotentiaries arrived for the meeting, they were shown into one room, the Russians into another, the Prussians into a third, Walewski wandering from one room to another. Clarendon and Cowley at last withdrew, protesting that they could take no further part in such a travesty, and requested an interview next day with the Emperor Napoleon. Clarendon was received by his Majesty next morning, finding him in such glee at the birth of his son, the Prince Imperial, on the 16th, and so anxious to celebrate the event by an immediate declaration of peace, as to be quite careless about the conditions upon which it could be obtained. This was discouraging ; but when Clarendon complained of Walewski's conduct of the proceedings, the Emperor was much discomposed, and undertook to make Walewski understand that he must act in concert with the British plenipotentiaries. Business went on far better after this, Buol remarking to Clarendon after their next meeting : ' Les Russes sont de fort mauvaise humeur aujourd'hui; ils sentent que Walewski leur a échappé des mains.'

At the twenty-first sitting of the congress, on 30th March, the Treaty of Paris was signed and ready for ratification. There were, indeed, two treaties—one whereby Great Britain and France were bound to protect Sweden and Norway against Russian aggression; the other whereby Great Britain, France and Austria became guarantors for the integrity of the Ottoman Empire. Neither indemnity nor cession of territory was exacted from Russia, so that M. de Bourqueney, French ambassador at Vienna, had some grounds for his caustic comment that there was ' no visible indication which were the victors and which the vanquished.'

The thing that gives me most pleasure, wrote Clarendon to Palmerston on that evening, is the position that England now occupies. It leaves us nothing to desire, and it is *so* different from what it was 6 weeks ago, when, owing to intrigues and lies, we were looked upon as the common enemy. . . . I suppose I must stay here at least ten days longer ; and if you would do a merciful act, prevent Malmesbury from postponing his Kars motion till I return, for I am so completely knocked up by my life here that I look with horror upon having to get up a blue-book the moment I arrive. . . .

These treaties were accompanied by a declaration which has proved more durable than either of them. It bound such Powers as should agree to abide by it to abolish privateering ; it established the principle that a neutral flag should cover an enemy's goods other than contraband of war; that, conversely and subject to the same limitation, an enemy's flag should cover neutral goods, and that blockades should be made effective before they could be observed. Undoubtedly Great Britain, as the chief naval Power, stood to lose most by these new conditions; the *Sun* newspaper put its sheets in mourning when the signature of the treaty was announced; and in the House of Lords Lord Derby, with all customary vigour, denounced the declaration as ' the Clarendon Capitulation '; but the peers supported the government, giving them a majority of fifty-four on a division : no other attempt was made to upset what had been agreed on in Paris; and the new conditions imposed by the declaration have become established as the maritime law of nations.

The Emperor of the French pressed Clarendon and Cowley to accept the Grand Cross of the Legion of Honour, but Clarendon explained that he must decline it; inasmuch as it was his duty as Foreign Secretary to refuse permission for other British subjects to accept foreign decorations, it would never do for him to set an example of breaking rules. But he received from his Sovereign something which gratified him far more than any number of stars and ribbons.

31st March 1856.—The Queen thanks Lord Clarendon much for his two letters of Saturday and yesterday, and we congratulate *him* on the success of his *efforts* in obtaining the peace, for to *him* alone it is due; and also to *him alone* is due the dignified position which the Queen's beloved country holds, and which she owes to a straightforward, steady, and unselfish policy throughout. Much as the Queen disliked the idea of peace, she has become reconciled to it by the conviction that France would either not have continued the war, or continued it in such a manner that *no* glory could have been hoped for us. . . . The Queen finds Lord Palmerston very well pleased with the peace, though he struggled as long as he could for better conditions.

The Queen proposed to raise both Lord Clarendon and Lord Cowley a step in the peerage; but both of them begged to be allowed to decline that honour.

Lord Clarendon to Queen Victoria.

Lord Cowley's reason was his extreme poverty, and the feeling that an accession of rank would only aggravate the inconvenience he already experiences from being a peer. . . .

Lord Clarendon felt that courtesy titles to his younger sons would be a positive injury to them in working for their bread, and he relied upon your Majesty's unvarying kindness for appreciating his reluctance to prefer himself to his children. . . . Lord Clarendon hopes it is not presumptuous in him to say that he would not exchange your Majesty's letters of approval for any public mark of your Majesty's favor.

Ladies are sometimes credited with a nicer appreciation of social grades than men commonly entertain, but in this case Lord Clarendon carried his wife's cordial approval in declining a marquisate.

I am very glad the offer has been made (she notes in her journal) ; it is the only public way the Queen can well acknowledge his services ; and I am glad it has been refused. I would not change the fine historical and much-loved name of Earl of Clarendon for all the marquisates in the world.

The Emperor, however, would not allow the Clarendons to leave Paris without the special mark of esteem described in this further extract from the said journal.

PARIS, 18*th April* 1856.—This morning an enormous van arrived at the hotel containing a splendid bit of Gobelin tapestry sent by the Emperor as a present to George, and some very fine books—*Iconographie Grecque et Romaine.* The tapestry was so large that it could not be got into the hotel, no door being wide enough. . . . It seems it was exhibited in the great French Exhibition, and was reckoned so fine that the Emperor would not allow it to be sold, tho' he had some great offer either from the British Museum or some other English institution. I believe he makes these presents of large pieces of Gobelin only to crowned heads or great potentates, so this is intended as a very special honor ; but alas ! I fear it is rather an inconvenient one, or may be so, if our dread is realised that we have no wall large enough to hang it on.

So ended the Crimean War, which cost the United Kingdom the lives of 270 officers, 22,467 men, and seventy-

six millions in money. The Black Sea had been saved
from becoming a Russian lake, and the Sultan's tottering
throne had been propped as a breakwater against Russian
aggression. Of the three Powers furnishing the props, the
goodwill of Austria was speedily chilled by the action of
her allies in the Mediterranean. In May the Emperor
Napoleon called upon Ferdinand II., better remembered
as King Bomba, to desist from the abominable cruelties
inflicted upon the constitutional party in Naples, and
received support from the British Foreign Office. To this
remonstrance, and to that addressed by Clarendon to the
court of the Two Sicilies, Bomba's minister Carafa addressed
a truculent reply, denying the right of any government to
interfere in the internal affairs of another state.

Lord Clarendon to Lord Cowley.

F.O., 28*th June* 1856.— . . . We have had a long discussion in
the Cabinet to-day about Naples, and it is *due to truth* to say
that Palmerston and I stood alone in favor of coercing Bomba.
Of course there are many plausible reasons against it : in the first
place, our right.   Then where will it stop ? to what will it lead ?
—probable revolution and necessity for upholding it—jealousy
of France if Sicily were to pronounce for us—whom to put in
Bomba's place if he were dethroned—why not go on and reform
the Papal government, etc. etc.   So after these topics had been
discussed *en long et en large*, it was decided to wait till the Notes
are presented to us by the Neapolitan ministers here and at
Paris.   This is staving off the difficulty for a very short time ;
and as I apprehend that we must lay the Neapolitan correspondence before parliament, we shall cut a very sorry figure for having
barked at such a wretch as Bomba and then not ventured to
bite him. . . .

Diplomatic relations were broken off by the withdrawal
of the British and French ministers from Naples, a proceeding which produced a strong protest from the Russian
government, Prince Gortschakoff taunting the Powers
which had coalesced against Russia with having ' assumed
for their motto the respect of right and the independence
of governments.' This notwithstanding, the British and

French fleets anchored in the Bay of Naples with the purpose of frightening Bomba into decent behaviour; but as bombardment was obviously out of the question, they sailed away again, the governments of Queen Victoria and the Emperor Napoleon contenting themselves with keeping the Sicilian court in diplomatic Coventry till the death of the King in 1859. So it ended, for the time, in barking at Bomba without biting; but there was one watchful intellect which drew encouragement from what had so grievously offended Austria and brought hope to Italian constitutionalists, namely, Count Cavour, the King of Sardinia's minister, of whom Lord Salisbury once said to Lord Cromer: ' Cavour always knew how to wait for a high wave to carry him over the bar of the river.' The wave was already rising; it wanted but a few years to raise it to its height.

Cavour's master, also, had views for exalting his kingdom in the comity of nations—views of which the nature is explained in the following letter from Clarendon to the Prime Minister.

BALMORAL, *6th September* 1856.—MY DEAR PALMERSTON,— Marochetti came here yesterday and I have had a long talk with him, the sum of which is that some time ago he made the bust of Princess Mary, who knew that he was about to go to Turin. She made herself so singularly agreeable to him, and set forth her mental and physical charms to such advantage, that he felt convinced she meant to be reported, which she accordingly was, to the King. His Majesty, as Marochetti said, would like the marriage exceedingly, and Cavour is most eager for it as the best thing that could happen to Sardinia; so when he (Marochetti) returned to England, he was charged to *tâter le terrain* and to ascertain whether a formal proposal from the King would be accepted; as H.M. would, of course, dislike to subject himself to a refusal.

Soon after his arrival in London, he was sent for to Osborne about the Queen's bust, and he then opened the affair to the Prince [Albert], who very properly told him that it ought to be communicated to the Queen's government, as the Queen in all such matters could only act upon the advice of her ministers, and that he (Prince A.) wished to hear nothing more about it. But in passing thro' London he sent word to Marochetti that he might come here and tell his story to me, if he thought proper : and that is what brought him here yesterday.

I was very frank with him, and told him the various difficulties which might be in the way of such an alliance : 1st, the refusal of Prince Napoleon on the score of religion,[1] the Queen having, with the entire concurrence of Princess Mary, declared that she would never give her consent to the marriage of her cousin with a Roman Catholic prince ; 2ndly, the objections that the people of this country might feel to the marriage of an English princess with a R.C. sovereign ; and 3rdly, the painful position that Princess Mary might feel herself in as the wife of a king of a religious, or rather a superstitious, people, who might look upon her as a sort of Ann Boleyn and make her life miserable. I said, also, that whatever my own opinions might be, I could say nothing without laying the whole matter before you and taking your directions.

I reported all this to the Queen, who approved, and told me that neither she nor the Prince would say anything to Marochetti ; but the Duke of Cambridge came here last night, and the Queen thinks I ought to make him acquainted with what has passed, and I shall do so as soon as the messenger goes. The Queen does not like the thought of it : she thinks it will be an embarrassment and a personal affair with the Emperor [Napoleon], whose *amour-propre* she had *ménagé* by placing the refusal of Prince Napoleon's offer entirely upon religious grounds. She is afraid that public opinion here, tho' favorable to Sardinia, would be adverse to a R.C. alliance ; and the Prince goes still further and says it would shake the Protestant character of the reigning family in England. On the other hand, the Queen fears the resentment of the Duke of Cambridge if she did anything to prevent a marriage which they will all desire ; and she says that, as Princess Mary is of age, she may, and probably will, take some steps to prove that she is free and able to marry the King of Sardinia if he is willing. The subject gives the Queen great anxiety, and she is anxious for your opinion and advice.

My opinion is that it would be a good thing for Princess Mary, an excellent thing for Sardinia, and not a bad one for England ; that the embarrassment with the Emperor might be got over by a simple statement of facts, and that if the young lady is de-

---

[1] Prince Napoleon, 'Plon-plon,' son of Jérôme Bonaparte, formerly King of Westphalia, had proposed for the hand of Princess Mary of Cambridge.

termined upon the marriage, it will be difficult for the Queen to impose her veto upon it, and that upon the whole, we ought to encourage the project rather than raise difficulties in the way.

By desire of the Queen, in which the Duke of Cambridge agreed, the decision was left wholly to Princess Mary herself.

Lord Clarendon to Baron Marochetti.

TAYMOUTH, 20th September.— . . . The Queen's first care was for the happiness of Princess Mary, and it was the wish of her Majesty and of her Majesty's government that the decision should be left to the unbiased judgment of her Royal Highness.

Princess Mary, having maturely weighed the matter in all its different bearings, has come to the conclusion that it is her duty, as regards both the King of Sardinia and herself, to decline the offer which you were empowered to make on behalf of his Majesty.

Princess Mary fully appreciates the many excellent and noble qualities of the King. She does not doubt that with him individually she could be happy, and she thinks that the alliance would be popular in England; but her Royal Highness feels that, as the Protestant Queen of Sardinia, she must be in a false position, and that a wife can never find herself thus placed without injury to her husband. Princess Mary is deeply attached to her religion, which is her first consideration in this world, and in the free and undisturbed exercise of that religion, however much it might be sanctioned by the King and supported by his Majesty's government, she feels that she would be the object of constant suspicion, that her motives would be liable to misconstruction, and that the King would be exposed to grave embarrassments which time would only serve to increase. . . . I am convinced that, in renouncing upon conscientious grounds the brilliant position which has been offered to her, and of which she fully appreciated the advantages, Princess Mary can only add to the respect which the King already feels for the noble and elevated character of her Royal Highness.

The match thus declined by Princess Mary was indeed a far more brilliant one than could be known at the time. Had Clarendon been able to foresee that the bride of the King of Sardinia would become the first Queen of United

Italy, his disappointment at Princess Mary's decision would have been keener than it was. But he probably underrated the disfavour with which the British public would have viewed the marriage, for, besides the disparity of religion, Victor Emmanuel had scarcely earned a reputation for austere morality.

On 4th June 1856 Lord Clarendon received the honorary degree of D.C.L. at Oxford, conferred by Lord Derby as chancellor of the University—the man whom Clarendon held in chief distrust politically among all the members of the Conservative Opposition. Lady Clarendon felt some misgiving as to the reception Tory undergraduates might give to the Whig peace-maker; but the result quite reassured her.

In August Clarendon went to Scotland with the Queen as minister in attendance. His first impressions of Holyrood were as discouraging as those Mary Queen of Scots must have felt when she first came from France; but the beauty of Edinburgh soon stirred his enthusiasm.

Lord Clarendon to Lady Clarendon.

28th August.— . . . The Palace, as it is called, is a ramshackle sort of place—ugly, dreary and cold. The environs of the town and the town itself would make your pencil jump out of your pocket to sketch them.

29th.— . . . I have had at least seven hours of the finest, freshest air I have breathed for many a long day. I am so little accustomed to the sort of thing that my face is rough and my eyes are sore from the wind; but I feel already that it has done me good. At 11 we issued forth in open carriages to drive thro' the town. The day was beautiful, and so beautiful a town I never saw. There is not such another in Europe, at least that I have seen. It gives one a notion of a city devoted to public monuments, and the prodigious natural capabilities all seem turned to the best account with the best taste. . . . We afterwards drove round the hills (on the top of one of which is the famous Arthur's Seat) by a sort of *corniche* road lately made, from which the panoramic view of the city and all its most prominent buildings, the rich, cultivated and wooded country on one side and the sea on the other, was strikingly beautiful.

When we returned the Queen and Prince lionised me all over the Palace, and we saw all Queen Mary's rooms and Darnley's, and where Rizzio was dragged out, and *of course* the stains left by his blood—the concierge knowing what everybody said and did at the time with astounding and impudent accuracy. I then worked hard at my boxes for two or three hours, interrupted by a long visit from Albert; and then we took the long drive—first to the Castle, where Mary was imprisoned after the battle of Pinkey (or Musselburgh),[1] and which is rather a fine ruin; then to Hawthorndene, an old castle belonging to the Drummond family. I never saw so lovely a place, built upon a cliff overhanging the Esk at about 150 feet; the banks thickly wooded with every variety of tree. We walked all thro' the glen and up to Rosslyn Castle, where there is the finest ruin of a chapel I have ever seen—I mean for the beauty of the workmanship; and such beautiful views. How you and the girls would have enjoyed it! I kept thinking of you the whole time. The *giro* was at least 18 miles, and as we kept on lingering at each thing, we got home very late. . . . The journey to-morrow will be about 10½ hours. They say that the air of Balmoral is as much superior to that of Edinbro' as that of Edinbro' is to Downing Street. I begin to feel very idle and disposed to forget foreign affairs. . . .

BALMORAL, 30*th.*— . . . Here everything is Scotch—the curtains, the carpets, the furniture are all of different plaids, and the thistles are in such abundance that they would rejoice the heart of a donkey if they happened to *look like* his favorite repast, which they don't. I am told that it is *de rigueur* to clothe myself in tweed directly. . . . It is very cold here, and I believe my feet were frost-bitten at dinner, for there was no fire at all there, and in the drawing-room there were two little sticks which hissed at the man who attempted to light them; and the Queen, thinking, I suppose, that they meant to burn, had a large screen placed between the royal nose and the unignited wood. She seemed, I thought, particularly grateful for such small jokes as my freezing state enabled me to crack. I have a very comfortable room, however, and am now sitting on the hob writing to you. . . . I must, however, be ready for kirk, where the *meenister* preaches for two hours and takes his large, rough greyhound into the pulpit with him, so no more at present.

2nd September.—I get to my room at about 11.15; but that

---

[1] It was neither; it was after the action on Carberry Hill.

does not give me much time for work, for I stick to my resolution of being *in bed* at one, having to be up at 8. There is no use coming here for health and doing just as if I was in London ; so, altho' I moan over the arrears that have already accumulated, I keep on never minding, and I am sure you will approve.

To Lord Granville he writes on 15th September : ' This place [Balmoral] is a sort of paradise, and has quite restored me to health ; but the Queen is so good as to insist upon my being in the air all day, and the consequence is frightful arrears. I have unopened boxes enough in my room to make a barricade if a revolution broke out in the Household.'

Lady Clarendon, also, was visiting in Scotland for the first time. Writing from Tulliallan on 7th September, where she was paying a visit to the Lansdownes—' I heard the Free Kirk service for the first time to-day. I do not like it. It is difficult to pray when one does not know what is coming *next*, and I do not like to be at the mercy of what an extemporary prayer may be. Also, I prefer kneeling in prayer to standing.' [1] As chance had it, Lord Clarendon was writing simultaneously to her ladyship *his* impressions of Presbyterian ritual :—

BALMORAL, *7th September*.— . . . We went to kirk and I don't like the service at all. There is a good deal of singing (very bad) and an exposition of part of a chapter of the Bible which is called a sermon, and then a prayer for everybody on earth who is a Christian, collectively and individually, and then comes a blessing with uplifted arms. The congregation appeared to be very devout and attentive, but there is no kneeling, and they never say the Lord's Prayer. The whole thing gave me more the impression of some saintly meeting at Exeter Hall, with Shaftesbury in the chair, than a church service. . . .

BALMORAL, *10th September* 1856.— . . . I am sorry that my concluding words that we should meet yesterday week will not come quite true, for this afternoon, after I had been with the Queen and the Prince for more than an hour, I was re-sent for and told that the Prince of Orange had written to offer himself, and it turned out that for one reason or another they couldn't

---

[1] Probably it was the Established, not the Free, Kirk which Lord Clarendon attended. In those days it was the universal custom in Presbyterian churches to stand for prayers and to sit for singing.

have him before Monday. The Prince then said we must ask Lord C. as a favor to stay with us till Wednesday, as it would never do for the Foreign Secretary to leave us the morning after the Prince of Orange arrived. Of course I could do nothing but bow assentingly, and we shall be another four-and-twenty hours before we meet. It's a great bore, but I could not help it.

I have been at work all day, but did not make much progress, as I had some long and disagreeable despatches to concoct. Things are going ill—the Russians won't yield the points that we must insist upon, and our policy is getting daily more at variance with that of France. Naples is becoming an ugly affair, and altogether I am in bad sorts about foreign matters, while the business arrears have accumulated to an amount that makes me sick. It was nearly 5 before I left the Queen, and she said—'Now what are you going to do, Lord Clarendon? not going back to your room, I hope, on this beautiful evening?' I asked whether I was ordered by H.M. to go out.—'You are,' she said, and so I was obliged to go on the hills. She seems more happy and free here, and is quite a different person.

11*th*.— . . . I am just returned from the Braemar Highland gathering, where I stood for two hours and came home afterwards in an open carriage. My fingers are so cold that I can hardly hold the pen. . . . I worked hard all the morning, but not with much success—I mean as to abating arrears; for Hammond, to do him justice, has sent me nothing that is unimportant, and every box is full of heavy matters which require much consideration and therefore time. It has been my drawback here to feel perpetually that I am doing what I like and not what I ought. I got your dear letter when I came home, and those few words saying you are very well are very precious. . . . We are to go a day-long expedition to-morrow from 11 to 8! In my heart I desire that waterspouts may prevent it. At night, too, a ball at the Duchess of Kent's!

13*th*.— . . . The Prince went out stalking. I took a walk before luncheon and have had the whole afternoon to myself, which I have dealt with in the usual way, *i.e.* not stirring from my chair; but I can't say I have made much progress, as I never remember having to deal with such a number of long, heavy questions. I suppose I must drag them all with me to Taymouth, where I shall probably not have much more time than here. . . .

12*th*.— . . . I have heard a rumour that the Queen intends

to make another day-long expedition *for me* to-morrow, but I hope it may prove unfounded. It is quite ridiculous how she keeps asking the ladies whether they are attentive to me and whether I am amused ! . . . I don't at all see our way out of the Russian and French difficulties ; we are in active quarrel with Mexico and Peru ; we are about to break with Naples and to declare war against Persia—trifles *not incompatible with anxiety*.

14th.— . . . It is a delight to me that you should be able to write that you are *very* well with the ' very ' right royally underlined.[1] I have liked this place very much, and everybody has been kind and tried to make it agreeable ; but I shall be so happy to be with you again. Short of a few hours, we shall have been separated for three weeks ! . . . I have worked a good deal to-day, but I have still *twelve* large brimful boxes of arrears. The Queen sent to me after luncheon to *desire* I would not sit poring over my boxes, so of course I joined the household walking-party. I have taken an immense fancy to Lady Augusta Bruce.[2] . . .

15th.— . . . I took a little walk this morning, but I have been all the afternoon with what they call here ' my beloved red boxes ' ; but such quantities of them pour in every night that I can make no way. Palmerston urges me not to return to London unless the business of the office renders it indispensable, of which I alone can judge. . . .

On the 17th Lord Clarendon rejoined his wife at Taymouth. She observes thankfully in her journal that she has never seen him looking in such good health since their marriage. After doing a little tour in Scotland they paid a visit of one night to Lord Brougham, who, records Lady Clarendon, ' received me in old chivalrous fashion on one knee at his door.' They returned to the Grove on 30th September, but on 2nd October Lord Clarendon was once more writing to his wife from the Foreign Office :—

My day has been pretty much what you may suppose— incessant interviews, and nothing very pleasant. Persigny was here for two hours, and I am afraid that, between Walewski's misrepresentations to the Emperor and the ignorance and

---

[1] An allusion to a characteristic in Queen Victoria's letters.
[2] Resident Bedchamber Woman to Queen Victoria. Married to Dean Stanley in 1863.

indolence of the latter in analysing the matters set before him, our relations with France are by no means in a good state. Persigny was as right-minded and as abusive of Walewski as one could desire, but that won't make crooked things straight. Even Palmerston, who was here for two hours also, having come up expressly to see me, was obliged to admit that the prospects were unpleasant. We went hopping from one topic to another in the different quarters of the globe ; but the operation did not bring much comfort ; tho' Palmerston as usual does not doubt that we shall pull thro' *somehow*, admitting at the same time that it would be very awkward if parliament were to meet to-morrow. . . . Cetto was here for ever so long too, and Reeve and Wilson, so you may suppose I have had *some* talking. . . .

3rd.—Another disagreeable letter has come from Cowley, and it is impossible not to feel that our relations with France are very shaky. . . . Madame de Lieven says that the Granville embassy has been complete ; beating all the others hollow.[1]

The routine of office work was broken by a summons to Windsor, whither Clarendon went alone, Lady Clarendon having lately lost her brother Charles. The usual daily letters were resumed.

WINDSOR CASTLE, *Sunday*, 19*th October* 1856.— . . . After church this morning Albertus Maximus sent for me to his room and did not let me go till after the third luncheon message, which consumed my best working time, and I could not shirk

[1] Lord Granville had been sent to represent Great Britain at the coronation of the Emperor of Russia. ' I am glad,' he wrote when it was over, ' to come away without the complete *fiasco* which I expected. My position as a complementary ambassador, and at the same time as a member of the government which was doing and saying very irritating things to the Court to which I was accredited, was anomalous. Great efforts were made to separate me from Wodehouse [ambassador at St. Petersburg], me from my government, the Queen from the government, Clarendon from Palmerston. All this of course I had to resist. Palmerston and Clarendon in my opinion have been too scolding lately. They are at everybody. They have tried by bullying to get out of difficulties caused by carelessness in the negotiations. They have almost broken up the French alliance, which now only depends on what is its best security—the importance to his own interests which Louis Napoleon may attach to it. . . . It weakens us in the eyes of Europe when our principal co-belligerent says that in a quarrel in which we impute bad faith to Russia we are in the wrong and the Russian government in the right. I think also that we have got into a scrape by our interference at Naples, and we seem now to be yielding to the wise reluctance of the French to take strong measures. Clarendon has behaved to me in a very friendly, straightforward manner.' I am anxious to have a little talk with him upon all these matters.'—Lord Fitzmaurice's *Life of Granville*, i. 216.

the walk in the afternoon, because I was summoned to it by Regina.   A messenger is come with more boxes, just as if I knew what to do with those already here !

FOREIGN OFFICE, 24*th October.*— . . . I can't say I have had a very delightful day, for I was met at the station by a messenger who, among other things, brought me a letter from Cowley saying that he had had a regular rumpus with the Emperor, and had been obliged to use quite as high language as H.M.   This is quite right for our dignity, but it does not help us out of the fix, and Cowley is much alarmed at the events which are or may be on the tapis, particularly as the Emperor is furious about our press and is going to commit the extreme folly of replying to it in the *Moniteur*.   Palmerston is very jaunty and won't hear of arbitration—says the Emperor is sure to yield if we stand firm ; but I don't share his opinion.   I feel that we *must* somehow or other put an end to the present state of things before parliament meets. . . .

27*th*.— . . . You will like to know that there is a shade of improvement in Cowley's letter of to-day.   He has had another long conversation with the Emperor, brought on by H.M. in a milder tone, in the course of which he admitted that he had done very wrongly and that he never until that moment had clearly understood the rights and the importance of the matter. For all that, we are not much nearer a settlement, but I *think* that a ray of daylight is perceptible.

It is amusing to turn from these weighty and ominous affairs to one creating no small agitation in a different sphere, and entailing the unpremeditated *début* of a young lady who has since had to enact a very exalted social rôle. It is thus described in her mother's journal :—

3*rd November* 1856.—This afternoon arrived a messenger bringing a card inviting George, me and Constance *for to-morrow* ! Imagine the flutter this produced !   Constance had but a linsey-wolsey morning dress fit to be seen. . . .   Off we went to Watford to get materials, and the maids, helped a little by a dress-maker in Watford, got up a silk morning dress and two muslin dresses for the evening, before two o'clock next day, at which hour we had to start for Windsor, where George joined us.   Our chick did look so nice, and her manners were *just* what they should be. She was much frightened, never having dined down stairs with company in her life—rather an awful beginning !

The work at the Foreign Office had grown to such dimensions as to exceed the power of any one man to transact it, wherefore it was decided to appoint an under-secretary. Clarendon, consulting Lord Granville about a suitable person for the post, received from him this succinct review of the young bloods of the Whig party :—

In my opinion a peer would be best for your purpose, an unparliamentary man the next, and a M.P. the worst.

A peer gives us a vote, and Wodehouse has established the precedent that he is not to speak unless desired.

A M.P. may easily get you into a scrape.

The only peers I have heard mentioned are

Lothian [1]—letter A, No. 1.

Somers [2]—moderate but agreeable to Lansdowne House.

Dufferin [3]—a poor creature, who does not require any bribe.

Aylesbury [4]—who is dying for it, but would not like his wish to be known. He is old to begin public business.

Lyttelton [5]—unpopular, uncouth, very clever and a first-rate man of business.

I have heard no one mentioned but Bulwer among those who have no seat in Parliament. You know his character, and he is unpopular at the F. O. I do not believe him to be a good routine man and he would sometimes get you into scrapes, but would undoubtedly be useful on occasions.

Of the M.P.'s mentioned, Sir R. Peel, a pleasant fellow, would be the worst under secretary except Dicky Milner.[6] Freddy Leveson [7]—nepotism apart—is popular, intelligent and would ride to orders. He is superior to his brother [8] in all respects, excepting pushing himself, but he has only had two months experience in a public office (as précis writer).

Shelburne [9] not so bad an appointment as it would seem. In small matters he is the most accurate and methodical man of business I know.

---

[1] Eighth Marquess of Lothian, died in 1870.
[2] Third and last Earl Somers, died in 1883.
[3] Fifth Baron and first Marquess of Dufferin, died in 1902.
[4] Second Marquess of Ailesbury, died in 1878.
[5] Fourth Baron Lyttelton, died in 1876.
[6] Third baronet, died in 1895.
[7] Hon. Edward Frederick Granville, the writer's brother.
[8] Lord Granville himself.
[9] Fourth Marquess of Lansdowne, died in 1866.

George Byng,[1] intelligent, priggish, huffy, speaks neatly, was very offensive to the government the last time he spoke.

Elcho,[2] clever, but without tact or discretion.

There was, of a truth, good and sufficient cause for reinforcing the staff of the Foreign Office, so greatly had the burden of correspondence been increased by accelerated communication and the growth of empire. Not only had perplexing difficulties arisen in enforcing the stipulations of the treaty of Paris, entailing innumerable despatches, but petty wars had to be waged during 1856 in China and Persia.

Lord Clarendon to Lady Clarendon.

Foreign Office, 19th December.— . . . I am dead knocked up, having had 6½ hours of interviews without a moment's interruption, and I have just completed four sheets of paper to Cowley. Palmerston in the most obliging manner came up from Broadlands at my request, and declared *he liked* doing so. We conferred together and agreed upon a line of frontier which ought to do for the Russians and which we might defend well enough in parliament ; but I daresay they [Russia] will reject it, because their real object is a notorious quarrel between England and France ; so I am not a bit more sure of a settlement than we were a fortnight ago. I think we have now pushed concession to its utmost limits and we have said our last word.

The same to Lord Normanby.[3]

26th December 1856.— . . . Nobody can have the least idea of the life of slavery I lead. Fourteen hours a day has been my average run of work for nearly four years. I have renounced all society : I cannot look into a book, and I do nothing but struggle against arrears. My only marvel is that more things are not neglected. There are excellent people in this office, many of whom work nearly as hard as I do ; but I cannot delegate responsibility, and I must therefore look into everything myself. If in the remotest corner of the earth any Englishman gets a well-deserved, but uncompensated, black eye, the news-

---

[1] Afterwards third Earl of Strafford, died in 1898.
[2] The present Earl of Wemyss.   [3] Minister at Florence.

papers and parliament immediately demand an enquiry into the conduct of the bloated sinecurist in Downing Street, who has no sense of British honor. There were 56,000 despatches sent and received last year, which perhaps will give you some notion of my life.

The same to Lord Howden.[1]

23rd December 1856.— . . . I asked Comyn to request Pidal never to give a thought to our newspapers *as representing the opinions of the government.* They are incurably blackguard, and they are so accustomed to deal with home matters in the strongest language, that it would not suit their customers (which is all they care about) if they dealt differently with foreign affairs. It is useless to attempt any check upon them, for there are but one or two that will receive an occasional hint. . . . I have never, since the beginning of the war, been so troubled and anxious about our foreign relations as during the last four months. Everything goes wrong in every part of the world and shows no disposition to come right. . . . The chief cause is the inexplicable conduct of the French government. I say inexplicable, because I firmly believe that the Emperor is of opinion that his own personal interest is bound up with the English alliance ; yet he does everything to weaken it here, to make it unpopular in France and to destroy its prestige all over the world. He does not *intend* this : he is only weak and incapable of foreseeing the consequence of his own and Walewski's acts. It is rather difficult, however, for people addicted to straight roads to march hand in hand with those who prefer tortuous paths. . . .

The same to Lord Stratford de Redcliffe.

16th January 1857.— . . . I agree with you that, in most cases, it is better to look forward than to look back, and I am quite willing to adopt that system and to postpone the explanations which you intend to enter into ; tho' I must say I am at a loss even to *imagine* why you should have been compelled to entertain a painful and bitter feeling. I am not in the habit of making professions, and indeed have not been called upon to do so with respect to you, as you have never given me reason

---

[1] Lord Howden was ambassador at Madrid.

to think that you were animated by any feelings of particular goodwill towards myself personally ; but I know that if I had been your oldest and best friend I could not have acted for you and by you differently from what I have done.   However, I won't go into the discussion that we have agreed to defer, but *let us have it well out some day*.

There is a melancholy interest in a note from Palmerston to Clarendon at this time.   Sir Robert Peel—*the* Sir Robert —left five sons, men of noble stature and commanding features, three of whom attained distinction, namely, the Right Hon. Sir Frederick Peel (1823-1906), chief railway commissioner; Captain Sir William Peel, R.N. (1824-58), who commanded the famous Naval Brigade in the Crimea, who was severely wounded at the second relief of Lucknow and died on his way back to England, and Arthur Wellesley, Viscount Peel (1829-1912), whom many remember with affection as Speaker of the House of Commons.   The eldest of the brothers, not inferior in talents, in personal charm, or in appearance to any of the others, sadly disappointed those who expected him to add fresh lustre to a great name. Everything was in the third Sir Robert's favour.   The hereditary principle is no monopoly of the House of Lords ; as the son of its former leader, Sir Robert commanded attention from the House of Commons, which was predisposed to welcome him.   He became a favourite at once ; men were sure of amusement when Peel was on his legs, but they soon learnt how fitful and unstable were his political principles.   In January 1857, being then a junior Lord of the Admiralty, he made a speech in Birmingham, in the course of which he passed some very injudicious reflections upon the court of Russia, whither he had accompanied Lord Granville to the coronation of Alexander II.   The affront was fiercely resented in the Russian and French press, and was discussed in parliament.   Palmerston thus expresses his disappointment to Clarendon :—

BROADLANDS, 16*th January* 1857.—I mean to write to Peel about his speech.   I am really deeply grieved at his repeated follies.   I had hoped that, with his talents, his wealth and the prestige of his name, he might become an able and useful public man, and a valuable member of some future Cabinet ; but I begin to fear that the case is hopeless, and that there is a want of ballast which will ever prevent him from sailing well.

Nevertheless, Palmerston gave Sir Robert another chance by appointing him Chief Secretary to the Lord-Lieutenant of Ireland in 1861; but Peel failed to re-establish his reputation as a statesman, and continued to the end beloved by men of all parties and trusted by none.

The Russian difficulty solved itself sooner than Clarendon had hoped for. On 28th December he received notice that the Russian government had agreed to the Moldavian and Bessarabian frontiers as delineated, and agreed to give up Bolgrad, which had been the chief bone of contention. That disposed of one bogey, but there was a whole troop of others ready to spring into action so soon as parliament should meet.

Lord Clarendon to Lady Clarendon.

30th January 1857.— . . . I have literally not one moment, for a cabinet was called suddenly to-day about Law reforms. The Attorney and Solicitor Generals were there, and when they went Palmerston produced the Queen's speech, for which of course I was obliged to stay, and I have left them sitting now (7 o'clock), not having written one word for the Eastern Mail or Paris.

2nd February.— . . . The cabinet of course was unpunctual —no operation so long as that of criticising and amending a Queen's speech. Persia, Naples and China stand in awful array next to each other, and will of course give rise to never-ending debates. . . . I don't know that opposition has yet taken any positive form, but there is a great deal of promised hostility. Gladstone is reported to be overflowing with economical venom, and Aberdeen admitted to Argyll that Graham meant to do all the mischief he could. . . .

The war in China was the matter which it was most difficult to defend. Lord Derby in the Lords, Mr. Cobden in the Commons, moved votes of censure upon Sir John Bowring, whose high-handed proceedings had brought about hostilities, and the government, in defending the action of

their agent, had to fight for existence. In the Lords they
scored a majority of thirty-six ; but in the Commons they
were beaten by sixteen, Lord John Russell riding full tilt
against his ancient colleagues, and Gladstone, for the
Peelites, entered in his diary that it was ' a division doing
more honour to the House of Commons than any I ever
remember.' [1] ' Lord John's speech,' wrote Clarendon to
Cowley, ' made a great impression, and his hostility to the
government, and especially to Palmerston, is of the most
venomous character. Yet if he turns out the government,
he has no more power to construct another than he has of
flying.'

Lord Clarendon to Sir H. Seymour.[2]

4th March 1857.— . . . The best way would have been to
dissolve or resign at once ; but the latter was out of the question,
first, because Palmerston is very popular, and the country would
have accused him of pusillanimity if he ran away from such an
unholy alliance and had not given the people a chance of pro-
nouncing. In short, as far as we can judge, dissolution has been
reckoned upon for the last 3 or 4 days if the government was
beaten.

2ndly. We could not resign against the wishes of the Queen,
who, as her confinement approaches, is very nervous and, in
fact, *could* not undertake all the anxious duties that a change
of government imposes upon the Sovereign. . . . We could not
dissolve at once, because not a farthing has been voted nor has
the Mutiny Act or any estimates been passed. We must therefore
announce dissolution and get money voted for a short period ;
but there are all the complications of Income Tax, tea duties,
etc., and the six weeks necessary for discussing these matters
will be very disagreeable with men so reckless and uncompromis-
ing as Gladstone, Dizzy, Lord John and others. . . . The conduct
and language of our public men are most damaging to our
national character and representative form of government all
over the world. . . .

It can scarcely be denied that the government had a very
bad case to defend in their Chinese policy. Bowring had
acted as an overbearing bully, bringing about a state of

---

[1] Morley's *Gladstone*, i. 564. [2] British ambassador at Vienna.

things which could only be solved by powder and shot. But Palmerston had won the confidence of his countrymen, few of whom were in a position to weigh nicely the justice of ministerial policy at the ends of the earth. Englishmen love what is downright and definite—some dominating personality who saves them the effort of making up their minds. Parliament was dissolved in April to take the sense of the country upon foreign policy ; when it came together again in May, the seats of Bright, Cobden, Milner-Gibson and other champions of peace were filled by supporters of the government. The verdict of the country was emphatically for ' old Pam.' The rift between the Whigs and their old allies the Peelites seemed complete. The Peelites had succeeded in sending Palmerston to the country, and they could not forgive Palmerston and his colleagues for winning a brilliant victory at the polls ; the Whigs were indignant with the Peelites for combining with the Tories in an attempt to turn them out. ' I went to a party at the Gladstones',' wrote Lady Clarendon in her journal on 29th April. ' Lady Palmerston would not go ; but then Gladstone has been more personally unfriendly to Lord Palmerston than to George.'

Lord Clarendon to Lady Clarendon.

OSBORNE, 29th May 1857.— . . . I sat next the Queen at dinner and never saw her in better spirits or more gracious. I had a long talk with her afterwards too, and she made me tell her what I thought of Palmerston's health, about which she was evidently anxious ; which is curious, considering how particularly she would have liked him to die two or three years ago. I can see she expects to have to *subir* Lord John one of these days, and does not like the notion of it one bit, as neither she nor his colleagues *can feel the slightest confidence in him.*

The Queen, as above mentioned, had desired to mark her sense of the services of Clarendon and Cowley during the Congress of Paris by raising each of them a step in the peerage ; but Clarendon, being devoid of social ambition, *noluit episcopari* ; and Cowley excused himself on the score of limited private income. Clarendon, however, changed his

mind concerning his friend, and persuaded him to accept
an earldom.

Lord Clarendon to Lord Cowley.

10th March.— . . . I want you very much to consider whether
you should not be made an earl.   We talked the matter over
at Paris, and I am therefore aware of your objections ; but I
have been reflecting upon it a good deal and talking it over
with Lady C., and we both agree—1st, that it would not be
more expensive to be an earl than a baron ; and next that it is a
decided advantage to girls, whether they marry or do not marry.
. . . I need hardly say that I have not said a syllable on the
subject to the Queen, and have only mentioned it to Palmerston,
who would have to recommend your promotion to H.M., and
he cordially agreed. . . .

Lord Cowley took the advice, and was advanced to an
earldom on 11th April.

Coming events cast no shadow over the spring of 1857,
and Clarendon began to enjoy some relaxation from the
strain he had borne since undertaking foreign affairs.

The same to Sir G. C. Lewis.

We are sailing before the wind just now—a victory over the
Persians reported (Outram of course not having heard of the
armistice) and peace with China certain ; at least so I suppose
Bowring says and thinks, as the termination of the telegram
sent via Cagliari and Turin finishes, as you will see by the enclosed, with ' no more reinforcements wanted.'   I did not send
this last part to the Times in case we might still think it right
when the news comes in detail to let some troops go, as the
peace may not be of the right sort. . . . Our success at home,
however, is still more important.   The absence of Cobden,
Bright, Layard and Milner-Gibson is of itself worth a dissolution, and I begin to think better of the next parliament than I
was disposed to do a few days ago, for the pledges required and
taken at many places were of the worst kind. . . . Granville is
just £7000 out of pocket for his embassy to Moscow.   He
got £10,000 from the Treasury, £6000 from this office, £5000
from the Duke of Devonshire, and it cost £28,000.   Do you

think you can do any more for him ?   His embassy was more
splendid and successful than any other, and I believe that in
that rivalry of expenditure he did the thing as economically as
possible, and it is hard that he should pay so much out of his
own (now very limited) resources ; but of course it is just the
sort of expense that the H. of Commons will criticise and like
to cut down.

CHAPTER XVII

ENGLAND DURING THE MUTINY

> 'In the year when the tempest of mutiny broke,
> And the Empire swayed like a storm-bent oak,
>   When the Sepoys showed no quarter,
>   When Islam had risen and Delhi fell,
>   And the plain was a furnace as hot as hell '—

all other matters, foreign and domestic, were thrust into insignificance by the gigantic Indian peril. London was *en fête* on 23rd June, celebrating the hundredth anniversary of Plassey—the victory which brought Bengal into the dominion of George III.—and none had any inkling of the tornado that was raging in the Far East. Yet while wine was flowing and rockets soaring in England, the Sepoy army was in full revolt, Delhi was in the hands of a disciplined force of 60,000 mutineers, and the British troops in India were but as a handful in the presence of the hosts of independent and tributary princes. The first tidings, already seven weeks old, reached London on 25th June ; Palmerston informed the Queen next day that an extensive mutiny had broken out among her native Indian troops, but that ' he had no fear of the results.' But in the following days, as details of massacre came to hand—of the butchery, not only of British officers and civil servants, but of their wives and children—loud and stern rose the cry for retribution. But where were the men and the means to exact it ? The grave lesson of 1854 had been learnt— and unlearnt. Establishments had been cut down to the barest peace footing. ' If we had not reduced in such a hurry this spring,' wrote the Queen to Lord Panmure, ' we should now have all the men we wanted.' Eight thousand troops were absolutely all that could be sent out from England.

Except as a member of the Cabinet responsible for the Empire, Lord Clarendon was not directly engaged in the measures taken to recover India. Indirectly, however, he had his share in them through the prompt action of Lord Elgin, whom he had sent out as plenipotentiary to settle the difference with the Chinese government. Elgin heard of the trouble in India when he arrived at Hong-Kong in July. He acted immediately as a weaker man might have shrunk from doing; he intercepted the reinforcements which were on their way to Canton, sent them to Calcutta, and followed thither himself in the *Shannon,* by which bold action he probably saved the British Empire in India.

The course of events at home may be traced in Lord Clarendon's letters to his wife, who was at a Continental watering-place during the summer :—

18*th July* 1857.— . . . Gladstone has repented of his abstinence and was as mischievous as ever about Persia and China, repeating all his old arguments in language even more offensive. I can't say that Master John Russell has been much behind him in this; but Palmerston pitched into both very well.

12*th August.*—Alas! the news of the taking of Delhi is not true. . . . The whole universe appears more occupied with this monster mutiny than with anything since the wars of Napoleon, and no wonder! for it is the most awful struggle between a mere handful of Europeans and an army trained, and disciplined by us, of more than 200,000 men. . . . The enormous distances are our great difficulty, because before our troops can reach India and begin their march of 1000 miles, the mutiny may spread beyond control, tho' I have no doubt about our mastering it in time. . . . On the whole, the conduct of foreign governments has been sympathising and friendly—just what ours would be to any of them under circumstances at all similar.

14*th.*— . . . It was lucky I wrote before I went yesterday to the House of Lords, for the bishops kept quarrelling over a Burials Bill and it was nearly 9 o'clock before Clanricarde's interpellation came on. I was able to give a satisfactory account of the proceedings at Osborne, which put an end to a very complicated state of things which might have given rise to events

out of all proportion to the causes from which they sprang.
There never was anything more fortunate than the Emperor's
visit at the moment it took place, for the agents in the East had
all become so excited, and had so committed themselves against
each other, that it required the strong and united decision of
England and France to restore order. . . .

15th.— . . . Gladstone is now in just as excited a state as
at the beginning of the session—the Divorce Bill being the
cause ; but from that he launches into everything else, and is
creating an amount of mischief, as well as delay, that you may
suppose irritates people in general, but more particularly those
wretched, overworked members of the government who are
daily 14 hours in the House of Commons.   Ferguson [1] declares
it can't be long before he ought to be in a mad-house, whether
his friends place him there or not.   Johnny, who wants to be
off to Minto, has now his sting out against everybody, so that
the public good, as well as the comfort of individuals, makes it
necessary that prorogation should not be delayed.   The fish
dinner is on Wednesday, and that is *something*.[2] . . .

17th.— . . . I dined with the Queen of Holland at her hotel.
She was gracious *beyond*— Nobody there but Sir B. Hall [3] (who
has been her lioniser in London) and Lady Wm. Russell.   We
were kept in sweet converse till 11.30, which was rather late for
one thinking of twenty unopened boxes at home !   The Queen
is evidently a very religious woman, as well as a most ardent
Protestant, and I hardly knew what to do when she launched
out against converts to Rome and her contempt for them—all
addressed to Lady William, about whose *going over* she evidently
knew nothing.   It was a scene for a play.   G. Lewis thinks that
Parliament *may* be prorogued on the 22nd, but I doubt it, because
it is in Gladstone's power still to make delay about the Divorce
Bill, and he is sure to abuse any power he has. . . .

In a letter to Lady Cowley the Queen of Holland refers
to this little dinner, all unconscious of the infelicity of her
discourse to Lady William Russell.

23rd August.— . . . You ask me if I like Lord Clarendon.   I find
him *the most charming of men*—so handsome—such a pleasing

---

[1] Dr. Robert Ferguson.
[2] As marking the end of the session.   Ministers used always to dine
together at Greenwich immediately before the prorogation.
[3] Sir Benjamin Hall (1802-67), First Commissioner of Works, created
Baron Llanover in 1859.

voice—so much simplicity of manner with his great cleverness. He was *very kind* to me, and you know, dearest Olivia, I *never* forget. He dined with me to-day week. After dinner, whilst he was discussing with Lady W. Russell listening to him, I was ready to cry because it was the last time I could see him. I admire, and always have admired, Lord Palmerston; but he has not the infinite charm of Lord Clarendon, which indeed is like no other. . . . I wish all the enemies could come to England and see these men. Prejudices would be cut short. Three years ago at Baden I remember to have declared my admiration for Lord Palmerston, on which somebody—and a clever man—said, ' Vous admirez donc Lucifer ! '

Bad news kept dropping in from India, and it required all Palmerston's buoyant confidence to sustain the spirits of his colleagues. Clarendon was more desponding than the others, just as he had been during the trying suspense of operations before Sebastopol. 'The Indian telegram makes me shudder,' he wrote to his wife on 22nd August, ' for all the details which the mail may bring of fresh atrocities and further mutinies. My colleagues are all more sanguine than I am; my own opinion having been settled for some time past that we shall lose India after a protracted and exhausting struggle to reconquer it.'

Meanwhile, matters in the nearer East had not been going smoothly. There had arisen much difference of opinion among the contracting powers in respect to the manner in which the provisions of the Treaty of Paris should be carried out. Lord Stratford's proceedings continued to give much anxiety to Lord Clarendon.

Lord Clarendon to Lord Cowley.

29th July 1857.— . . . How I wish that Stratford had taken Lyons's good advice about coming away. Half the difficulties which now exist at Constantinople are owing to the *rix* between him and Thouvenel, and his doing the right thing always in the wrong way. He has behaved very ill to Bulwer throughout. If he would have acted cordially with him, his own position at Constantinople would have been strengthened. He may, perhaps, resign in a pet upon the Pisani affair, and a fine end that will be to his long career. . . .

20th August.— . . . Stratford seems determined to defeat us,
and I believe he would think his own personal triumph in this
struggle would be *cheaply* purchased by dividing Europe into two
hostile camps and cementing an alliance between France and
Russia, founded upon the extinction of Turkey.

Lord Clarendon to Lord Stratford de Redcliffe.

20th August.—I am much annoyed at the intelligence, dated
18th and 19th from Constantinople, which has reached us through
the French Embassy here and through Musurus. Not only does
it appear that no official communication has been made to the
Porte by you and the Internuncio, and that we are consequently
in the position of appearing to have broken our promise to the
Emperor [Napoleon], but the part of the agreement which we
promised him should be kept secret for the time has been shown
totidem verbis of Musurus's despatch, to Thouvenel, who, of course,
has reported it to his government. . . . This renders our position
with regard to France most painful and humiliating, as the
Emperor is entitled to say (though I trust he will not *think* it)
that we have not kept faith with him, and *that*, as I need hardly
tell you, is a position we don't mean to accept.

Moreover, the present state of things at Constantinople is
exactly what Russia desires. If she had had the arrangement of
it herself, it could not have better suited her purpose, which is to
embroil us with France. . . . We have to look to eventualities
in other parts of the world, and it is our duty not to increase the
number of our enemies at a moment when all the energies of this
country must be strained to the utmost, and when it is fearfully
doubtful whether all the exertions we can make will avail in the
monster struggle in which we are about to engage in India. You
seem to be creating for us as much embarrassment as the nature
of the case admits, as of course the Porte does exactly what you
advise. It is an unenviable responsibility you are taking upon
yourself. An ambassador is not bound to act upon instructions
in which he does not agree, and his course is then clear ; but he
has no right to prevent those instructions from being executed,
and I hope, within the next 48 hours, to hear that you have put
an end to the delay which ought not, as far as H.M.'s ambassador
is concerned, to have existed.

Stratford's bearing towards the French ambassador at
Constantinople had been the cause of most, if not all, of

the trouble with the French government; but personal intercourse between the Emperor Napoleon, Queen Victoria and Lord Clarendon proved more effective in bringing them to an understanding than leagues of correspondence. The Emperor visited the Queen at Osborne in August, and matters were agreed between them in a very short time.

Lord Clarendon to Lord Normanby.

17th August 1857.—You will have been glad to see that good things were done and bad ones averted at Osborne. A very black cloud hung over the alliance when the Emperor came there; but all was sunshine before he departed. He appears to have obtained a momentary triumph, and he has one—*quoad* the form, which is what Frenchmen really care about; whereas we who look to the substance have obtained what we wanted—viz., the renunciation by the Emperor of his project of uniting the Principalities under one Prince. This latter fact, however, is for manifest reasons to be considered quite confidential for the present; the Emperor wants to take his own measures for inducing his confederates to back out of the project with him; so pray say nothing about it. . . .

Towards the end of August Clarendon went as minister in attendance to Balmoral, and kept his wife regularly informed about his proceedings.

EDINBURGH, *28th August.*— . . . You will like a line to say that we arrived here without let or hindrance in 10½ hours, the only disagreeable thing being the dust—the pleasant thing being that I had no boxes, and I read the *Edinburgh Review* right thro' from one end to the other, which is a lark I have not had these four years.

BALMORAL, *31st.*— . . . We walked—the two Ladies Grey and I—to Abergeldie to inscribe our names at Madame Mère's,[1] which is always de rigueur the day after arriving. . . . I had an excellent fire in my room when I came home, which made me suffer all the more from the intense cold of the drawing and dining rooms, the Queen seeming to have no more intention of a fire than she would have in London a month ago. . . . Soon after I went to my room the messenger arrived bringing very

[1] H.R.H. the Duchess of Kent.

melancholy Indian news. . . . The tone of letters from Calcutta
and the three Presidencies has undergone a great change.
Things there are looked upon as very grave and certain to be
more so. The demand for more troops—alas ! many more
than we can send—is most urgent, and makes one feel how
powerless the troops we *have* sent will be, tho' we shall denude
ourselves at home and almost invite insult by our helplessness.
. . . The Queen has not the same apprehension that I have of
losing our Indian Empire ; she believes that with time and
money we shall reconquer the country. I don't. . . .

1st September.— . . . The morning here was spent in what
is called ' leastering,' which is spearing salmon in the Dee. It
was a gay scene, but rather cruel and very poaching.[1]

3rd.— . . . We are all going now to Braemar for the gathering of the clans, as it is called—*i.e.* about 150 fellows in kilts
are brought from the neighbourhood and engage in Highland
games—throwing weights and dancing flings—which might be
all very well if one had not seen them before and had nothing
else to do, which is not my case, and if it was not raining torrents
as it now is. . . . It is really astonishing how so many boxes
can arrive brim full of despatches, without containing any information worth the carriage. All our foreign agents have now
a mania for writing which requires to be checked ; but I suppose
I should offend them mortally if I told them not to write except
when they had something to say. . . . Palmerston tells me that
he has proposed to the Queen to offer a dukedom to Lansdowne,
and the Queen tells me this morning that she approves. I am
glad of it ; tho' I shall be surprised if he accepts. . . . Macaulay
was astonished at being offered a peerage ; but did not hesitate
a moment about accepting it, and asked to be allowed to retain
his name, which he is quite right in doing.

5th September.— . . . I had a long letter from Palmerston
this morning full—not of hope, but of *certainty* that, altho' the
next three or four mails will bring bad news, yet that we shall
reconquer India in 5 or 6 months and add immensely to our
position in the world by doing it all off our own bat. Confidence and courage are fine things and contain in them elements
of success ; but they are bad when, as with Palmerston, they
lead to neglect of the means of which success can be attained.

6th.— . . . I heard a most admirable and eloquent sermon
at kirk this morning from a Mr. Caird who preached here two

---

[1] Leistering salmon is now prohibited by law.

years ago a sermon which the Queen asked him to print and
which has been translated into three languages and sold by
the thousand all over Europe. The Queen has just given me
a copy and I long for a spare ¼ of an hour to read it.[1] He is a
modest, unassuming, very ugly young man, speaking with the
broadest Scotch accent, but possessing a power of illustrating
his thoughts such as I have rarely heard. . . .

7th.— . . . I have been out the whole day on an expedition
with the Queen, and we are only returned now—7.20. It was
to the famous hill of Lochnagar, and it would have been very
pleasant if it had not poured torrents the greater part of the
time. There were places where riding was quite out of the
question, and as I have walked a good deal on rough ground,
have been thoroughly drenched and came home for the last
¾ hour in a carriage with wet feet, I shall be rather lucky than
otherwise if I have neither a cold nor the gout to-morrow. I
feel better, however, to-day than I have any day yet. Lady
Churchill was of the party, and, poor woman, has to dress directly
to go fourteen miles to a ball at Mar Lodge. Pleasant ! . . . I
had a letter from Palmerston this morning who seems to have
made up his mind to throw over the East India Company, and
asks me while *I am shaving or walking* to think what sort of
government should be established in place of it ! He has a
jolly way of looking at disasters. . . .

9th.— . . . I never can drive out of my head that great
disasters are still in store for us, and that when Bombay and
Madras are in the same state as Bengal we shall be found utterly
unprepared to meet the further crisis, altho' we have had notice
and warning enough. . . .

Referring to Blair Atholl, where it had been arranged he
should meet Lady Clarendon and Lady Constance Villiers,
he continues :

I hardly know the Duke, and, as I see the Duchess means him
to show me good sport in the forest, you must tell her that my
habits are not those of deerstalking, that my shooting days are

---

[1] John Caird (1820-98) was at that time minister of Errol, presently
to be translated to Park Church, Glasgow. In 1873 he was presented by
the Crown to the Principalship of Glasgow University. The sermon of 'two
years ago' was from Romans xii. 11—'Not slothful in business, fervent
in spirit, serving the Lord.' It was published by the Queen's command
under the title of *Religion in Common Life*, and was pronounced by Dean
Stanley to be ' the greatest single sermon of the century.'

over, that I am more or less gouty, that I don't want to go to
the forest, and that I prefer not to be put in a kilt, which
I believe is required of all visitors at Blair. I rely upon
you for all this. At Invercauld here the guests have to wear
kilts and all the paraphernalia, and they look miserable.
Lord Cowper was in one the other day and didn't venture to
show himself.

9*th*.— . . . Lavradio [1] did not appear before dinner as expected yesterday, and we all thought he had done wisely in
stopping somewhere, for the wind and torrents of rain were
really awful, beyond anything of the kind I remember ; but at
1.30 this morning he arrived, and when, after waiting ¾ hour at
the door, he was at last admitted, they say that no drowned rat
ever looked half so drowned as he. . . .

11*th*.— . . . It has been agreeable enough here ; the Queen
and Prince have, as usual, been very kind, and I have had a
good deal of time to myself, which was lucky, as I had a great
deal of work ; but I have not liked it so well as last year because
it has not done me the same good. The weather has been
detestable, and I have never been fairly quit of gouty feelings,
so I don't mind a change ; tho' if it had not been for you and
Constance I should certainly cut off south, not being in trim for
my favorite pastime of country-house visiting ; but I don't
know that Downing Street would improve my spirits. . . .

We packed off Lavradio this morning. He carries off with
him poor notions of Highland climate. The fireless drawing-
room last night shrivelled him into nothing, and the Queen
had the windows open while we were at dinner ! He is
going to Germany to make a formal proposal from the King
of Portugal for the hand of Miss Hohenzollern-Sigmaringen,
which is absurd enough three months after the marriage has
been settled.

HADDO HOUSE, 13*th*.— . . . I had rather a dreary drive
here of eight hours, as it rained the whole time and the road
was so detestable that I could hardly read. Aberdeen is never
very *hot* in his manner, but he was evidently pleased to see me.
We had a good cosy talk in the evening about foreign affairs.
He is just like Palmerston (and I suppose every one else who
has been Foreign Secretary), in caring about them more than
anything else. I daresay I shall be just the same when I leave
them.

---

[1] The Portuguese Minister.

Lord Clarendon to Lord Granville.

DRUMMOND CASTLE, 23rd September.— . . . I cannot but think that the last Indian news is disastrous instead of cheering—increasing pressure upon diminishing means of resistance is everywhere apparent, and I fear that irreparable mischief may be done before our insufficient reinforcements can arrive. I wish Mars would think how Delhi might be stalked instead of deer. . . . I have suggested to Palmerston to telegraph to the Queen for permission to announce an honorary distinction to Havelock who has done more for India in the last four months than all others put together. He is a Queen's officer and a C.G., he ought at least to be K.C.B.

After all, Clarendon was induced to go to the hill when he was at Blair, and shot a stag in a drive in Glen Tilt. On 25th September he went off to the south, leaving Lady Clarendon and her daughter to pay some more visits, and the daily letters were resumed.

FOREIGN OFFICE, 29th September.— . . . I send you a long telegram which arrived in the night. It shows the extreme danger to which Havelock and his handful of exhausted heroes are exposed. I understand that Cawnpore is quite indefensible ; and if it is retaken by the rebels and Havelock destroyed, there will be no hope of saving Lucknow and Agra. The moral effect of that makes one tremble. In the whole Bombay Presidency there are not at this moment 200 European soldiers !

To Sir G. C. Lewis.

F. O., 28th September 1857.— . . . The spirit of the country is thoroughly roused, as you say, but I don't think it has been turned to account. I am not exactly prepared to say how that might have been done ; but we have resorted to no other measure than the recruiting sergeant, and altho' he has been more successful than we expected, yet it is absurd to believe that voluntary enlistment at the rate it is now going on will furnish made soldiers in the number we now require immediately. At this moment, every man below 5 ft. 5 in. is excluded from the ranks, and yet I don't believe that there is a Zouave or Chasseur-de-Vincennes who is 5 ft. 4 in., and they are the best troops in France. The King of the Belgians has proposed that the government or the Company should have the pick of his army to the extent of 10,000 men for a limited period, and that they should be ready in a month (we or the Company paying clothing, etc.) ; but Palmerston would not hear of it, because it is important for our national honor to win off our own bat. . . . Palmerston opposes everything that is out of the beaten track, and I own that his want of energy, and his system of hoping and believing, instead of acting, have disappointed me woefully.

To Lady Clarendon.

1st October.—I have been the whole afternoon at the cabinet. All the news has been read, and I think it *very bad*. The mutinous spirit is evidently spreading. I have no doubt it could be checked if Havelock found himself at the head of 5000 men and if Delhi were taken, or, in other words, if a miracle were performed in our favour, upon which we have no right to speculate. I was not at all satisfied with the language at the cabinet. Except poor Labouchere, who turned up his eyes like a duck in thunder, no one seems the least alive to the transcendent gravity of the crisis. As for Panmure, with his foolish red-tape objections, I could have knocked him down. With the exception of lowering the standard to 5 ft. 4 in. and ordering 10,000 more militia, nothing new has been decided upon, and I really feel unhappy.

A clamour was got up at this time for the recall of Lord Canning, Governor-General of India. Calcutta was in the throes of panic, calling upon Canning to make savage reprisals upon the mutineers, and to seize the dethroned King of Oudh who was living quietly near Calcutta. Of all Dalhousie's acts the annexation of Oudh was that which gave the British conscience most cause for uneasiness. It was bruited that the King of Oudh was about to join the insurgents. 'Clap him in prison!' shrieked people and press. Instead of doing so, Canning received the King and his vizier to live as his guests in Government House. This caused a frenzy of indignation. 'Clemency Canning' must be removed : send us a man of some courage. Canning's courage never flinched ; but he did what so many less conspicuous citizens failed to do—he kept his head all through the turmoil.

Lord Clarendon to Sir G. C. Lewis.

5th October.— . . . The feeling of want of confidence in
Canning seems to be based upon no better grounds than that a
man with insufficient means cannot grapple successfully with
monster difficulties. For my own part, I think he has done as
well as a man could in such circumstances, and I could suggest
no one whose antecedents would offer a prospect of wiser or more
energetic policy. Elgin may be cleverer, but he is deficient in
the very qualities which with truth you assign to Canning.

Lord Clarendon to Lord Palmerston.

DOWNING STREET, *4th November* 1857.—MY DEAR PALMER-
STON,—Granville showed me to-day a letter from Clanricarde
respecting the attacks upon Canning. He told me that he
intended to say something this evening at the Mansion House
in defence of Canning, though not in a controversial spirit or
in a manner to commit the government, but merely asking for
fair play and that an absent man should not be condemned
without a full knowledge of the facts upon which public opinion
ought to be formed. I must say I think it is time that some check
should be put upon the run which is made against Canning, which
had its origin in the necessary measure he adopted for preventing
the mischievous excesses of the Press at a moment when, for
aught he or any one else knew, the whole of India might have
risen in open insurrection against England.

If this organised system of attack upon him continues until
parliament meets, without any authentic vindication of his
proceedings, not only injustice will be done to him, but his
power of usefulness will be destroyed. He himself will be discouraged, and friends and foes alike will cease to respect a
governor who will appear to have lost the support of the government and people of England. Granville will, no doubt, say what
is proper and useful ; but he cannot speak in the name of the
government, and he has not the weight and authority with the
public *which you alone possess.* Moreover, what he says this
evening will positively do harm unless it is backed by you on
Monday ; because, as you are known to the whole world as the
chivalrous defender against all comers of those who serve you
faithfully, people will watch to see whether Granville's opinions
are endorsed by you, or whether they are to be attributed solely
to his personal friendship for Canning.

I am the more induced to think it expedient that you should give Canning the benefit of your public approval, because I have been at some pains to find out what public opinion really is upon the humanity question, as it is called, and I am convinced that the cry for vengeance has been overdone.   Nobody wishes that a single mutineer, still less a single perpetrator of outrage, should be spared ; but it is not to be denied that the language of many newspapers has been sanguinary and ferocious, thereby misrepresenting the national character. This effect has been very apparent abroad, and I have no doubt that we shall soon see a reaction ; indeed I think it has begun. . . .

5th.—I wrote the above last night, and have this morning read Granville's speech, which is very good and does not, I think, in any way commit the government ; but it does not alter my opinion about the importance, on public grounds, of your good word for Canning.

Palmerston replied next day after reading Granville's speech :

I think Granville's speech very good, and I will say a few words on Monday in defence of Canning.   My own feeling about him is that there are things evidently done by himself alone which do him great credit, and that there are things apparently done in his name by his council, which require much explanation. As to the twaddling order or proclamation, I am sure he never wrote a word of it, but only adopted the rigmarole of other people.

The good news of the recapture of Delhi on 20th September did not reach London till 26th October, when it inspired Palmerston to adopt a needlessly defiant tone at the Lord Mayor's banquet on 9th November.

Lord Clarendon to Lady Clarendon.

10th November.— . . . For once in my life I am very sorry I did not speak, for I could have supplied some shortcomings in Palmerston's speech.   He talked of the ' dreadful consequences ' which would have befallen any Power that had attacked us in the notion that we were weak.[1]   I should have spoken of the

---

[1] While all the forces of the Crown were employed in suppressing the Indian revolt.

friendly feeling which has been exhibited towards us by foreign Powers and the foreign press. Of course, I might have managed it with the Lord Mayor, but as I am always slow about volunteering a speech, the time went by. I don't care as regards myself, but I have certainly missed an opportunity of doing a bit of public good, and one too that was much wanted. I am very sorry, and there's an end of it.

Lord Clarendon to Lord Cowley.

F. O., 11*th November* 1857.—Thanks for your long and interesting letter of yesterday. I marvel how you find time to write, for well I know what the scramble of rural royalty is. The history of the Imperial cold is really curious, and not the least curious part is his having the taste for such puerile pastimes, and the courage to engage in them, surrounded as he knows himself to be with hostile critics. What a story the hunt would make for the newspapers! and what a subject for illustration the *hare* and the *hounds* would furnish to *Punch*!

Our friend is an odd little fellow. It is impossible not to like him and not to feel that he has qualities which would make him a most reliable friend if he had good advisers about him. But a man who is so indolent and ignorant as the Emperor, and has so much unavoidable business to do, must depend upon others, and should have a Nestor for a Foreign Minister, instead of a man with an empty head and an abundant abdomen like Walewski, who leads him into quagmires from which others have to pull him out all covered with mud. I can't forgive him, however, for believing in our treaty with Austria, as it is a proof that he does not know or understand us, which is an unpleasant reflection. If you have the opportunity, I think you should impress upon him the necessity of bringing to book his informant who had *seen* the treaty signed on 6th June. We ought to do this for his own sake, because the man who crammed down his throat a lie which had not, like most political lies, the shadow of a foundation, must have reckoned upon his gullibility to an extent which was personally offensive. Moreover we owe it to ourselves to hunt up this disgusting intrigue to its source.

For some weeks matters had been going from bad to worse in the city. By the second week of November the country was in the midst of a financial panic; one great

house after another came crashing down, and on the 12th
the government decided to suspend the Bank Charter Act.

I quite concur as to the necessity for this measure, wrote
Clarendon to his wife, but one consequence of it is absolutely
diabolical, viz., that parliament must be called together.   We
are all agreed that if, having broken the law, we allowed nearly
three months to pass without seeking to be indemnified, parliament would meet in justly bad humour with *everything*, even if
it did not pass a vote of censure. . . .

13*th November.*—*The letter* has had an excellent effect in
restoring confidence, and things are easier to-day.   The great
discounting house of Alexander, which is only second to Gurney's,
was to have stopped payment last night, as the Bank of England
could give them no assistance.   *The letter* enabled the Bank to
go to their relief and they are saved—at least for the present.[1]
The Bank discounted two millions yesterday, and was left at
night with only £250,000 of notes !   It must have stopped payment this morning before 12 o'clock, so that there never was a
more fortunate or better timed measure.   It is all G. Lewis's
doing, and he deserves infinite credit for his judgment and
courage.

17*th.*— . . . It was a blackish cabinet to-day, for the news
from the country, particularly from Wolverhampton, was bad.
So it was from Scotland, and George Lewis shook his head
ominously about events that are oncoming.   Then there is a
letter from Sir Colin Campbell which is not a little alarming, as
he considers the position of Outram and Havelock *most critical*,
and sees no chance of relieving them.   Very disagreeable ; but
Palmerston did not seem to care much !

19*th.*— . . . I am just returned from Windsor and, as you may
suppose, find a pretty accumulation of boxes and letters.   The
Menagerie [2] behaved very well.   They crawled the whole length
of the Throne Room on all fours with their noses to the floor,
and the Queen boasted much to me afterwards of having kept
her countenance. . . . I had a long audience, at which the
Queen expressed great alarm about Palmerston's health. . . .
She was full of the evil consequences of his dying or resigning to
the country and herself, and then let out that *she would look to
me* ; which I was very glad of, as it gave me by far the best

---

[1] The letter authorised the Bank to issue notes beyond the legal limit.
[2] The Siamese ambassadors, whom Clarendon had been to Windsor to
present to the Queen.

opportunity I could have of proving to her *the utter impossibility* of such an arrangement. She was very bitter against Lord John ; but I told her she could not escape him if the Tories were unable to form a government. . . .

20th.— . . . Oh such a day of it as I have had ! but when haven't I ? It is past 6.30 and I am only just out of the cabinet and nothing written for the messengers. Then I dine with Granville to meet Delane and Russell,[1] for the latter is going out to India as *Times* correspondent, and G. thinks it useful for him to start with good impressions and a good *entrée* in his mouth. But imagine all the mischief in store for us from that fellow, who of course will want a second crop of Crimean laurels grown upon the ruins of everybody's reputation.

1st December.— . . . Palmerston, for some reason best known to himself, *forgot* to bring with him [to the cabinet] the Queen's Speech, which, tho' agreed to yesterday, was to be read over again to-day ; consequently I don't know how the Reform paragraph stands, but G. Grey says he is better satisfied with it than he was. I think Reform will be the rock on which the government will go to pieces. . . . I am going to Granville's full dress dinner, but my thoughts will be at Hatfield this evening.[2]

Lord Stratford de Redcliffe having resigned the embassy at Constantinople Clarendon felt some trepidation as to the mood in which the formidable ambassador might return to England. However, all went well ; Clarendon entertained a genuine respect for Stratford's undoubted ability and the extraordinary energy with which he had applied himself to an exceedingly difficult and prolonged task. The asperities of correspondence disappeared in the cordiality of meeting ; Stratford's services were recognised by the Universities of Oxford and Cambridge, each of which conferred upon him an honorary degree, and in 1869 he received the Garter—the highest distinction that can be conferred upon a peer. Clarendon was prepared for his first interview with

---

[1] Afterwards Sir William Russell, the pioneer of war correspondence in journalism.

[2] Where his daughter, Lady Constance, was to go to her first ball. There is a touching note about it in Lady Clarendon's journal : ' Constance was exceedingly admired, immensely danced with, and had great success. She looked like a rosebud. I felt so proud of, and I trust so thankful for, such a dear child.'

Stratford by a private note from Lord Howard de Walden, British Minister at Brussels, which he acknowledged thus :

12th January 1858.—I was much obliged to you for letting me know the *animus* with which Redcliffe Pasha was about to visit the mother country, as it enabled me to meet him in a kindred spirit, and until I got your letter I did not know whether he was coming here with his sting *out* or *in* ; but I was prepared for either course. Our relations together have not been very friendly of late, and I had announced to him that he should only receive *official* correspondence from me in consequence of some *boutade* in one of his private letters.

He was born and bred in the old anti-Gallican school, and he is not a man to modify an opinion or to admit that altered times and circumstances can justify any deviation from a long-established policy. He has, therefore, consistently and unremittedly hated the French and done his utmost to thwart them ; and, having for a numbers of years occupied the Eastern dunghill without competitors, he could not find an inch of room upon it for the French ambassador, who, being backed by 150,000 men, thought he might have *locus standi* there. I have a great respect for Stratford's talents and a great dislike of his character, but I bear him no ill will. . . . I believe Lady Stratford left Taymouth because I came there, but I did not inquire much about it, and I did not know that I had been so severely lashed by his daughter. When one has stood in the pillory of office as long as I have, one gets very indifferent to the missiles of abuse or praise that are hurled at one. . . . I ought to add that Stratford's demeanour fully bore out your announcement. He was very friendly and agreeable ; but there were some subjects which we both instinctively avoided.

The Indian upheaval brought the nation to a sense of the anomaly of a vast dominion, containing a population more than five times as numerous as that of the United Kingdom, being governed by the directors of a trading company. The time had come when the administration should be transferred from the Company to the Crown, a measure involving disturbance of so many vested interests that none but a strong ministry could undertake it. And Palmerston's ministry was strong in virtue of the unbounded popularity of its head ; so strong that as Palmerston walked

home from the House with the Attorney-General Sir Richard
Bethell, after Disraeli's opposition to the introduction of the
Bill for the Better Government of India had been defeated
by 318 votes to 173, his companion compared him to a
Roman consul in triumph, and said that somebody should
be told off to remind him that he was mortal.

Palmerston had to wait exactly four-and-twenty hours
for the reminder, which came from the quarter least likely.
Orsini's attempt on the life of the Emperor and Empress
of the French in the Rue Lepelletier took place on 14th
January 1858.[1] Orsini, after a romantic escape from
prison in Mantua, came to London—that universal Alsatia
for desperadoes—and, being well-looking and of engaging
address, became a bit of a lion, much petted by people
with more leisure than sound sense. Presently he was
seen no more in London, and was next heard of as one of
those wounded by the explosion of his own bomb.

Not unnaturally, there was a flare of indignation in France
against the miscreant who had been harboured in England
while maturing his plot. The French government addressed
a reasonable and temperate request to Queen Victoria's
government that measures should be taken 'to provide
such a guarantee of security which no State can refuse to
a neighbouring State, and which we are entitled to expect
from an ally.' Palmerston, accordingly, caused a bill to
be prepared which, while preserving the right of asylum,
provided that conspiracy to murder should constitute a
felony. The Conservatives supported the government
against Kinglake the historian, Roebuck and Lord John
Russell, who opposed the introduction of the bill, and
nothing seemed less likely than that any difficulty would be
met with in passing it. Unluckily before it came up for
second reading on 19th February the tone of the French
press had become so violent in denunciation of *perfide
Albion*, even the official *Moniteur* describing England as ' a
den of conspirators,' as to rouse an angry spirit in retalia-
tion. When the Radical Milner-Gibson moved a hostile

---

[1] The attempt failed, but the explosion killed ten bystanders on the
spot, and wounded no fewer than one hundred and fifty-six others.

amendment, he received the support of Gladstone and the Peelites ; whereupon Disraeli, discerning a chance of inflicting a defeat on the government, spoke against the bill which he had supported ten days before, and—*proh pudor !* led 146 Conservatives into the ' No ' lobby, thereby placing ministers in a minority of 19—234 to 215.

Lord Palmerston at once resigned, and Clarendon, having handed over his charge to Lord Malmesbury, who took the seals of the Foreign Office under Lord Derby, betook himself, with no slight sense of relief, to the sylvan tranquillity of The Grove and the society of his wife and children, of whom he had seen so little for the past five years.

Among the many private friendships into which Lord Clarendon was brought through his official duties, none appear to have received warmer expression than that which was borne towards him by Queen Sophia, the consort of William III., King of Holland. Having failed of happiness in her own married life, she was all the more eager to cultivate friendship with those who won her esteem. Her quick intellect kept her in sympathy with the private interests of others as well as in touch with passing political events. European unrest caused her much anxious foreboding for the destiny of her husband's realm as well as for her native duchy of Würtemberg.

The Queen of Holland to Lord Clarendon.

STUTTGART, 17*th May* 1858.— . . . I find public opinion in this part of the world in such a state of excitement that 1848 and '49 were hardly inferior to it. Austria plays a desperate game, calling forth a perfect dissolution of the present state of Germany. . . . I do not believe that the Emperor Napoleon wants to attack Germany. I do not see the necessity of going headlong to war. We all rely on England to keep and preach neutrality. Buol's fall is a concession to Russia : Bach is to follow. Russia is urging war. She will not go to war : she hopes to weaken all parties and to reap the fruits. The only way to prevent her triumph is to localise the war in Italy and prevent a general conflagration. You are to have a perfect inundation of Russian princes and princesses this summer in England—for what aim, Heaven knows ; but *I* know that Russia is [*illegible*] France, and

I cannot conceive how the [*illegible*] mind of the Emperor could
be taken in those snares. . . . I have never seen—at no time of
my life—such a dark, hopeless prospect.

The Hon. Emily Eden to the Earl of Clarendon.

EDEN LODGE [1858].— . . . Lord Brougham was my only
Sunday visitor. He was very tame and *proper*, perhaps because
he talked nothing but French. He has not yet acquired that
perfect accent which will enable him to join my gallicised class.
Considering that he is such a great master of English and makes
such a hash of French, I rather wish he would confine himself
to the vernacular. He seemed to be all right about politics ; at
least he thought everybody else wrong, which is the nearest
approach to right that can be made just now. Lord John is
out of favour ; Roebuck ditto ; and he was extremely anxious
to know if Lord Derby really meant to go on governing the
country with a minority. I could only give him the consolatory
intelligence that Lord D. neither governs the country nor *is*
in a minority. He says it is melancholy to him the way
absolutists and foreigners generally crow over the failure of our
free institutions ; but you will hear all his sentiments from
himself. . . . Lady Westminster brought her new son-in-law
to show me yesterday. Agnes looked really pretty with happiness.[1] The Buccleuchs have had a great alarm about their
eldest girl, for which you will pity them.[2] I thought when
the Duchess was here on Friday that they were trusting to
homeopathy with an alarming faith ; and it appears that Dr.
Bell had entirely overlooked a pleurisy under which Victoria was
suffering. Ferguson and Bright are now attending her.

The Emperor of the French took the unusual course of
inviting the Lords Palmerston and Clarendon, leaders of
the Opposition, to visit him at Compiègne. Their acceptance of the invitation, upon which they did not decide
without some hesitation, excited much unfriendly comment
at the time.

Lord Palmerston to Lord Clarendon.

BROADLANDS, 31*st October* 1858.—MY DEAR CLARENDON,—I
have received this morning the invitation to Compiègne and I

---

[1] Lady Agnes Grosvenor was married in 1858 to Sir Archibald Campbell
of Succoth.
[2] Lady Victoria Scott, afterwards Marchioness of Lothian.

conclude you have received yours also.   It is for six days—from the 15th to 20th of November.   What do you mean to do ?   We must, of course, do the same.   Being comfortably settled at home, we should, if left intirely to chuse, prefer staying where we are ; but it seems difficult to assign any valid and sufficient reason for declining the invitation of a Sovereign when the distance is so small and the intention so friendly.

Perhaps some of our Radical friends would rather not see us too intimate with Napoleon ; on the other hand, our being on personally friendly terms with him may be politically useful to us individually, and to the country—if we should come into office again.   And if we were to decline the invitation, we might perhaps create an unpleasant feeling in the Emperor's mind.

2nd November.— . . . The more I think of our Compiègne invitation, the more I wish to get off if it could be managed without offence to the Emperor.   It would be a considerable bore to go thither, and one cannot say how our going thither might, under all the circumstances, be taken by our Liberal friends and the public at large.   On the other hand, one should be very sorry to do anything on the subject which could be taken amiss by the Emperor.   I shall be glad to receive your opinion on the matter.

Lord Clarendon to Sir G. C. Lewis.

ASHRIDGE, *5th November* 1858.—I have waited to thank you for your most interesting letter of the 30th until I had been to Windsor and had a chance of picking up some news at head-quarters.   At no time during the last six years have I found the Royal Pair more friendly and confidential.   I believe there was no question which they would not have answered if I had thought it decent or discreet to interrogate them.   However, in the course of three long conversations with Prince Albert he volunteered some information—*inter alia*, that he was better pleased with Stanley [1] than he had expected ; that he had found him very quick and candid, not avoiding discussion and never resorting to sophistry ; but ignorant of the British constitution and indifferent about precedents and forms, which he treated as belonging to a bygone state of things and not to be taken into account nowadays. . . .

---

[1] Lord Stanley, who had been appointed to the India Office.

The helpless state of the Navy alarms them very much. Upon a thoro' investigation things turn out much worse than was expected. They see no reason for immediate apprehension about France ; but they have lost confidence in Louis Napoleon, whose conduct at Cherbourg showed a marked difference in his feelings, even towards the Queen.

. . . They were greatly surprised, as everybody will be, at Gladstone's wish to go to the Ionian Islands.[1] The Queen had had a long letter from the saint of his idolatry, the Duchess of Sutherland, explaining his wish to solve some difficult questions there, and admiring his motives, which made H.M. merry at the Jesuit's expence. . . .

. . . They were, on the whole, pleased with Bright's speech as likely to promote Conservatism and to prevent his being walked with arm-in-arm by Cabinet ministers.[2] They were still more pleased, however, with the speech of their friend Fairbairn, the Mayor of Leeds, who, tho' a Radical and risen from the ranks, pitched handsomely into J. Bright. On all sides I hear that that worthy has overshot the mark, and did not even hit the fancy of the working-men at Birmingham. Aberdeen, who, you know, was much Bright-bitten, writes to me that 'his last exhibitions, altho' containing much truth, have failed entirely to increase my trust in his practical wisdom.'

The Duke of Bedford, who was here yesterday, told me that John's state of mind worried him to death and made him wish to have nothing to do with politics. He is in the habit of writing his impressions to the Duke, who says he immediately puts his letters in the fire in order that there may be no record of such foolishness and injustice. His father years ago said that John's failure thro' life would be want of judgment, and his brother considers that the prophecy has been strictly fulfilled. He thinks that the coming together again of Palmerston and J. R. is an absolute impossibility.

---

[1] 'At the beginning of October, while on a visit to Lord Aberdeen at Haddo, Mr. Gladstone was amazed by a letter from the Secretary of State for the Colonies [Bulwer Lytton], which opened to him the question of undertaking a special mission to the Ionian Islands. . . . To the new proposal Mr. Gladstone replied that his first impulse on any call from a minister of the Crown . . . would be to place himself at the minister's disposal.'—Morley's *Gladstone*, i. 595.

[2] Bright spoke on 27th and 29th October in the Birmingham Town Hall. On the first occasion he delivered a violent attack on the House of Lords ; on the second, he described British foreign policy as nothing but 'a gigantic system of outdoor relief for the aristocracy.'

We are asked to Compiègne from the 15th to the 20th and have accepted, which is perhaps a foolish thing to do under present circs. ; but I could find no good excuse for declining, and I should not like to offend the Emperor.

The visit to Compiègne took place, not without attracting a good deal of adverse criticism from the press and other sources. ' I think,' wrote Lord John Russell to Sir Charles Wood, ' that Palmerston and Clarendon have done themselves infinite harm by going to Compiègne. They must hereafter be considered rather as courtiers of the Tuileries than subjects of St. James's.'

Delane of the *Times* wrote to Bernal Osborne, M.P., as follows :

. . . ' As to the suns of our late firmament, they are all obscured. Did anyone ever hear or imagine such folly as this visit of Palmerston and Clarendon to Compiègne ? Not that it now makes much difference to either, but because people see that they need not bolt the door against their return [to office]. I enclose, *in confidence,* Palmerston's excuse for himself. Clarendon's is much to the same effect—if possible, still more lame. I think you may safely recant your allegiance to both these luminaries. No star shines very bright above the horizon ; but these two seem to have hopelessly set.'

I have not come across any account under Clarendon's own hand of what took place during the visit, nor is it easy to see any other motive in the Emperor receiving a visit from two leading members of the Opposition, except that, foreseeing the early return of their party to power, he aimed at putting them off the scent of the secret treaty he was negotiating with Cavour at that very time.

Charles Greville has recorded a conversation he had with Clarendon on his return—' for the first time for many a day, when he told me a great deal that was interesting, just as he used to do formerly.' [1] The chief matter discussed by the trio at Compiègne was the French occupation of Rome, which the Emperor declared it passed his wit to see how it could be brought to an end. He said that the dearest wish

---

[1] *Greville Memoirs,* 3rd series, ii. 215.

of his heart was the regeneration of Italy, to accomplish which France had become the ally of Russia and Sardinia against Austria. Clarendon warned him that Austria would spend her last florin and sacrifice her last man in defence of her Italian possessions, and that the danger of disturbing the peace of Europe was very serious.

Stricken in years, whereof he now numbered three score and four, and in fast failing health, Byron's 'travell'd thane' still corresponded with some of his old colleagues; but even his cool judgment and long experience did not help him to peer further into the Italian millstone than anybody else.

Lord Aberdeen to Lord Clarendon.

ARGYLL HOUSE, *2nd November* 1858.— . . . I have been condemned by the doctors to return to London in order to improve my climate, although it is not very obvious how writing by candle-light and being half stifled with smoke is to do it. However, I must not complain. If I were inclined to grumble I should not lack matter both abroad and at home.

Your assurance of the disposition of the Emperor Napoleon is quite satisfactory, and I fully believe this disposition to be sincere; but I have no great reliance on its continuance. . . . I have always anticipated as much evil as good from the French alliance. It has given a sanction to our Neapolitan policy, and, without it, France would not have acted such a part at Lisbon in such a cause. . . . You did not extend your journey to Vienna, and I have heard very little about their doings; but I hope they have not lost your good opinion since you ceased to encourage the tormenting policy and ambitious projects of the Sardinian government. The ill-will of France [towards Austria] is undisguised; but I am not much afraid of its effects, so long as the Austrians retain their fine army. It may suit the Emperor Napoleon to give the Italian revolutionists hopes of assistance, without pledging himself; but although he may advance to the verge of a rupture, I scarcely think he will do more. He is too much of a Sybarite, and values his position too much, to risk the loss of all in such a cause. I care comparatively little what he may do either for or against the Turks. Fortunately we are beginning to see the egregious blunder of which we have been guilty, and to appreciate at its true value the integrity and independence of the Turkish empire. . . .

The Reform puzzle seems to admit of no solution. . . . I believe Lord John, on the whole, to be the safest guide in this matter, although I feel no great confidence. . . . I rather incline to the belief of your continental friends that we are in a rapid course of *Americanisation.*

Is this to be our euthanasia ?

This is the latest letter from Lord Aberdeen which I have found in Lord Clarendon's correspondence : perhaps it was the last, for he died on 13th December 1860, whereby Clarendon lost one of his kindest and best friends.

Lady Theresa Lewis to Lord Clarendon.

HARPTON, 24*th November* 1858.— . . . I want very much to hear a little more about your Compiègne visit. . . . I am glad it was not one of the riotous parties when ladies defend fortresses and mounds, and gentlemen pull them by the feet to make them lay down their arms, for your young companion P. would probably have joined in that fun too. . . . I sincerely hope that your visit may have been of some *real* use in a public point of view, and I am glad the Emperor should have seemed aware of the sacrifice you and Lord Palmerston made in accepting his invitation at the present moment. If he takes in the *Saturday Review* and other papers he may be still better able to appreciate the amount of self-sacrifice by English statesmen of the late'government in appearing to sanction his proceedings by accepting his hospitality at this particular moment. I have no doubt that, if the present government were turned out, it would be much easier for you and Lord P. to deal with him for having gone to Compiègne ; but, so far as Lord P. is concerned, I should think he had placed another very large nail in the coffin of his premiership. *His* services are not valued by his party so highly as to make them anxious to overlook any very unpopular acts. But what I care about to my heart's core, and *far* more than you do and quite as much as Katty *can* do, is that this visit should not be looked upon by the Liberal party in an injurious light so far as you are concerned. . . . It is with your own friends and with leading men of the Liberal party that it is important you should not let unjust or exaggerated views exist of the motives or objects of your visit.

It is for this reason I was anxious you should ask Lord John [Russell] to The Grove and talk *openly* to him on the subject of the Compiègne visit. He is easily won by confidence being shown him, and it is *much* better he should not be hostile to you about this. It would not be the part of a sister who loves you as I do if I were to say—' Never mind—it is only the nasty newspapers, and they are not worth reading.' I should *like* to take that view, but I am confident that the impression is strong and general, and that it is no more safe to be disregarded than was the prejudice against Lord Clanricarde. The *Saturday Review* was right in one thing : public men cannot treat themselves or their deeds as unimportant or as if they were private individuals ; and it will not do to disregard a public feeling, whether just or unjust, once it has been created. The article in the *Saturday Review* was odious and *bitter*, so I suppose it was Mr. Harcourt's.[1] You know Mr. Delane and Mr. Cook of the *Saturday Review* and various other editors, and you might through a third person ascertain the amount of feeling that has been created, and deal with it accordingly ; but I should like to see it subside, if possible, before parliament begins. . . .

Lord Clarendon's reply to his sister has not been preserved ; but here is an account of some of the proceedings at Compiègne in a letter to the Duchess of Manchester,[2] with whom he maintained regular correspondence :

THE GROVE, 27*th November* 1858.— . . . I think I left off writing to you when I was sent for to go a-gunning at Compiègne, but the *chasse* was given up as it rained too hard, and the day was got through by such pastimes as a *conversation spirituelle* kept up by 30 people, football in the gallery and quadrilles on horseback in the *manège*, and the Emperor doing the lance exercise and other equestrian feats *à la Franconi* for the amusement of the Court. The next day was fine and we had a *chasse au tir* ; each *tireur* had 4 guns provided for him with 4 loaders in cocked hats ; the beaters were a squadron of lancers in boots and spurs, with a trumpeter who signified to them what they were

---

[1] Afterwards the Right Hon. Sir W. V. Harcourt.
[2] Wife of the seventh Duke, after whose demise in 1890 she married the eighth Duke of Devonshire.

to do.   It was a pretty gay scene, but I believe that most of
the creatures had been turned out the day before, or were let
out of traps as the Emperor approached.   In the evening we
had a charade, at which 'grand presence' of Mary Craven [1]
was much wanting.   She would willingly have yielded to the
Imperial entreaties to stay, but Mons[r]. le Mari would not hear
of it.   I doubt whether the entreaties were backed by the
Walewska,[2] who began to think it was high time she should be
off. . . .   Princesse Mathilde was in high good humour, chaffing
everybody, and Hertford [3] in particular.   She could make nothing
of Palmerston, who sat next her at dinner and was exclusively
occupied with the comestibles. . . .

Lady Theresa Lewis to Lord Clarendon.

HARPTON, 1*st December* 1858.—I think the account of No. 2's
début very satisfactory.[4]   It would have been a great pity if
she had been too shy to enjoy herself.   You must have felt
rather a fish out of water, for I see by Katty's list of the company that, with the exception of Lord Cowper, you were invited
to an unmixed ministerial party. . . .   I think Lord John
[Russell] had the impression, and so, I heard, had the Duke of
Bedford and Lord Palmerston, that Lord Derby would be afraid
of offending his own party by bringing forward a Reform Bill
that would be likely to satisfy the Liberal party.   I think that
may have been Lord Derby's intention ; but my belief was
and is that, tho' Lord Derby may intend this or that, he will
do by every other measure precisely what he did about the
Jews, about the India Bill, about Lord Canning, about everything.   Sooner than lose the race he is running, he will do what
his jockey Dizzy thinks will succeed, never mind *how*.   ' Go along
Teapot, never mind the Lid ! ' is the motto for their plan of
action.   Dizzy is to the Cabinet what Fagan was to the street-
boys—very instructive ; Bulwer is his Usher ; Lord Stanley
the promising pupil who earned the title of Artful Dodger by
his aptitude.   Lord Derby laughs loud and enjoys the fun like
Charlie Bates, and men like Walpole and Pakington innocently
fill little Oliver Twist's part of picking out the marks of the

---

[1] Wife of the second Earl of Craven and sister of Lady Clarendon.
[2] Madame de Walewski, the Emperor's reigning favourite at the time.
[3] Richard, fourth Marquess of Hertford (1800-70).
[4] Lady Alice Villiers, Lord Clarendon's second daughter, afterwards
Countess of Lathom.

pocket-handkerchiefs, not knowing how they were acquired, but feeling a wondering respect for the bigger boys who were so industrious and clever in bringing home so many new articles. It is a Fagan Cabinet and a Ministry of Dodgers. . . . I wish I thought there was any prospect of parliament being met with more decided union in the Liberal party : but Lord John believing that Lord Palmerston sanctions or orders articles to be written against him, and then Lord Palmerston supposing the *Daily News* pleases Lord John by attacking the Compiègne visit, is not the way to improve the personal or public position of either. After all, possibly neither really dictated any of the offensive articles. I believe Lord John to be much less inclined to that work than our late premier. I quite agree with you in thinking Wm. Harcourt odious in temper and in bitterness ; but I do not think him such a very great ruffian, as I have my doubts about those Compiègne articles being his, because I find that there is a much more direct interest than his in that paper to cry down the Emperor. The Orleans party have got possession of its French politics. . . . Still, I do regret that you went to Compiègne, as it is of much more consequence to England that honest men should not be misinterpreted than that they should run the risk of slightly offending the Emperor, who would make war upon us to-morrow if it suited his purpose. Of course, as you went on public grounds, I can only hope you were right ; but you can hardly expect those to whom you are a first-class object can like any step that attaches abuse to your name.

I thought the constitution was considered in a bad way yesterday, as they said medical aid was to be called in by making Sir Benjamin Brodie a peer. If it is so, I propose that Locock should be called to the same House by the title of 'Babbicome.' [1] Every one would feel the propriety of the title.

The press never exercised a more potent influence in politics, foreign and domestic, than it did in the second and third quarters of the nineteenth century, and party leaders were careful to convey to the public through chosen channels the views which they considered salutary on the questions of the day. That influence certainly has not since diminished, but the trajectory has been

---

[1] Sir Charles Locock was a famous accoucheur.

flattened, and the number of those who now turn for light and leading to the *Edinburgh* and *Quarterly Reviews* must be small indeed.   But in the 'fifties these great periodicals exercised a notable sway over educated opinion, and their editors kept in constant touch with the heads of the parties which they represented respectively.   Sir George C. Lewis had resigned the chair of the *Edinburgh Review* when he succeeded Gladstone as Chancellor of the Exchequer in 1855 ; but he resumed his connection with it as a contributor so soon as he was again out of office in 1858.   The Derby-Disraeli government being known to have in contemplation a measure of parliamentary reform, Clarendon deemed it essential that the views of the Liberal party on that ever-recurrent question should be adequately laid before the nation, and he appealed to Lewis to undertake the task.

Lord Clarendon to Sir G. C. Lewis.

THE GROVE, 14*th December* 1858.—Reeve has been here, and we had a good deal of talk about reform.   I told him your sound and solid reasons for thinking a measure expedient at this moment, and he is *very* anxious that you should undertake an article for the next number of the *Edinburgh*, as the review, in his opinion, would abdicate its functions as an organ of the Liberal party, and disappoint its friends if it was altogether silent upon the question which, a fortnight before the meeting of parliament, will be occupying all men's minds.   He says that no one has the same amount of knowledge—statistical and other—upon the subject as you, and that, without actually proposing a measure, you might do much to guide opinion as to what should be avoided as dangerous and what might be done with safety and advantage. . . . The Whigs are in a very ragged state, but I believe you might rig them out in new uniforms and make them look decent for parliament by an article which should well pepper the Tories, and show how accurately the Whigs in 1832 estimated the requirements of the country and the temper and character of the people, and that they can point to the long list of beneficial measures which have been since carried, while the Tories can only point to their opposition to these measures and to their falsified predictions of anarchy

and spoliation 28 years ago.[1]   The Whigs must therefore be
surer guides in their own paths than the Tories whom nobody
trusts, or the Radicals whom everybody fears.   Moreover,
Gladstone's impudent, insolent articles in the *Quarterly* ought
to be *relevés*, and the Whigs, having a case so good and national,
ought not to let judgment go against them by default.   The
opportunity for spice and pepper is excellent, and should not be
lost. . . . Charles is in a state of fiery indignation at Lowe's
speech, which I thought showed great ability and moral courage.
Charles says that any blockhead can speak the truth, but that
nobody wanted it and Lowe will never be forgiven by the party.

20th.—I thought that Lord John would not like an article
in the *Edinburgh* ; but I did not expect such petulant opposition
to it, and his deference to that tricky fellow Graham is absurd
and cannot be sincere.   Palmerston, too, will probably deprecate
an article as embarrassing to himself.   It is difficult to know
how to steer among a parcel of men who are guided only by
personal motives.   Their rivalries set the Reform question in
motion, and upon them the government will be safely floated
over the question and the session. . . . It would be unwise to
begin the session with Lord J. in a passion . . . but as Reeve
will probably write the article himself, you might point out to
him the things he should avoid. . . .

I shall not be the least surprised if a consul-generalship is
offered to Cobden ; and, if he accepts it, I will engage that he
will be the worst in the service !

Clarendon's next letter to Lewis shows how wide still lay
the chasm between the Whigs and their Radical auxiliaries.
Bright had rudely jarred the equanimity of moderate
Liberals by delivering at Birmingham on 27th October a
violent denunciation of the House of Lords, resuming the
attack at Manchester on 10th December.

19th December.— . . . I did not read Bright's speech at
Manchester with great attention, but I thought it able and

---

[1] Lord Clarendon's enthusiasm for his party here leads him into less
than his customary fairness to political opponents.   By the Factories
Act of 1844 the conditions of juvenile labour were greatly improved, notwithstanding vehement opposition from Whigs and Radicals.   Lord
Brougham tried to bring ridicule upon it by asking why washerwomen
and wet nurses were not to receive protection under the bill, and John
Bright, newly elected for Durham, denounced it as ' miserable legislation
on principles false and mischievous.'   After all, the repeal of the Corn Laws
was also the work of a Conservative government.

apologetic. I marked the part about the House of Lords as reaffirming more emphatically what he had said sarcastically, and almost playfully, at Birmingham. I consider the Monarchy, the House of Lords and the Established Church, as bound up together, and the whole as the most perfect of the various imperfections called governments ; so that I differ root and branch from Bright. So differing, I shall look with great distrust on the advice he gives as to the means of attaining an end which is not the end I wish to reach. His may be the best and quickest route to America ; but I don't wish to go to America. I am sorry the Whigs cannot come to some agreement, but Palmerston and Graham have willed it so. . . .

Lord Howden to Lord Clarendon.

PARIS, 8*th December* 1858.— . . . You tell me that Bright has been of great use to the government, which I fully believe. He has put the old Liberal party into a very difficult, not to say damnable, position. They must chalk out something for themselves as a visible sign of existence, and it is not easy to say what. If they don't, they will have the fate of the Liberal party in Spain, which has been squeezed into nothing between two wedges, or they will be obliged to live by having continually other children's pap forced down their throats. I don't think we were ever in so bad a way, for such has been the immorality and the unnatural commerce going on lately that we shall still appear Radicals to the Conservative country gentlemen, and regular old Spoonies to such a fast association as Stanley, Bright and Co.

Lord Palmerston to Lord Clarendon.

94 PICCADILLY, 27*th November* 1858.— . . . Many thanks for your very interesting letter. I am glad to hear that Derby adopts and approves all our foreign policy, especially considering that when he told his son to decline the offer which I made him, the refusal to join us was placed specifically upon an intire disapproval of our whole system of foreign policy.

I infer from what you say of Derby's language about Reform that their bill will be a moderate one, though as Dizzy will have a hand in it, it is pretty sure to have some absurd provisions.

The prosecution of Montalembert has undoubtedly been a great mistake, and one is revolted at the idea of his being im-

prisoned for six months for having written with so much eloquence and so much truth.[1]   But sympathy with him in this
country will be somewhat alloyed by dislike of his ultra-Catholic
opinions ; and in France the bulk of the nation will not find so
much fault with a punishment which they will think well deserved by his praises of England. . . .

BROADLANDS, 19*th December.*— . . . As to the Emperor of
the French, it is quite true, as you say, that at the time of his
great popularity he was doing things, in the way of sending
people off to Cayenne, much more tyrannical than anything he
is doing now : but the gentlemen of the press were not then so
hard pressed as they are now in France, and they now cry out
as lustily as a pig carried to market. . . .

As to Reform, I am quite sure that we ought to lie quite still.
Any attempt to come to an understanding with John Russell,
or anybody else, would answer no good purpose.   With Johnny
we (or at least I) should be sure to differ, and our difference
might be upon points which the government bill and the course
of discussion might perhaps not bring absolutely before parliament for decision.   By far the best way is to wait and see what
the government bill may be, and then to deal with it according
to its merits.   There are many reasons which make it desirable
that some Reform bill should be passed this next session, and I
should not be disposed to quarrel with it for its shortcomings
unless they were great and manifest.   John Russell, I hear, wants
to add a million to the existing voters.   This would be very much
to swamp property and intelligence. . . . He at length deems
Bright a dangerous man.   I suppose this means that he thinks
him a dangerous ally, because he [Bright] is losing his hold
upon the country by unmasking his revolutionary yearnings.
I wish I could believe that Johnny is enough alive to the
dangerous tendency of the measures with which Bright says
he would be content as a first step towards his further objects.
But Johnny wants to add another million to the present number
of electors on the plea of interesting so many more men in the
constitution of the country.   Would not the introduction of
such a mass of ignorance and poverty tend to alter that constitution, not for the better but for the worse ?

[1] Montalembert was prosecuted for publishing a pamphlet in which he
extolled the freedom of debate in the British parliament and contrasted
it with the restraint imposed upon members of the French chambers.   He
was sentenced to six months' imprisonment, but received a free pardon
from the Emperor.

Clarendon's sixtieth birthday did not pass without the customary exchange of greeting between him and his sister.

Lady Theresa Lewis to Lord Clarendon.

THE PALACE, HEREFORD, 12*th January* 1859.—MY DEAREST GEORGE,—This is the day which brought the great blessing of your birth to your family, your friends, and, I must say, to your country, and you must have a word from your *very* affectionate sister to tell you how she loves and admires and values you. Years seem to have the effect of binding us the more closely to each other as other ties are snapped. I can safely say, without being deficient in affection for husband and children, that they never diminish those feelings between sister and brother which stand alone and make a chapter apart from all other beings. . . . I am here with the two girls for a Hereford ball—George shirking at home, supposed to be doing accounts with his steward (whom he will probably not see !) . . . There is to be a very radical meeting here to-morrow, when the city members are to be told that Bright is the right man, and that nothing can go down without the ballot. They are very radical in this town. . . . I hear Scholefield would not attend any of Bright's meetings and will have nothing to do with his bill.[1]

Lord Clarendon to Lady Theresa.

THE GROVE, 13*th January* 1859.—It 's worth completing another year in one's downward course to get such a very dear letter as I had to-day from you. A birthday is an occasion for reviewing and renewing one's feelings towards those one loves as I do you, and it is therefore very pleasant, though I could wish that it took 24 months to make one a year older, as I can't bear the express train by which time seems now to be going. Go it fast or slow, however, I feel as you do that it binds us more closely together, and that love between brother and sister can be ardent and constantly increasing, and run in parallel lines with love for husband, wife and children, without the least fear of their coming in conflict with each other. . . .

Lord John seems to be in a state of feverish excitement, scarcely knowing *à quel saint se vouer*. He says that Derby can't be trusted

[1] William Scholefield, M.P., was John Bright's colleague in the representation of Birmingham.

with a Reform bill, that Malmesbury is unfit for the oncoming European crisis, and that the H. of Commons will not bear any longer being led by such a swindler as Dizzy—*ergo*, the government must go out—*ergo*, he must come in ; but between Johnny's lip and the cup which he proposes to drink for his country's good, many a thing may happen.   In the meanwhile, I shall not be surprised if he comes out with a pastoral letter to the Pope, and that he and Palmerston should fraternise in Italy, reserving to themselves the right to cut each other's throats at home.   If the result of the session is not to divide the Liberal house still more against itself and to make it fall lower than it has already done, I shall be agreeably surprised.

Heaven help the poor Madrasians with that ravening wolf Trevelyan put over them to establish a new order of things.[1] His appointment is a job, 1st, to get rid of him (which is a natural desire), and next, to provide for that pauper Orangeman Hamilton[2] and the recruited prig Northcote,[3] who, however, has one of the clearest heads, and is the best man of business I ever had to do with.   He was at the Board of Trade when I was there.

[1] Sir Charles E. Trevelyan of Wallington (1807-86), assistant Secretary to the Treasury 1840-59, appointed Governor of Madras 1859, created a baronet 1874.

[2] George Alexander Hamilton (1802-71), Financial Secretary to the Treasury, appointed Permanent Under-Secretary in 1859 *vice* Sir C. Trevelyan made Governor of Madras.

[3] Sir Stafford Northcote (1818-87), created Earl of Iddesleigh 1886.

CHAPTER XVIII

OUT OF OFFICE

Now, my co-mates, and brothers in exile,
Hath not old custom made this life more sweet
Than that of painted pomp? Are not these woods
More free from peril than the envious court?'
As You Like It, ii. 1.

JOHN BRIGHT, having overcome the malady which had laid
him aside from political war for two years and more, undertook a campaign in the north of England and in Scotland
during the closing months of 1858, travelling from platform
to platform in vain endeavour to rouse the masses to agitate
for parliamentary reform. Demagogues (nor is it any
slander upon the John Bright of those early days to classify
him as a demagogue) are wont to level their fiercest in-
vectives against landowners, land being at once the most
visible and vulnerable form of property ; accordingly Bright
made landowners in general and the House of Lords in
particular his chief objective. When he carried his arms
into a wider field it was but to declare that the foreign policy
of Great Britain was ' neither more nor less than a gigantic
system of outdoor relief for the aristocracy.' [1]

Rhetoric of this kind alarmed the Whigs as much as it
inflamed the Tories. The Duke of Argyll having spoken
at Dundee in refutation of Bright's statements about landowners, Clarendon wrote to him on 27th November.

I read with great pleasure and admiration your speech the
other day in answer to Bright, who, it must be admitted, has
done service by showing how little steam is to be got up for
Reform. It may be said of him, as Lord Byron once said of
his mother-in-law, Lady Noel, ' She has been dangerously ill—
she is now dangerously well again ! '

---

[1] Speech to his constituents at Birmingham, 29th October 1858.

Bright's northern tour proved a signal failure. Those who had the vote showed no feverish anxiety to have their influence watered down by the admission of half a million new electors ; those who were still unenfranchised could not be persuaded to express dissatisfaction with things as they were. They listened willingly enough to a great master of speech—an oration by John Bright was an intellectual treat for northern understanding—but the people made no response to the summons for a crusade. Wise and disinterested rulers would have interpreted such apathy as a sure symptom of contentment, and have left matters alone ; but be rulers as wise as they may, party leaders cannot afford to be disinterested. Lord Derby and Lord John Russell, indeed, were conscientiously anxious to settle the franchise on a broader basis ; they were equally anxious to take the settlement out of the hands of the Radical party ; but it must be confessed that there is little, if any, evidence in the private correspondence of other leading men of either party that they were guided by any higher motive than party advantage. This may not be so discreditable as it seems in cold blood ; for when men are convinced that the destiny of their country is safest under the guidance of their own party, they are apt to regard country and party as convertible terms.

The Derby-Disraeli Reform Bill was introduced on 28th February. Next day, J. W. Henley, President of the Board of Trade, and Spencer Walpole, Home Secretary, resigned office ; a month later, the government were beaten on an amendment moved by Lord John Russell, who, in Palmerston's absence, was leading the Opposition—a truly factious amendment, craftily drawn to secure the support of those who considered the bill went too far in lowering the county franchise to £10 as well as of those who complained that it did not also lower the borough qualification. Bright protested in the name of democracy against reducing the county franchise, because it would increase the influence of landowners ; Palmerston, who wanted no reform, gave his 'cordial support' to Russell's amendment, because he objected to the proposal to transfer to the borough constituencies the votes of county freeholders residing in boroughs ; so Bright and Palmerston voted in the same lobby from opposite motives. Lord Derby obtained the Queen's consent to a dissolution, and, although the Conservatives scored a net gain of some thirty seats in the general election, that only brought up the strength of the party in the House of Commons to within fifty of the Liberal-Radical-Peelite Opposition.

Hon. Emily Eden to Lord Clarendon.

EDEN LODGE [*Easter* 1859].— . . . I have a great mind to send you back your own letter ; it was so exceedingly amusing. I am sure you would like to read it. Moreover, it is the latest news I have had of anything beyond my own gates. I presume London is entirely empty, what with Easter and what with elections ; for the one or two visitors I have had were relations or elderly ladies come to town for a day's shopping, and utterly incompetent to give me an atom of news for you. I doubt if they were aware that there was a coolness between France and Austria. Don't things look rather worse than ever to-day ? [1] and is not our Louis Napoleon a greater villain than ever ? hatching this offensive—I may say *very* offensive—and defensive treaty with Russia under pretence of arranging a congress. Moreover, I feel the force of suction into this vortex on our blessed selves. I suppose if Austria goes to the front door to defend it from French burglars, that Russian thieves will attack the back door, and then that we shall be obliged to appear as police and get frightfully injured with crowbars. The police always get the worst of it in a robbery. I am indulging in fond hopes that, if the French Emperor goes on a distant fighting expedition, France may request him not to come back again. Is not that possible ?

I always forgot to tell you what you must have heard till you are tired—of the immense sensation your speech made last week. I heard of nothing else, both in talk and writing. Do keep constantly speaking, and put all those things straight which Lord Derby states crooked. . . .

Thursday.— . . . Things look blacker than ever this morning ;

---

[1] War was declared at the end of April 1859, and was concluded by the battles of Magenta (4th June) and Solferino (24th June).

indeed L. N., the leading villain of the plot, seems to me to have invented a new patent black, quite unmatchable, in which he has dyed himself. I feel like the *Times*—intensely curious to know the date of that treaty. In fact I should like to read L. N.'s private letters for the last year or two, just to know how much fun he has had with us, his poor dupes. And then Lord Derby goes to the hustings armed with Lord Malmesbury's clear-sightedness, diplomacy and dignity. Funny!

Talking of letters—Lena made me look out for her some of the old letters I wrote in 1825. Interspersed with other topics, I have preserved a few very good jokes of yours; but you will be sorry to hear that what particularly struck me in you was your singular wickedness. I am always apologising to poor Mrs. Colville for it, evidently thinking it very amusing all the time. ' *Were* you so very wicked, Lord Clarendon?'

That question is a parody. A giantess at a fair died accidentally, and the showman in desperation hired the first tolerably tall woman he could find in the village to take her place. The neighbours gave their shillings in ignorance, and when they got in all they said was, 'Dear me! only Mrs. Tucker. But *are* you so very tall, Mrs. Tucker?' 'No,' said she, 'not particularly, but the real giantess is dead.' I hope you will say the same. . . . Was Strawberry pleasant? and how is Frank W. herself [1]—political, fashionable, theatrical or what?

Are you so very wicked, Lord Clarendon?

Lord Clarendon to Lady Clarendon.

GROSVENOR CRESCENT, 25*th May* 1859.— . . . I met Craven [2] at the door of the Travellers and walked with him as far as Aberdeen's, with whom I staid till 7.30. He is always most friendly and agreeable. The war has taken complete possession of his mind and he can think of nothing else. He expects the move against the government to be successful, but does not, like other rational beings, see how any government formed by Palmerston can be carried on. He says, however, that the Queen will certainly send for P. in preference to Lord John. He expects to be consulted by the Queen when the time comes for her to act, and he asked me whether it was quite impossible

[1] Frances, Lady Waldegrave, died in 1879.
[2] William, second Earl of Craven, whose wife was Lady Clarendon's younger sister.

that I should attempt the pleasant task. You may suppose
what my answer was! He said Gladstone came to him every
day and that he certainly was prepared to join Palmerston. I
see by the newspapers that Mrs. Gladstone has a party to-night,
and I should have liked to go there and have some talk with
him—or *her* (as she appears to be his political agent); but I
can't find any invitation here, and Jacob knows of none, so of
course I cannot. . . . I had my bath, dined in my dressing-
gown on a tray in the sitting-room and am now setting in for a
good read. Next to being with my own dear belongings, I call
that perfect comfort, and a slight improvement upon dining
and supping with Princesses.

Lord Derby's ministry fell on the third night of the new
session before an amendment to the Address, moved by
Lord Hartington, expressing want of confidence in the
advisers of the Crown. What chiefly contributed to the
defeat was the suspicion that the Conservative ministry
was secretly in sympathy with Austria in defending her
possessions in Lombardy against the combined attack of
France and Sardinia. Palmerston was warm in good
wishes for Italian unity, and although at a meeting of the
various sections of the Opposition on 6th June, when the
hostile amendment had been agreed upon, a strong opinion
was expressed in favour of absolute neutrality in the war
then in progress, the great weight of national feeling was
in sympathy with Cavour's policy. The following letter to
Lord Clarendon, written during the general election, explains
Palmerston's innermost feelings upon the Italian question.
The original is in his clear, bold hand throughout, without
a single erasure, witnessing the unabated vigour of this
veteran of seventy-five.

94 PICCADILLY, 24*th April* 1859.—I have this morning only
received your letter of the 21st with an account of your visit to
Windsor. I think you are unjust towards the Emperor of the
French. Cowley's mission to Vienna was a most unbusiness-
like proceeding. Our government ought, before it took so public
a step as to send to Vienna our ambassador at Paris, to have
obtained from Napoleon some formal and official acceptance of
our mediative character. A mission without official instructions

from hence and with no official character could lead to no definite result; neither did it obtain from Austria anything positive. And the proof of its vagueness is in the fact which you state, namely, that Cowley on his return to Paris had no distinct communication to make to the Emperor on the part of the English government, and that he was annoyed to find that the Emperor did not manifest the slightest interest about his mission, or even any curiosity to know what he had done. The Emperor, no doubt, knew from Bourqueney all that Cowley could have told him, and that was nothing but vague and general assurances.

In the meantime the Emperor had taken a businesslike step which nothing that had passed with our government precluded him from doing. He had asked the Emperor of Russia to propose a congress on Italian affairs, and that was no new idea of Napoleon's, for I have heard him suggest it in almost every conversation I have had with him on European affairs at any time for several years past. This step did not, in fact, set aside our mediation, because our mediation had never been distinctly offered or accepted; nor did it set aside any acquiescence of Austria, if such acquiescence was considered as having been given to the views of Napoleon; it only provided a meeting at which those views might be formally stated and that acquiescence might be formally expressed. But, at all events, the suggestion of a congress proceeding, as it now appears to have done, from Napoleon, seems to me a proof that the French Emperor was not so bent upon war as he is generally supposed to have been.

My belief is that, for many years past, Napoleon has had a fixed desire to improve the internal condition of Italy by freeing as much of that country as possible from the crushing weight of Austrian domination, and that he has at various times thought of various ways of attaining his object; but that his object has been one and the same; and I must say that the end he has had in view is much to be wished for.

But now the scene has changed. Everybody has been openmouthed about the aggressive attitude of France and Sardinia, about to pounce upon that innocent lamb Austria. Now it turns out that Austria is the aggressor, and that it is Austria that is fully prepared, while Sardinia and France are not equally ready for the conflict. I have heard some details connected with these affairs which I believe to be correct.

It is said that Apponyi had urged Derby to state in parliament

that if France and Sardinia attacked Austria, England would
side actively with Austria ; and Derby was assured that such
a distinct declaration would ensure peace.   Derby could not
go so far, because parliament and the country would not
have borne him out ; but he promised that he and Disraeli
would hold the language which they actually did hold on
Monday last.   Their statements were put off from day to
day in expectation of a messenger Apponyi was waiting
for from Vienna, who was to bring him some more definite
announcement of the intentions of Austria.   Apponyi said
that this man would certainly arrive on Friday morning, so
that the government might make their statement on that
day ; but he was stopped at Calais by telegram from Vienna
in order that he might not arrive until after the ministerial
statements announced for Friday.   He came early on Saturday
morning or in the course of Saturday, and he brought to Apponyi
information of the summons intended to be sent off on Monday
to the Sardinian government.   But Apponyi having obtained
from Derby the promise to make the sort of threatening declaration against France which was made on Monday, withheld from
Derby the knowledge of the step intended to be taken at Turin,
and left him to thunder out against France the denunciations
which Austria was at the very moment about to deserve for
herself.

The excuse made for the Austrian government is that interrupted letters and papers were put into the hands of the Emperor
of Austria, proving that France and Sardinia intended to become
the aggressors in the beginning of May, and that the Emperor
of Austria therefore thought it best to strike the first blow.
This may be so, but on the other hand Massimo Azeglio says that
Napoleon told him a few days ago, as he passed through Paris,
that he had not more than 30,000 men ready to enter Piedmont
immediately to co-operate with the Sardinian troops.   However, it may be said that Napoleon only found out lately how
much less prepared he is than he imagined himself to be, and
Malakoff says that his Emperor is badly cheated and imposed
upon in all that regards his army.

We dined yesterday at Shaftesbury's and met the two Azeglios,
who said that they had at 11 o'clock in the morning received a
telegram from Turin making no mention of the Austrian summons
and that they had in answer sent a message to ask whether it
had or had not been received.   At about ten o'clock they received

the reply announcing that the summons had been received that afternoon, so that the three days' grace will extend to next Tuesday night.   It is evident from this that the Austrian government have paid no attention to the remonstrance which our government sent them on Friday by telegram upon receiving Augustus Loftus's announcement of the intended summons, because there is telegraphic communication from Vienna to Milan, and there would have been time to stop the delivery of the summons if the Austrian government had been disposed to do so, for the message probably left Milan yesterday morning or Friday night.

Still, it is possible that during the three days of grace, the Austrian government may be induced to withdraw or modify its demand, although one must own that it would be very difficult to retract so public and decided a step, the more so because the Austrian government knew when it sent the summons, that Sardinia had accepted the general principles of a disarmament, and the summons seems now to point specially to the disbandment of the Italian volunteers from other parts of Italy—a demand which Sardinia can scarcely comply with.   The Sardinian parliament had yesterday conferred dictatorial powers on the King during the crisis.   If war comes on, the French troops will in three days have made some way towards a junction with the Piedmontese, and though the Austrians may possibly get to Turin, they will soon be driven out again, and such a war once begun, Napoleon cannot for his own honor and that of France stop till he has sent the Austrians back into Germany.

We have, therefore, a hedge against Fate.   If this squall blows over, we shall have peace, and that will be one good thing : if war ensues, we shall have Italy freed from the Austrians, and that would be another good thing.   In any case we must stand aloof and not engage in the war.   But there will, no doubt, be some outbreak or other in some part or other of Italy.   Men's minds there are too much excited to remain quiet, and even if this immediate crisis is got over, some other will arise unless remedial measures are promptly taken by the Italian [?Austrian] government, and that is not a very likely event.

I am off to-morrow to Tiverton.   Two opponents have shown themselves there, one after the other ; but both have retired after trying the ground, and I do not expect a contest.   Our calculators reckon that the government may gain 10 or 12 seats, but that will not give them the majority, to obtain which for them they made the Queen offer up her fervent prayers to Heaven.

Lord Derby accepted defeat and resigned, which brought the Queen into the dilemma of choice between Palmerston and John Russell. Unaware that these two lords had agreed, before the meeting on 6th June, to act together in the event of either of them being called upon to form a government,[1] and dreading to offend either of them, the Queen sought a way out of her difficulty by sending for Lord Granville. Palmerston loyally agreed to serve under Granville, who was thirty years his junior ; but Lord John declined to join the government except as Prime Minister or, at least, leader of the House of Commons. As Palmerston could not reasonably be asked to resign the leadership of the Commons, except to go to the House of Lords, which he declined to do, Lord Granville gave up the attempt to form a Cabinet, and the Queen laid her commands upon Lord Palmerston. Lord John joined him, but only on condition that he should have the Foreign Office ; and Lord Clarendon, feeling a strong disinclination for any other department, begged to be allowed to stand out.

From Lady Clarendon's Journal.

13*th June* 1859.—Clarendon received a note this morning from Lord Palmerston to say that Lord John had consented to join him, but claimed the Foreign Office. He asked Clarendon to come to a meeting at his house at 12 o'clock. The meeting consisted of Lord Palmerston, Clarendon, Sir G. C. Lewis, Sir George Grey and Sir Charles Wood.

It seems that Lord Palmerston, tho' offering Lord John Russell the choice of offices, told him that the Queen and he himself wished Clarendon to be at the Foreign Office, owing to his long experience, etc., but Lord John said he must have *that*. When Lord Palmerston asked him whether he claimed it *as a right*, he answered that he *did*.

Lord P. and the others most earnestly and repeatedly urged

[1] See Lord Palmerston's letter to the Queen (Martin's *Life of the Prince Consort*, iv. 453).

Clarendon to take some other office, Ld. P. strongly pressing the Colonial Office upon him, and Lord Granville in the most disinterested way urging him to take the Presidency of the Council and leadership of the House of Lords ; but Clarendon was firm. He said that, had he been required for the Foreign Office, where his experience might really have made him useful, he would have made the personal sacrifice in spite of his extreme reluctance to take office ; but that he thought the offer to Lord John was exactly what ought to have been made. His own dislike to office, he said, was well known, and he did not feel that he was called upon to take any other office where he was not necessary, and where new men might be placed with advantage to the government.

In the afternoon the Queen wrote to Clarendon to come to her. Instead of a few minutes, she kept him nearly two hours. Her conversation—her sorrow that she was not to have Clarendon's services and her gentle, but earnest, urging of him to take some office, were very touching ; but he showed her that it would not be essential to her service and unnecessarily painful to himself.

The Queen expressed her opinion that the present arrangement could not last. 'If I could but hope that, if it fails, I might count upon your taking the Foreign Office, Lord Clarendon ? ' Of course George had only to assure Her Majesty that his services would always be at her command when, using his own discretion, he thought he really could be of use to her.

14th.—Gladstone has insisted upon having the Chancellorship of the Exchequer ! Why he who voted in the last division with the Derby ministry should not only be asked to join this one, but be allowed *to choose his office*, I cannot conceive, or rather—I *can* conceive, because I know that it is for his power of speaking. They want his tongue to help and they dread it in opposition. And so, tho' G. Lewis had accepted the office, . . . he has been requested to make way for Gladstone, which accordingly he has done and accepts the Home Office instead.

Lord Palmerston to Lord Clarendon.

94 PICCADILLY, 13*th June* 1859.—MY DEAR CLARENDON,—I saw John Russell yesterday evening. He joins our government, but I am sorry to say claims the Foreign Office. I wish much that this had been otherwise. Pray come here a little before 12.—Yrs. sincerely,   PALMERSTON.

Same day, later.—I am exceedingly sorry for the determination which, by the few words you said as we were going upstairs and by a letter I have had from the Queen, you appear to have taken. Your determination will inflict a great loss on the government—both in council and in parliament; but under these circumstances, as I wish at our meeting to-morrow to persuade John Russell into a sounder view as to the chancellorship, he might object to the opinion of a person who was not going to be a member of the government. When I asked you to come and help us, it was under the impression you were still open to conviction.

Lord Clarendon to Henry Reeve.

GROSVENOR CRESCENT, 13*th June* 1859.— . . . You have always taken such a kind and friendly concern in my affairs that I think you will like to know how I stand. Palmerston, by the Queen's desire, insisted on my returning to the F.O., and I felt that, though most unwilling to accept the offer, I had no sufficient plea for declining it. But when Palmerston very properly placed any office at the disposal of Lord John, he claimed the F.O. as his right, which did not surprise me, as he has unbounded confidence in his diplomatic talents and happens to know that he is the only man who can pull us through the crisis successfully. I gladly recognised his right and the superiority of his claims to my own. I was most warmly pressed by Palmerston and my former colleagues to take any other office; but for that I am no necessity, and I was sure I should best consult the public taste by making way for some one who had not been in Palmerston's former government.

The Queen sent for me, and very kindly tried to shake my determination, but that had not been lightly taken, and she did not succeed. So I am still free, and great is my happiness thereat.

Having failed to secure Clarendon as a colleague Palmerston invited Charles Villiers to join him, and met with better success.

94 PICCADILLY, 4*th July*.— . . . I am very glad that your brother Charles has accepted the Poor Law Board with a seat in the Cabinet; and, after the precedent set us by Derby of father and son in the same Cabinet, there can no longer be any

objection to having two brothers at that mystical table in
Downing Street. . . .

Lord Clarendon held strong views on the Italian question,
which subsequent events have proved to be mistaken.
He was sceptical about the possibility of a united kingdom
of Italy, differing *toto cœlo* from Palmerston on that matter.
Perhaps his experience in Madrid had shaken his faith in
the capacity of the Latin race for constitutional monarchy.
Nevertheless, throughout the anxious summer and autumn
of 1859, when Palmerston himself was losing faith in Louis
Napoleon's sincerity, and when the British volunteers were
being organised to repel the invasion which seemed to be
the object of the extraordinary military preparations in
France, Palmerston constantly took counsel with Clarendon
upon the European situation and prospects. Clarendon
embodied in a memorandum his objections to Palmerston's
project of setting the King of Sardinia on the throne of
United Italy, which he thought would never receive support
from the Emperor Napoleon. He suggested Ferdinand,
ex-King of Portugal, as a suitable ruler for any Italian
kingdom that might take shape out of the chaos prevailing.

Being thus at variance with his old chief on the question
which dominated all others in European politics of the time,
Clarendon congratulated himself more than ever on his
escape from office. He continued to correspond confidentially with his old friend Lord Cowley, ambassador at
the Tuileries, who took the same view as himself about
Italian affairs. This correspondence was no doubt irregular,
and having come to the knowledge of Lord John Russell,
a circular was sent out from the Foreign Office to the whole
British *corps diplomatique*, directing them to refrain from
writing to anybody upon public affairs, and to confine their
communications to the Foreign Office. Cowley, being in
England at the time, made inquiries of his friends in the
department, the result of which convinced him that the
circular was *à son adresse*, and in consequence discontinued,
for a time, his confidential letters to Clarendon.

Clarendon's reluctance to resume office, his unconcealed

The Honble Charles Villiers. M.P.

C. P. Villiers

LONDON: EDWARD ARNOLD.

delight at escaping from it, had their source in the charm of his family circle. Two of his daughters had already come out, and Lady Clarendon's journal reveals how their father was perpetually making plans for them and with them, organising private theatricals, taking them on expeditions, and so forth. But it was on behalf of a niece that his attention was most earnestly claimed in the summer of 1859, namely, Thérèse Lister, elder daughter of his beloved sister Lady Theresa Lewis. Young Mr. William George Granville Harcourt, a barrister with prospects, perhaps, but little practice as yet, had fallen deeply in love with this young lady. He was of ancient lineage, tracing descent from the royal house of Saxony in the ninth century—no objection, therefore, on that score, nor, perhaps, on that of means, for he had but to apply wisely the ability that God had given him to ensure his independence. But that ability had been applied hitherto in a manner that had made him many enemies.

In 1855 Mr. Beresford Hope, with J. D. Cook as partner, started the *Saturday Review*, a journal professing independent politics and soon commanding attention by the fearless pungency of its articles. It became known that Harcourt was the writer of certain of these articles, which went far to justify the title of *Saturday Reviler* bestowed on it by those who felt their withers wrung. Lord Clarendon having made no secret of his disgust at these articles and his dislike for the writer, Lady Theresa requested Harcourt to discontinue his visits to Kent House. But things had gone too far between the young people : Lady Theresa might reasonably have wished for her daughter a better match, in a worldly sense, than a barrister, as yet briefless ; but when she found that her girl had given away her heart, all her objections crumbled away.

Lady Theresa Lewis to Lord Clarendon.

KENT HOUSE, *5th August* 1859.— . . . Lady Waldegrave was wrong. Mr. Harcourt asked leave, as I got out of the train, to call at Kent House, from which he knew himself to be excluded at our music on account of . . . the articles in the *Saturday Review*. He came, as he said, to discuss the great Kent House subject and to know if he must always be excluded. . . . Well, we had it out about his detestable articles. I told him quite plainly all I had thought and do think of that style of anonymous attack by one gentleman upon another. He tried to defend the system upon the usual newspaper principles ; but alleged as his best defence that he had given it up and never meant to resume it. Then came his frank avowal of attachment to Thérèse, which he said he would not feel at liberty to make to her without first knowing whether your feelings towards him would be a bar to my consent, as he had no right to introduce discord where there was such entire unity ; and that if he could not hope to obtain your good-will, which he had left in Lady Waldegrave's hands to try and obtain, he could not expect that I should allow him to speak to Thérèse.

He also thought it right that we should know his means before he ventured to ask her. . . . He said he had taken up parliamentary business, which is the most profitable and most certain, . . . but I did not enter into the ways and means. . . . I could give him no answer till George comes back from this odious voyage. Thérèse is head over ears in love with him. . . . She cannot bear the idea of the object of her affection being disliked by any of her family ; she feels sorry to give up her favorite abstract hopes of living a great deal in the country and having a country place ; the uprooting from home she cannot contemplate without being almost ready to burst out : but the one thing she sticks to is that she could *not* give him up. . . . Nobody could have behaved more honorably than he has done in this matter, and I am free to confess that this week's visit has immensely changed my opinion of his character and temper. He is very clever, and Alice [1] says, I think with some truth, that it will be very difficult for Thérèse to attach herself to an inferior man after the devotion and tenderness of so clever an admirer as William Harcourt. . . . Alice has caught the infection and is very nearly in love too ! . . . I said everything that was disagreeable and severe to him yesterday for three hours, and he said at the end that he thought the way he had borne it must at least prove to me that his temper was that of an angel. . . .

KENT HOUSE, 15*th August*.—Many thanks for your letter.

[1] Lady Theresa's second daughter, who married Sir Algernon Borthwick (afterwards Lord Glenesk) in 1870.

It was looked for with great anxiety, tho' it did not contain any other information on *the* subject than that there was no more to give.

To my great relief, I got my dear husband home yesterday afternoon.   He is kindness itself to Thérèse [1] upon the subject. He rather likes Mr. Harcourt, and likes, I think, the idea of her marrying a man who has plenty of brains ; but, whilst we were talking over the matter, I got a long letter from Mr. H. himself which has put our young lady in a great fluster.   He seems to have brooded over our conversation and fancied it was preparatory to rejecting him.   He thinks he is again to encounter the trial of an adverse family, and dreads, like a burnt child, that he shall meet with the same fate a second time, and that he would spare me the pain of telling him so : that he had felt so discouraged by his conversation with me that, unless he had misunderstood my meaning, he could only hope that when he had overcome his passion, he might at least be admitted to her and my friendship.

Perhaps I was more discouraging than I intended ; but in truth I felt quite bewildered as to what course to take.   I have all the year looked with dread upon the prospect of his winning, and not returning, her affection.   Your very strong expressions against him—my own only very lately removed impression . . . the fear of his temper and the doubt how her papa or her brother or my brothers would view the affair (for they had not changed their opinion of him, as I have done, on many material points) made me afraid of encouraging his hopes.   On the other hand, when we discussed personalities (which was before he had revealed his love for Thérèse) I spoke out *quite* plainly as to my feelings with respect to the propriety of political attacks peppered with personal injustice.   He is no doubt a very sensitive man ; but I think that the dread of being refused, after all he suffered before, has operated rather strongly upon him.

I wrote him a kind letter, such as George and Thérèse approved, telling him what time he would find George at the Home Office or here, etc.   If he is not satisfied with that (if George is satisfied with the rest), he must be of too morbid a nature to make my child happy, and I shall feel it better for her to suffer now than hereafter. . . .

HARPTON, 18*th August* 1859.— . . . Mr. Harcourt came yesterday about 11 o'clock and spent all the morning with

---

[1] His stepdaughter.

Thérèse, and then drove in the carriage with us, dined and staid till ½ past 11 and was at the station this morning at ½ past 9 to wish the young lady good-bye till Tuesday, when—tell the girls —he comes back and looks forward to seeing and making acquaintance with his new cousins. . . . Thérèse's happiness is so great that I suppose it would have been wise to let her marry him had he only had a travelling caravan to offer her ; but, as I have great faith in the power of brains and industry, I trust she may have all sorts of worldly blessings. And now for what I know you and Katty will care most to know—we are *very* much pleased with him, and the more I have seen of him, the more confident I feel that he is worthy of her. Lady Waldegrave and Mrs. [*illegible*] are right in saying that his faults are on the surface, and they are far less apparent as you see him more. . . .

' I cannot say,' wrote Sir George Lewis from the Home Office, ' that I feel any great confidence in W. Harcourt's professional prospects ; but marriage cannot fail to be a stimulus, and it is too late now to recede.' In the end, all doubts and difficulties were overcome, and the marriage took place on 5th November following.

In August Clarendon paid a visit at Osborne, where he had the bad luck to be laid up with gout.

Lord Clarendon to Sir G. C. Lewis.

THE GROVE, 11*th August* 1859.— . . . It was very provoking to be tied to my chair at Osborne, but very flattering to be the object of royal solicitude. I could not have experienced greater kindness in the house of my nearest relative. . . . The Queen thinks of nothing but foreign affairs, and spoke to me with great bitterness about Palmerston and J. Russell. She said she was unhappy and in a state of constant nervousness from the fear that some trick would be played her, and that, without her being able to prevent it, the country would be engaged in a wrong policy. Lord John, she said, had not written one despatch which she did not wish he had *not* written ; but she admitted that he had adopted all her numerous corrections with good humour, and that, as yet, his letters had not been rude as formerly. I tried, and not in vain I hope, to moderate her views and those of the Prince on the subject.

To Lady Theresa Lewis.

THE GROVE, 11th August 1859.— . . . If the Queen had been my sister instead of my Sovereign, she could not have been more kind—sending the first thing in the morning to know how I had slept, and when she was at dinner sending to inquire what I had got, and whether I would not like some of this or that which they had downstairs. . . . Her old feeling against Palmerston is quite returned, and she spoke with bitterness of him and Lord John. 'I can't say I am happy, because I am not. I live in constant dread that some trick will be played me and that the country will be entangled in a policy that will be wrong and unfortunate. I have given up arguing with Lord Palmerston, and now I only protest. Lord John has not written a single despatch that I did not wish he had abstained from writing, and my only comfort is that, as yet, he has adopted all my corrections with good humour and that his letters to me have not been rude as they used to be ; but I don't know how long that will last,' and a great deal more in a like strain. It is evident that these two men sit upon her mind like lead, and give it a permanent indigestion. . . . I saw Palmerston on Tuesday and put some water into his wine, for he was very unjust about the Austrian tendencies of the Prince, who is as much alive to the brutal stupidity and shortcomings of the Austrians as Pam. himself ; but the latter dubs every one Austrian and anti-English who won't go all lengths with him in trusting France and backing Sardinia.

Hon. Emily Eden to Lord Clarendon.

THE PARSONAGE, CHILD'S HALL [1859].—I get up every morning under the fond delusion that I am going to write to you, because, if I don't, you will not write to me, which would be dreadful ; but somehow days that are quite quiet and uninterrupted seem to last only six hours, and it is always time to go to bed again just as I am going to begin to occupy myself. I must say I like this little place, tho' it is not a soil that grows letters. It is so quiet and cheerful, with a constant tourbillon of soft air blowing that is very refreshing.

I did not exactly know how to set about wishing you joy of Thérèse's marriage.[1] I do not suppose it is an alliance you

[1] Lady Theresa's daughter, married to Mr. (afterwards the Right Hon. Sir W. V.) Harcourt.

would have chosen; but still I am glad it is settled, for Theresa was very nervous about it last time she was here (the day before he proposed), and, as it was obvious that Thérèse was regularly in love, anything is better than a disappointment. I am all for happiness, and if Thérèse finds it in comparative poverty and positive Harcourt, she is old enough to know her own mind. I am glad he has given up writing for the press. I should hate having the *Saturday Review* for my son-in-law. In short, I am very glad of anything that makes dear old Theresa happy; but, between ourselves, it was she who originally taught my young ideas to shoot in the direction of thinking Mr. Harcourt detestable. However they can easily be trained in another direction.

It was more easy to answer the Duchess of Buccleuch's letter. She seems intensely delighted with Dalkeith's marriage, and indeed both families are equally pleased.[1] Lady Cowper had been over to Brocket, and, considering that she had quite set her heart on having Lady Louisa for her daughter-in-law, she is most magnanimous in her view of their happiness, and says— 'Dalkeith is a young man quite after my own heart—so refined and pleasing, and so good. I do not know which of the two is most lucky.' I feel certain that, if there is another daughter, Lady Abercorn will marry her to the Prince of Wales. The old Duchess of Gordon[2] must go on working away in her coffin for her granddaughters as she did for her daughters.

The Duke of Bedford was here on Thursday, looking thin and ill, more completely bit with Lord John than ever. I am sure you will be glad to hear that his visit cost him nothing. He wrote to offer himself, but said he had no carriage in London; whereupon I offered him mine, which is at Eden Lodge. This delighted him, and he asked if he could have it again when he came to town. It is a great thing to assist the struggles of virtuous poverty, and, anyhow, I should be glad to do anything for the old dear; but if, in any future state of existence, I become Duke of Bedford with £200,000 a year, I think I shall keep a one-horse fly of my own in London. . . . *Semi* continues to flourish.[3] The oddest people take to it. Lord Lansdowne wrote me a very pretty note about it, and said it had been a

---

[1] The present (sixth) Duke of Buccleuch married Lady Louisa Hamilton, daughter of James Marquess (afterwards first Duke) of Abercorn.

[2] Jane Maxwell, married the fourth Duke of Gordon in 1767, died 1812.

[3] *The Semi-detached Couple*, a novel published by Miss Eden in this year, which met with a popular favour.

great amusement to him in his convalescence. I should not have thought he would have the remotest idea what it meant. . . . It is very odd so many grave men should take to it ; but I am flattered by it, and there never was a folly (for I think it an *insigne* folly to print) that has brought so few unpleasant consequences. . . .

Having brought the reader into touch with matters matrimonial, we may by anticipation record another matter of moment even nearer to the Clarendons than the wedding of Lady Theresa's girl, namely, the engagement of their second daughter, Lady Alice Villiers, to young Lord Skelmersdale, who had succeeded his grandfather as second baron in 1853. The first break in a family so devoted to each other as that at The Grove could not fail to cause mingled feelings of rejoicing and regret ; but the most anxious mother could not desire a better marriage for her daughter, whether in a worldly or a personal point of view. They were married on 16th August 1860.[1]

Lord Howden to Lord Clarendon.

PARIS, *8th July* 1860.—Your letter, my dearest C., gave me immense pleasure—firstly, on account of the fact you impart, secondly, because you at once thought of me in a thing that touches you. . . . Now, if I was such a vulgar fellow as to go to a jeweller's shop, and afterwards such an impertinent one as to send your daughter what I had bought, you would think of me just what I should think of myself ; but when I tell you that the old-fashioned and badly mounted affair I send with this belonged to my mother, and when I tell you with the truest truth that I reserved it, when I gave the other things to my cousin Selina Vernon,[2] for a daughter of yours whenever she married, I feel sure that both you and Lady Clarendon and Lady Alice herself, in favour of it having belonged to one so dear to me, will allow me to offer it on this occasion. I wish it was more in accordance with the present fashion, and a prettier concern altogether ; but then it would not be what it is. Tell Lady Alice, my dear C., with my affectionate regards, that she

---

[1] Lord Skelmersdale was created Earl of Lathom in 1880, and died 19th November 1898, having survived his wife less than a year.
[2] Lady Selina Meade, daughter of third Earl of Clanwilliam, married in 1854 Granville Vernon, M.P.

has all the good wishes of a very affectionate heart, which has never opened itself so completely as at the times when all its sympathies have been with you.   Yours always,

HOWDEN.

Clarendon's eldest son, Lord Hyde,[1] having reached his fourteenth year, was now at Harrow, and spent part of his holidays at Harpton, the country house of Sir George and Lady Theresa Lewis in Radnorshire.

Lord Clarendon to Sir G. C. Lewis.

THE GROVE, 28*th August* 1859.—I cannot let Hyde go without a line of thanks to you for allowing him to increase our already too great encroachment on your hospitality ; but he enjoys the thought of going to Harpton as much as his sisters do being there. He is a good boy and I can see no wrong tendencies in him.   He is of some promise too, as Vaughan told me he could not speak quite satisfactorily of him, for altho' he was much higher in the school than any boy of his age, he never did his best, or anything like it, till just at the end of the quarter, when he made a rush for his remove, and got it easily.

I wish the best years of his life were not spent in forgetting French, making bad Latin verses and acquiring nothing that will fit him to be a prominent or useful member of society.   I have long been of opinion that our public schools do not keep pace with the requirements of the age ; indeed they seem to ignore or be indifferent to them ; and altho' of late years some reformation has been forced upon them by public opinion, yet it is always unwillingly adopted by masters who seem to be as much attached to routine as they are to dead languages.   I admit, however, that the universities must take the lead, and that, until they do so, schools are powerless, even if well disposed to improve.

I enclose a letter which I cut out of the *Morning Star* of yesterday, as I entirely agree with the writer about flogging, which is a remnant of an unenlightened age.   Surely it is better to appeal to the head or the heart of a boy than to his *derrière*.

Ministers had but a broken holiday during the autumn of 1859, for the unsettled state of Europe made it necessary for the Cabinet to meet very often.

---

[1] The present Earl of Clarendon.

Lord Granville to Lord Clarendon.

16 BRUTON STREET, 13th September 1859.— . . . I went to
Yorkshire for some grouse-shooting, came back to Aldenham,
and was summoned to an interesting and important cabinet, of
which you must have heard from Charles Villiers. . . . Palm.
is inclined to go the whole hog about Italy and is in a fool's
paradise about the Emperor of the French. Persigny swallows
all Palm.'s notions, *thinks* they are his own, and offers them as
the Emperor's. . . . It is a good illustration of the value of
human prophecy that, whereas we all feared danger from the
disunion of the two great statesmen,[1] our chief difficulty now
is their intimate alliance. . . .

Lady Theresa Lewis to Lord Clarendon.

HARPTON, 26th September 1859.— . . . It is very worrying to
have George called away so often for the cabinet ; but I am
most thankful, for the credit of the government, that the cabinets
are held, and that we are not at the entire mercy of offhand
despatches and random shots by our leader Robin Hood and
his colleague Little John, which might be very fatal, and these
frequent meetings are at least a check. . . . It is very evident
from all I hear from George that your absence is an immense
loss in the cabinet, not only in your particular office, but in
keeping the Q[ueen] and P[rince] straight, and making others
behave well to them also. I suspect little Johnnie is rude
and the Q. and P. distrustful, which don't make a very
happy family.

The Emperor of the French, being fully as anxious to
get free from the war with Austria as he had been to scramble
out of that with Russia, determined upon making peace at
any price. Desiring to have the support of Great Britain,
he confided to Lord John Russell the terms which he wished
to convey to the Austrian government through the British
Foreign Office. But when Palmerston and Russell saw the
proposed conditions, they would have no hand in a bargain
which left Italy almost as far from being united as ever.

[1] Palmerston and Russell.

So the two Emperors took matters into their own hands. Meeting at Villafranca on 11th July 1859 they signed a treaty whereby Austria ceded Lombardy (saving the Quadrilateral) to the Emperor Napoleon, who undertook to hand it over to the King of Sardinia ; the duchies of Tuscany and Modena were to be restored to their former rulers, Venetia was to remain Austrian, but also a member of an Italian Confederation under the presidency of the Pope. The King of Sardinia was satisfied with the possession of Lombardy, and signed the treaty, but his great minister Cavour resigned, indignant at the trick whereby the Emperor of the French had sold the cause of United Italy whereof he had proclaimed himself the champion.

It may easily be understood that neither Palmerston nor Russell could brook this settlement. ' Italy for the Italians ' had been their purpose in the benevolent neutrality they had observed, and they declined Louis Napoleon's proposal for a European Congress until they should be satisfied that Austria was not to form part of the Italian Confederation, else the Italian question was as far from settlement as ever. They were prepared to form an alliance with France for the expulsion of Austria from Italian soil. Clarendon, ever sceptical about the scheme for United Italy, was strongly against any departure from strict neutrality. Palmerston conferred with him, wrote to him, argued with him, as freely as if he had still been at the Foreign Office ; but Clarendon would not be convinced. A fresh move of the Emperor Napoleon altered the situation. At Christmastide a pamphlet entitled *Le Pape et le Congrès* was published in Paris, and was sold by tens of thousands, for it was an open secret that it was from the hand of Louis Napoleon himself. It was urged in this pamphlet that the Pope should resign the States of the Church, a proposal so outrageous in the eyes of Austria that she refused to attend the projected Congress unless the pamphlet were officially repudiated by the French government. Louis Napoleon refused to do this, his foreign minister resigned, and the Congress was abandoned.

Lord Palmerston to Lord Clarendon.

94 PICCADILLY, *2nd December* 1859.— . . . The refrain of the
Austrian song to us is—If you love us and have any regard for
us or for making us happy, do for Heaven's sake help us to continue to tyrannise over the Italians and to make them as unhappy for the future as we have made them in the past. The
truth is, there is a passion in the human heart stronger than the
desire to be free from injustice and wrong, and that is the desire
to inflict injustice and wrong upon others, and men resent more
keenly an attempt to prevent them from oppressing other people,
than they do the oppression from which they themselves may
suffer.

BROADLANDS, *4th January* 1860.— . . . The pamphlet was
naturally calculated to astonish and discompose those who have
not had confidential conversations with the Emperor Napoleon,
and who judged of his intentions and feelings simply by their
own belief that he was intirely dependent at home upon the
Catholic priesthood of France. But you and I who, during the
last few years, have from time to time had long conversations
with Napoleon on the affairs of the world, know very well that
the pamphlet expresses nothing more than the ideas and schemes
which have been in his mind for many years and which we have
heard from him frequently when we have met him.

As to which is the best ally for England—France or Austria
—there can be no hesitation in making the choice. As friends—
Austria has taken our subsidies, engaged not to make peace
without our consent, been immediately beaten and made her
own peace without any communication with us. France has
stood by us in war, has brought war to a successful issue, and,
though not steady to us in negotiations for peace, has in the main
acted by her engagements. If we chuse our allies according to
the mischief they might do us in war and according to the
advantage we might therefore derive from having them as friends
instead of foes, Austria could do us no possible harm as an enemy :
France could injure us seriously.

But I cannot admit that we are acting hostilely towards
Austria by rescuing the unhappy Italians from their grasp. The
Austrian anger with us on that account is much like the indignation of the Southern States of the American Union against
the Northern for presuming to think that slavery is an un-
christian condition and that slaves ought to be made free.

The best solution of the existing Italian difficulties would be that the Pope should refuse to join the Congress because Napoleon refuses to disown the pamphlet : that Austria should refuse to come without the Pope : that Russia and Prussia should decline to come without Austria, and that thus there should be no Congress : that France should say that she and Sardinia will not permit the employment of coercion in Central Italy, and that the Italians of those central states, left to themselves, should carry out their determination of uniting themselves to Piedmont. There would thus be made a respectable little kingdom of Northern and Central Italy, capable to a certain degree of defending itself against Austria, and therefore so far independent of France. The Italians would be happy ; Europe would be freed from one great source of danger to its peace, and the government who had brought about this result would have occasion to be proud of their work.

Lord Clarendon to Lord Palmerston.

THE GROVE, *8th January* 1860.— . . . We may not think Austria has any right to consider us hostile, but it is rather too much to expect that she should share our opinion ; and, in judging for others, one ought as much as possible to look at things from their point of view.   Despotism is a system of government, and a horrible one ; but like all other systems it has its laws and its usages, which are pretty much the same everywhere.   Nicholas marches Poles 1500 miles in irons to work underground for life. L. Napoleon sends Frenchmen to die of fever in Cayenne, has a *loi des suspects*, and suppresses all thought.   Austria spies and imprisons and flogs men, women and children, and the Pope and the King of Naples do still worse ; but none of these sovereigns will admit that they are acting otherwise than their divine rights entitle them to act for the preservation of their own absolute power over their people, although every one else knows that their system is revolting to humanity and fatal to the happiness and well-being of their unfortunate subjects.

I never much liked the notion of a Congress or felt any confidence that it would lead to useful results ; so I am not sorry that it must be given up ; but I have not shared, and cannot now share, your opinion that the annexation of Piedmont would be a safe or final settlement of the Italian question, tho' it is possible that no other present solution of the difficulty may be found.

In the first place—what does annexation really mean ?   The Italians may desire it now as the most effectual means of preventing the return of their former rulers ; but I doubt if any one of the States desires to be incorporated with, or to form part and parcel of, Piedmont.   Each may wish to have Victor Emmanuel as King ; but each intends to maintain its own laws and institutions, and to have its own system of representation and taxation.   From our knowledge and experience of the Italian character, I think it impossible to expect that such a system would work well or would give Piedmont the strength that she would derive from a united people.   My chief objection to the scheme, however, is that Austria, no matter what straits she may be reduced to, never will consent to the arrangement. She may be too poor and too weak to resist it by force, and it is probable she will not attempt any such folly ; but she will protest against it, intrigue against it, threaten from a distance all who lend themselves to it, and declare that she will bide her time to recover what has been taken.   This will produce mistrust and intrigues in the annexed States, and Piedmont, altho' apparently made more powerful, will be more dependent upon France than she has ever yet been.

France will necessarily become the dominant power in Italy, which I consider a very bad arrangement for England, because France is always restless and aggressive, and the freedom of the Mediterranean and the safety of our possessions in that sea will never again be what they have been from the day that France takes the place of Austria in Italy.

With respect to which is the best ally for England—France or Austria—I entirely agree with you that the former may do us much harm and that the latter cannot do us much good ; but France will always keep us in hot water and Austria we need never think about.   In the one there can be little confidence and with the other no community of interest or action.   Louis Napoleon for the moment *is* France, and we must do our best to keep well with him.   He has done nothing as yet of which we can positively complain, except throwing us over after the peace and taking part with our common enemy ; but he has done much to alarm us as to his ulterior intentions, and, as he has really no moral sense, I hope we shall be warned by the experience we have had of him, and never again trust him beyond what may be absolutely necessary for maintaining friendly relations with France.

Sir G. C. Lewis to Lord Clarendon.

HOME OFFICE, *9th January* 1860.—I have been attending poor Macaulay's funeral in Westminster Abbey. Shelburne was unable to come, and I was asked to take his place. The pall-bearers were the Chancellor, Duke of Argyll, Stanhope, and Lord John, David Dundas and myself; Carlisle and the Speaker also followed the body. The service was chiefly chaunted, which made it less impressive by making it unmeaning. The tones of the organ were solemn, but what the choristers sang might have been the psalms of the day. There was something very sad in the contemplation of such a vivid and brilliant intellectual power being suddenly extinguished. Monckton Milnes has just returned from Bowood, and I am told that he describes Lord Lansdowne as showing his satisfaction at having outlived Macaulay, which seems to me a singular feeling and quite unlike what usually affects the old who see their juniors die before them.

I have been at a sort of committee of the cabinet where I saw Granville, and I dined last night at the Admiralty where I met Gladstone and the Chancellor. Neither the latter nor Granville is inclined to agree to a treaty with France to guarantee Central Italy against Austria, and my impression is that if the same proposition is renewed, and we are told that we must accept it or break up the cabinet, the *latter* alternative will be preferred. Palmerston writes me word that if the cabinet *altogether* reject Lord John's proposal, he will resign and the cabinet must be dissolved. What virtue there may be in 'altogether' I know not. A mitigated proposition might be adopted; but the crude article which was presented last Tuesday will, as it seems to me, be rejected by the cabinet gorge.

I must say I think it extremely inconvenient to have an ambassador at Paris who talks to the Emperor as if he was a French Secretary of State, or at most as if he was *amicus curiæ,* and who involves us in serious difficulties by conversations which must influence our conduct, but which we cannot disclose.

Lord Clarendon to Sir G. C. Lewis.

THE GROVE, *10th January* 1860.—I thought of you yesterday and of the cold you would probably catch in Westminster Abbey; but I hope my presentiment may not have been realised. The burial service well read, I think, would have been more impressive

than the music, which must have interrupted the train of thought
that poor Macaulay's sudden death was calculated to inspire.
I am not much surprised at Lord Lansdowne feeling the satisfaction you allude to, but I am so at his showing it.   The severe
fits of gout I used to have when I was young always gave him
pleasure, as it made him think that his own infirmities did not
proceed from old age, and in the same way he now likes to
flatter himself that in personal vigor he exceeded Macaulay.

The feeling in the Cabinet against being entangled in the
Italian embroglio was too strong to let Palmerston have his
way.   No trait in his character was more impressive and
effective than the power to bide his time.   When his policy
failed to receive the support of his colleagues, he either
found means to make it inevitable without their assent, or
waited till events brought them to a like view to his own.
When, for a time, the opinion of the majority prevailed
against him, he never nursed a grudge.   He might strike
back on the moment, as he did in his famous 'tit-for-tat with
Johnny Russell,' but when the occasion was past his inimit-
ably cheerful friendliness was without a cloud.   It is strange
that Clarendon, who had known Palmerston so long and
intimately, should have been deceived, as the following
letter to Sir George Lewis shows, into imagining that the
Prime Minister was going to throw over the cause of Italian
unity merely because his colleagues flinched from the risk
of war.   Palmerston's purpose was as firm as ever ; though
he would veil it prudently until the autumn recess, when
inquisitive members of parliament should be scattered to
their homes, and Lord John should be free to show what
the sympathy of the Liberal party was worth to Italy, as
he did by the historic despatch of 27th October.[1]

[1] Writing to Sir James Hudson, British Minister at Turin, after Garibaldi
had saluted Victor Emmanuel as King of Italy, Lord John reviewed the
motives which he considered to justify the rising in the Roman and
Neapolitan States, and concluded : ' Such having been the causes and
concomitant circumstances of the revolution of Italy, Her Majesty's
government can see no sufficient grounds for the severe censure with
which Austria, France, Prussia and Russia have visited the acts of the
King of Sardinia.   Her Majesty's government turn their eyes rather to
the gratifying prospect of a people building up the edifice of their liberties,
and consolidating the work of their independence, amid the sympathies
and good wishes of Europe.'

Lord Clarendon to Sir G. C. Lewis.

THE GROVE, 11*th January* 1860.—I am very much obliged to you for your account of the manner in which your crisis vanished into thin air yesterday. I have not often been more anxious than during the last 24 hours, and it is an immense relief that we have escaped the ridicule of breaking up the government and the disgrace of lashing ourselves to France in a war against Austria, with nothing better to show for it than the Roman gleanings of Mr. Odo Russell. If the majority of the cabinet had not done its duty a week ago, we might at this moment be far enough on in an agreement with France to have made retreat extremely difficult, if not a cause of quarrel. But you must have your eyes and ears open for the next dodge, as you may be sure that Austria in a state of voluntary quiescence will not be sufficiently humiliated to satisfy Palmerston and Azeglio, and they will go on driving at annexation until the Emperor *nous envoie promener*, or demands from England some guarantee of the arrangement we think indispensable.

Talk of humiliation, however ! P. and J. R. have their fill of it ; and they must be conscious now that, roar they never so loudly, there is a counterblast in the cabinet always ready to shut them up. . . .

CHAPTER XIX

GLADSTONE'S BUDGET, RELATIONS WITH FRANCE, ETC.

> ' To the statesman of sterling merit fame is of no more account
> save in so far as it wins for him the confidence of the public,
> thereby clearing the way to carry out his purpose.'
>
> PLUTARCH, *Agis*.

THE session of 1860 remains memorable for Mr. Gladstone's
budget, which searched the hearts of the Whigs almost as
severely as those of Conservatives. When he took over
the Exchequer in the summer of 1859 he had to face a deficit
of five millions, owing to increased military and naval
expenditure incurred under apprehension of French invasion. This Gladstone met by raising the income tax
from fivepence to tenpence. The budget of 1860 was
framed in accordance with a commercial treaty with France
which Cobden, holding no official position, but acting in
concert with Gladstone, had negotiated with the Emperor
during the autumn. Under this treaty, which had not yet
received parliamentary sanction, Great Britain undertook
to abolish all duties on French manufactured goods, and to
reduce those on French wines and brandy in consideration
of French duties on British manufactures being reduced.
The budget provided also for the abolition of the paper
duty and the increase of income tax to tenpence.

There is perhaps no test of magnanimity in parliamentary
life more searching than for a strong man to be left out of
office and to refrain from any act or speech embarrassing to
his former colleagues. There is assuredly nothing with
which innumerable instances have made one more familiar
than the spectacle of an ex-minister rising in his place to
denounce the policy of the Cabinet in which he once sat—a
spectacle as exhilarating to the Opposition as it is galling

to the Government. To such a course of action Clarendon never felt the slightest temptation. As a diplomatist, he disagreed with the Italian policy of Palmerston and Russell; as a Whig, he distrusted Gladstone and disapproved of his finance; and if, from his armchair, he expressed these feelings freely in correspondence, he did so chiefly to those of his old colleagues who, being still in the Cabinet, shared his misgivings and, well knowing their man, continued to communicate with him as confidentially as if he had still been a Minister of the Crown.

To certain women, also, he expressed himself with great frankness; confidential friendship with feminine intellects he always cherished as the very salt of existence; but never by private word or public act did he ever anything to weaken the authority or credit of a Liberal ministry.

To the Duchess of Manchester.

The Grove, *7th January* 1860.— . . . I wish you had been able to stay ½ an hour longer this morning and have talked about Charles's letter, which was very important, and my sister got just such another from G. Lewis. Some *mezzo termine* will perhaps be found, and I rather expect it will; but at this moment the government is in extreme peril from internal combustion. John Russell has neither policy nor principles of his own, and is in the hands of Palmerston, who is an artful old dodger and whose monomania against Austria has reached the point of phrenzy. He knows well what he is about, tho' I am sure that he utterly miscalculates the feelings of the country and the support he is likely to obtain. The Emperor has committed a monster mistake by his *brochure*, for the proposed spoliation of the Pope sets the Catholic Church thro'out the world against him, and the recognition of revolutionary principles which that spoliation involves sets all established governments, except ours, against him; but if he is at daggers drawn with all Churches and States, he must be more dependent on us, and his extraordinary eagerness now to be well with us and to make any sacrifice for the purpose, shows how embarrassing his [position] has suddenly become. Yet this advantage Palmerston would throw away, and place England in the honourable position of canister to the Imperial tail, to be dragged wherever the

Emperor chooses to go, and to declare war against Austria, upon the assumption—*without a particle of proof*—of her intentions towards Italy, and all this for the purpose of making Sardinia more powerful, without any security that the annexation to her of Tuscany and the Duchies would be a satisfactory or permanent settlement of the Italian question ! He may have his own personal reasons, and they may be very pleasant ones, for the *politique adultère* ; but they are not national, and England cannot reasonably be called upon to pay and bleed to be hated and isolated in order that the Dorchester squire may be kept constant in his affections.

The present intention of Pam., J. R. and Gladstone is to cram this policy down the throats of their twelve colleagues, and, if they won't swallow it, to resign : if they *will* swallow it and the H. of Commons *won't*, then to dissolve parliament. But three dissolutions in three years is what the country won't swallow, so that either way the government will come to an end, unless the three knock under. Until the contrary is a *fait accompli*, I shall continue to expect a patch up, tho' it will be a hollow one, for I imagine Johnny is getting sick of the humiliations he has had to endure, and of others which are in store for his conceit.

Cowley came here to-day on his way to Pembroke Lodge. . . . He found extreme bitterness at Windsor : the Prince called the Emperor a ' walking lie,' and he seemed disposed to place two of H.M.'s ministers in the same category. I asked C. what the Queen would do in the event of the Cabinet agreeing to adopt Pam.'s policy and requiring that it should be indicated in the speech from the throne. He said she would refuse point blank to do so, let the consequences be what they might ; so we may be on the eve of great events. We know already that Russia and Prussia disapprove of our wanting to make any stipulations respecting Italy before the meeting of Congress (which will *not* meet), and that they must therefore disapprove still more of the policy which P. now proposes.

Pray burn this letter directly, like a good woman as you are, for its contents are almost too confidential for writing about.

Lord Clarendon to Sir G. C. Lewis.

THE GROVE, 11*th January* 1860.—I shall be agreeably surprised if Cobden's treaty is not most improvident as a fiscal measure and most injudicious as a political one. We shall lose

an enormous deal of money and be accused of bribing France
to leave us quiet.

27th.— . . . The feeling against the treaty seems to wax
stronger, and I doubt whether it will be carried—*i.e.* whether
parliament will consent to the additional taxation necessary for
giving effect to it, altho' every one will be alive to the gravity
of rejecting a treaty with France.   People were saying to-day
that Gladstone might be backed against Lord John for up-
setting a government. . . .

2nd February.— . . . The treaty seems to be rather gaining
ground in public opinion, and, when cooked with Gladstonian
sauce, will, I daresay, be swallowed by the H. of C. altho' with
a sense of the indigestion to come. . . . Monteagle was talking of
the budget and I asked him if he thought the moral army would
be gratified by the removal of the paper duty.   He said Gladstone
was audacious enough for many things, but he (M.) would bet
me any money that he had not dared to think of *that*.

Lord Clarendon to Henry Reeve.

THE GROVE, *2nd February* 1860.— . . . The annexation of
Savoy to France is a serious affair ; not only because it makes
Italy French, but because it is the first step towards the *re-
maniement de la carte* which we know has long been germinating
in L. Napoleon's mind.   We have been done brown in the affair,
and how Lord John proposes to get himself undone I am at a
loss to imagine, though I believe he thinks it will be sufficient
to remind the Emperor of some *disinterested* passages in one of
his Italian proclamations ; but the only result of that, I expect,
will be to change the colour of our Foreign Secretary from its
present brown to verdant green.

When we made our first convention with France on going to
war with Russia, we did not know our ally as we do now ; but I
thought it would be prudent to put in a clause that neither Power
should get any benefit for itself from the war.   He accepted the
proposal cheerfully—said it was a grand precedent, etc. etc. ;
but when I read over the convention with Walewski prior to
signature, the clause was omitted, and I had it restored.   From
that moment, however, I felt that *grab* was in our friend's mind,
whenever the opportunity offered, and we shall see the ' idea '
developed on a grand scale before we are much older. . . . To
give the Devil his due, I must say he *makes proof* of moral courage

in dealing with his Holy Father. That article in the *Constitutionnel* is a great fact, and it establishes a new era. Papal insolence and encroachment have increased since '48 intolerably, and L. N., by shearing the temporalities and denying the infallibility of the Pope, takes the right way of abating the nuisance.

Lord Cowley to Lord Clarendon.

PARIS, *7th February* 1860.—I had intended, if I had had time, to have written you a line about the commercial treaty. I do not understand these matters much and will not be bold enough to give an opinion as to its results ; but it would be a very unwise proceeding on the part of the Opposition to reject it. I presume that they look to coming into power again and mean to remain on good terms with this country. If so, they should take care. The Emperor has never forgiven the vote on the [*illegible*] question,[1] and looks upon the Tory party as his bitter enemies. If they oppose the treaty and come into power in consequence, I fear that they will make their relations with this country very difficult. You are so much consulted by all parties that I thought you might like to know this. I do not think that I should be justified in writing to Malmesbury on the subject, or I would do so. . . .

Lord Clarendon to the Duchess of Manchester.

GROSVENOR CRESCENT, *9th February* 1860.— . . . I have just been dining at the Palmerstons' with a swell mob—duchesses, marchionesses, countesses all of a row to meet the Orange Boy.[2] I felt quite rural and shy amidst such fine folks, and managed to conceal myself at dinner behind the ample proportions of the Duchess of Somerset,[3] who now requires at least a place and a half. People like the Prince of Orange, and wish him success with Princess Alice, and won't hear of his not having come about her. There was a monster party afterwards, and it was quite tiresome to look at all the old faces again and to think that these dull diversions were beginning once more. . . . The discussion last night in the House of Lords was important—debate it could not be called, as everybody was of the same mind and sang in chorus. The Emperor was *wapped* tremendously, and Shaftes-

---

[1] The vote on the Aliens Bill after the Orsini plot.
[2] The Prince of Orange, who had come to England as suitor for the hand of Princess Alice.
[3] Jane Sheridan, wife of the twelfth Duke : Queen of Beauty at the Eglinton Tournament: d. 1884.

O

bury, to my surprise, punished the King of Sardinia quite as
much as he did L[ouis] N[apoleon]. . . . Derby's was an excellent speech, but I doubt if anything will stop the Emperor's
intention to possess himself of Savoy.   He said two days ago—
'L'Europe boudera, mais l'Europe ne me fera pas la guerre.   I
must think first of my own interests, and their tendency is to
annexation.'   This is the morality of 600,000 bayonets, and a
pleasant lookout for Europe!   He asked Thiers the other day
what he thought of his position in quarrelling with priests and
protectionists at the same time.   Thiers said—'Votre Majesté
me fait l'effet d'un homme qui ne marche qu'en s'appuyant sur
deux béquilles, et qui les jette par la fenêtre!'   Rather good, and
so is another saying of his—'Eh bien; que l'Empereur avale le
Pape, pourvu que ça l'étouffe!'

Charles Greville to Lord Clarendon.

BATH, 10th February 1860.— . . . I conclude from
Palmerston's announcement last night that Gladstone will
speak to-night. . . . Certainly public affairs were never in a
more deplorable state, or more full of doubt and anxiety for the
future.   How much better it would have been if no reconcilia-
tion had taken place between Palmerston and John Russell,
and how much has been sacrificed for that object.   But the
Whigs had persuaded themselves of its absolute necessity, and
that there was no other way of getting back to office, that it was
considered the happiest thing in the world when it was effected.
They probably would not have recovered office quite so soon,
but the delay would not have signified much, and we should not
now have J. R. at the Foreign Office nor be hampered with his
pledges on the reform question.   The dilemma in which we now
stand, as you put it, is very embarrassing; but is it so certain
and indispensable that the government must resign if Gladstone
is defeated?   If it is true that the stipulations of the commercial
treaty are that it is to depend on the approbation of parliament,
and that the budget and the treaty are to be taken together, I
think Gladstone *may* be defeated in some manner which will
not necessarily involve any quarrel between the two countries,
and which need not compel the government to resign.   If
Gladstone and J. R. choose to do so alone, there would be no
great loss. . . . The Poodle has just detected two tall chimneys
vomiting forth smoke, which he says they ought by law to

consume, and he is gone off to inform against them. Mrs. Poodle says Frederic does nothing but run after all the pretty women. I tried to console her by assuring her that *he never caught any of them !*

14*th.*— . . . Now that I have recovered from the effects of Gladstone's ' stunner,' I am much struck by the various blots and objections you point out. The Speaker writes me ' Derby was in the gallery to hear the speech. I am told he listened with profound attention and looked very serious and black at the end. The plan is so large it will have to be taken or rejected as a whole. The first will be its fate.' I expect this likewise, for it will be impossible to reject it as a whole and dangerous for anybody to attempt to mend so complicated a piece of machinery ; but Delane writes me—' Gladstone's speech was admirable, but there is much in his scheme which it will be very hard for a government without a majority to carry. It took all his go to force his tariff through the House, and Palmerston has not [a majority of] nine to rely on.' For all this, I adhere to the Speaker's view, which seems to be yours also. I don't like the prospect you shadow out of Gladstone's future, and can only hope the *volvenda dies* may bring about some combinations which may serve to avert the realisation of his notions, which are the more dangerous in such a very good and conscientious man !

As to Savoy, the Emperor may well say that Europe will *bouder*, but submit.[1] *We* have had our *bouderie*, and have announced our intention to submit ; and if we are passive, who else is likely to make a show of more active resistance ? I rather enjoy throwing the whole blame on Palmerston and J. Russell. It serves them right for meddling at all and making England the humble servant of Cavour and the Italian patriots. . . .

Lord Clarendon to the Duchess of Manchester.

GROSVENOR CRESCENT, 2*nd March* 1860.— . . . I did a bit of Locock last night and assisted at the nativity of the Russell mouse ; but it is clearly not my vocation, for, to my shame, I must own that I went to sleep. The statement was made and received with a flatness that well reflected the apathy of the country, whose only care about reform is to have as little of it as

---

[1] Referring to the annexation of Nice and Savoy by France.

possible and as quickly as possible to get rid of the detestable question. The Conservatives made no sign of ill-humor, and were perhaps satisfied at the Bill being no worse ; but on thinking of this bill and the one of last year, the dishonesty of party spirit comes out in fine relief. A twelvemonth ago we were told that it was intolerable arrogance of the Tories to attempt a measure of reform and to pollute the ground consecrated to Whigs, and that it would be treason to the people to allow Derby's bill to be read a second time ; and now we have a bill differing only from the one of last year by the low rate of franchise which is introduced, not because it is approved by the Cabinet, or even by Johnny himself, but for the sole purpose of saving his consistency ! He had, contrary to the entreaty of his friends, chosen to announce that franchise before the dissolution, thinking it would do good to himself and harm to his opponents ; therefore, *and for no other reason* this franchise is now proposed. You will understand what the democratic operation will be, and the enormous addition it must make to the town constituencies, when I tell you that every man paying half-a-crown a week for his house will have a vote ! . . .

While Johnny was bringing to bed, his other mouse—the Italian one—was being squashed by the iron heel of our ally, as you will see by the Imperial speech. For the last six months we have, as we thought, been doing Louis Napoleon very cleverly ; when all at once with a *chiquenaude* he demolishes our house of cards. The speech is a triumph over our scheme for settling Italy, and all but an open avowal of intention to take the first step in disturbing the territorial arrangements deliberately devised against France in 1815. I understand that it is so considered at Paris, and grave complications are feared, although the slap in the face to us causes great satisfaction. Persigny openly talks of the folly of Palmerston and Lord John concealing what they had known all along—that the Emperor meant to have Savoy if they persevered in the undue aggrandisement of Piedmont, and he is particularly pleased that all the world must see that the verbiage of the House of Commons *ne tire à rien.* . . . I have no doubt that Palmerston will now do as he always does by everything else he don't like, viz., swallow it and appear to like it very much. Only the night before last he told me that the Italian question never looked better, and that the Emperor's proposals about Tuscany were merely absurdities to cover his retreat ! . . .

Lord Morley has described step by step the fight which Gladstone had to wage in the Cabinet on behalf of his budget.[1] Sir George Lewis's correspondence supplies a few supplementary touches.

Sir G. C. Lewis to Lord Clarendon.

HOME OFFICE, 12*th April* 1860.—There was a decisive cabinet to-day on the budget. The majority clearly wished to make no reduction, but to renew the existing taxes, and to hold any surplus which might accrue. Gladstone stated in the most resolute manner that he would not propose any budget in which there was not a reduction of taxation. The question was then put to the vote whether the paper duty should be repealed, on which there were 14 votes against, and 2 for, the repeal—the two being Gladstone and Milner-Gibson. A majority afterwards decided in favour of a repeal of a penny of the income-tax, against a reduction of the tea duty. The cabinet then broke up. Judging from Gladstone's dogged manner to-day, I should say he meant to resign if he cannot have his own way. . . . Lord John showed no disposition to support the repeal of the paper duty.

13*th.*—Gladstone to-day entirely altered his tone. He was extremely bland and conciliatory, and denied that he had insisted on anything or refused anything, although his language was perfectly clear and was fresh in the recollection of everybody present. At the same time he shifted his ground, admitted that it was difficult to maintain the entire income-tax, and therefore proposed to repeal a penny of it, and *also* the paper duty. After some hesitation this proposal was acquiesced in, rather than agreed to. The budget will be generally regarded as what it is—reckless and hazardous, and intended merely to discharge the bad political debts of the government.

HOUSE OF COMMONS [*no date*].—I was forced to leave the cabinet on Monday before it was over. The chief events which it produced were an agreement to propose a pacific resolution on the paper duty question, and another threatened resignation by Gladstone. The resolutions are in to-day's paper. . . . My expectation is that they will be carried by a large majority. At all events there is nothing which the House of Lords need resent. The precedent will now be established that the Lords *can* inter-

---

[1] Morley's *Gladstone*, vol. ii., pp. 18-41.

fere in an extreme case. I hear that Bright is anxious that
Gladstone and Gibson should not resign, and that he will not take
any course forcing a disruption. . . . Gibson does not conceal
his wish to remain in : Gladstone seeks to attain his object by a
constant repetition of threats to resign, but they have ceased to
have any effect.

Clarendon did not conceal from his brother-in-law the
uneasiness he felt about the Italian question.

GROSVENOR CRESCENT, 21*st* *May* 1860.— . . . I really cannot
express all I feel at the manner in which the Cabinet has been—
is—and will continue to be treated about foreign affairs. I feel
so strongly because I soon became aware how easy it was for a
Foreign Secretary to act dishonestly towards his colleagues without being detected ; and I therefore always took especial care
never to write or say a word that I did not *wish* them to know.
I have no doubt that a deep game is now playing, which may
succeed with the Court, but which will utterly fail as regards
L. Napoleon and other governments.

Palmerston had vigorously opposed in the Cabinet
Gladstone's proposal to repeal the paper duty, which
involved a sacrifice of £1,200,000 in revenue, but on this
question the Prime Minister was out-voted, and wrote to
the Queen to say that, if the Lords threw out the bill ' they
would perform a good service.' [1] The Lords did so, on the
motion of Lord Monteagle, formerly Whig Chancellor of the
Exchequer ; thereby raising the constitutional question
whether they had any right to deal with a money bill.
Gladstone, Russell and Milner-Gibson were for decided
action—resignation or what not ; the rest of the cabinet
deemed that protesting resolutions by the House of Commons
would meet the occasion, and that was the course adopted.

Lord Clarendon to Sir G. C. Lewis.

GROSVENOR CRESCENT, 2*nd* *June* 1860.— . . . I think the
government have taken quite the right course about the vote of
Monday, as the Derby, Whitsuntide and £1,200,000 saved may
put a good deal of water into the Radical wine ; but of course

[1] Martin's *Life of the Prince Consort*, v. 100.

all will depend upon the manner the country views the matter.
I am very glad you had determined not to be responsible for
any violent measure against the Lords, for if you had resigned,
others must have done so likewise, and the government would
have been broken up or the intention would have been abandoned.
J. R., however, has told several people that, if he had had his
way in the cabinet, he would have prorogued parliament yesterday, and then have brought in the same bill, and that if the
Lords had rejected it again, he would have dissolved and appealed
to the country against them.

If Frankie[1] had been so petulant about anything, he ought
to understand I should have put him in the corner with a
fool's cap on for half-an-hour.   Aberdeen told me yesterday
that Gladstone was for dissolution or *any* violent measure, but
that he had had his day and that his colleagues (meaning, I
suppose, S. Herbert and Newcastle) would not submit any
longer to his dictation. . . . Thirty of the Liberal side voted
with Mountkite.[2]

16*th*.—Aberdeen saw Gladstone on Monday and tells me that
he is *rabid*.   He admits that he cannot leave the government
on the increased China expenditure, or the fortifications ; but
he thinks the cabinet will not agree to any course very hostile
or offensive to the Lords, and that if he resigns on that he shall
have opinion with him, *and* probably Lord John who, he says,
has used much stronger language than himself on the subject.
Aberdeen told him that if the cabinet took the course he desired
' they would deserve to be dragged by the heels through the
mud from one end of London to the other.'   This mild opinion
of his ' patron ' (as G. always calls A.) seems not to have alarmed
Gladstone. . . . I think it is well that you should know this, tho'
you may perhaps be already aware of your crafty colleague's
intention. . . .

P.S.—If this note reaches you while you are at the cabinet,
you can show it confidentially to Palmerston if you think proper.

Palmerston and Gladstone both spoke on the resolutions
of protest.   ' A strange and memorable debate,' wrote Sir
Robert Phillimore ;   ' Palmerston moving resolution con-
demnatory of the Lords, and yet speaking in defence of
their conduct !   Gladstone most earnestly and eloquently

---

[1] Lord Clarendon's third son, then aged eight, now the Hon. Sir F. H.
Villiers, British Minister at Brussels since 1911.   [2] Lord Monteagle.

condemning them, and declaring that action and not resolutions became the House of Commons, and that though
he agreed to the language and spirit of the resolutions, if
action were proposed, he would support the proposal.'
Clarendon wrote to Lewis :

G. C., *6th July* 1860.— . . . Gladstone's speech is a great
inconvenience, and it is difficult to calculate what may be its
consequences. Bright clearly intends to raise a flame in the
country, but I doubt whether there are materials for a flare-up.
If not, then it is probable Gladstone will not resign. I sincerely
hope he may remain ; 1st, because such a speaking power as his
will be very dangerous in opposition, not only to the government,
but to the *res publica* ; and 2nd, because he ought to be personally
responsible for the financial difficulties he has created, and
scramble out of them as best he can, instead of aggravating them
to his successor, which he would be able and most desirous
to do.

The frank confidence which Palmerston had felt in Louis
Napoleon from the moment he became Emperor of the
French had been souring for some months into suspicion
for which it is not easy at this distance of time to detect
the grounds.[1] Anyhow, it was confirmed by the cession of
Nice and Savoy, an act which Lord John Russell warned
the House of Commons was probably only the preface to
further aggression. Palmerston considered the danger of
invasion so serious that, in view of the neglected condition
of our defences, he introduced a bill to provide nine millions
to be spent on fortifying Portsmouth, Plymouth, Chatham
and Cork. This brought him into violent collision with his
formidable colleague, who had charge of the public purse.
Gladstone vowed he would resign rather than consent to
such expenditure. Lewis explained to Clarendon how this
difficult corner was turned.

KENT HOUSE, *19th July*.— . . . The Gladstone drama has
now, I think, pretty well reached its *dénouement*. He has sent
round a paper sketching out the conditions on which he will
accede to the fortification scheme. Those conditions will not be

[1] See Palmerston's letter to the Duke of Somerset (Ashley's *Life of
Palmerston*, ii. 190).

accepted, at least the principal ones ; but, having left the high ground of 'insuperable objection' and having begun to parley, he is not likely to hold out much longer. *Château qui parle et femme qui écoute, l'un et l'autre va se rendre.* The cabinet has now pretty well taken the measure of his foot, and I trust they will not be such simpletons as to surrender again at discretion to his threats. As far as the country is concerned, the resignation of Gladstone and of Lord John would rather add strength to the government ; but it would produce a revulsion in the House, which would render it difficult to reach the end of the session.

It is extremely doubtful whether the Emperor Napoleon ever seriously contemplated the invasion of England. It is but justice to hear what he described as his real sentiments and intention, as set forth in a letter to M. de Persigny, preserved among Lord Clarendon's papers. He always felt more confidence in Clarendon than in either Palmerston or Russell, and probably instructed Persigny to communicate the letter to him.

The Emperor, Napoleon III., to M. de. Persigny.

St. Cloud, *le* 25 *Juillet* 1860.—Mon cher Persigny,—Les choses me semblent si embrouillées, grâce à la défiance qui a été semée partout depuis la guerre d'Italie, que je vous écris dans l'espoir qu'une conversation à cœur ouvert avec Lord Palmerston remédiera au mal actuel.

Lord Palmerston me connaît ; et quand j'affirme une chose, il me croira.

Et bien : vous pouvez lui dire de ma part de la manière la plus formelle que, depuis la paix de Villafranca, je n'ai eu qu'une seule pensée—qu'un but—c'était d'inaugurer une nouvelle ère de paix, et de vivre en bonne intelligence avec tous mes voisins, et surtout avec l'Angleterre. J'avais renoncé à la Savoie et à Nice, et ce fut l'accroissement extraordinaire du Piémont qui me fit revenir sur le droit de réunir à la France des provinces essentiellement françaises.

Mais, dira-t-on, vous voulez la paix et vous augmentez démesurément les forces militaires de la France. *Je nie le fait de tous points.*

The Emperor here explains in detail the scale of the

imperial army and navy, showing it to be not out of proportion to that of the other Great Powers.

Cela dit, he continues, je n'ai depuis Villafranca rien fait, ni
même pensé, qui peut alarmer personne. . . . Maintenant
arrivent les massacres de Syrie, et on croit que je suis bien aise
de trouver une nouvelle occasion de faire une petite guerre ou
de jouer nouveau rôle.   C'est vraiment me prêter bien peu de
sens commun.   Si j'ai tout de suite proposé une expédition,
c'est que je sens comme le peuple qui m'a mis à sa tête, et que
les nouvelles de Syrie m'ont transporté d'indignation.   Mais
ma première pensée a été de m'entendre avec l'Angleterre.
Quel intérêt autre que celui de l'humanité peut m'engager à
envoyer des troupes dans cette contrée ?   Est-ce que par hasard
la possession de ce pays me rendrait bien fort ?   Est-ce que je
ne gémis pas bien souvent de voir l'Algérie absorber depuis 30
ans le plus pur de notre sang et de notre or ?   Je l'ai dit en 1850
à Bordeaux et je n'ai pas changé d'avis depuis.   J'ai de grandes
conquêtes à faire, mais en France.   J'ai encore à organiser ce
pays moralement et socialement ;   j'ai à développer toutes ses
ressources intérieures qui languissent encore, et ce but ouvre un
assez vaste champ à mon ambition pour que je m'en contente.
Il m'a été difficile de m'entendre avec l'Angleterre au sujet de
l'Italie du centre, parce que j'étais engagé par la paix de Villafranca ; mais pour l'Italie du sud je n'ai point d'engagements,
et je ne demande pas mieux que de m'entendre avec l'Angleterre
sur ce sujet comme sur les autres ; mais, au nom du ciel, que les
hommes éminents qui sont à la tête du gouvernement poussent
à côté des jalousies mesquines et des défiances injustes !   En-
tendons-nous loyalement comme des honnêtes gens que nous
sommes, et non comme des larrons qui veulent se duper ré-
ciproquement.
En résumé : voici le fond de ma pensée.   Je désire que
l'Italie se pacifie, n'importe comment, pourvu que je puisse
m'en aller de Rome, et qu'on évite toute intervention étrangère.
Je désire beaucoup ne pas aller seul en Syrie ; d'abord, parce que
cela sera une grosse dépense, et ensuite parce que je crains que
cette intervention n'engage la question d'Orient ; mais d'un
autre côté, je ne vois pas comment je pourrais résister à l'opinion
publique de mon pays, qui ne peut comprendre qu'on laisse
impunis, non seulement les meurtres des chrétiens, mais l'in-
cendie de nos consulats, mais le déchirement de nos drapeaux,

mais le pillage des monastères qui étaient sous notre protection. Je vous ai dit toute ma pensée, sans rien déguiser ni sans rien omettre. Faites de ma lettre l'usage que vous voudrez : le style n'est pas soigné, mais il n'est que plus sincère. Croyez, etc.   NAPOLÉON.

Lord Cowley had resumed correspondence with Lord Clarendon, unmindful or neglectful of the injunction he had received from the Foreign Office.

Lord Cowley to Lord Clarendon.

PARIS, 25th June 1860.—There is no truth whatever in the report of my having had another row with the Emperor. He has fought very shy of any discussion with me since our famous shindy,[1] but he is as civil as possible. . . . I am satisfied that no immediate mischief is intended, and I still think that the Emperor's object is not to quarrel with us. Query—how long will it be our object not to quarrel with him ? Our government seem determined after all to have a conference on the Savoy question, which I cannot but think an error. . . . However, John Russell has changed his mind so often on the subject, that he may change it again. . . . Matters do not seem to be very comfortable with the government; but I suppose they will now weather the session. I am glad that you are out of it all, and yet I cannot help thinking that, had you been in your old place, much mischief would have been prevented. As to Lord John, one never knows where one is with him. One day it is one thing—one day another. Sometimes I am a week or more without hearing from him privately, and I never know whether the silence proceeds from *insouciance* or from *bouderie*. . . .

In July the Queen invited Lord Clarendon and his eldest daughter to Osborne.

Lord Clarendon to Lady Caledon.

GROSVENOR CRESCENT, 9th July 1860.—As there is nothing I enjoy so much as a visit to Osborne or Windsor, I need not say what pleasure your letter has given me, and I must beg you to

---

[1] Lord Cowley had to complain of the Emperor's rudeness to him at Court, and the Emperor in turn complained angrily of the attacks upon him in the English press.

make known to the Queen how grateful I am for her kind intention that Constance and I should go to Osborne, and her consideration in not asking Katty, who is just embarking in the anxieties of the trousseau, in which she will get no assistance from Alice, who declares that she will think everything beautiful, provided that her more interesting occupation is not disturbed by enquiries as to her wants and wishes. The young lady, notwithstanding her doubts and hesitation is very calmly, but very desperately, in love, at which Paterfamilias does not wonder, for Skelmersdale is charming, and the more we know and learn of him the more we have reason to confide in his amiable and honorable character, and in our darling child's prospects of happiness. . . .

Writing to Lewis, Clarendon gives him an account of the visit.

G. C., 16*th July* 1860.— . . . Constance and I passed three pleasant days at Osborne, as the host and hostess were, if possible, kinder than ever. I had a great deal of conversation with them, which I hope may have been of some use. Palmerston is in favor, and they are both pleased with his civility and attention. They dislike and distrust Lord John very much ; but still they are glad that Gladstone did not succeed in dragging him out of office, which would have been *a great misfortune* ; for although Palmerston had promised them to carry on the government without those two men, yet it would have been uphill work, as they would certainly have allowed Bright to join them and have headed a fierce Radical opposition. The Queen, however, thinks that the government would be stronger and inspire more confidence if Gladstone ceased to be a member of it, and it was clear to me that she would accept his resignation with satisfaction.

In the following note to Henry Reeve, Clarendon writes complacently about what was considered fifty years ago the *ne plus ultra* of speed in travelling.

THE GROVE, 30*th September* 1860.—I returned here last night, without touching at Grosvenor Crescent. If I had gone there, I should have been at home ten minutes within the 20 hours from Paris ; which is a fair rate of speed when one remembers that in pre-railway days one travelled hard, and got much shaken, to arrive at Paris in three days ; and in pre-steamer days I was once 18 hours in getting from Calais to Dover.

by air now less than two 1932

The journey is now timed to occupy less than seven hours from Charing Cross to the Gare du Nord.

The engagement of Lady Alice Villiers brought a warm note of congratulation from Emily Eden.

EDEN LODGE, 1860.—I am so very, *very* glad. I do not know how to say all I feel about it, except that you and Lady C. *know* the share I take in all that concerns your happiness ; and as that is bound up in your children, I own I am in a state of joyful excitement. I feel sure dear Alice will be happy : the Wilbrahams are such a good race, and so amiable and domestic. Everybody says he is charming. As for Alice not being sure she was in love yesterday, how she must laugh at that wild idea to-day, and how she will assure that deluded young man for the rest of his life that she fell in love with him the first time she saw him, which is probably true. . . . How deaf everybody is, and how tiresome they are in consequence. Madame de Flahault, Charles Greville, Lord Brougham, Locock,[1] Lord Lansdowne— all the people I see habitually are as deaf as posts, and do not care how much trouble they give with it. Do not let *us* grow deaf ; or, if we do, let us make a solemn vow not to say— ' What ? ' or ' Eh ? ' but just bear it quietly. Lord Brougham is just gone : luckily he talked without ceasing, which makes his deafness less fatiguing than it might be, and his conversation a thought more tedious than it ought to be. . . . I am so glad the Prince of Wales has arrived.[2] I always thought they would have to put Jonah, Duke of Newcastle, overboard before the ship could make any way. Poor man ! he will hear that Lord Lincoln has left England, having raised £28,000 to pay his gaming debts, for which he has given post-obits to the amount of £230,000. . . .

Some further scraps from Miss Eden's gossipy letters during the autumn of 1860 may serve as *entremets* to tougher political viands ; but whereas the good lady very seldom vouchsafed a date to her correspondence, the sequence can only be found by internal evidence.

TERRACE HOUSE, RICHMOND [*no date*].— . . . So many people tell me their secrets, from thinking that I lead rather a

---

[1] Sir Charles Locock, the surgeon and fashionable ladies' doctor.
[2] The Duke of Newcastle went as Minister in Attendance on the Prince of Wales, who, in July, paid a visit of state to Canada and the United States.

recluse life, that I have got into the habit of keeping them—till they creep out of themselves. I think I told you that the Duchess of Buccleuch had asked me several times to repeat to the Derbys a number of interesting facts respecting Mr. Talbot's attachment and constancy, and the certainty he felt (very justly) that Emma [1] never would marry anybody else, tho' she would never marry without her father's approbation, etc. etc. I told the Duchess that if a very intimate friend like Lady Derby did not speak to me of what I knew was on her mind, it would be quite impossible I should speak first—not to say impertinent. She said: 'Oh, she will come and see you at Richmond, where there will be no interruptions—surely you can then.'

It was a prophecy : for as soon as Lady Derby arrived, she sent Emma out with Lena, and then poured out all the misery she has been going through the last two years—seeing her daughter's health and spirits failing without a word of complaint. Indeed, the mother and daughter never spoke on the subject by Lord D.'s wish, and he would not allow Lady D. to speak to any human being about it. But the day before she came here she told him she could bear it no longer, and she wished to consult a friend, as she was pleased to say, upon whose judgment and affection she could rely, and he was graciously pleased to say—' If you mean Emily Eden, you may speak to her.'

Such a blessed opening ! So then I told her all the Duchess had said, which would, she said, have great weight with him. I also begged her to inform him that, so far from the world blaming him for allowing his daughter to make a poor marriage, it was blaming him now for allowing her to be unhappy ; that, as poverty was the only objection he had to Mr. Talbot, he could easily obviate that by putting his hand in his waist-coat pocket and giving her the loose change he probably always carries there. And then there was another strong argument I suggested to Lady Derby—that it was all very well to be prudent for your daughter at 18 or 19, when she knew but little of life or her own mind ; but that at 24 a woman was a woman and ought to be allowed to chuse for herself what would make her happy. Emma Stanley has not the least taste for the *gauds* of life. In short, there was plenty to be said on her side, and I made great use of Theresa's example and the Harcourt happiness. I fortunately remembered that you had said that, if your daughter

---

[1] Lady Emma Stanley, only daughter of the fourteenth Earl of Derby.

were *really* and truly attached even to a poor curate, you and
Katty would do all you could to make her happy. This was a
very effective hit : Lady D. made me repeat it twice. She went
off in great spirits, saying that she should repeat to Lord D.
every word we had been saying. I have no doubt he had previously made up his mind to consent, but evidently had a
curiosity to know what people would say—a strange weakness
in him. Oh, dear me ! how stupid rich people are. If I could
write another book, it would be solely to show that no millionaire
can buy happiness for himself, except by buying it for other
people. But that grand truth is unrevealed to people who have
never known what it is to be poor. Lord Derby was a hard,
obstinate boy when he was at school at Mitcham nearly half a
century ago, and he seems to me to be more hard, more obstinate
and more *boy* than he was then. I have had such happy letters
from both mother and daughter ; the latter suggests bringing
Mr. T. to see me.[1] . . .

VILLETTE, BROADSTAIRS [*no date*].—There—I have had my
cigar and now I can write. It is all very well to talk of the sin
of luxury and the merit of self-denial and of roughing it. I can
put up with a great deal. I don't mind a small cottage, with a
few earwigs walking about it ; I keep pet dogs which never
mind a word I say ; and servants who carry out the system of
the dogs to the fullest extent, and go on never minding ; I have
wretched health, and I have lost one of my knitting needles ;
the upholsterer has cheated me (because he says his foreman
cheated him) to such an amount that I am obliged to give up
my pet scheme of a small greenhouse ; and the cook says the
grouse will not keep. Still, I bear an equal mind ; but if once
my cigars are touched—if I can't have my tobacco regular—if
the weed fails me— ! ! ! But *you* know, my dear Lord Clarendon,
what that sensation is. All philosophy gives way—*ça casse
bras et jambes*—and leads to the belief that all commentators
have misunderstood *Othello* as thoroughly as all the rest of
Shakespeare's plays ; for, when Othello said that his occupation
was gone, he simply implied that he was out of cigars. . . . I
really and truly am trying tobacco as a remedy (Locock insisted
on my doing so), though I cannot say with any particular success,
though I think I breathe better for it ; nor with any great
delight as yet, seeing that I loathe the smell of tobacco and that

---

[1] The wedding came off all right between Lady Emma and Mr. (afterwards Col. the Hon. Sir) W. P. M. Chetwynd Talbot, K.C.B., brother of the
eighteenth Earl of Shrewsbury, 11th October 1860.

I suppose I do not manage the process well. The smoke gets into my eyes and down my throat, and probably Ramsgate cigars are of a strong seafaring character. However, *I have taken to smoking*, and I thought you would triumph, considering all my *fleers* at your habits. . . . The Gladstones are jewels of neighbours, and I like her very much indeed. She is in and out of the house at all hours—comes in at the window and sits down to write her letters here, because she cannot find a vacant table at home ; and an hour afterwards comes back because the governess is out of sorts. They often come in to tea, because, as it appears to me, their household arrangements are on the most lodging house scale—what may be called *slammerkin*. But anyhow, she is very good natured and easy, and feels to me more like a niece than a new acquaintance, she is so thoroughly at home here, and she appreciates Villette,[1] sits out in the verandah looking at the moon and sea, surrounded by geraniums and mignonette, and looking in at my pink satin room, she thinks it ' ideal,' which is a favourite Tractarian word.

I remember your snubbing Theresa Lewis when she said she did not think Mr. G. pleasant, and now you may snub me. I daresay he *is* very clever, and he is good natured, doing his best to bring his mind down to the level of mine—but fails. He is always above me, and then he does not converse—he harangues —and the more he says, the more I don't understand. Then there is something about High Church people that I can't define, but I feel it when I am with them—something Jesuitical—they never let themselves go ; and, to complete my list of sins, there is the same degree of parvenuism about him that there was about Sir R. Peel—something in the tone of his voice and his way of coming into the room that is not aristocratic. In short, he is not frivolous enough for me ; if he were soaked in boiling water and rinsed till he was twisted into a rope, I do not suppose a drop of fun would ooze out. But, having said all this in the strictest confidence, I go back to the point—that I have been wonderfully fortunate to have such good neighbours, and they have given my Broadstairs quite a different tone. . . . How curious that meeting of the Emperor [L. Napoleon] and our Albert. Some years ago the extreme politeness of his making the Prince get into *his* carriage first would not have been so palpable. . . .

[*No place, no date*, 1860].— . . . Lady M. Compton always

[1] Miss Eden's villa at Broadstairs.

seems to me to keep up the ball of amusement with greater vigour than anybody except Lady Waldegrave ; which reminds me to thank you for that admittance to Strawberry Hill. Lena had so set her heart on seeing it, and the day after she came back we drove there, meaning to be received by a housemaid in curl papers to whom we could give ourselves all sorts of airs ; instead of which there was a train of powdered menials and a most imposing groom of the chambers ; so I suggested driving back again. But the imposing man said my lady was out, and affably volunteered to show us the house. As Lena said the staircase was easy, I got up to the picture gallery, which amused me intensely. I think Lady Clarendon's and yours excellent, and Lady Waldegrave's and the Duc d'Aumale's ditto, tho' of course I cannot judge of their likenesses ; but I must say I thought most of the others detestable. The Duchess of Sutherland, Lady Clanricarde and Lady Shaftesbury will give posterity the impression that they were very plain women ; and as for dear Lady Morley, I should hate to sit in a room with such a caricature of her. To be sure, it is hard to put any pictures of this day in a room with Sir Joshua's. What a painter that man was ! I think that portrait of H. Walpole's niece one of the most lovely things I ever saw. Of course I could not see the rest of the house, but I saw enough to satisfy myself that, if it were not for love of Horace W. and the reminiscences attached to him, Strawberry Hill is not a place I covet. . . .

Lady John [Russell] came back two days ago, and called here yesterday. She liked Scotland ; but is rather perturbed in mind because the Queen never called on her, tho' she was always calling on the Farquharsons [*illegible*], etc. It *is* rather odd. She expects Lord John on the 16th. He has shot a wild boar. Just conceive the indignation of the wild boar, if he had a moment's consciousness before death, to see the very small *human* who had murdered him. Such a *rugissement* as he must have made about it ! The Flahaults keep up their daily attentions with the most amiable perseverance, and I am devotedly attached to them all. Lady Shelburne came here after Mary F.'s marriage [1]—much pleased with it. I had a most amiable letter from Lord Lansdowne yesterday about *Semi-attached* ; but he cannot believe that there ever was such a detestable

---

[1] Lady Mary Fitz-Maurice, daughter of William Earl of Kerry, who died in the lifetime of his father, the third Marquess of Lansdowne. She married General the Hon. Sir Percy Herbert, 4th October 1860, who d. 1876.

woman as Mrs. Douglas.   I have assured him that it is merely
respect for him that prevents many charming women from showing him that they can *dénigrer* each other quite to that extent,
and that Mrs. D. was claimed by everybody as the exact portrait
of their most intimate friend.   Lady Cawdor says she knows
three Mrs. Douglases, which is rather a large allowance of ill-
nature for a small circle.

I am so curious to know the history of that mysterious young
clergyman you are going to marry off.   He must be somebody's
natural son—not yours, or Montagu's,[1] or Lady C.'s, I hope ;
but somebody's.   The late Lord Morley's,[2] probably ; he had a
large supply of such articles.

EDEN LODGE, *6th November* 1860.—I hope I shall see you soon,
but in the meantime I have an anecdote that will not keep—
even in this bitter weather.   The Duke of Bedford proffered
himself to luncheon to-day, and I was extremely glad to see
the poor old thing.   I really believe he walked here through
the fog and east wind ; at all events he walked part of the way,
for he arrived at the door quite exhausted and shivering.   We
fed him up, and then gave him some hot coffee, and he sat a long
time pitying himself so much for having to walk *towards* the east
wind, that, tho' I scorned myself for it, I could not help offering
him the carriage, tho' it had been out all morning with one of
the Colviles.   This charmed him, and he begged Lena to go with
him.   He coughed so much that she suggested lozenges.   ' You
have not any with you ? ' he asked.   She said no, but it would
be easy to stop at a chemist's and get some.   So they stopped at
De Castro's, and when the man brought out a box of jujubes, the
Duke hesitated, and then said to Lena, ' I suppose you mean to
make me a present of them ? ' to which she assented, and then
he took them with the greatest delight, and thanked her repeatedly, because, he said, Lady Palmerston had given him
some, but he had taken them all and really did not know what
to do.   Now would anybody who was writing a novel dare to
put in that trait ? . . . Did you know that Skittles[3] had joined
Garibaldi's army under the care of a Mr. Redfern, and that she
claims the glory of having won the Volturna fight ?   She says

[1] Montagu Villiers, Bishop of Durham.
[2] Lord Clarendon's maternal uncle.   The marriage referred to was that
of Bishop Villiers's daughter Amy to the Rev. Edward Cheese, his
chaplain, and rector of Haughton-le-Skerne.
[3] A beautiful horsewoman, original of the type ' pretty horse-breaker.'
She still lives in London, retaining many of her old friends—on a different
footing.

Garibaldi continually consulted her, going on saying—'Now Miss Walters, what do you advise, etc. etc ? ' Madame Dellatoura [1] disputes the crown with Miss Skittles ; but as *she* was an active combatant, flashing her sword about in all directions, of course, she could not direct the evolutions of the troops. . . . Lord Cawdor is dying of a very small carbuncle on his arm, which has suddenly mortified. [2]

Instant in season and out of season, Lord John Russell at the beginning of the session of 1860 had extorted from an unwilling Cabinet consent to his bringing in another Reform Bill. He insisted, moreover, upon introducing it upon the anniversary of the bill of 1832—the 1st March— whereby he only brought into sharper relief the utter apathy of the House and country upon the question. He got his second reading without a division ; but the attention of all parties was absorbed by the budget, and he was fain to withdraw the bill to the great relief of all concerned. He let it be known, however, that he intended to bring the measure forward again in 1861. Clarendon, who knew by experience that the work of the Foreign Office was in itself enough to tax the powers and consume the whole time of any one man, had little patience with Russell in attempting the impossible by undertaking the conduct of what must be a highly contentious measure wholly unconnected with his proper department, and he thus communicated his feelings to Lewis :

THE GROVE, 10*th October* 1860.— . . . The Duke of Bedford is here, wonderfully improved in health. When I saw him in July, I though it was for the last time ; but now. . . . I see no reason against his living on. He tells me that Johnny is de- termined to mount his reform hobby again and that Palmerston had been obliged to promise that the question of Johnny's re- deeming his supposed pledge should be discussed and settled at the first cabinet in November. I said that, as J. R. had brought in a revolutionary bill, disgusted his friends, alarmed the country, wasted the public time and made an ignominious retreat, it seemed to me he had done quite enough in the way of pledge

---

[1] I have not succeeded in identifying this lady, one of the figures who flashed into prominence in the lime-light of the Italian stage.

[2] He died on 7th November 1860.

redemption without again dragging the government thro' the mud in order to discover that the country would be quite as indisposed next year as it was the last to a comprehensive measure of reform. The Duke agreed, but said John was unreasonable and would not consider that he had redeemed his pledge until he had taken the sense of the House upon *a measure*. He asked me what I thought would be the feeling of the cabinet upon John's *difficulty*. I told him I had no means of knowing, but that as the majority of the cabinet were sensible men, I should expect them to prefer not to run their heads against such a brick wall as another reform bill, and that the invitation to do so would be scouted. . . . Are you aware that J. R. means to go to the House of Lords ? He intended it this year, if he had carried his reform bill, and the other day in passing thro' London from Scotland he told the Duke he had made up his mind. . . . He feels that with Palmerston and Gladstone in the H. of C. and no inclination anywhere for reform, he is nobody and sinking fast ; so if he is not allowed to have his own way when the cabinet meets, I expect he will say that his colleagues have put an end to his career of usefulness in the H. of C., and that as a member of the H. of L. he can devote himself better to the management of our foreign policy. He will, of course, supersede Granville, but he will not succeed so well there as leader, tho' possessing much more ability than Granville, and he will not have temper for the pokes that Derby will delight in giving him.

Charles Greville, well versed in political meteorology, wrote in the same spirit to Clarendon :

NEWMARKET, *6th October* 1860.— . . . This morning I have a letter from the Duke of Bedford in which he says—' I have a letter this morning from Palmerston on the reform question. The substance of it is that he considers John [Russell] quite free to take his own course to go on with or to abandon it as he may decide for himself. Palmerston writes only as the question concerns himself personally, and adds—" What course the government may think it right to pursue must be considered in November." ' I hope the government will have the good sense to set their faces against any attempt to bring on again a measure distasteful to the House of Commons and to the country, which only ultra-radicals require and which most people regard as pregnant with mischief. . . .

Events in Italy had been moving swiftly in the direction most desired by Palmerston—most dreaded by Clarendon. In May Garibaldi and his thousand had taken possession of Sicily under protection of the Piedmontese fleet ; the King of Naples fled from his capital on 6th September ; Victor Emmanuel's army entered the Papal States a few days later, and by the end of the month had occupied all the fortresses therein. France and Russia marked their disapproval by recalling their ministers from Turin ; Protestant Prussia confined herself to a formal protest addressed to the Piedmontese government.

Lord Palmerston to Lord Clarendon.

BROADLANDS, 10th October 1860.— . . . I believe in the honesty of Garribaldi [sic] and in his singleness of purpose. He wants to unite all Italy under Victor Emmanuel. He put off annexation that he might retain the Sicilian and Neapolitan forces in his own hands, to wield them against Rome and Venetia. He has probably by this time discovered that an impromptu army such as his is no match for regular troops such as the French and Austrians, and he will leave Rome and Venice alone for the present, at least.

But Austria cannot permanently hold Venetia, even if she abandons her cruel and tyrannous system of crushing, not governing, that province. She would do wisely to sell it for 20 millions sterling, which she might probably get for it.

One does not know what to wish as to the Pope's staying in, or going away from, Rome ; but as long as the French troops remain he will probably stay there, and he and they will go away together, if ever they do go. Napoleon has a difficult game to play between his Catholic priests on the one hand and the Roman stilettos on the other.

I believe in the consolidation of Italy into one State, though many doubt its being accomplished ; and I think that such an arrangement would, on the whole, be the best for Italy and for Europe. Florence would make a good capital and, in a sanitary point of view, better than Rome.

Charles Greville breathed the very spirit of the old Whigs in writing to Clarendon on the situation :

LONDON, 13th October 1860.— . . . Cavour's speech, as given

in the *Times* of to-day, is a marvellous exposition of the Sardinian policy and intentions. Are we to sanction and uphold an open violation of every principle which has hitherto been deemed sacred, and by the maintenance of which the moral elements of the world have been held together ? Is our *policy*, too, so changed that we can regard with satisfaction and approbation a course of conduct by which the very existence of Austria will be directly or indirectly threatened ? . . . There was a time when such cynical effrontery would have excited a just indignation here ; but the British public is in one of its fits of foolish enthusiasm for Garibaldi, and this, together with a not unnatural abhorrence of the King of Naples, father and son, make them insensible to every consideration of sound policy, as well as of political honor and good faith. The *Times* too, which is used to lead, or mislead, public opinion, is itself in a great state of perplexity and inconsistency—abusing all the Sardinians *say* and approving of all they *do*. . . .

Cowley, on the other hand, though he had always shared Clarendon's disbelief in Italian unity, seemed prepared to accept it as *fait accompli* :

CHANTILLY, 12*th November* 1860.—I was very glad to get your letter giving me some of Palmerston's views, for as for learning them (or indeed the views of the government in general) in any other way, I might as well be in California. . . . You may well say that the success in Italy is miraculous ! Had Garibaldi met with any real opposition, he must have been destroyed. When the Sardinians went to his assistance, his army (if it ever ought to have been called one) was utterly disorganised. If Cavour can make anything really constitutional of this new infant kingdom, his success ought to cover a multitude of sins ; but I fear that it will be found that, for at least some time to come, a military government will be necessary in Naples. . . . The best thing Victor Emmanuel could do would be to fix the seat of his government at Naples, until he can get to Rome. The latter, however, will not be so easy a task. I cannot believe that the Pope will go, tho' I wish with all my heart he would ; for so long as he stays the Emperor cannot abandon him and bring away his troops. He may diminish them. I hope he will do so—but bring them away altogether is an impossibility. . . . I am amused at Palmerston's roundabout way of becoming convinced that the Emperor did not want to quarrel with us; but it was always so with him since I have served under him: he will trust to any one rather than to his own agents. . . .

To the last Lord Cowley remained convinced that real Italian unity was impossible, or, if by some miracle it were to be brought about, that it was contrary to British interests to encourage it. He expresses this opinion very strongly and at great length in one of his contraband letters to Lord Clarendon:

CHANTILLY, 6*th December* 1860.—I am more obliged than I can say by your letter of the 4th from Ashridge, and the hints you give me respecting Johnny's forthcoming despatch. He had prepared me for it . . . and, with his usual satisfaction with his own work, he had told me that it was a despatch which should settle the Venetian question with the concurrence of all Europe. I had been led, however, to expect something else than what you say it is, inasmuch as I had written to him to say that it would, in my opinion, be useless to attempt to deprive Austria of Verona, but that it might be hoped perhaps to induce her to abandon Mantua and Peschiera; and that then some arrangement might be made for neutralising the Venetian territory. . . . Johnny answered that he very much agreed with me that Venice might be made a free port under a Doge, and that a sum of money might be given to Austria for the two fortresses. . . . I do not believe that Austria can abandon Verona, and Augustus Loftus adds that she cannot abandon Peschiera, as, without possession of the latter, Verona can be turned. Whatever may happen, I hope from my heart and soul that Venice may not become an appendage of Sardinia. Nothing will ever persuade me that Italy will be English in her policy: she must of necessity be French; nor that she will like France, but she will be afraid of her, and therefore do her bidding. In working for Italian unity, we are working for the creation of another maritime Power in the Mediterranean, and I maintain that that is not good policy for England. We do not want maritime assistance there as it is, even if we were sure of having that of Italy when required, and we run the risk—in my belief we incur the certainty—of finding it thrown into the opposite scale.

A few private letters keep us in touch with the family at

The Grove till the close of 1860.   First comes one from Lady Theresa :

KENT HOUSE, 17*th December* 1860.— . . . The Windsor visit was not particularly lively, but I am sufficiently a courtier always rather to like a visit there than not, and I was curious to see the object of so much love and happiness as the Prince of Hesse.   The charm is not on the surface, for what he is really so like that I cannot believe he is not one of them, are those German boys and youths that make up the bands of music in the streets.   He has got just that out-of-doors, weather-beaten sort of face that they have, all looking as if the cold wind swelled the eye-lids and reddened the nose-bridges.   None of the family proposed presenting us to him, and of course we could not ask such an honour, so I got no further than the looks ; but the happiness and perfect contentment of Queen, Prince [Consort] and Princess Alice is quite unmistakable.   Princess Alice says one cannot always be thinking of rank and riches : happiness don't depend upon them only ; and she seems so much more calmly happy than I ever saw her before.   Grannie Missus [1] and the Consort were very civil, and in very good sort.

And this, of doubtful date, from Emily Eden :

. . . Your letter gave me such real warm pleasure I want to thank you for it.   It is a great point in life to have a real genuine friend—just what you have been to me, neither more nor less, for several centuries. . . . I am convinced that you and I are good-tempered people, because we have never had a tiff with each other—no little notes of explanation—it has always been a smooth path. . . . Lady Shelburne says that Lord John [Russell] was full of mischief—utterly without principle, and, in short, I am afraid he was *tout simplement* Lord John.   I cannot abide your speculation that, next year, Lord P[almerston] may play Lord John's part over again.   I think him too highminded for that, and might I trouble you, as a general rule, never to quote the Bear [2] to me, nor even to mention that there is—or even has been—a Bear.   He and the Poodle [3] were, when I was alive, almost the only two people in the world I disliked. . . . These two never did me personally any harm ; but I never could see why the Bear was not only allowed

---

[1] H.R.H. the Duchess of Kent, who died just three months later.
[2] Edward Ellice.   [3] Right Hon. George Byng, M.P.

to assume that he advised and managed and thwarted and
assisted all the distinguished men of the age, but was also the
authority by which every assertion was to be met and refuted.
' The Bear says the country does not like it' : ' the Bear thinks
Lord Grey a fool' : ' the Bear says the Queen is unpopular,' etc.
etc.   It is very trying, and I am so old and worn out, I cannot
bear it any longer (I did not mean to make a pun !) . . .
[*Cœtera desunt*].

CHAPTER XX

IN RETIREMENT

'Qui semel aspexit quantum dimissa petitis
Praestent, mature redeat repetatque relicta.'
                                        HORACE, *Ep.* I. vii. 96.

IN January 1861 Lord John Russell urged Lord Clarendon to undertake a mission to Vienna with the object, first, of treating with the Austrian government upon the cession of Venetia to the newly-formed kingdom of Italy, which should pay to Austria £20,000,000 or £30,000,000 ; second, to press for such reforms as would satisfy those Italians who would continue as Austrian subjects ; and third, to use his endeavour to dissuade Austria from a war of aggression upon Sardinia. Clarendon replied at considerable length on 20th January, declining the mission because, first, any proposal to cede Venetia would be rejected with scorn by Austria ; second, the advice of a foreigner upon the domestic affairs of Austria would be received ' just as you would receive Apponyi's at the Foreign Office if he offered advice about the ballot or the restitution of Church property to the Roman Catholics of Ireland ' ; and third, he—Clarendon—considered that Austria had a fair *casus belli* against Sardinia as being responsible for the acts of Garibaldi. ' You will say, however,' he continued, ' that you don't propose to me to go to Vienna direct, but to Berlin in order to compliment the King and to invest him with the Garter. To that I must answer that the three persons who within my recollection have carried Garters to sovereigns are the late Lord Hertford and the present Lords Wilton and Bath ; and tho' I have no vanity, still I have no fancy for being No. 4 on that list.'

The early months of 1861 witnessed the unification of Italy, the British government being the first to give official recognition to the young kingdom on 31st March. To that result Great Britain had contributed in no grudging measure, albeit that three-fourths of the cabinet had been opposed to Palmerston's policy. One may speculate upon the line Clarendon might have taken had he been Foreign Minster instead of Russell. To the last, he considered that Palmerston was acting like a Conservative at home and a Revolutionary abroad; in writing to Charles Greville he referred to the victorious minority in the cabinet as 'the three confederates,' Palmerston, Russell and Gladstone; nor have I found in his subsequent correspondence any admission that he had backed the wrong horse. It is easy to see in the light of after events how far astray was his judgment in this matter. His exclusion from office at this time, deplored by his friends as a misfortune, may in truth have been one of the luckiest chances that ever befell him. If it has been truly said that the man who never makes a mistake can never accomplish anything else, it is no ill fortune that absolves him from responsibility for the consequences of his mistake.

Private theatricals being always a favourite pastime of the Villiers family, Lady Theresa Lewis writes an amusing description of those at Nuneham:

NUNEHAM PARK, *20th January* 1861.—MY DEAREST GEORGE, —I conclude you and K. will expect some account of our visit here, so I shall begin to-day tho' the post is gone.

We found here a very large party—Lady Canning, Harriet and Car Stonor, General Peel and his two daughters, Lord Sefton, Evelyn Ashley, Parky Alderson, Sir Henry Cotterell, Victor Van de Weyer, Mr. T. Stonor (these twelve persons all went away next day), the [*illegible*] Glyns, the Norreys, the Duc d'Aumale, M. d'Estançon (that's not right), the Enfields, the Moneys, Mr. Chichester Fortescue and Mr. Ward Braham who have staid on and all go to-morrow. *The Dowager* was well acted—*very* well—by Waldegrave and Lord Enfield. Lady Enfield and Miss Money acted—the first fairly, the other *wonderfully*, considering what an awkward, silent stick she was a short

time ago. The little piece called *Q in the Morning* [?], acted by
Lady Sefton and Norreys was uncommonly good; and then
came an extravaganza written by Lady Waldegrave's brother
Ward Braham, called *The Mutiny of the Houses*—very clever and
very much to the taste of our hostess. Ward Braham, dressed
as a fairy, comes on earth to visit country houses, and summons
before him certain personated châteaux whose merits are freely
discussed. Nuneham, Strawberry Hill, Little Strawberry, the
Priory (where the coals come from) and [*illegible*], the object
being to show that Nuneham is dull, stiff and inhospitable,
except when cheered by Lady Waldegrave, and the preference
given to *all her* places—Strawberry Hill in particular. I was
told that our *host particularly* enjoyed the piece (this being the
second representation). His face gave no signs of delight; but
this might be from the intensity of his pleasure.

I had no idea of how inferior the little theatre is in effect to
that of the Grove this year; it looked quite *mean* in comparison,
and really so—not because I saw it with the jaundiced eyes of
a rival theatre and company. The management was excellent,
being by Mr. Braham—so different from Granville Vernon.[1]

It was rather a bore losing all the *jeunesse* yesterday, as of
course there was dancing in the evening with three girls and not
one young man dancer. However, the evening passed . . .
the Duc d'Aumale is quite charming, as usual, and I like his
friend very much too. . . . Sir H—— C—— was more inclined
to take part with everybody in conversation than I have ever
seen him before. I asked Lady Waldegrave if she thought he
had recovered his spirits, and she said that now he knew there
was *no* hope for him she thought he made up his mind to his
disappointment. She said Constance had given her leave to
tell ' Selina ' that there was *none*, so that she thought, tho' he
was still in low spirits at times, he would get over it quite
now.[2] . . .

In her next letter Lady Theresa refers to Lord Derby's
serious illness which had wrought apprehension among
Conservatives:

KENT HOUSE, 13*th February* 1861.— . . . It is evident to
me that the Opposition wish to keep very quiet and are not on
the look-out for an innings just now, and that the particular

---

[1] Granville Vernon, M.P. (1816-61), died on 1st February in this year.
[2] He had proposed unsuccessfully for Lady Constance Villiers.

reason for this state of things is their knowledge that Lord Derby *could not* undertake the labour of office just yet. . . . I think the Tories must be looking very anxiously to his restoration to vigour, for they have not got another man in their party that could take his place. . . . Dizzy is only tolerated as *his* foreman, but would not carry on the business on his own account, for they do hate him cordially.

In a letter from Charles Greville may be heard the muttering of the hurricane that was about to break upon the United States :

LONDON, 26*th January* 1861.— . . . I called on Lyndhurst this morning and read your letter to him. He says there is no doubt but that Anderson is the Queen's subject. Brougham writes to L. from Cannes that he can't come over to the meeting of parliament. He recommends that the North should make some *small* concessions to the South, without giving up any principle. This is useful advice to two parties exasperated as these are, when one is doubtful whether the North will make *any* concessions, and certain that *none* would be accepted by the South. . . . I am persuaded that the North will not go to war, at least not to compel the South to remain in the Union, and therefore that the separation will be consummated. Whether what remains of the Federal government will quietly submit to have all the forts and arsenals, all stores, ammunition and arms, taken possession of by the revolted States appears more doubtful, and upon this they may be brought into hostile collision. Sooner or later it seems impossible they should not quarrel and fight, whether there remain two great republics, or one large one and a number of small independent states. Any war will be almost sure to interfere with the cotton crops, and this is really what affects us and what we care about. With all our virulent abuse of slavery and slave-owners, and our continual self-laudation on that subject, we are just as anxious for, and as much interested in, the prosperity of the slavery interest in the Southern States as the Carolinian and Georgian planters themselves, and all Lancashire would deplore a successful insurrection of the slaves, if such a thing were possible.

Gladstone, determined to get rid of the Paper Duties, skilfully outmanœuvred the Lords in his budget of 1861 by including all the financial proposals for the year in a single bill, instead of drawing separate bills for each subject as had been the practice hitherto. Assuming that the power of the House of Lords was constitutionally confined to accepting or rejecting money bills and debarred from amending them,[1] he calculated that this would leave them no alternative except to pass his whole budget or create a financial deadlock by rejecting it. As it turned out, Gladstone encountered more difficulty with the Commons than with the Lords (who passed the Bill without a division), and more difficulty in the cabinet than in either House of Parliament. 'The budget,' he recorded, 'was the subject of a fierce discussion [at the cabinet], in which Lord Palmerston appeared to me to lose his temper for the first and only time.'[2] Of the cabinet on 12th April he noted— 'Cabinet, 1-3. Very stiff. We "broke up" in one sense and all but in another.' It looked as if Gladstone must be allowed to resign this time ; but the considerations mentioned by Clarendon in the following letter to Lewis prevailed with Palmerston, who yielded with perfect good humour, as was his wont when he had to yield. But he would not allow the Paper Duties to be made a government question in the Commons, where their abolition was only effected by a majority of fifteen votes.

Lord Clarendon to Sir G. C. Lewis.

Grosvenor Crescent, 13*th April* 1861.—If Gladstone went out and you were to take his place, I am sure the funds would rise and that a feeling of security and confidence would be general throughout the country ; so I cannot quite think the Cabinet is *in extremis* ; but it would have great difficulty in getting on against the desperate and unscrupulous league of Gladstone, Dizzy and Bright that would be formed within a week. . . . Gladstone must be very ignorant of public opinion to think that he would be allowed to meddle with the paper duty, and very indifferent about it when he seeks to propose a budget that everybody would condemn, instead of one that might be received with satisfaction.

---

[1] A doctrine to which Lord Derby refused assent.
[2] Morley's *Gladstone*, ii. 39.

In July the House of Commons parted with one of its most distinguished men in the person of Lord John Russell, who, despairing of the lukewarmness of his party towards reform, betook himself to the House of Lords. Sir George Lewis notes the event in his almost daily bulletin to Clarendon :

HOME OFFICE, 24*th July.*— . . . The new Earl took leave of the House of Commons last night. Some foolish people wanted to get up a valedictory debate in the House, which would inevitably have called forth a torrent of abuse from some such man as Bowyer or Hennessey. Eulogies on moving the writs of a dead man are borne ; but eulogies on the living are intolerable.

Pascitur in vivis livor, post fata quiescit.[1]

Charles Greville's failing health had caused him to discontinue his journal in 1860, being, as he wrote on the last page thereof, ' entirely out of the way of hearing anything of the slightest interest beyond what is known to all the world.' But he still visited Miss Eden, who reports as follows to Lord Clarendon, neglecting, as usual, to date her letter :

EDEN LODGE, [1861].— . . . I have been through a visit from C. Greville this wet day—crosser than any number of tongs. If he had not been deaf his visit would have been charming from the finished perfection of crossness. It really makes me laugh, and then I am obliged to find a false excuse for laughing. He was not glad the Federals were beat : why should he be ? They still had an army of a million. He did not believe a word that was said against General Butler : why should he ? Yes, he liked his nephew's marriage very well ; but as he had never seen the young lady—never knew of her existence—he could not much care—why should he ? Oh dear me ! how fatiguing it must be to take life *si de travers* ; but he looks so ill, I suppose that accounts for it. You probably know that Mrs. Hope has settled £10,000 a year on the Lincolns, besides their own £5000 ;[2] so with £15,000 a year and that house in town that destitute young couple are not much to be pitied. . . .

---

[1] Spite battens on the living ; after death it subsides.
[2] Lord Lincoln, afterwards sixth Duke of Newcastle, married Henrietta Adela, daughter of Mr. Hope of Deepdene, 11th February 1861,

Miss Eden's next letter refers to a visit which Princess Alice, who was a great friend of Lady Constance Villiers, proposed to pay at The Grove.

VILLETTE, BROADSTAIRS, —— . . . I think with you that Princess Alice's day at The Grove is rather more difficult than if she came for a week, which might be laid out according to the approved royal pattern. But it is difficult at this time of year to fill up a day amusingly. I think you ought to let her find you affectedly *in the rough*, and make her suppose that is real English private life when not expecting royalty—Lady C. fussing about the dairy and holding out a hand covered with cream to the Princess—you in a blouse surrounded by labourers. The girls in their brown holland frocks and dark gauntlets would then hand the Princess up to the *ci-devant* schoolroom and offer her one of those wretched chairs (which must have been invented by a despairing governess), and ask her if she would like a cup of tea from the housekeeper's room. I think that style of thing might answer.

The Italian settlement had cleared the Eastern horizon, but in the far West the prospect was darkening daily. First came the trouble about Mexico, where Congress had suspended payment of interest on the national debt for two years. A convention was signed in London between Great Britain, France and Spain, which Powers were to co-operate in protecting their subjects in Mexico and in compelling the republic to discharge its obligation to the bondholders.

Lord Clarendon to Sir G. C. Lewis.

GROSVENOR CRESCENT, 4*th October* 1861.— . . . It would have been very wrong if war against Mexico had been declared without the knowledge of the Cabinet ; but it would have been Palmerstonian. I remember once his agreeing with me that Vera Cruz ought to be blockaded, and desiring me to write accordingly in the Queen's name to the Admiralty. I said— 'Surely not without bringing it before the Cabinet ? '—' Oh, ah ! the Cabinet,' was his answer, ' very well ; call one then, if you think it necessary.' The matter, however, was patched up without a blockade.

The war now, if war there is to be, will not be in order to get our bondholders paid, but to chastise the Mexicans for murdering and robbing British subjects of every class unremittingly for a long series of years, and for violating every engagement they have entered into with the British government. The objection—almost a fatal one—to such a war is the absolute impossibility of reaching the people you want to punish. All you can do is to occupy 2 or 3 seaports, which are so pestilential that you are certain to kill more men of your own than of the enemy.

Lord Clarendon, who never shared Lord Palmerston's faith in *the power* of the French Emperor to keep good faith, had his belief in him further shaken by his action in the Mexican dispute. He seems to have communicated his distrust of him to the Queen of Holland, who warmly defended him against suspicion.

HOUSE IN THE WOOD,[1] 17th *August* 1861.—You will be astonished at receiving so soon again a letter from me ; but I feel in duty bound to communicate the copy of a letter I have just received from the Emperor, to whom I had written telling him how much we all wished for peace, how much we all deplore his armaments. This is his answer : [2]

'On prétend que je dois avoir quelque dessein caché puisqu'en parlant sans cesse de paix je poursuis des armaments gigantesques. A cela je dirai avec toute la France—il faut que l'Europe ait des desseins bien machiavéliques puisqu'elle affecte sans cesse à donner pour prétexte à ses armaments nos *prétendus* préparatifs gigantesques. En effet, je nie de la manière la plus formelle ces armaments gigantesques. Tout ce que je fais est en plein jour ; l'Europe doit le savoir. Pourquoi donc sans cesse jeter l'alarme sans motif ? Je fais tous mes efforts pour mettre l'armée de terre et de mer sur un pied respectable. Eh bien : je le dis sincèrement, sous ces deux points de vue la France n'a pas de forces en proportion avec sa population et ses ressources. Si je considère le matériel de la flotte, en faisant abstraction de ses navires plus ou moins bons qui sont en station sur tous les points du globe, je ne pourrais pas armer plus de dix vaisseaux. Pour le personnel, il me manque 200 officiers de marine. Quant à l'armée de terre—j'ai 400,000 hommes sous les armes, et c'est le chiffre indispensable en temps de paix ; car, retranchez

---

[1] Huis-ten-bosch, House in the Wood, a seventeenth-century palace.
[2] It is in the Queen's own handwriting.

70,000 h. nécessaires en Algérie, 30,000 à Rome, en Chine et Cochin-chine, 23,000 gendarmes (qui ne font pas partie de l'armée active), 12,000 ouvriers d'administration, 30,000 h. employés dans les dépôts pour instruire les recrues, il reste 235,000 h. comme armée active, ce qui est peu de chose pour la France. Et maintenant—quand l'Angleterre a quatre fois plus de vaisseaux que nous—quand la Prusse avec 18 millions d'habitants peut mettre sur pied 300,000 h.—on viendra me dire que je fais des armaments gigantesques ! C'est vraiment ou de la folie ou du mauvais vouloir. Je demande pardon à votre Majesté d'entrer avec Elle dans ces détails ; c'est qu'Elle comprendra combien je suis peiné de voir des relations qui devraient être si cordiales se refroidir sur la supposition de faits si diamétricale-ment faux. Aussi, quelles que soient les défiances, je remplirai mon devoir de souverain, et tout en cherchant à maintenir la paix, je ferai tous mes efforts pour améliorer les forces du pays qui, je le dis en toute conscience, sont insuffisantes.'

These are facts, not words. I feel them to be true ; and because I feel it, I hasten to repeat them to you.—Believe me, truly and sincerely, Yours   SOPHIA.

Loo, 27th August 1861.—. . . Thank you for all the kind and true expressions you use with respect to my son. This boy is a strange character ! He is the real Orange—there is no Russian or Brunswic or Wurtemberg in him. I wonder sometimes—but it is so ! and for the Orange there is a destiny to fulfil in this world—a destiny which has been bought by the blood of the first [? prince] and the sufferings of the sons. You, the relation of Queen Mary—you must be their ally.

I am sorry your faith in the Emperor is so much shaken. I more than believe—I feel him to be honest. But he may be pulled into dishonesty by perpetual doubts and bickerings. I once heard the story of a woman who was doing no wrong, but who heard herself so much calumniated by public slander that she went into wrong deliberately, saying, 'As it is said, I do it !' You see already the effect that Roebuck's speech has made—ainsi du reste. He [the Emperor] wants peace, which he likes ; his nature is not for war and strife ; but he may be brought into a dogged determination by perpetual doubting and re-criminating . . .

On the death of Sidney Herbert in August 1861, Sir George Lewis left the Home Office to become Secretary of

State for War.   Clarendon, though he set no high value
on education in the classics, entertained a just opinion of
Lewis's scholarship, and asked him for an opinion about
the performance of his eldest son, Lord Hyde.[1]

HARPTON, 14*th October* 1861.—Hyde's Greek exercises show a
considerable proficiency in the language.   Regarded as com-
positions they are fair, but not remarkable.   If he could let
me have some of his Latin verses, I should be glad to see them.
They are easier, and in some respects show better how a boy
can dance in chains.   I am going up to town to-morrow for a
cabinet on Wednesday, which is doubtless called for the Mexican
affair.   I wrote to Hammond to know what had been done, and
it seems that we have proposed to France and Spain a joint
operation for compelling Mexico to perform her engagements,
which I take for granted she is not willing to do.   War, therefore, is the inevitable consequence of such activity.   It is a pity
that we cannot leave the matter in the hands of the Americans.
A free State established by the Northerners in Mexico would have
a fine effect in equalising the balance of power in the Gulf of
Mexico. . . .

The last sentence refers to the stipulation made by the
British government before agreeing to the convention that
the United States should be invited to join it also ; but
President Lincoln's government had their hands too full to
let them attend to Mexican affairs.

Sir G. C. Lewis to Lord Clarendon.

HARPTON, 27*th October* 1861.—Our cabinet, though it might
as well not have been called, was not quite harmless.   Nominally,
we were summoned in order to decide upon the Mexican question ;
but practically the question was already decided, for proposals
had been made to the French and Spanish govts., by which we
were bound, and which engaged us to a joint occupation of the
country for the purpose of collecting the custom duties.   How,
when we have once embarked in this *galère*, we are to get out
of it, surpasses my imagination to conceive.   I anticipate mis-
understandings about the amounts to be reimbursed and the
division of the miserable spoil.   If we wished for more territory
within the tropics, there would be sense in our proceeding, for we

---

[1] The present Earl of Clarendon.

might seize a province by way of compensation for this Pacifico affair on a large scale; but as we have already got as much as we well know what to do with, our proceeding seems to me most impolitic. It is, moreover, quite certain that this measure will give deep offence to the United States govt., who will think that we have taken advantage of their weakness in order to gain a footing in Mexico, and to impede their *manifest destiny* of extension in that direction. Indeed, I feel pretty certain that the U.S. would have contrived to prevent this intervention, if their hands had not been full of their own affairs.

In addition to this Mexican business, the Cabinet agreed to interfere in the Morocco loan, and to give a quasi guarantee to a loan by an engagement to collect it by British agents. Both these scrapes seem to me quite gratuitous, and to spring out of a disinterested love of getting into hot water. . . . I suppose Palmerston will give us his views about Reform; but I do not expect that he will propose a bill for this session. The torpor of the country and the ill-disguised reluctance of the House render a repetition of the experiment highly uninviting. . . . Palmerston has been inspecting the fortifications on the southern coast. The officer who accompanied him told me that one day he was 8 hours on horseback.

. . . Graham's death was unexpected,[1] but from what he said to me when I last saw him, I feel sure that he thought ill of his chances of life. His importance and usefulness as a politician were not equal to his ability both as a reasoner and a speaker. Nobody discussed a subject in private better than he did. The article in the *Times* about him was singularly inappropriate and ignorant.

With the subsequent course of this quarrel—the satisfaction of the demands of Great Britain and Spain and the withdrawal of their forces so soon as the Emperor Napoleon's design of setting up a Mexican empire under Maximilian of Austria became manifest, we have no further concern in this narrative. Before the convention had been arranged, Lord Clarendon (who, though technically out of office, could never get *procul negotiis*) had been sent to represent the Queen at the coronation of King William I. of Prussia.

I wish you joy, wrote Lord Granville, and am delighted to

---

[1] Sir James Graham, died on 25th October 1861.

hear that your ladies are going.   Don't forget to make the
Admiralty take your carriages and horses to Hamburgh. . . .
I had a letter from Eliza[1] in a state of delight at your going,
and desiring me to write to you ' in the same sense ' ; but what
that sense was she omitted to specify.   For tourists, it would be
better to content themselves with Berlin, and imagine the
coronation.

The Americans certainly seem inclined to pick a quarrel with
us ; but I doubt their going far enough even to oblige us to re-
cognise the Southern States.   A step further would enable us
to open the Southern ports, but a war would nevertheless be a
great calamity. . . .

Of all men, Clarendon most detested pomp and ceremony,
whereof some measure was inseparable from the function
he had undertaken, so he begged Russell to ascertain from
the Queen how much would satisfy her as meeting the
dignity of the occasion.

I can tell you, replied Lord John on 6th October, without referring to the Queen, that she does not wish you to vie with the
Frenchman in pomp and magnificence.   I ask'd her some time
ago, and I said, ' Some dinners will be necessary,' to which she
assented.   The House of Commons, too, ought not to be dipped
beforehand in wasteful extravagance.   I should advise some
large dinners and a table for thirty people every day, whether
you dine or not.   Cowley suggested that you should visit Paris
on your return, unless the Queen objected.   H.M. said, ' But
I do object.   It will diminish the compliment to Prussia.'   So
that is not to be thought of.

Lord Clarendon to Henry Reeve.

HARPTON COURT, 22nd September 1861.— . . . I would have
gladly escaped the Prussian job, which is not much to my taste ;
but the Queen insisted, and the Viscount [2] and the Earl [3] attached

---

[1] Students of political memoirs must be familiar with the practice of
statesmen, especially diplomatists, of referring in intimate correspondence
to the most exalted personages under pseudonyms. ' Eliza ' and ' Joseph '
were the terms employed to designate Queen Victoria and the Prince
Consort ;   nor was there the slightest disrespect intended thereby ;
although in the trial of Rochester and Sir Thomas Overbury their enemies
did allege it as an offence that ' they had cyphers and jargons for the King
and Queen and the great men of the realm.'   The device is probably as
old as statesmanship.

[2] Palmerston.   [3] Russell.

political importance to it; so I yielded, and Lady C. and
Constance and Emily are (also on Royal recommendation) to
accompany me. The two latter are of an age to like a lark,
which is more than their respected parents do.

I need not say that my hope of doing any good by a flying
visit in the midst of a carousal is exceedingly small; but I
know the King well, and shall have no difficulty in telling him
what I believe to be the truth concerning his duties and his
interests; which I am sure he will listen to obligingly and forget
immediately. . . .

This mission to Berlin was not altogether devoid of
anxiety; considerable friction had taken place between the
British and Prussian governments, arising out of the rough
handling of a British traveller, Captain Macdonald, by the
railway officials at Bonn, and his imprisonment for resisting
them. The affair was taken up by the English press, and,
high as the value which Clarendon set upon a free press as
one of the surest safeguards of liberty, the abuse of its
freedom was very often a source of anxiety to him in dis-
charging public duty. ' It is quite unnecessary,' he wrote
to Queen Victoria from Berlin on 21st October, ' to inform
your Majesty of the enormous and wanton mischief done by
the articles in the *Times*, which offend the whole [Prussian]
nation, and particularly the army, as they are studiously
reproduced with comments in the German newspapers.
They mortify all those who desire to promote a good understanding between the two countries, and, *if anything could
do so*, they would damage the position of the Crown
Princess.' He went on to suggest that the Queen should
direct Lord Palmerston's attention to the mischief that was
being incessantly wrought by the contemptuous and in-
sulting tone adopted by the *Times* in every reference to
Germany and German institutions. Writing to her Majesty
three days later, he returns to the same subject in words
which bear as grave significance to us at the present as they
did to our sires half a century ago.

The mischief is incalculable that all the recent articles have
done us with a people who ask no better than to be our friends,
and who are indignant that we should meddle with their affairs

for no other purpose than insult. If anything could make the
Liberal party defend the King's exposition of Divine Right, it
would be the attacks upon it in the *Times*, for they say truly that,
although in principle they agree with the article, yet they must
spurn every opinion given with a manifest intention to offend.
Lord Clarendon is all the more annoyed at the *Times*' system,
because it evidently preys upon the Princess Royal's spirits, and
materially affects her position in Prussia.

The Queen followed Lord Clarendon's advice and wrote
to Lord Palmerston as ' the only person who could exercise
any influence over Mr. Delane, and, even if this should not
be much, it will be important that that gentleman should
know the mischief his writings are doing.' [1]

Delane's reply was almost incredibly impertinent.

' MY DEAR LORD,—I shall be very glad to give the
Prussians a respite from that most cruel of all inflictions—
good advice.'

Palmerston drew the Queen's attention to the difference
between a free press and one under more or less control, as
all continental journals then were, and to the constant
misunderstanding to which this difference gave rise through
the ministers of foreign States believing that what appeared
in English journals was published under sanction and with
the approval of the government.

Notwithstanding this disturbing element, Clarendon met
with a very friendly reception from the King and Queen
of Prussia. The Princess Royal (who had married the
Crown Prince of Prussia in 1858) informed Queen Victoria
that they made ' a marked difference between their marked
cordiality to him and the stiff etiquette with which the other
ambassadors are received.' The King desired him to accept
the Order of the Black Eagle, which, it may be remembered,
Frederick the Great bestowed upon Clarendon's grandfather,
the first earl.

There is a notable paragraph in one of Clarendon's letters
to the Queen, written at Berlin on 20th October.

Lord Clarendon took the opportunity of warning the Queen
[of Prussia] respecting the Emperor [Napoleon] and his *idée fixe*

---

[1] *Queen Victoria's Letters*, 25th October 1861.

—that his dynasty could only be secured by the territorial aggrandisement of France.   Lord Clarendon expressed his conviction that if the King had resembled M. de Cavour, some strong proposals would already have been made to them, but that the Emperor's plans had been foiled by the honourable character of the King.   There ought, nevertheless, to be no delusion here ; but, on the contrary, a careful avoidance of the traps which cajolery and flattery were setting for Prussia, because at any moment the Emperor might think it necessary for his own purposes in France to seize upon the left bank of the Rhine, and that all classes in France, no matter to what party belonging, would be delighted at his so doing, and his popularity and power in France would be enormously increased by it.   The Queen agreed, but was under the notion, which Lord Clarendon was able effectually to dispel, that the dilapidated state of French finances would prevent the Emperor from undertaking war upon a large scale.[1]

To Sir George Lewis, Clarendon wrote in a lighter vein.

BERLIN, 30*th October* 1861.—I have not been able to write sooner, for I have led a life of continuous racket and have never had a moment to myself.   I have scarcely been out of uniform, and have come to the conclusion that being a personage is the most irksome of all rôles that a man can play.   I am not sorry, however, that I came, as it seems (modesty apart) to have given pleasure and to have been taken as a compliment.   The coronation at Königsberg was an interesting ceremony.   I have not done much business, as everybody is in the same whirl as myself, and Bernstorff is completely bewildered by his new office and his ignorance of everything that belongs to it.   However, I am to have talks with him and the King before I go.

I am let off the visit to Vienna, which is a relief.   I would have gone there to please Lord John ; but it would have been

---

[1] The above is an extract from one of the letters referred to by Lord Granville in the following note to Lord Clarendon :

16 BRUTON STREET, *Saturday evening*.—The Queen sent for me this morning and told me that you had written some very able and interesting letters recording the conversations of the Queen of Prussia and of the Princess Royal.   It had struck her that if Palmerston or John Russell were not perfectly discreet about their opinions, it might be very injurious to the Queen of Prussia and to the Princess Royal, and she told me to ask you to give the Premier and Lord John a hint on the subject. . . .

The rest of Lord Clarendon's correspondence with the Queen on this occasion, or part of the rest, is printed in *Queen Victoria's Letters*, vol. iii.

a wild-goose chase, and I hate meddling in other people's affairs
and offering advice that is not asked for.   Then if I had gone to
Vienna and not to Paris (which the Queen objected to), we should
have been accused of some intrigue and getting up a German
coalition against France. . . .

Writing on the same day to Clarendon, Lord John shows
due appreciation of the rise of Prussia among the nations.

30*th October* 1861.— . . . The King of Prussia has before him
one of the most glorious enterprises monarch ever undertook.
If he had a little more of his ancestor Frederic and less of his
brother Frederic William, he would be at the head of Germany
in less than two years.   But he must neglect the little winnings
to be had in Sleswig and play the great game !   I should like to
be in his place.

Clarendon returned to England in November.   In one
of his numerous letters to Henry Reeve, there is a pleasant
note of a visit from Princess Alice to The Grove.   Her
Royal Highness was a great friend of his daughters.   ' The
poor little birds in royal cages,' he remarks, ' do love a day
of liberty and to try their own wings.'

Clarendon found that, during his absence from England,
relations with President Lincoln's government, which had
been in a dangerous state of tension ever since Lord John
Russell had announced in May the recognition of the
Southern States as belligerents, had been brought to the
very verge of rupture by what became known as the *Trent*
affair.[1]   Whether this was or was not a breach of international law, as it then stood, is a doubtful point.   The
belligerency of the Federals and Confederates having been
recognised by Great Britain, it was argued that she had no
right to complain if the Federals exercised the right of a
belligerent to stop and search neutral merchantmen.   On
the other hand it was a violation of that immunity from
search which the United States had always claimed for

---

[1] Messrs. Mason and Slidell, envoys of the Confederate States to Great
Britain and France, having run the blockade of Charleston, embarked at
Havana on the British mail steamer *Trent*.   Captain Wilkes of the
Federal Sloop of war *San Jacinto*, fired across the bows of the *Trent*,
boarded her and made the envoys prisoners.

themselves, and had declared war against Great Britain in 1812 for her disregard of that claim. Anyhow, indignation at such an affront to the flag was immediate and general in England; instant reparation was demanded, and the government prepared for the worst. On 10th December Sir George Lewis wrote to Clarendon from the War Office :

We are making all our preparations on the assumption that there is to be war. They will cost a great deal of money ; but, if we have war, everybody will approve of them ; and if, by some marvellous inspiration of good sense and moderation, Lincoln's govt. yields to our demands, and preserves peace, the public will probably think that the preparations had something to do with the decision of the American govt. My belief, however, is that Lincoln will commit himself before he receives our despatch.

While Lewis was writing these lines, there was gathering over the Court of England a cloud, which, when it descended a few days later, involved the whole nation and absorbed the attention of public men even more urgently than the question of peace or war. The Prince Consort had been lying ill for several days at Windsor, and his malady assumed a serious aspect, baffling the skill of the Court physicians. Clarendon had from the first entertained a very high opinion of the Prince's motives, sagacity and tact ; moreover the intimate terms of friendship to which he had been admitted had created mutual affection between them. It was, therefore, with profound anxiety that Clarendon waited for news from the sick-chamber on personal, as well as public grounds.

Lord Clarendon to the Duchess of Manchester.

THE GROVE, 14*th December* 1861.—MY DEAR DUCHESS,—You will of course hear from London more than I can tell you about the Prince. When I was there yesterday [1] the anxiety was extreme. . . . That article in the *Times* is quite like a death knell. I can think of nothing else, and yet I can't bear to think of all the consequences that his death must entail. I am sure you will have the same feeling, for you know, just as I do, what the real relations were between him and her, and how different they necessarily were from those of any other man and wife ; for no

[1] Windsor Castle.

other woman has the same public responsibility or the same
motive for being absolutely guided by the superior mind of her
husband. This habit, or rather necessity, together with her
intense love for him, which has increased rather than become
weaker with years, has so engrafted her on him that to lose him
will be like parting with her heart and soul.

We know, too, how her mind trembled in the balance a few
months ago, and yet the affection she had for her mother, compared to that for the Prince, is as one to a million, and a national
calamity may be close at hand—the loss of her reason would be
nothing else. However, there may still be hope, tho' I fear not
much. The day the news of the King of Portugal's death
arrived, he [the Prince Consort] was moralising upon it, and asked
me if I did not, like him, wonder at the cause of good men being
cut off in the midst of their usefulness, while bad ones were left
to do harm without interruption and with apparent impunity.
He little thought how soon his enquiry would become applicable
to himself. . . . There was nothing new in London about
America, nor will there be till we get the President's message,
which is expected to-night or to-morrow ; but all the private
accounts lead to the belief that our demand for satisfaction will
be rejected and that war is inevitable. If the Americans are
determined upon it, and if, as I believe, they have been looking
for an opportunity to quarrel with us, the sooner it comes, the
better, as we are not likely to have a better case to go to war
about, nor shall we ever be better, or they worse, prepared for
war. Lyndhurst is quite of this opinion, and he has a letter from
your host [1] approving all that has been done, which I am very
glad of, as it is of immense importance, when we are about to
engage in such a struggle, that the world should see we can lay
aside all party differences and unite as one man for the public
good.

The Prince Consort died on the same day that Clarendon
wrote this letter, in the very prime of life, being only forty-
two years of age. ' A national calamity,' wrote Clarendon
to Sir George Lewis, ' of far greater importance than the
public dream of. And at what a moment has it occurred !
His sagacity and foresight would have been more than ever
valuable if we are to embark in a long struggle and all its
contingent questions.'

[1] Lord Derby.

It is well known that this estimate of the Prince Consort's value to the nation was not generally held. ' Do not imagine,' says Hazlitt, ' that you will ever make people friends by showing your superiority over them. It is what they will never forgive.' The Prince had lived down much of his early unpopularity ; he had won the sincere regard of those intellectual equals with whom he came in personal intercourse ; but for the mass of the Queen's subjects he was *too good*. It is scarcely to the credit of human nature that, ever since the days of Aristides, people prefer an ideal with a few flaws in it. It almost seems as if, to become a really popular hero, one should not let himself be suspected to be perfectly free from some frailty, or at least some foible.

Some degree of disfavour the Prince was certain to incur by his laudable energy in reforming the extravagance and wastefulness which the Georgian tradition had imposed upon the Queen's household. He found forty housemaids at Windsor and as many at Buckingham Palace receiving £45 apiece in wages. He reduced this to an initial wage of £12, rising to a maximum of £18. The great rooms in these two palaces had to be lit by hundreds of candles, whereof the unburnt portions were the perquisite of one among the upper servants. This had been stretched to a license for taking all the candles daily, whether they had been lighted or not. When the Prince put an end to this abuse, he was denounced as meanly saving the candle ends.

More serious, because more reasonable, was the jealousy felt by ministers and members of parliament regarding the part taken by the Prince in State policy. We now know that his influence, though freely exerted, was always for good—a beneficial counterpoise to party polemics.

Peel, wrote Clarendon to a correspondent, certainly took the Prince into counsel much more than Melbourne, who had his own established position with the Queen before the Prince came to this country ; but I cannot tell you whether it was Peel who first gave him a Cabinet key. My impression is that Lord Duncannon, during the short time he was Home Secretary, sent the Prince a key when the Queen was confined, and the contents of the boxes had to be read and signed by her.

Clarendon always entertained a very high opinion of the Prince Consort's motives, sagacity and tact.

Lord Clarendon to the Duchess of Manchester.

17th December.—I was in London the whole of yesterday, and you will perhaps like to know the information I collected. . . . The account of his death and of the hours preceding it in the second article of the *Times* yesterday is quite correct. The Queen sent directly for the Duchess of Sutherland, for whom she has always had affection and respect, and who, perhaps, was as useful to her in the first moments as any person she could have seen. Between the most intense paroxysms of grief, the Queen was calm ; but it must have been quite heartbreaking when she went to his room to see her prostrating herself before his clothes, and then appealing to the Duchess as to his beauty and the perfection of his character. Her dominant idea, however, is duty to *him*, and her whole desire is to do what he would wish and think right for her to do in her present position. She seems to remember how much he disapproved and warned her against such extravagant grief as she manifested at her mother's death. If she can support herself in this frame of mind, it is all one can hope for ; but as yet it is, of course, early days for believing that her nervous system may not give way.

Princess Alice has shown a strength of mind and judgment, as well as tenderness, throughout, that are beyond all praise. The Prince of Wales, too, behaved quite beautifully. He threw himself into his mother's arms and said his whole life should be devoted to endeavouring to comfort her and diminish the anguish of her bereavement.

I could hear nothing about the Princess Royal, but I am afraid it will be the misery of her life not to have seen her father before he died. He thought ill of himself throughout, and the whole of last week felt sure he would not recover. It is sad to think, but I fear it is true, that he had not the benefit of the best medical aid. Holland and Clark are not even average old women, and nobody who is really ill would think of sending for either of them. Jenner has had little practice and experience, and they would have been all if Palmerston had not written a letter of such fierce remonstrance that Watson was sent for.

But Watson (who is no specialist in fever cases) at once saw
that he came too late to do any good, and that the case had got
too much ahead to afford hope of recovery. . . . One cannot
speak with certainty ; but it is horrible to think that such a life
may have been sacrificed to Sir J. Clark's selfish jealousy of every
member of his profession.

It is a great mistake the Queen going to Osborne, where every
single object must be associated with him.   It would have been
better to go to the White House or to have accepted the Duchess
of Sutherland's offer of Clifden.

When I came back last night I found that Miladi had written
to you.   It is a great vexation to forego the pleasure of seeing
you here ; but under all the circumstances I am sure you will
think we are right not to have a large, gay party within a week
of that poor man's funeral.   I would sooner be accused of
courtiership than that the Queen should for a moment think
me ungrateful for all the kindness I have for so many years
received from her and the Prince.   I know, too, that her whole
occupation will be observing the marks of respect that are shown
to his memory.   I am nevertheless grieved not to see you :
there are so many things about which I should have liked to
talk to you.

Palmerston has been shocked by the event beyond what you
have supposed possible, and is *very* far from well.   He over-
taxes his strength, and unless he makes some change in that
respect, he cannot last long.

The news from America is thought by the government, and
indeed by everybody, to confirm the notion that war is inevitable,—Ever yours sincerely,   CLARENDON.

From Lady Clarendon's Journal.

Clarendon had for so long been on such intimate terms with
the Prince that he could appreciate the extraordinary qualities
which were combined in him—extensive and most correct
learning, excessive simplicity and diffidence, with the greatest
energy and activity of mind.   His ambition was free from selfish
motives, wholly directed to furthering the interests of the
country which had adopted him and of the dynasty of which
he was the chief stay and support.   He maintained an honesty
of purpose and purity of conduct seldom, if ever, met with in
the young and prosperous—a head which was not turned by

greatness and a heart which was not hardened by the undeserved unpopularity which, at various times, he incurred from
an ignorant public which did not understand his merits and
could not believe (because he was not a British subject) in the
motives which have ever influenced him.

From Sir G. C. Lewis.

18*th December* 1861.— . . . I have a note from Lady
P[almerston] saying that he has got the gout in both feet, but
that his general health is good.   There is to be a meeting to-day
at the Council Office to make the alterations in the Liturgy.
This ought to be done by a council, but I suppose a less formal
procedure will now be adopted.   I know that the celebrated
alteration by which Queen Caroline's name was omitted was
made at a council. . . . The impression, so far as I can collect
it, is that the last mail from America is decidedly threatening,
not encouraging.

19*th*.— . . . We were told yesterday by G. Grey that the
funeral would be on Monday morning ; that there would be a
special train from Paddington, by which you could doubtless
come ; that we were to wear, not uniforms, but plain black
evening dress, with trowsers and boots.   Those who have orders
are to wear them. . . . Granville told me that the Prince never
recognised the Prince of Wales, so that he must have passed
the last day in a state of unconsciousness.

Lord Clarendon to Lady Caledon.

THE GROVE, 18*th December* 1861.— . . . The poor dear woman
seems to have no other idea than duty to *him* and to do everything that he would think right for her to do in her present
position as regards both the children and the country.   Moreover she bears in *useful* remembrance how much he deprecated
her extravagant manifestations of grief at her mother's death,
and she seems determined to avoid a renewal of them.   This
is as good a frame of mind as could be hoped for, and much better
than was expected.   I only hope she may have strength to
persevere, but she will be severely tried at Osborne, where every
object is so entirely associated with him.   Sir G. Grey saw
her on Monday and says nothing could be more touching than
her grief and her determination to be calm. . . .

Princess Alice has shown wonderful tact and judgment, as

well as tenderness, and the Prince of Wales, when all was over, threw himself into his mother's arms and said his whole life should be devoted to comforting her and endeavouring to make her feel her bereavement less. She has desired that all papers for signature should be sent to her as usual. On the whole, therefore, I hope that she will pass safely thro' this great crisis of her life. I had a line from the Queen of Prussia yesterday to say it was quite impossible for the Princess Royal to travel, so I suppose she is *in a state* ; but how I do pity her, poor child, adoring her father as she did and not to have been able to see him once more.

Miss Emily Eden tried to attune her letters to the prevailing melancholy, but that was a key in which she never could pipe for long, and she soon relapsed into her customary *causerie*.

VILLETTE, BROADSTAIRS [*no date*].—I am getting Mary to copy a few lines addressed to the Queen, which appeared in a magazine you are not likely to see because it is very *good*, and you know goodness is *not* your line. I suppose no woman in affliction was ever so felt *for* and *with* as the Queen. . . . There was one little story of Princess Beatrice you may not have heard. Mrs. Bruce writes to me—' Princess Beatrice is a most fascinating little creature ; she said to me to-day : " I had such a funny thought to-day, just for my own amusement, but it turned out an *un*proper thought so I would not let it think." ' [1] I suppose the poor child had thought of going to the play or of some diversion which did not suit a house of mourning. I had a letter from Ann Cooper quite *excédée* with the bore of her visit to Hatfield, which certainly sounds very tiresome. She says she had nothing but a straight-backed cane chair in her room whereon to throw herself to repose from her bore. But she has a devoted attachment to Lady Salisbury.

The New Year brought no immediate relief to the strain of apprehension about an American war.

Sir G. C. Lewis to Lord Clarendon.

WAR OFFICE, 8*th January* 1862.— . . . We remain in much the same state both as to intelligence and expectations. According

---

[1] Princess Beatrice was then between four and five years old.

to the last account from Lyons, the American Cabinet had decided nothing. The 30th was to be their last day, and Thouvenel's despatch had been delivered. Mercier had been extremely friendly, and so far as he was individually able, had anticipated Thouvenel's despatch. Lyons himself still thought it extremely improbable that they would agree to surrender the two men within the time limited.[1] Head thinks it likely that Seward will calculate on the surrender of the men being so unpopular as to compel his resignation, and that he will for this reason decide in favour of a refusal. It seems to me that the chances are equally balanced, but that the probability is slightly in favour of peace by some means or other.

23rd.— . . . I called on the King of the Belgians yesterday by appointment at Buckingham Palace, and had a conversation of some length with him. He is likely to remain there several days longer. The account which he gave of the Queen is, on the whole, satisfactory. It is evident that she is prepared to exert herself to see people ; but for some time to come she will see them *singly*. She fears anything like society or an assemblage of people, however small. . . .

Writing from The Grove on 31st January to Lewis, Clarendon gives a diverting description of Lord Palmerston's visit of condolence to Osborne :

I had a letter from Hayward [2] this morning. He has been at Broadlands from the 24th to the 30th, having staid the last day to keep Delane company. He says that Palmerston is as well and sound in wind, limb and digestion as he ever was in his life. . . . He (P.) seems to have gone to Osborne in a brown greatcoat, light grey trowsers, green gloves and blue studs ; which, I think, will not have escaped royal observation !

From Lady Clarendon's Journal.

3rd February 1862.—C. sent for to Osborne, altho' not in office, ostensibly to meet King of Belgians, but really from the Queen's desire to see him as a friend. It was a trying interview, the Q. désolée in tears, but Princess Alice told him next day that his visit had given her mother much pleasure, particularly as he had not tried to offer *consolation*, but on the contrary had said that

---

[1] They had done so, however, although Lord Lyons's telegram announcing the release of Mason and Slidell, dated 27th December, did not reach Downing Street till 8th January.

[2] Abraham Hayward, essayist (1801-84).

all attempt at consolation was a mockery. The Q. showed embarrassing emotion.

Lord Clarendon to Sir G. C. Lewis.

HINCHINBROOK, 12*th* *February* 1862.— . . . I am rather annoyed at some private letters of Cavour's being published, as he has grossly exaggerated what passed between him and me in some private conversation at Paris. It is quite true that I expressed sympathy for Italy and disgust at the brutalities of the Austrians (Bologna had then been *seven years in a state of siege*, and you know what that means in the Austrian code) ; but it is absolutely false that I ever told him or led him to suppose that we should go to the relief of Piedmont if she would declare war against Austria ; for even if I had not been certain that Piedmont would have been smashed past redemption in a single-handed fight with Austria, I should never have thought of committing the English government to such a course without instructions—*or with them.*

Gen. the Hon. Charles Grey to Lord Clarendon.

OSBORNE, 20*th February* 1862.—MY DEAR LORD CLARENDON,— The Queen desires me to tell you how earnestly she hopes that you will consent to form one of the committee to whom she wishes to look for advice in the selection of artists to be employed in the choice of a design, as well as in the direction of its execution. She has been so long in the habit of looking upon you as a friend, and is so convinced of your attachment and devotion to herself and to her dear husband, that she counts confidently upon your entering cordially into her feelings and giving her your best assistance towards making the proposed monument worthy of its object. . . .

The Queen has asked Lord Derby and Sir Charles Eastlake to be the other members of the committee, and she believes that the country will have entire confidence in a committee so constituted. Believe me, yours very truly,   C. GREY.

In the course of his reply, agreeing to act on the committee, Lord Clarendon said :

I stop not to enquire whether others might not be better qualified than myself for taking part in this national labour of love ; but in zeal and devotedness I will yield to no one. Nothing can be more consonant to every feeling of my heart than to share in any work which has for its object to honor the memory of the great Prince whom we have lost.

The task thus undertaken was as difficult as it was delicate. Between a sensitive Sovereign on the one hand and a critical public on the other, there was small prospect of giving general satisfaction. The nature of the difficulties may be illustrated by a few passages in Lord Derby's numerous letters on the subject to Lord Clarendon :

KNOWSLEY, 14*th August* 1862.—I have received this morning a letter from the Prince of Wales which, indeed, I may as well enclose to you, expressing himself as much pleased with our Report, and promising, in due time, a contribution of £2000 towards the suggested ' Hall.' I conclude there can be no objection to the announcement of the fact of his having signified his approval and promised the subscription. . . . It will appear in good time to counteract any bad effect which might be produced by an article (which, if you have not read, I beg you will) which appeared yesterday or the day before in the *Morning Post*, attacking the whole scheme in the most unmeasured terms, accusing us of jobbing (!), favouritism and I know not what else, and expressing an opinion that it would be scouted by Parliament. Now whatever may be the merits or demerits of the plan, it is not likely to have fair play if it is violently condemned at the outset by a paper which, however small its circulation, is supposed to derive its inspiration from Palmerston. If we have, unwillingly, accepted a responsibility which ought properly to have belonged to the Queen's government, I think we might have at least expected that we should not be subjected to attacks on the part of its avowed organs. . . .

19*th.*— . . . From a printed slip sent to me this morning ' with the Author's compliments,' you and I are likely to be excused *quoad* the jobbery, as being mere tools in the hands of Sir Charles Eastlake,[1] who, in prospect of what he is likely to meet with, is, I hope, not very thin-skinned.

20*th.*—This morning's post has brought me the enclosed, which I should have considered satisfactory had it not been for the Queen's pencil note inside. This leaves on us the responsibility of deciding, with an expression of H.M.'s wishes in favour of a course to which our judgment is opposed. . . .

---

[1] President of the Royal Academy and Director of the National Gallery.

22nd.— . . . The plan, which I received this morning, identifies Mr. Rigby Wason with the 'slip,' which, it appears, has been sent to you as well as to me. I cannot say that the mode which he has adopted of recommending his own view is of the most conciliatory character. I do not dispute but that Burlington House is in many respects a preferable site to Hyde Park in the neighbourhood of Kensington ; but it must be re-collected—first, that we had, and have, no reason to suppose that Burlington House would be made over to us ; and next, that the Queen's expressed wish was in favour of a site as near as possible to that of the late Exhibition.[1] As matters now stand, I think we have nothing to do but to wait till the Architects send in their proposals ; after which, the question must rest, where I think it should have done from the beginning, with the Queen's government. . . .

24th.—I presume that with the return of this letter of Grey's, our brisk interchange of notes will have a pause for the present. I am amused to see how Grey[2] lays the ground for letting the blame rest with us if the result should be *nil* or worse ; in short if 'it does not turn out better than he expects.' . . .

ST. JAMES'S SQUARE, *29th April* 1863.—A letter from Charles Grey yesterday contained this ominous paragraph : ' My object in now writing to you is to disabuse you of any idea you may entertain that you are *functus officio.* The Queen chose you also to advise on the details of execution, and on these I shall have to write you a letter.'

I answered this from the H. of Lords, and expressed an earnest hope on my own part, and I knew I might add on that of my colleagues (though I had no opportunity of consulting them) that H.M. would reconsider her determination ; and I pointed out the absolute impossibility of our exercising that intelligent and incessant superintendence over the progress of the work which would be indispensably required. I urged again the great importance of keeping within the estimates, and I expressed my approval of the only step which has yet been taken in calling on Scott[3] to separate his estimates for the building and the sculpture. The Queen was to see him, I think, to-day ; when she would also

---

[1] The Exhibition of 1862 was held on the space then vacant between Kensington Gore and Cromwell Road.

[2] Gen. the Hon. Sir Charles Grey, Private Secretary to the Queen.

[3] Sir George G. Scott, architect (1811-78). He designed the Memorial as a kind of ciborium to protect the statue of the Prince ; but his design for the Albert Hall was rejected.

inform him that *she had accepted* Mr. Kelk's offer to execute the
design, and to keep it within the estimate ! It remains to be seen
how Scott will receive this intimation, given without any reference to his opinion. . . . I anticipate no end of embarrassments
if we are compelled to act, nominally, as advisers. Every point
will practically be decided by others, and we, without the power
of imposing any effectual check, shall be held responsible for every
blunder, and, above all, for the expenditure of the money. . . .

So soon as the Duke of Newcastle's Commission on
Elementary Education had presented its report in 1861,
Mr. Gladstone persuaded Lord Palmerston to appoint
another Commission to deal with the great public schools—
Eton, Harrow, Winchester, and others. Lord Clarendon
was called upon to preside over the inquiry, which he was
very willing to do, having long been painfully impressed by
the methods of education at some of these schools, besides
disapproving of instruction being confined almost exclusively
to Latin and Greek. Most of May and June were spent in a
tour of inspection.

More than once during the spring and summer he received
summons from the Queen at Osborne, and mindful of the
jealousy excited at the beginning of the reign by Her
Majesty continuing to send for Melbourne after he had left
office, Clarendon was not without some misgiving as to what
ministers, especially the sensitive Russell, might feel about
this mark of preference. The Queen told him frankly that
she desired to see him as the intimate friend of her husband ;
for although she had received unbounded kindness and
sympathy from hosts of people, he—Clarendon—was the
only one who quite understood and entered into her feelings.
She told him that her mind was strained to its utmost limit
—that she had never before had to think, because the Prince
used to read and arrange everything for her, saving her all
trouble, explaining to her things which she had to sign, etc.,
and that now she had to do all that for herself.

On 16th June Her Majesty charged him with a somewhat
delicate mission. She desired him to tell Lord Derby that
she was not in a fit state of body or mind to undergo the
anxiety of a change of government, and that if the Opposi-

tion succeeded in turning ministers out of office, they would do so at the risk of sacrificing her life or reason. She added that this applied only to the current session of parliament, after which she trusted to recover strength for whatever course events might take.

Clarendon had an opportunity the same evening of communicating the Queen's message to Lord Derby whom he met at dinner with the Skelmersdales. Lord Derby seemed taken aback. ' I didn't think,' he said, ' that she was so fond of them as *that* '—not an unnatural remark, considering how lately the Queen had both distrusted and disliked Lord Palmerston. Clarendon, however, assured him that likes and dislikes had nothing to do with it ; but that a Cabinet crisis, in the existing state of the Queen's health, might bring about a crisis of a graver kind.

Clarendon's old friend Lord Howden, who had reached the rank of lieutenant-general in the army, retired from diplomacy in 1859 and spent the rest of his life at Bayonne, whence he wrote frequently on men and matters generally.

Lord Howden to Lord Clarendon.

CAMBO PAR BAYONNE, 6*th May* 1862.— . . . This is really a beautiful spot. Three Brittannick females have just passed my window—one with a hat exactly like a plate, another like a soup-tureen, and the third like a sauce-boat with the asparagi sticking out of it. . . . Did you ever read *La Reine Margot* by Dumas ? I think it is one of the most dramatick novels I ever read, and wonderful from being a dialogue from beginning to end. I have a great mind to turn it into a play. It is sadly immoral, and would not do for the English stage. You will say—how do I come to ask you this question *àpropos des bottes* ? It is not quite so. I am rather full of it, for I have amused myself by translating it into Spanish. . . . A journalist at Madrid gave me £40 for it as a *feuilleton*. I don't think the *Fiscal de novelas* will let it appear. . . . I am inclined to think the Old Woman of the Vatican will beat you all after all. It is Idea *versus* Fact, and, if facts are hard things, ideas are very

tough also, and therefore less easy to be broken.   There is much
sectarian feeling on all sides mixed up with the Italian question.
My distance from Exeter Hall allows me to proclaim my entire
conviction that religious indifference is a far better state than
religious fanaticism.   On a little examination of motives and
habits of thought, I find quite as much intolerance among
Anglicans as among Romans or Mahometans.

In the autumn of 1862 the titanic conflict in North
America had been raging for a full year and a half.   Even
during its early stages those in Great Britain best situated
to forecast the result had formed the opinion that it would
prove impossible to restore the Union by force.

Lord Lansdowne to Lord Clarendon.

BOWOOD, 14*th February* 1862.— . . . Is not the news of this
morning sufficiently bad for the Federals to afford a promise of
some good ?   I cannot bring myself to believe that the mobocracy
of New York, much less the middle classes or those who have
one particle of common sense left in them, can wish, if they do
not forbid, the commencement of a new expedition for the
subjugation of the South, with increased taxation and increased
conscription looming before them.   I conclude that they have
been made to understand that we—*i.e.* England, France and
Russia—are ready to do them a *douce violence* the moment they
give us a hint to that effect.

It would be idle to deny that Englishmen regarded the
course of the war with complacency so far, and so far only,
as it promised the disruption of the powerful, and not always
friendly, transatlantic Republic.   Nevertheless, no civilised
government could contemplate with indifference the awful
carnage and devastation inflicted upon each other by the
Federals and Confederates ; least of all, the government
of a nation with such near affinity to both combatants in
blood, in language, and in creed.
Moreover, circumstances might arise any day through
the force of which Great Britain might be dragged into the
dispute, in which she had so narrowly escaped being involved
as a consequence of the *Trent* affair during the previous

winter. Nor could there be left out of account the severe
and increasing distress in northern England arising from the
stoppage of cotton imports owing to the blockade of the
southern ports. On the whole, the public showed patience
and forbearance, all the more easily because everybody
thought that the end could not be far off, and that the war
must end in the victory of the South and the break-up of
the Union. Except Bright and Cobden, there was hardly a
public man in Britain who entertained, or at all events
expressed, any doubts about that. Thus it came to pass
that when Mr. Gladstone, speaking at Newcastle on 7th
October, committed what he noted thirty-four years later
as 'the most singular, palpable and least excusable' error
of which he ever was guilty, by declaring that Jefferson
Davis had made a nation, and that all the world must see
that the Northern States must drink of the cup which they
were still trying to hold far from their lips, although men
were staggered by this amazing indiscretion on the part of
the Chancellor of the Exchequer, they saw no reason to
differ with his diagnosis.[1] Nor did Lord Clarendon, in the
prized tranquillity of The Grove, discern the outcome of the
throes of a continent more clearly than men who had to
grapple immediately with events. In the following letters
to Sir George Lewis he refers to the independence of the
South as '*fait accompli* whatever may be said to the contrary,' though he feels more anxious than some of his former
colleagues to avoid either giving offence to the North by
precipitate recognition of that *fait*, or incurring a rebuff by
an unsolicited offer of mediation.

In proposing about the middle of September that the
government should offer mediation between Federals and
Confederates on the basis of recognising the independence
of the Southern States, Palmerston won eager assent from

---

[1] 'We know quite well that the people of the Northern States have
not yet drunk of the cup—they are still trying to hold it far from their
lips—which all the rest of the world see they nevertheless must drink
of. We may have our own opinions about slavery; we may be for or
against the South; but there is no doubt that Jefferson Davis and other
leaders of the South have made an army; they are making, it appears, a
navy; and they have made what is more than either—they have made
a nation!' (Morley's *Gladstone*, ii. 81).

Russell and Gladstone. Fortunately the rest of the Cabinet, sensible of the extreme delicacy of the situation, could not be brought to agree with their more intrepid colleagues. Lord Russell circulated a memorandum, explaining that he was convinced that it was the duty of the European Powers to intervene, and stating that the Cabinet would be asked to come to a decision at a meeting to be held for the purpose. That meeting never was held, for Sir George Lewis circulated a counter-memorandum, objecting to what he once referred to as ' the most singular action for the restitution of conjugal rights he had ever heard of.'

Lord Clarendon to Sir G. C. Lewis.

THE GROVE, 24*th* *October* 1862.—Thanks for sending me your memorandum on the American question, which I have read with great satisfaction. Johnny always loves to do something when to do nothing is prudent, and I have no doubt that he hoped to get support in his meddling proclivities when he called a Cabinet for yesterday ; but its postponement *sine die* is probably due to your memorandum. You have made so clear the idiotic position we should occupy, either in having presented our face gratuitously to the Yankee slap we should receive, or in being asked what practical solution we had to propose after an armistice had been agreed to at our suggestion, that no discussion on the subject would have been possible, and the Foreign Secretary probably thought it would be pleasanter to draw in his horns at Woburn than in Downing Street.

A proposal from us to mediate would be attributed, I expect, to a forlorn hope of getting out cotton during the fortnight or month that the armistice would last, and this would be an additional reason for rejecting it and laughing at us. . . . At the same time, I think that we ought to make up our minds, from an impartial spectator's standpoint, what arrangements would be desireable and so far practical as to have a chance of being accepted by the belligerents. . . . Between being asked to mediate and volunteering the offer there is all the difference in the world, and in the event of some great disaster to the Federal cause and an appeal being made to us or to the French Mission at Washington, I think we ought not to be unprepared with an answer. It would be necessary to agree with the French government on the subject, and the first condition of agreement should be that neither government should accept the proposal without the other.

. . . We have not yet recognised the Southern States (whose independence is a *fait accompli*, whatever may be said to the contrary), because it is not our interest to quarrel with the North ; and we submit to great privations, because it is our policy to remain neutral, and not because we doubt the utter inability of the North to impose its yoke again upon the South. The French, who have no such fears about a quarrel with the North, have long since thought that the time was come for recognising the South, and they would have done so if they had not been restrained by deference to our wishes and interests.

26th.—The Foreign Secretary's *blatt* exhibits considerable soreness, for which you are specially bound to make allowance, as it was you who procured abortion for him. He had thought to make a great deal of his colt by Meddler out of Vanity, and you have shown his backers that the animal was not fit to start and would not run a yard if he did. He is therefore taken back to the country, where he must have a deal more training before he can appear in public again. Seriously, although I think it was fortunate that the matter did not come to discussion in the cabinet (for there is generally an oozing out of what passes there, and a difference of opinion upon such a grave subject would have done harm), nevertheless, as the arrivals of the ministers for the purpose of attending a cabinet were announced in all the papers, I think a cabinet should have been held, if only to ask each other how they did, and to agree that no subject, foreign or domestic, required deliberation.

There will now be all manner of jibes at the cabinet not venturing to face itself. Johnny must have been hard put to it for an argument when he talked of the armies retiring to winter quarters, as in the time of Louis XIV. He might have remembered that last year all the most active operations, particularly those which depended on the aid of gunboats, were conducted in the winter.

I should say that your speech at Hereford was nearly as effective in checking the alarm and speculation caused by Gladstone's speech, as your memorandum was in smashing the Foreign Secretary's proposed intervention, and that you did so without in the smallest degree committing either the government or yourself with respect to the future. I was as much surprised, therefore, as yourself to observe that, in Palmerston's opinion, your speech was open to any of the objections taken to Gladstone's. I don't mean to be uncharitable, but when I read the passage it occurred to me that Gladstone, in defending himself to P., had suggested that you also had exceeded the limits of discretion.[1] In your place, I should not think it worth while to offer any explanation to Palmerston ; but if you do, I need scarcely ask you not to let him suppose that his indiscreet murmur to me had been made known to you. . . .

Lord Palmerston to Lord Clarendon.

BROADLANDS, 20th October 1862.— . . . Many thanks for your letter giving me an account of Derby's language on things in general. It is as satisfactory as, in his position, it could be expected to be. What he said about Gladstone's speech is quite true. A minister, whether speaking in or out of parliament, ought to confine his remarks to the past and the present, and to steer clear of the future, unless he is authorised to announce the result of some cabinet decision. The same remark has also been made upon part of Lewis's speech.

As to Derby's intentions for next session, nobody has a right to ask what they are ; but he will be unable to resist the pressure of Disraeli and the most impatient of his followers, aided by the blandishments of Cobden, Bright and Co. But a House of Commons defeat will not kill us, and we shall still have in reserve an appeal to the country, which I think would be in our favor. . . .

. . . As to the American War, it has manifestly ceased to have any attainable object as far as the Northerns are concerned, except to get rid of some more thousand troublesome Irish and Germans. It must be owned, however, that the Anglo-Saxon race on both sides have shown courage and endurance highly honorable to their stock.

Whence it may be seen that Palmerston, though too sagacious to publish his opinion abroad, differed not at all from Gladstone in his estimate of the outcome of the American Civil War.

---

[1] Lord Morley (Life of Gladstone, ii. 80), says he was informed that Lewis went to Hereford 'at Lord Palmerston's request,' to put things right. Lewis certainly expressed in his speech a strong opinion that the Confederates had not established their independence, and were not entitled to recognition on any accepted principles of public law.

Sir G. C. Lewis to Lord Clarendon.

KENT HOUSE, 11*th November* 1862.—Lord John [1] opened the Cabinet yesterday by stating that Flahault had called on him the previous day and had read (without communicating) a despatch from his government making the following proposal to Russia and England, namely, that they should join with France in a request to the two American belligerents to suspend hostilities for six months by sea and land. It was not contemplated to suggest any terms of pacification or to offer mediation. He added that he had received a telegram from Napier informing him that the answer of Russia had already been sent, and it was that she declined to be a party for the joint representation, but that she would support it by her minister at Washington, provided it would not cause irritation.

Having made this statement, Lord John proceeded to explain his views on the question. These were, briefly, that the recent successes of the Democrats afforded a most favourable opportunity of intervention, because we should strengthen their hands, and that if we refused the invitation of France, Russia would reconsider her decision, act directly with France, and thus accomplish her favourite purpose of separating France and England. He therefore advised that the proposal of France should be accepted. Palmerston followed Lord John, and supported him, but did not say a great deal. His principal argument was the necessity for showing sympathy with Lancashire, and of not throwing away any chance of mitigating it [*sic*].

The proposal was now thrown before the Cabinet, who proceeded to pick it to pieces. Everybody present threw a stone at it of greater or less size, except Gladstone, who supported it, and the Chancellor and Cardwell, who expressed no opinion. The principal objection was that the proposed armistice of six months by sea and land, involving a suspension of the commercial blockade, was so grossly unequal—so decidedly in favour of the South, that there was no chance of the North agreeing to it. After a time, Palmerston saw that the general feeling of the Cabinet was against being a party to the representation, and he capitulated. I do not think his support was very sincere : it certainly was not hearty. . . . I ought to add

[1] People continued to speak of him as ' Lord John,' although he had become Earl Russell.

that, after the Cabinet had come to a decision and the outline
of a draft had been discussed, the Chancellor uttered a few
oracular sentences on the danger of refusing the French invitation, and gave a strong support to Lord John.   His support
came rather late. . . . I proposed that we should *tâter le terrain*
at Washington and ascertain whether there was any chance
of the proposal being accepted.   Lord John refused this.   He
admitted there was no chance of an affirmative answer from
Washington.   I think his principal motive was a fear of dis-
pleasing France, and that Palmerston's principal motive was a
wish to seem to support *him*.   There is a useful article in to-day's
Times throwing cold water on the invitation.   I take for
granted that Delane was informed of the result of the Cabinet.

To understand the following note from Sir George Lewis
readers will remember that he and Lady Theresa continued
to occupy one half of Kent House, and Lord and Lady
Morley the other.   Villiers Lister was Lady Theresa's son
by her first marriage ;   he was now about to marry Miss
Fanny Coryton, Lady Morley's daughter by *her* first
marriage.

HARPTON COURT, 26*th September* 1862.— . . . Villiers had
great temptations to make a fanciful marriage ; but he has done
very wisely in leaving nothing to chance in a matter which
necessarily has a good deal of the lottery in it.   The Scotch
say that ' it is better to marry over the midden than over the
muir,' and certainly a marriage from Kent House B to Kent
House A complies with this proverb. . . .

Lord Clarendon to the Duchess of Manchester.

THE GROVE, 20*th November* 1862.—MY DEAR DUCHESS,—The
spirit moves me to ask you how you are before I set out for the
metropolis, where I have been and must go every day this week
for the Schools Commission, which, as far as travelling goes, is a
great bore, but as respects the business has been most interesting.   We have had before us all the biggest swells in science—
Dr. Carpenter, Sir Charles Lyell, Farraday [*sic*], Hooker, Owen,
and Max Müller.   I don't know when I have been so interested
as in hearing the opinions of these eminent men, each from his
own point of view, upon the deplorable neglect of physical
science and natural history in our system of public education,

and the national loss that is sustained by forcing all minds into the same groove and compelling everybody to study the classics, without a thought or a care whether there is any aptitude for such studies, and whether a natural taste for other and equally, if not more, important studies is not thereby repressed and its development altogether crushed. The chief task of examining these giants fell upon me as President, and I never felt more shy, as of course I did not want to expose my own ignorance more than was necessary. We are now going to have a very different batch of witnesses, viz. boys who have left school long enough to be able to judge whether their time was well or ill employed, and yet not long enough to have lost their schoolboy impressions. Can't you fancy all this being very interesting, when we consider the immense national importance of the education of the upper classes in these days of active and general competition, and the stick-in-the-mud system of our great public schools, which places the upper classes in a state of inferiority to the middle and lower? Heaven knows whether we shall be able to effect any good; but the existing state of things calls loudly for enquiry and reform. . . . I must beg your Grace to believe that I *can't stand* not hearing from you upon the plea that your letters are stupid!—of all excuses in the world for *mauvaise volonté*! Ever yours sincerely, *quand même*,

CLARENDON.

CHAPTER XXI

CHANCELLOR OF THE DUCHY OF LANCASTER

'Rerum
Fluctibus in mediis et tempestatibus urbis.'
Horace, Ep. II. ii. 84.

IT is perhaps time to give some description of The Grove—
that home to which Lord Clarendon always repaired so
gladly for repose in the intervals of a life of almost incessant
strain.

The earliest record of the property shows that it belonged
to the family of Heydon in the first half of the fifteenth
century. In the reign of George II. it was owned by Arthur
Mohun, third Viscount Doneraile, who turned the old
Catholic chapel into a kitchen, and is, or was until lately,
believed to haunt the park in consequence. Old people
used to say, when the deer moved at night, 'that's the
wicked lord on his ramble.' From Lord Doneraile The
Grove passed by purchase to Thomas, first Earl of Clarendon
in the second creation. Of the original house, if anything
remains it is hidden by repeated additions and reconstruc-
tions. The present mansion is a rambling, but substantial
structure of brick; built, as all country-houses ought to
be, without a sunk basement, standing on a well-timbered
hill facing Cassiobury Park, whence Earl Thomas brought
his bride, and whence the demesne is separated by the
winding river Gade. The two parks combine to produce
the very ideal of English landscape. Parallel with the
river runs the Grand Junction Canal, whereon deep-laden
barges with brilliantly painted sterns and rudder-heads
slip silently along—a tranquil traffic which has suffered
no change since railways began to rattle and roar through

the vale. Noble trees adorn both parks. John Evelyn
has left it on record that he advised Lord Essex in the
planting of Cassiobury ; it is probable that The Grove was
planted at the same time, for there is nothing to choose
between the stature and bulk of the trees on either side of
the river. Yet have I space to notice one tree only amid
the sylvan glories of The Grove, and that because it is the
only species of a genus unique among the green things of
the modern world, existing nowhere in a wild state, and
preserved unchanged from the Permian age through the
pious practice of the Japanese, who plant it beside their
temples, and the cultural care of the Chinese, who cherish
it for its beautiful foliage. This is the Gingko or maiden-
hair tree (*Gingko biloba*), whereof a fine specimen stands
solitary on the flat beside the river, where once was the
kitchen-garden of The Grove, before it was thrown into
pasture. This remarkable tree is now 68 feet high and
10 feet in circumference of bole at 5 feet from the ground,
and is still growing vigorously.

Of the portraits which Lord Chancellor Clarendon caused
to be painted of his contemporaries, many came to Earl
Thomas through his wife, the granddaughter of the last
Earl of Clarendon in the older line. These pictures he
brought to The Grove, including no fewer than twenty-one
by Vandyke, and others by Lely, Cornelius Jensen, etc.
Vandyke's group of Charles II., James II., and Mary Princess
of Orange was presented by Charles II. to Lord Chancellor
Clarendon. The portrait of Katharine of Braganza is the
identical canvas sent by the King of Portugal for Charles II.'s
approval before his betrothal. Therein may be seen the
singular lock of hair which the Infanta wore over her forehead, and which, says Bishop Burnet, excited the mirth of
English ladies. A full historical account of these portraits
and the rest of those which the first earl brought to The
Grove may be found in Lady Theresa Lewis's interesting
volumes—*The Lives of the Friends and Contemporaries of
Lord Chancellor Clarendon.*[1]

The fourth earl during his residence in Madrid bought

[1] Three volumes, published in 1852.

THE GROVE IN 1913.

a number of paintings by Spanish artists. Three of these, large canvases by Herrera representing incidents in the life of S. Buonaventura, hang in the entrance hall, whereof one side is entirely covered with the fine Gobelin tapestry, a reproduction of Raphael's cartoon of the Miraculous Draught, which, as recorded in Lady Clarendon's journal, was presented to Lord Clarendon by the Emperor Louis Napoleon after the treaty of Paris.

Among other memorials of Lord Clarendon's long public service may be noticed a large gold vase in the drawing-room, the gift of Los Patriotes Españoles on his leaving Madrid. It is of gold, not silver gilt, with silver ornament added. Here also is the large casket of gold, pearls and stones—all native Irish—given to Lady Clarendon by the ladies of Ireland at the close of her husband's viceroyalty.

A delightful task awaits the book-lover who shall receive commission some day to catalogue the library at The Grove, whereof the foundation was laid, and the bulk of the contents collected, by the first Earl of Clarendon, the friend of Frederick the Great and Voltaire. There they stand, thousands of volumes in orderly array—works in history, biography, and *belles lettres*, a fine collection of Greek and Latin classics, of French memoirs and Spanish literature, the latter being profusely illustrated with woodcuts, nearly all within easy arm's length (no small merit in a country-house library). Library, said I? The two libraries at The Grove suffice to hold but half the collection, which has overflowed into the drawing-room, whereof the walls are clothed with bookcases to half their height, providing that most restful and decorative of backgrounds—russet calf, soft-hued morocco struck with dim gold, and, no whit less full of promise to the bibliophile, plain grey and brown paper backs. But one sighs for a catalogue, for as a book without an index so is a library without a catalogue.

With old paintings and books of all ages, there still lacks something to make an ideal country home, to wit, flowers, and these are here in profusion. The garden of The Grove is but a roofless apartment in the suite of reception-rooms,

Lady Theresa Lewis to the same.

KENT HOUSE, *25th November* 1862.— . . . I have seen
George at the War Office and have just brought him home. He
has seen the Princess Alexandra, and thinks her very pleasing,
but *not a beauty*—rather too thin ; but the interview was short,
and he does not see well.

(George now dictates) : I had not time to write to you to-day
after my return. I have seen Palmerston this morning : the
result is that there is *no chance* of the throne of Greece for Prince
Alfred being entertained by our government. The Queen herself
is strenuous against the idea, and Lord Palm. has consented to
act in that sense. What he wishes is that the Protocol excluding
members of the three royal families should be strictly observed.
. . . I hear Lady Yarborough is going to marry Mr. Monson,[1]
much younger than herself. She is a pretty little woman still ;
but Charles [Villiers] does not like *him*—says he lives at Brooks's,
pretends to be even ultra in his Liberalism, and then votes
against the government on every opportunity. . . .

The question of the crown of Greece had been brought
about through the revolution whereby Otho, King of the
Hellenes, had been deposed, and the nation called upon by
the Provisional Government to elect another king. The
voting was well-nigh unanimous in favour of Prince Alfred,[2]
who had become well known in Athens when serving in the
Mediterranean squadron ; but, other considerations apart,
there was the convention of February 1832, whereby Great
Britain, France and Russia had bound themselves not to
put forward any member of their respective royal families
as eligible for the crown of Greece.

The following note from Lewis refers to the cession of
the Ionian Islands to Greece, which islands had been placed
under British protectorate by the Congress of Vienna in
1815 :

WAR OFFICE, *7th December* 1862.— . . . The Cabinet yesterday was not well attended. The Dukes of Newcastle and Argyll,
Stanley and C. Wood were absent. Newcastle, under the cir-

---

[1] Eldest son of the sixth Lord Monson, whom he succeeded in 1862 ;
he was created Viscount Oxenbridge in 1886. His marriage with Lady
Yarborough (widow of the second earl) did not take place till August 1869.
[2] Created Duke of Edinburgh in 1866.

cumstances, was an important hiatus.   Granville was present.
Lord John opened his case briefly, and not forcibly or clearly.
Palmerston supported him in a few sentences : the Cabinet then
discussed the question.   The general feeling was in favour of
the cession.   The Chancellor laid it down with much solemnity,
that the measure would be tremendously unpopular, but nobody
seemed to share this view.   The result was that the Cabinet
consented to steps being taken for obtaining the consent of the
four Great Powers to the cession.   If this consent should be
obtained, the question was to be submitted to the Ionian parliament for their consent.   The ex-King of Portugal is the candidate
whom we are to try to carry.

Kinglake had been at work on his great history of the
Russian war, the appearance of which was anticipated with
some eagerness by the public, and, as it seems, with some
trepidation on the part of those responsible for the War
Office in 1854-5.

Lord Dalhousie to Sir Charles Wood.

BRECHIN CASTLE, 29th November 1862.— . . . I don't know
whether you are aware that whoever got possession of Lord
Raglan's papers after his death placed them in the hands of Mr.
Kinglake, who has been threatening ever since to publish what
he calls a history of the Crimean campaign.   Murray the book-
seller has declined to embark in it, and I hear that Kinglake is
trying to get Messrs. Blackwood in Edinboro' to bring it out for
him.   Both Newcastle and I will be able to keep our own heads
with our own sticks ; but such a publication, based upon such
papers, might be of the greatest possible inconvenience so far
as it might affect the good understanding with the Emperor of
the French.   I think it might be well if you mentioned the matter
to Palmerston.

Reeve asked Lord Clarendon to review the first two
volumes for the April number of the *Edinburgh*.   He
declined, for the reasons given as follows :

THE GROVE, 11th January 1863.— . . . There are many
reasons why I should not like to review the work ; but I am
equally obliged to you for the offer, and I shall, of course, communicate to you unreservedly my opinions upon it. . . .

23rd.— . . . Although I 'm sure it is unnecessary, yet it occurs to me to ask you not to quote my opinion of Kinglake's book ; as, for the present and for a variety of reasons, I should prefer its not reaching him in an indirect manner. . . .

25th.—Hayward has written to ask my opinion of the book. He is at Broadlands, and says that Palmerston is, on the whole, well pleased with the portrait of himself, and that Lady P. is enchanted. I think as you do of the second volume. There is nothing finer that I know of in the English language than those successive battle pictures. He beats Napier out of the field. The *Times* does not seem to like the portrait of itself. I thought the article yesterday ingenious. I shall hear shortly what effect the book produces at Paris. Persigny will, of course, prohibit its entrance, but he will not be able to shut out all the papers that contain extracts. . . .

25th February.— . . . Kinglake would induce people to believe that the Emperor was under an urgent necessity to turn away the intention of his subjects from his action at home, and that he therefore dragged us into the war fourteen or fifteen months after the *coup d'état*. It would, I think, be worth while to get some facts respecting his status in France at that time. If I am not mistaken, he was in no trouble or danger at all ; for the nation had accepted him as a sort of deliverer from the *Rouges*, the fear of whom had been terrifying people out of their senses.

Lord Clarendon went on to give so many suggestions as to the line Reeve should take in dealing with the book, and afterwards made so many additions and alterations on the proofs, that the article may almost be taken as coming from his own hand. The immediate result was a rupture of friendship between Reeve and Kinglake for three years. Clarendon's part in the review was not known till the publication of Reeve's *Memoirs* by Sir John Laughton in 1898, by which time the public had many other matters pressing more straitly on their attention than the Crimean War ; but that article in the *Edinburgh* remains, in virtue of its real source, the most authoritative vindication of the motives of the Aberdeen government in going to war.

Lord Clarendon to Henry Reeve.

GROSVENOR CRESCENT, *4th March* 1863.—The article quite comes up to my expectations and I like it very much. I cannot

think it obnoxious to the charge of dullness ; but on that point
I may not be an impartial judge as the diplomatic details are to
me intensely interesting. You have not spared Kinglake ; but
you have not hit him harder than he deserves, for the right way
of dealing with such an historian is to smash his work as a history,
and thereby take the sting out of personalities and misrepresenta-
tion that are too numerous for refutation in detail. . . . Pray
quote Kinglake's reasons why information was not procured—
Lord Stratford's mind being unable to go beyond diplomacy,
and Lord Raglan not thinking it gentlemanlike to have to do
with spies. I believe that the 10th vol. of the Great Duke's
correspondence, just published, is full of spy letters, and it
might be worth while to allude to this (if the fact is so [1]) with
reference to his pupil,[2] who was always trying to follow his
example, and who must have been at his elbow all the time
that he was making use of these spies and getting information
wherever he could. It was unpardonable both in Lord R[aglan]
and Lord S[tratford] to have remained in such ignorance when
there must have been plenty of Greeks and others ready to go
to Odessa or elsewhere and procure information respecting the
number of the Russian troops.

A passing notice might also be taken of Raglan's system of
not trusting the government he served, and not sending them
information which they might carry to a newsman. . . .

On 14th April 1863 the House of Commons, on the Prime
Minister's motion, adjourned out of respect for the memory
of the Secretary of State for War, Sir George Cornewall
Lewis, who had died the day before at the comparatively
early age of fifty-six. Upon Clarendon Lewis's death fell
as a blow of peculiar severity, for not only had his brother-
in-law become the most intimate and esteemed of his male
friends, but Lady Theresa, for whom Clarendon's affection
was almost passionate in its intensity, was thereby widowed
a second time. Lewis was, indeed, well worthy of friendship,
and one of his colleagues in the Cabinet has well described
the qualities which gained for him the esteem of men of all
parties :

Lewis, although he had never been prominent as a party
politician, had a great and just reputation, not only for learning

---

[1] It was so : see the reports of spies printed on pp. 55, 59, 68, 82, 100-5,
166-7 *et passim* of Wellington's *Despatches*, vol. x.   [2] Lord Raglan.

and literary ability, but for judgment and wisdom. He became one of the most valuable of all our members, not so much in finance, as in all the questions of international law which a great war and prolonged negotiations were bringing to the front. His calm, judicial mind, and the utter absence in him of political passion of any kind, made him an invaluable counsellor. I have never seen in any man, except in Lord Aberdeen, a mind so singularly dispassionate, combined with such wide knowledge and perfect integrity of character. He was one of the very few men I have ever met in the world whose formed opinion on any difficult question would be to me in itself a very strong presumption in favour of any course which he approved. He was a real authority on a whole range of subjects, equally helpful in thought and action. He had a quiet and very grave manner, with a demeanour so staid and thoughtful that the saying ascribed to him that ' life would be very pleasant if it were not for its amusements ' is a perfect translation of the impression made by his intercourse with the world. He was a great addition to the Cabinet.[1]

The Queen of Holland to Lord Clarendon.

HAGUE, 24th April 1863.— . . . Sir G. Lewis's death seems to have been felt by all as a calamity ; ' a safe man,' as public opinion qualified him, is indeed no ordinary praise ! Public esteem is of still greater value than public admiration. But what I say has been repeated many times. However, I wish to repeat that any event in your public and private life cannot leave me indifferent. I had a strange visit to-day—Mr. Spurgeon, the Baptist preacher. He preached in one of our churches yesterday : I did not choose to go, but I wished to talk to him. I found eloquence, talent, I hope faith, but a good deal of conceit and self-admiration—as much, and perhaps more, vanity than the more worldly people. In the public the enthusiasm was not kindled. He leaves to-day to preach in other towns of this country. . . . Tho' unknown to Lady Clarendon, will you kindly express to her all the part I take in her loss.

The abrupt end of Clarendon's close and constant correspondence with his brother-in-law leaves us without any direct clue to his views upon the Dano-German question, which was brought into an acute phase in this year by the

[1] Duke of Argyll's Autobiography, i. 540.

death of Ferdinand VII. of Denmark and the accession of
Christian IX., father of the Princess of Wales. We have
heard Clarendon condemning the indignity of a power that
barks without any intention of biting ; must he not, then,
have blushed for England when Palmerston, after announcing to the House of Commons on 23rd July that if any
attempt were made to infringe the territorial rights of the
Danish crown, the invaders would discover that it was not
with Denmark alone they would have to contend, 'found
that, of all his colleagues, Russell alone was ready to support
his chief in taking up arms for Denmark, and that without
allies, if need were '

In August there was held a conference of German
sovereigns and princes at Frankfort, on the initiative of
the Emperor of Austria, to discuss a project for reforming
the Bund. Only Prussia was unrepresented there—an
ominous exception ; for nobody thought of attributing
the absence of the King of Prussia to the indolence or
negligence of his dread minister. Clarendon, having gone
to Wiesbaden for the waters, was asked by Lord Russell
to go on to Frankfort in order that he might witness un-
officially the proceedings of the confederacy.

4th October.—I did so, he wrote to Lord Howden, and was
interested and amused. It was an opportunity which may
never occur again of meeting the sovereigns of Germany, great
and small. . . . The impression made upon me by the Emperor
of Austria was very agreeable. He had none of the proud
manner of which, at one time, we heard so much ; but, on the
contrary, he was frank and gentlemanlike, and told me the
difficulties in which Germany was placed by such an effete institution as the Diet and the advances making by democracy,
which for the first time were dangerous, because the people
had reason and justice on their side. It may be that some good
will come, perhaps before the close of the present century, from
a public avowal by congregated Sovereigns that their subjects
had grievances of magnitude, and that delay in redressing them
was full of dynastic danger.

In another letter Clarendon described the Emperor as
' not a bad coachman and looks well on the box, but I begin

to fear that he will be unable to drive the team he has harnessed together here ; and if they upset his coach, it may be serious, as Plebs will then start one of his own, and their Jehu will drive furiously.' . . . He tried to convince the Emperor of the advantages of Free Trade, both as a lubricant in government and a cement for the alliance of States.

As the Emperor expressed a hope that the alliance between the two countries [Austria and Great Britain] might now become closer, I said that nothing so much promoted political alliances as the cultivation of reciprocal interests, and that our example was well worthy of imitation by Austria.   Without the previous abolition of the Corn Laws, I observed, we should perhaps not have weathered the difficulties of '48, and without the free interchange of our products with the whole world we should not have met the cotton famine in '63 with an increased revenue.   Politically and financially, these were the results of Free Trade, and as such they appeared to me peculiarly applicable to Austria.   The subject seemed rather to interest him, and he said he clearly saw that Austria should follow in the footsteps of England.

On his return journey Clarendon stopped in Paris and held some long conversations with the French Emperor and his minister Drouyn de Lhuys on the subject of Mexico and Italy, all of which he reported at length to Lord Russell, who was spending his holiday at Meikleour. ' Your very interesting letters,' he wrote, ' confirm what I always thought—that a hundred spies cannot ascertain so much as an English gentleman in whom Princes and Ministers believe that they can safely trust.'

But in describing to the Queen the proceedings at Frankfort Clarendon seems to have carried frankness beyond the verge of discretion. ' Clarendon,' wrote General Grey to Sir Charles Wood, ' managed to irritate the Queen a good deal by the contemptuous tone in which he spoke of Germany ; and, by his account, she gave it him pretty sharply, telling him he forgot the stock she came of, and he should not speak that way to her. . . . The Crown Princess was still more angry with him ; but I think it very possible *she* may have deserved a little rebuke.' . . . The effect of this little unpleasantness was to be felt in a later year.

As a minister *en retraite* Clarendon enjoyed more leisure than usual for correspondence with friends.

Lord Howden to Lord Clarendon.

1st August 1863.—I was reading the other day at Cambo an old journal and I copied out of it this page or two which I thought might amuse you.

'MONTEVIDEO, 10*th July* 1847.—Garibaldi came to see me— a small, thin, interesting-looking man, apparently about five-and-thirty, having somewhat the look of a Parisian *Rapin*, with a full-grown beard, light hazel eyes and long brown hair hanging down his neck, not giving one at all the idea of a ferocious bandit or capable of the cruelties he is said to have committed, or permitted, at the capture and sack of Colonia. In speaking of Pereira, who had just been named chief minister by the government of Uruguay, and who was leaving the room when Garibaldi entered it, the latter said—" He is a rich man, and therefore well spoken of." I did not quite understand this remark coming from him ; but I supposed he meant that Pereira was too well off in the world to be suspected of being easily bribed, an accusation so easily and constantly made here right and left. I answered that I hoped Pereira had a better foundation for his good name than his money-bags : that surely good opinion was not a necessary consequence of riches, for I had heard, even from his enemies the Rosistas, that he (Garibaldi) was as poor as he was brave, and that in his case, as a chief who had had opportunities of being otherwise, the publick opinion of the country, quite as much as myself, must indubitably think the better of him for it. On my saying this, to my surprise and as a peep into the human heart, Garibaldi blushed crimson up to the eyes.

' Now, psychologically, why did he blush ? Was it at receiving a compliment of any kind from a stranger ? was it because he really was very poor ? (not that I believe he had ever read Juvenal—

> Nil habet infelix paupertas durius in se,
> Quam quod ridiculos homines facit).

' Was it, peradventure, *that he was not poor*, and that he had quietly feathered his nest under cover of a disinterested reputation ? Somehow or another, I hardly think this ; but some men are ashamed of being thought rich, others of being thought poor,

and Garibaldi may be among the latter.   Certainly his outward
man well justified [1] his good reputation.   He had on a thread-
bare, once-black *redingote*, buttoned to the chin without the
vestige of a shirt or waistcoat, and he kept twirling in his fingers
a little greasy cap such as the German students wear.   He spoke
little and he seemed discontented ; but he pleased me from something peculiar in his manner, and that in spite of the cataracts
of abuse I had heard poured on him at Buenos Ayres.'

PARIS, 13*th September.*— . . . I have just finished Sir G.
Lewis's book on the Astronomy of the Antients.   How admirable
it is : of what vast erudition and of how little dogmatism ! . . .
The only literary topick here of the moment is Renan's *Life of
Jesus*.   I do not like it.   If you are in a philosophical mood, it
is too hypothetical—if you are irreligious, it is too conceding
(what the Spaniards call *accomodaticio*)—if you are devout, it
is too destructive. . . . With regard to writing by post, there
was a time when my correspondence was thought interesting.
Olozaga told me he had seen a file of my letters copied at the
Ministry of the Interior [at Madrid] ; but I have a great idea
that nobody takes the same trouble now.   However, if you ever
had anything you wished to send me without any chance of
violation, you had better enclose it to Cowley.

From the Hon. Emily Eden.

EDEN LODGE [1863].— . . . It strikes me as a very gouty
year.   To-morrow, if it is fine, I shall make my drive a grand
gout progress, and ask after you, and Lord Derby (who has
arrived at a slight use of his left hand), and Shelburne [2] (who had
arrived at the whist stage).

I see what Princess Louise means about the ' enforced idle-
ness ' of the Prince of Wales, which may lead to evil.   The
Prince Consort would have devised some work for him—made
him Regent of Scotland or a clerk in the Audit Office or bailiff
of the home farm—something distinguished that would have
kept him out of harm.   I think it so wise of the Duke of Devonshire to have got Lord Hartington made a Lord of the Admiralty.
It will be a counter-irritation to Skittles !

RICHMOND [1863].— . . . I have been seeing another friend
of yours, Lady Cowley,[3] who is at Twickenham with her sister,

---

[1] ? Accorded with.
[2] Succeeded as fourth Marquess of Lansdowne in 1863.
[3] Olivia, daughter of Baroness de Ros and wife of the first Earl Cowley.

Mrs. Broadhurst, and very good-naturedly found me out and paid me a long visit. What an odd thing to see an old friend so utterly unchanged by the wear and tear of life—the same joyousness—the same good-nature—the same little corkscrew curls— a great deal of the same beauty. I never saw such a woman. . . . It was a most satisfactory interview with a new friend, and, except for all those children, she might be Olivia de Ros still. You must hear much more gossip at the Grove than I do here, and I suppose you know about a handsome Mrs. Bulkeley's affair with that detestable Colonel Armytage, and that her husband and he have fought. It is a pity the husband did not kill him just a little, for he is always making mischief, and poor Fenella goes on liking him all the same.[1] Lord Normanton, aged 78, marries that giddy young thing Sylvia Doyle, which is fortunate, for with her youth and inexperience she might get herself talked about.[2]

The other day we saw a party of sportsmen in Richmond Park, which turned out to be the firm of Wales, Cambridge and Greece. The beaters signed to us to keep back, so we followed at a foot's pace, saw them shoot 20 partridges, heard Cambridge objurgate and swear to a vast amount, thought Wales very pretty, and Greece nothing particular,[3] and came away much edified. When the Duke of Cambridge lets himself out in a loose shooting-coat, I think he reminds me of the dear lost Henry VIII., of course minus the six wives.

In the following letter the Queen of Holland refers to Lord Russell's despatch of 25th November declining the invitation of the Emperor of the French to a congress of European Powers to deliberate upon the conflict then raging in Poland, the strained relations between Austria and Italy, the chronic anarchy in the Danubian principalities, the occupation of Rome by French troops, and the demand made upon Denmark by Austria and Prussia for the cession of Schleswig-Holstein. Clarendon, feeling hopeless of any agreement among the Powers upon so formidable an array of conflicting interests, had expressed general approval of Lord Russell's despatch ; but Queen Sophia, thoroughly

[1] Colonel Armytage, grandson of Sir G. Armytage of Kirklees Park : was in the Coldstream Guards, and married the Hon. Fenella Berkeley, daughter of the first Lord Fitzhardinge.
[2] This marriage did not take place.
[3] George I., King of the Hellenes.

alarmed by Bismarck's aggressive attitude, expressed her disappointment strongly :

HAGUE, 13th January 1864.— . . . You ask my opinion about Lord Russell's answer. I must candidly express that I think it *deplorable*. It is the deathblow of an alliance which ought to have dominated the world, managed the affairs of the Continent, assured us an era of peace. It is over. England wishes to forget that the Emperor has been her faithful ally, that he helped her in the *Trent* affair, that he fed your people in the commercial treaty.

You answer him with scorn. You deeply move and insult public feeling in France, always ready to turn against you, and your present proposal of conferences in the Danish question proves the *ultimate necessity* of settling the disturbed state of Europe. The Germans are wrong in their violent pretensions ; but it is no easy matter to give to understand to a *people*, who wishes to become a *nation*, that whatever they claim or urge is wrong and folly. If the congress had been a Tower of Babel, at least it would have taught to lurking democracy the sincere desire of the Governments to do something to settle claims and wrongs which are growing daily more clamorous. I believe the Emperor will look on in silence and peace ; but I always feel afraid of an ultimate alliance between France and Russia. . . .

I have no courage to read over what I have written. I hope my contradiction has not displeased you ; but I feel the world is getting more unsettled and feverish than ever. Come what may, I know, dear Lord Clarendon, that we remain friends, and I am ever truly and faithfully yours,   SOPHIA.

When the Duke of Newcastle resigned the Colonial Office in March 1864, Palmerston asked Clarendon to come and see him. He said that the only reason he had for not inviting him to take the vacant department at once was the growing jealousy of the House of Commons about so many of the chief offices of State being held by peers. Accordingly, he dared not do so, as the Whips told him that, should a hostile motion be made on the subject in the Commons, it would be carried against ministers. ' Wherefore,' said Palmerston, ' I propose to have Cardwell appointed to the Colonial Office, and if you will kindly consent to take the Duchy of Lancaster it will be a most friendly act, for the whole Cabinet are clamouring to have you back.'

Clarendon answered that he entirely approved of the Secretary of State being in the House of Commons. As for himself, he greatly preferred being out of office, and the only consideration that would induce him to resume it was that the government were not likely long to survive the discredit brought upon it through the Mazzini business, which, he thought, had been grievously mismanaged. He asked Palmerston whether he did not think Lord Wode-house [1] would be of as much use as himself as a prop. ' Not at all,' said Palmerston, ' he has not a tenth of your ex-perience ; besides, it is you that the Cabinet wants.' ' Very well,' sighed Clarendon, ' *la nuit porte conseil.* I 'll let you have my answer to-morrow.'

Lord Clarendon to Lord Granville.

THE GROVE, 22nd March 1864.— . . . You must have had hundreds of protests against Lowe, whose name seems every day to smell less sweetly in the nostrils of the country.[2] A proposal to take the Duchy of Lancaster which Palmerston made me yesterday was nearly as unsavoury to my nostrils. . . . I did not give P. a definitive answer, as there was no hurry, and no arrangement can be made till parliament meets and Cardwell's writ can be moved. My detestation of office is so great, and has increased so much during the last five years, that I would not give P.'s proposal a moment's consideration if I did not believe that the days of the government were numbered, and that it is *uncivil* not to take an oar in a sinking boat. . . . I advised Palmerston most strongly to put Wodehouse in Cardwell's place, but he would not. . . .

24th March.— . . . I sent my acceptance to Palmerston. As you know how genuine my hatred of office is, you will understand how much it cost me to make the effort you recommended. If the government had been prosperous and sailing before the wind, I could not have brought myself to say Yes ; but seeing breakers

---

[1] Created Earl of Kimberley in 1866.

[2] Mr. Lowe, as Vice-President of the Council, had displeased both the country and his colleagues by his educational policy. The House of Commons passed a vote of censure upon him on 12th April, in consequence of which he resigned.

ahead, I could not refuse an oar in the boat with old friends. . . . The generous public will think me very greedy for the sweets of office, and Palmerston very wicked for not bringing forward any of the latent talent that is always talked of, but never appears, as it is withering away under the scornful pride of Whig aristocracy.

Lady Theresa Lewis to Lord Clarendon.

STAUNTON PARK, 25*th March* 1864.— . . . This morning brings me Katty's letter saying your acceptance has gone. I need therefore do little more than tell you how very glad I am you have decided as I feel to be right. There must always be many occasions in which a man of any weight in public life or in a profession must *s'effacer*, and not think of what is agreeable to himself. . . . Your services are asked for in the Cabinet which represents the party to which you belong ; the head of that Cabinet is the only man in political power to whom you have always said you owed some obligation for the hand he extended to place you on the ladder in your youth ; a ladder on which you afterwards ascended by yourself. You know that the Queen needs the support of ministers on whom she can trust, and that she bitterly feels the change in her position since this ministry was formed. The loss of her husband has changed her from a powerful sovereign (which she was with the knowledge and judgment of her husband to guide her opinions and strengthen her will) into a weak and desolate woman with the weight of duties she has not the moral or physical power to support. Death has robbed her of an active, intelligent, zealous minister and persuasive speaker in Sidney Herbert, and of the wisdom, knowledge and experience of my beloved husband ; and now illness incapacitates the Duke of Newcastle from adding his honesty and experience to her counsels. No doubt the state of Europe is very critical, and that England needs the guidance of men of experience, ability and foresight to save her, if possible, from being involved in these dangers. Your own opinion of such a Cabinet as Lord Derby would bring in cannot inspire you with the slightest confidence. . . . All that remains for Lord Palmerston to do is to endeavour to add strength to his government by recovering to his aid one whose services neither he nor most of his colleagues ever willingly forewent, and I do not think it would have been the part of a good citizen, of a good subject and good friend to the Queen, or of a steady adherent to party ties and private friendship, had you not accepted an oar in the boat when breakers are ahead. . . . The office of Chancellor of the Duchy is utterly unimportant ; but it is your *advice* that is far more important than administration of an office in the present crisis. . . . I have been anxious since I got your letter yesterday morning for fear you should decide otherwise than you have done ; tho' I hoped your duty and affection to the Queen would have its influence. . . .

'I keep thinking of that last ministry' [Lord Derby's], wrote Emily Eden, ' to reconcile myself to the idea of my friends being again in office. It is a prodigious blow to all their comfort in life in all ways. I am sure that in another and wiser world, ambition is *the* vanity we shall most wonder at—so unsatisfactory and such hard labour. It is a grovelling propensity too, a hankering after abuse and ingratitude. However, never mind ; there you are and we must make the best of it.'

Lord Clarendon to Lord Howden.

6th April 1864.— . . . As five years of freedom had augmented my inveterate dislike of office, you may suppose that I made a gallant resistance, quite *à la Danoise* ; but at last I could not help taking an oar with old friends in a boat which they believed to be sinking, and in which they fancied I might be of some use. If the government had been as clear of some of the worst shoals a fortnight ago, nothing would have induced me to say Yes.

The *Times* of 4th April made uncharitable comment upon Clarendon's appointment, assuming that he had no higher motive than personal ambition, and that his acceptance of the Chancellorship of the Duchy—' the cushion of the Cabinet '—proved that he endorsed the whole foreign policy of the government, than which nothing could well be further from the truth. Clarendon felt a good deal nettled by this attack.

' Palmerston,' he wrote to Lady Clarendon on 5th April, ' was full of flattering speeches at my joining, but I cut them pretty short, as I am sure that if he had taken the ordinary trouble that was due to one who had obliged him, Delane would not have ventured to write as he did. I told Palmerston that in a few lines there was a concentration of everything that was offensive and annoying to me ; moreover I said this so sharply that *he* was annoyed, and owned that the article had surprised him very much, as he had himself written to Delane to announce the changes, which makes it clear that he either said something disparaging of me himself, or left me to be dealt with by the malignity of Delane and Lowe. . . . I have a pressing letter from Johnny asking me to assist him at the conference.[1] That will be an awfully long business and a most unsatisfactory one, I am sure, as we shall be the only people there not bent upon defeating the objects for which they profess to meet. Of course I could not decline. . . . I have accepted a dinner for you and me at Stafford House on 13th April. I concluded, of course, that it was to meet Garibaldi, and Johnny tells me that it is, and that he and Palmerston have agreed to go there.

If the relations between the Prime Minister and the *Times* newspaper strike one as somewhat strange in these days, still more so must the action of the Sovereign in writing an anonymous letter to be published in that journal. It appeared in the *Times* of 6th April, and consisted of a vigorous remonstrance by Her Majesty against the complaints about her seclusion ; explaining that the cares of State taxed her strength to the utmost, and stating that the rumours about her intention to resume drawing-rooms and other social functions were unfounded.

'*Anonyma's* communication to the *Times* yesterday,' wrote Lord Clarendon to his wife on 7th April, ' has produced a very painful impression, and is considered very *infra dig.* for the Queen. It is her own writing, and Grey took it straight from Windsor to Delane. By chance he met Puss [2] on the way, who urged him to consult some of the ministers before the Queen so committed herself, but he would not hear of it. . . . Lady Palmerston told me that Pam had made up his mind to speak seriously to her on the subject ; but I am sure he won't.'

Garibaldi arrived in London on 11th April, and had all the town at his feet. The Clarendons met him next day at a luncheon given by the Dowager Duchess of Sutherland at Chiswick. Lady Clarendon notes in her journal that

---

[1] Held in London in April by the plenipotentiaries of Austria, Prussia, Russia, France, Sweden, Norway and Denmark to endeavour to settle peaceably the dispute between Germany and Denmark.
[2] Lord Granville.

far too much fuss was being made about the hero—the ladies curtseying to him as if to royalty.

On the 13th Clarendon went off to Paris, commissioned to try and arrive at some understanding with the Emperor about the approaching conference on the Danish question. During his absence he kept Lady Clarendon well *au courant* with his proceedings :

16th April 1864.— . . . The sensation about my visit is on the increase and is really too absurd.   Fancy our caring a straw about any Frenchman coming to London or his being asked by everybody whether he was satisfied with the Queen.   This was the case, however, with me last night at the magnificent banquet and subsequent ' swarree ' that the Cowleys gave in my honour, and I talked more in those four hours than I have done in any four days of late.   I found myself a personage, and can only hope that I behaved as such, and that five years much more pleasantly engaged at the Grove did not make me appear rustic. The compliments were too absurd and almost offensive from their exaggeration—my return to the government was of European importance—the salvation of the alliance with France—the means of bringing the Emperor to a true view of his own interests —and bosh of that sort without end. . . . I had very long talks with Persigny, Fould, Rouher and Walewski—all satisfactory as regards peace and the English alliance.

The *accueil* of the Emperor yesterday was never warmer. He said he was delighted to have the opportunity of frankly stating his views upon all things to an *ancien ami*, and he made out just the case I expected, exactly as I stated it to J. R. at Strawberry in January—for doing nothing *in re* Denmark.   I think that my explanations about the congress and our reception of Garibaldi were satisfactory to him, but they were both necessary.   I could not get him to abandon his idea about a *plebiscite* in the Duchies, but he will only bring it forward when all other plans have failed.   People complain of my going away as soon as Monday ; it is quite lucky that I have the Conference on Wednesday to plead for my departure.   The worst thing here is the quantity of visits I must pay under pain of giving dire offence.

I find among the Dips. here a prodigious distrust of the Emperor, whose intellect is thought to be deteriorating (though I saw no evidence of it) and a dislike to Drouyn.

The patient reader will have received the impression from Lord Clarendon's correspondence that the statesman whom he distrusted and disliked more than any other member of the Conservative Opposition, was Lord Derby. But locksmiths are not the only craftsmen at whom Love laughs ; he delights in flouting the prejudices of grave politicians. It was therefore quite in accord with his practice that he should cause Lord Derby's second son, the Hon. Frederick Arthur Stanley,[1] and Lord Clarendon's eldest daughter, Lady Constance Villiers, to become enamoured of each other. Their wedding took place on 31st May 1864, affording subsequently emphatic refutation of the sinister augury which a silly superstition attaches to marriages in that month.

From Lady Clarendon's Journal.

16*th April* 1864.— . . . Lord Palmerston was warmer and more eulogistic of Clarendon than I had ever heard him before. He told me that his mission to Paris had been of immense use . . . for he had got the Emperor to give up his idea of a *plebiscite* in the Duchies except *en dernier ressort*, and that *dernier ressort* would never come, for they must never allow it to do so. It would be abominable for those men to meet round a table and separate without stopping bloodshed, and something *must* be arranged by the Conference. . . . He talked in the most flattering way of the great advantage it had been to his government Clarendon joining it—that his great experience and talents in conducting affairs with foreign countries, his knowledge and weight with foreigners, his tact and way of saying things without giving offence, were all of the utmost use and importance ; and he added, laughing, that he never heard Clarendon talk so much nonsense as he did the other day when he hesitated to admit that he could do any good by joining the government.

Lord Howden to Lord Clarendon.

BAYONNE, 4*th June.*— . . . The French papers talk of the abdication of Queen Victoria. I am beginning to think there may be something in it. I have always thought that, with

---

[1] Succeeded in 1893 as sixteenth Earl of Derby.

the turn her mind took from the beginning of her widowhood, she would have done well, for her own interest, happiness and *reputation*, to have abdicated on the day her son came of age. She would *then* have left a great name and a great regret. If she abdicates *now*, she may still gain peace and what the Greeks call ἀταραξία ; but the fugitive moment—that deity in all things—is past ; the *àpropos* is gone. . . . I should like a new reign to begin by a fused government of you and Lord Derby. Under such circumstances there could be no reason whatever that such a combination should not take place, and without the shadow of a reproach to you in *then* lending yourself to a like inauguration. You could not have done so at the tail of Palmerston's political existence ; but it would be a totally different case in the *tabula rasa* of a young sovereign. I don't know anything in the world that would interest me so much as to see the realisation and the march of such a ministry arising out of such a conjuncture. The evening of my life would be its best hour.

By this time the Austrian and Prussian troops had occupied Holstein and Schleswig. Austria and Prussia had been parties to the treaty of London in 1852 conjointly, therefore, with Great Britain, France, Russia and Sweden, guarantors of Denmark in possession of the duchies. Sympathy with Denmark ran strongly in England, all the stronger because the beautiful Danish princess had so lately become Princess of Wales. Palmerston's brave words spoken in the previous summer seemed to leave no room for doubt that the government were ready to fulfil the treaty obligations ; but the utmost force that Great Britain, her navy apart, could land on the continent was 20,000 troops ; Russia was not prepared to move ; was Great Britain to encounter single-handed an Austro-Prussian army of 200,000 or 300,000 ? There remained France ; would she take the field ? Clarendon's first duty after rejoining the Cabinet in March was to go on a special mission to Paris in order to sound the French Emperor as to his intentions. Now the Emperor was in ill-humour with the British government by reason of Russell's refusal to join a European congress ; he gave Clarendon plainly to understand that he would not go to war to maintain the artificial settlement of 1852, whereby two German duchies had been arbitrarily annexed to Denmark. So, although Palmerston and Russell still remained ready and anxious to defend Denmark, they were overborne by their less intrepid colleagues, and the two aggressors were left to quarrel over the spoil. Indignation waxed hot in England ; but it cannot be argued that Great Britain alone, of all the parties to the treaty, was bound in honour to take up arms against two of the other parties, while the remaining three parties stood aloof. The responsibility was joint, not joint and several. That, at least, is all that can be urged in palliation of a somewhat cloudy page in our history.

On Lord Russell's invitation the conference assembled in London on 25th April, an armistice having been arranged between the belligerents ; but Bismarck succeeded in preventing the plenipotentiaries coming to any agreement, for he declined to admit that the treaty of London was still in force ; he declared that it had been voided by the war which he had himself provoked. The conference broke up on 22nd June ; hostilities were resumed, and Denmark was left to make unaided what terms she could. In defending the government against a motion of censure in the House of Lords, Clarendon said that, although he had not shared the responsibility of ministers during the events which led up to the invasion of Danish territory, he approved of the course they had followed in their endeavour to bring about an amicable settlement—an endeavour which would have succeeded had they been able to secure the co-operation of the other Powers who were parties to the treaty of 1852.

The Chancellorship of the Duchy being an office almost devoid of departmental cares, he who holds it is liable to be asked to take up any odd job for the government. Clarendon had brought to a successful issue the inquiry into the condition of public schools ; but he declined Lord Granville's invitation to pursue investigation into a different educational level.

WIESBADEN, 12th August 1864.—MY DEAR G.—At this moment it would be impossible for me to fix the sum that would induce me to get upon a Middle Schools drag.   I will only say generally that it must be something that I could settle upon Hyde, and thereby raise him from the pauper to the millionaire class.   I am very glad, however, that you meditate such a commission, as I know it is wanted and will give satisfaction.   Lyttelton would make a very good chairman—the only one of the late lot who would.   Devon [1] is weak, Northcote pedantic,[2] Thompson idle, Twistleton quirky,[3] Vaughan mad ; [4] yet they all had merits and worked usefully together, except Vaughan who, tho' a man of real genius, is unmanageable.

Lady Theresa Lewis to Lord Clarendon.

TEMPLE NEWSOM, 25th September 1864.— . . . We left Hickleton [5] with great regret on Friday.   All that friendship and kindness could do to make us feel at home and to make me not mind being more or less unwell all the time I was there both Sir Charles and Lady Mary did ; and all their nice sons are so well bred, so naturally obliging and civil, that I found an arm whenever I moved and a constant desire to make me comfortable, as if I had fallen into a new nest of nephews.   Charlie Wood is a charming youth—very handsome, very accomplished and refined, very pleasing. . . . This is a magnificent possession [Temple Newsom]—an Elizabethan house.   The owners, Meynell-Ingrams, are the kindest people possible. . . .

HARKNESS, SCARBOROUGH, 30th.— . . . I cannot remember the place from which I wrote to you last.   I think it was Temple Newsom.   From there we went to Studley.   Lady de Grey, as you know, is with the Princess of Wales, but Mary Vyner and her [illegible] sons Clare and Reginald were there.   Mary V. is scarcely recognisable ; she is perfectly grey, still in weeds (I think it is about four years since H. Vyner died), no crinoline ; in fact her appearance is that of a farmer's wife. Yet when she talks and smiles there is the same kind, gentle, loving look she always had, and she was so affectionate and cordial that it was very pleasant seeing her again.   Lord de Grey was charming as he always is as a companion, and so attentive and kind. . . .

[1] William, eleventh Earl of Devon (1807-88).
[2] Sir Stafford Northcote, created Earl of Iddesleigh in 1885.
[3] Edward T. B. Twisleton (1809-74).
[4] Henry Halford Vaughan (1811-85), professor of modern history.
[5] Sir Charles Wood's place near Doncaster.

WENTWORTH HOUSE, 17th October 1864.— . . . I think our hostess here one of the most charming little people I know. She is as simple and unpretending as a child, very intelligent, and manages everything in this enormous house and *principality*; but she never looks as if she were at all busy.[1] She has 12 children, of which seven are at home. Their eldest son, Lord Milton, is quite the strangest looking creature you ever saw. He has been living a wild life with savages in North America and going through all sorts of hardships which one cannot understand how he endured. . . .

FIR GROVE, 8th December 1864.— . . . Poor Lord Carlisle! I do not think the *Times* article will be gratifying to his family, and tho' much of it was true, there was a peculiar press-vulgarity about the blood-royal of the Whigs, and aristocracy, and Howards and noble birth, etc. etc. The truth was, poor man, that he had a mind capable of just so much cultivation as to yield a very pretty flower-garden ; but the soil was not deep enough for forest trees. As long as the plants and shrubs looked well, it was thought it could bear heavier work, and when the trees of larger growth did not find sufficient depth for their roots, the poverty of the soil was discovered and the ornamental flower-garden was despised.

[1] Wife of the sixth Earl Fitzwilliam and daughter of Sholto, nineteenth Earl of Morton.

CHAPTER XXII

THE FOREIGN OFFICE ONCE MORE

Quae regio in terris nostri non plena laboris ?

'Ο φεύγων μύλον ἄλφιτα φεύγει.[1]

THE year 1865 was pregnant with ill or good for the British Empire, memorable beyond other years for the death of Lord Palmerston, who had stood so long as a breakwater against the surges of democracy, and for the definite adoption by Mr. Gladstone of doctrines which should one day rend asunder the Liberal party as widely as Peel had rent the Tories. In the previous year Palmerston had taken Gladstone sharply to task for his sudden and startling declaration in favour of manhood suffrage ;[2] from that moment the Cabinet became the battle-ground of irreconcilable forces, 'almost as rough,' to quote Gladstone's own words, 'as any of the roughest times.'[3]

Lord Howden to Lord Clarendon.

PARIS, 19th August 1865.— . . . I hear from good authority that Palmerston is not at all flourishing, and that for the latter part of his sojourn at Walmer he has been unusually languid, endeavouring to counteract it by stimulants and tonics. I opine, in my distant ignorance, that Lord John will not, even if he could, succeed directly to P., but that he will do what he can to have Granville, as a man of straw, placed in that position ; enabling him to hold the F.O. and do what he likes without control. My hope is that the Queen will see through this and send for you. You very probably would prefer keeping aloof ;

[1] He who shirks the grinding misses the meal.
[2] See correspondence between Palmerston and Gladstone, Morley's *Gladstone*, ii. 128-30.   [3] *Ibid.*, p. 140.

but with the majority in the new parliament and the utter *telum imbelle sine ictu* of the Tory party, you would have a comfortable start.

I cannot tell you how happy what you said about your sons made me ; for, after all, any man *qui post terga reliquit sexaginta annos* must seek his real happiness in private, not in publick, life.

The Clarendons having proposed to spend some weeks at Wiesbaden in the autumn, the Queen of Holland exacted the pledge of a visit.

HOUSE IN THE WOOD,[1] *8th June* [?] 1865.—DEAR LORD CLARENDON,—I am so grateful for your kind promise of coming to see me here that I must hasten to thank you from my whole heart. You must come to my house—to the room of your great kinsman King William III., where you shall find all his *reliques*, discovered by me, and where I do not doubt some of his spirit—the spirit of the great Whig King—will visit you.

I have no other idea of leaving this, except for a few days at the end of June to visit my father at Wiesbaden ; but I shall be returned here the first days of July. We are expecting the Emperor of Russia in this month of June, for one day, and this prevents me from fixing the exact date of my trip to Wiesbaden.

This letter being only a letter of thanks, I will add nothing more, except that I remain,—Ever faithfully yours,

SOPHIA.

The septennial sands of the parliament of 1859 had well-nigh run out ; dissolution took place in July, and the electors once more registered their confidence in ' Old Pam,' now in his eighty-first year. But when the new House of Commons met in February 1866, that venerable figure was there no more.

Lord Clarendon to Lord Granville.

THE GROVE, *21st October* 1865.— . . . He died at the best moment for himself—in the plenitude of his political and intellectual power, just after the triumph awarded him by the country at the elections, without suffering or change of habits, or loss of consciousness—plucky and *Palmerston* to the last moment.

---

[1] Huis ten bosch, the House in the Wood, a seventeenth-century palace now constituted as the Palace of Peace.

He held a great bundle of sticks together : they are now unbound and there is nobody to tie them up again. . . . The Queen, in anticipation of the event, wrote to J. R. that she should charge him with carrying on the government. I got a letter from him yesterday asking me to lighten his labours by returning to the F.O., and I have felt ever since as I do on board a steamer in a gale. The idea of it is nauseous to me beyond what I can express. I went up yesterday to see if I could not get this cup to pass away from me ; but J. R., tho' it was his day for London and he had made many appointments, thought it pleasanter, as I am sure it must have been, to remain at Pembroke Lodge. . . . I wrote to him that, if invited, I would accept.

Lord Granville replied, strongly remonstrating against his friend's reluctance to return to the Foreign Office.

PARIS, 22nd October 1865.— . . . I cannot conceive why you should object to going to the F.O. With your active mind, why should you dislike work which you do so well ? I shall be in town on Tuesday to attend the funeral on Wednesday. Will it not be necessary, independently of the cattle plague, to summon parliament ? Everyone will dislike it and it will do no good, but it was only the acknowledged majority in favour of Palmerston's government which made us agree that it was not necessary to do so. . . . I wrote to J. R. telling him that I would cordially give him the little assistance in my power. I shall ask him, as I presume others will, not to make many *coups d'état* without consulting the Cabinet.

Thus unwillingly did Clarendon go into harness once more.

Long before this parting of old comrades, Palmerston had dismissed all that suspicion of Clarendon as an intriguing rival which at one time had put their friendship in jeopardy. Of late years there had been none of his colleagues in whose judgment and loyalty he put more perfect confidence than in Clarendon's. The frequency and freedom of the letters he wrote to him are sufficient proof of that. I have been at pains to count those written to Clarendon in Palmerston's own hand during a single year—1857. They number three hundred and ten, ranging over the whole field of politics, foreign and domestic, diverging not infrequently into personal matters. Some of these letters are exceedingly long, written *currente calamo*, without a preliminary draft and with hardly an erasure or alteration from first to last. The writer's thoughts are sometimes epigrammatically expressed. Thus : ' When people come to the point to which you wish to bring them, you ought not to be too nice about the road which they have chosen for getting there.'

Again : ' No powerful nation can ever expect to be really loved or liked by any other. The interests and views of nations perpetually clash, and men are apt to be angry with those who stand between them and the accomplishment of their wishes.'

Palmerston has been condemned as *chauviniste*—carrying, or wishing to carry, his imperialism into overt aggression. He certainly believed in not barking unless one were ready to bite ; but the following letter to Clarendon shows how far he was from entertaining dreams of sheer aggrandisement. Long as the rich territories of North Africa had withered and languished under Oriental misrule, and greatly as Palmerston prized the alliance with France, he emphatically refused to be drawn by that alliance into schemes of conquest. The dominant principle in his foreign policy was the maintenance of the honour of England, her influence in the councils of Europe, and the integrity of the dominions of the Crown.

PICCADILLY, 1*st March* 1857.— . . . As to the Emperor's schemes about Africa, the sooner Cowley lays in his ground of objection the better. It is very possible that many parts of the world would be better governed by England, France and Sardinia than they are now, and we need not go beyond Italy, Sicily and Spain for examples. But the alliance of England and France has derived its strength, not merely from the military and naval power of the two States, but from the force of the moral principle upon which that union has been founded. Our union has for its foundation resistance to unjust aggression, the defence of the weak against the strong and the maintenance of the existing balance of power. How, then, could we combine to be unprovoked aggressors—to imitate in Africa the partition of Poland by the conquest of Morocco for France, of Tunis or some other State for Sardinia, and of Egypt for England ? How could

England and France, who have guaranteed the integrity of the
Turkish Empire, turn round and wrest Egypt from the Sultan ?
A coalition for such purpose would revolt the moral feelings of
mankind and would certainly be fatal to any English government that became a party to it.

Then as to the balance of power to be maintained by giving
us Egypt—in the first place, we don't want to have Egypt.
What we wish about Egypt is that it should continue attached
to the Turkish Empire, which is a security against its belonging
to any European power.   We want to trade with Egypt and
travel through Egypt, but we don't want the burthen of governing Egypt, and its possession would not, as a political, military
and naval question, be considered in this country a set-off against
the possession of Morocco by France.

Let us try to improve all these countries by the general influence of our commerce ; but let us all abstain from a crusade
of conquest which would call down upon us the condemnation
of all other civilised nations.

Part of Clarendon's aversion for office no doubt arose
from the effect upon his health of the unreasonable hours at
which he chose to transact business.   A martyr to gout
from early life, he never gave himself half a chance owing
to his inveterate habit of sitting smoking and writing
despatches hours after he should have been in bed.
Palmerston tried, without success, to make him reform
his time-table.

PICCADILLY, 22nd May 1857.—Peel said that no man should
give advice till he is called in, and you have not called me in,
but I am called in by the interest which we all take in your
health.   What, then, would be your objection to the following
suggestion ?   You want more air and exercise ; much, you
cannot have ; a little you might, and every meikle makes a
muckle—a little every day tells in the course of the year.   Why
should you not provide yourself with a steady hack with good
action, who would give you no trouble when on him and not
prevent you from thinking over the draft you are next going to
write ?   Why should not the aforesaid quadruped be at your
door every morning just as you finish your breakfast ?   and
why should you not ride him to the end of Hyde Park and back
again ?   It would take you only half-an-hour, but that half

hour, if daily taken, would have in some degree the good effect of Balmoral air.

From her invalid sofa in Kensington Gore Miss Eden describes a visit from the aged Brougham, vindictive as ever against those whom he considered his unfriends :

EDEN LODGE [1865].—Lord Brougham came last Friday. I do not think he is more childish than he was last year, but he is considerably more detestable. The Palmerstons are his great grief ; he cannot understand—could I ?—what the papers meant by making such a fuss about that old man ; a very moderate speaker and a man of moderate ability, whom the Tories allowed to remain in his place because they were not ready to take it, etc. His language about Lady P. was too disgusting, and I said at last that I did not understand how any one could talk disrespectfully of the dead ; still less how they could speak of a broken-hearted woman so cruelly. And then, as usual, I told him I was very tired and he had better go, which he did. He is a great beast, if he were not 87.

So Leopold is gone. He was very nearly a great man, and at all events a very lucky one. I do not think the Queen can make an excuse of his death for not opening parliament six weeks hence. . . .

From the Queen of Holland.

Loo, 26*th October* 1865.—I hope you received a short note I sent from Dresden as soon as I heard of Lord Palmerston's death. Yesterday I read in the papers your appointment as Minister of Foreign Affairs. I rejoice to see you in the high position, for which no one is so well fit as you are. I rejoice for Europe, who can rely on your wisdom and experience ; but I regret it for your health, and (allow me to impress it) I regret it for myself, for I know I shall have still less chance to enjoy your society and to receive your kind letters. Forgive me the selfish expression. A life such as mine is poor and dreary, and I cannot miss a friend.

However, may God bless all your enterprises, your works and vigil for the grandeur of your country and the peace of Europe ! Your fame and glory are so well settled, they need not increase ; I only hope your health may not suffer.

I left Dresden on Monday. Being very unwell, I travelled à *petites journées*. . . . I am still coughing and feverish, and for illness *home* is the only place. . . . What changes since I left England ! I am very sorry for Lord Palmerston. On the whole, the foreign press has been *convenable*—little abuse and expressions of respect and consideration.

Once more, God bless you ! I remain, ever and always, yours sincerely,   SOPHIA.

Well was it for Lord Clarendon that he undertook the Foreign Office when he did, for there is no surer or safer anodyne than hard work. Hardly was he established once more in the familiar Downing Street rooms than he was called on to bear the poignant grief of parting with his sister Lady Theresa, who from childhood had been his closest confidante and most kindred spirit. In the piles of correspondence whence the present narrative has been woven, I have found but one reference to this sorrow. It occurs in a letter to Lady Salisbury :

8th November 1865.— . . . I went to Oxford yesterday to see my poor dear sister. She was so shrunk and changed I should hardly have known her, and her weakness was such that even with my ear close to her lips I could hardly distinguish what her whisper was intended to convey. My brother left Oxford at 12 to-day, and says that it was then but a question of hours and that all will be over this evening. Alas, alas ! You can have no idea how I loved her and what a blank her death will create in my existence—for as long as it lasts.

Lady Theresa died on 9th November at the Principal's Lodgings, Brasenose College, aged sixty-two. Of all the personalities which the preparation of these pages has brought under review, none has appeared to the compiler so entirely fascinating as hers. Beautiful, but ever taking thought for others rather than for herself ; lively, but never frivolous ; accomplished, but too gentle to despise others ; enduring repeated sorrow, but always serene—she embodied Brantôme's favourite phrase of *une grande dame de par le monde.*

> Surely He pities who made the brain,
>   When breaks that mirror of memories sweet,
> When the hard blow falleth, and never again
>   Nerve shall quiver or pulse shall beat.
> Bitter the vision of vanishing joys ;
> Surely He pities when death destroys !

One by one Clarendon's confidential correspondents were being called away. Nobody could take the place of Lady Theresa in that relation ; but about this time he began to communicate very frequently on political questions with Lady Salisbury. This lady was the second wife of the second Marquess of Salisbury, the head of a leading Tory house ; but she was also a daughter of the fifth Earl de la Warr, descended, therefore, from that first Duke of Dorset of whom Lord Shelburne said that ' he had the good fortune to come into the world with the Whigs and partook of their good fortune till his death.' Lady Salisbury remained a Whig *au bout des ongles* all her days, and thought it no treason to admit the Whig Foreign Secretary to a knowledge of how things fared in the Tory camp. They called their letters ' paper *coses.*' On 26th November Clarendon wrote to her :

. . . I had to take down [to Windsor] a white and a black man (Spain and Hayti) yesterday to present their credentials. . . . When I asked my sable companion if he had seen the Princess of Wales, he replied—' Oui, milor, je l'ai vue deux fois—chez Madame Tussaud ! ' . . . You will have seen that Forster has accepted,[1] and he did so gladly. I am told that under a rough Yankee sort of exterior he is an amiable man, who will be all the better for friction in office with his betters. . . .

3rd December 1865.— . . . I returned to my old *galère* with nausea, and am now dead sick of it. The total impossibility of ever doing anything else or anything that I like is too bad, and I despise myself for not being able to imitate my predecessor's [2] example, but I cannot. I have not his enviable nature. I can't leave papers unanswered and people unseen because they bore me, and I am just as great a fool now as I was seven years ago. . . . As Lowe always takes care to be in hot water himself, he can't imagine how two or three can be gathered together without being so likewise; but I never assisted at cabinets more entirely harmonious than those held since Earl John has put his little hand to the helm. It is not out of any particular regard or respect for him ; but each man seems to feel his share of responsibility, and that union is the best chance

---

[1] Right Hon. W. E. Forster (1818-86) entered office for the first time as Under-Secretary for the Colonies.   [2] Lord John Russell.

is most important that you should be at hand to guide Gladstone in all parliamentary explanations, and you can rely upon Cowley acting like a clerk under your instructions.

From the far West, also, peace seemed on the point of being broken owing to the impatience of the United States government about the *Alabama* claims, still outstanding. Nearer home, but linked with the American dispute, the Fenian conspiracy commanded anxious attention, and received it in the shape of a fresh coercion bill for Ireland. Upon none of these rocks was the government to be cast away, but upon one marked on every chart, strewn with the wreckage of former administrations. Lord Russell was possessed with the belief that his honour and that of his party were bound up with the question of reform ; he was in his seventy-fourth year—' an old man in a hurry,' to quote a phrase coined for one of his colleagues twenty years later. That colleague, Mr. Gladstone, was perhaps the only member of the Cabinet earnest in demanding a reform bill ; outside the ministerial circle there were few signs of anxiety for further change. 'A little steam,' wrote Clarendon to Granville three weeks or thereby after Gladstone had introduced the bill—

. . . A little steam, but not enough for the required momentum, seems to be getting up for the Bill. My agent here, who is a Liberal and knows everybody in the county, says it will lower the tone of the H. of C., which is already too low ; that no one wants reform and that people ask why they can't be let alone, instead of being forced to oppose a government that they would like to support. If you happen to have a good answer to this, please to let me have it.

Russell deeply resented the tone of the *Times* on reform, reflecting as it did the general feeling of the country.

Lord Russell to Lord Clarendon.

PEMBROKE LODGE, 26*th April* 1866.— . . . As to the *Times*, I am aware that Mr. Delane was very angry that I did not ask to kiss his hand instead of the Queen's when I was appointed to succeed Palmerston ; but I would rather not be in office than hold it on such humiliating conditions. It is true Palmerston constantly saw Delane, and the *Times* was of great use to him ; but when P. was at the Foreign Office, especially during the Pacifico business, the *Times* fired at him six times a week, and Palmerston burnt it. It all ended in Reeve going to Palmerston to announce that the hostility of the *Times* was over, and to ask that Mrs. Reeve might be invited to Lady Palmerston's parties. This Palmerston told me himself. . . . The best way of meeting Delane is not to give him any information that is not given to all the Liberal papers. . . .

All men now looked upon the government as doomed : the question of the hour was how long they would care to stave off that doom, and who would be Russell's successor. Young Charles Wood [1] wrote to his father, who had just been created Viscount Halifax on retiring from office :—

20th April 1866.— . . . I had a very pleasant dinner at Lord Russell's and afterwards went to Mrs. Gladstone's party. They had written up ' Sortie ' over some folding doors, and I need not say the world at once remarked that it was doubtless the *sortie* of the government which was anticipated.

Next day, Mr. Brand, Chief Whip, writes to him rather more hopefully.

It blows hard : I think, however, that we shall carry the second reading of the Franchise Bill. . . . You will be shocked at some of the names scored as voting against us. Bright has done it all by patronising us. . . . The Whigs hate Bright ; moreover, many distrust Gladstone. Lord Russell is very unpopular ; since Palmerston died he has greater proclivities for Bright . . . the fact is, we have been resting too much on the Radical leg. Palmerston's plan was to rest upon Whig support, and the Radicals had no choice but to follow. R.'s plan has been to rely upon Radical support, and the Whigs immediately take fright and desert to the Tories. P. used to follow my advice : R. scarcely ever. You can imagine my position between Lord Russell on the one hand and Gladstone on the other. . . .

The Cabinet agreed to resign should the hostile motion to be moved by Lord Grosvenor, a dissentient Liberal, on the second reading not be defeated by at least ten votes

---

[1] The present Viscount Halifax.

(Lord Clarendon pressed for fifteen). The majority for the government was only five on that division ; but Russell and Gladstone managed to persuade their colleagues not to resign, Clarendon strongly dissenting.

Certainly (he wrote to Lady Salisbury a month later), here our all-absorbing Reform Bill is indeed a *misère* compared with the two millions of men armed to the teeth by bankrupt governments, preparing to cut each other's throats and set all Europe in flames, *for nothing*, or rather for the gratification of one man—Bismarck—who says he would rather go down to posterity as Attila than as John Bright.

The battle over the bill ended in June by the intrepid Lowe and his Adullamites placing ministers in a minority of eleven on Lord Dunkellin's amendment in committee.

Then arose the question—should they resign, dissolve or re-establish themselves by asking for a vote of confidence. Clarendon, so resolute for resignation after the second reading debate, now advocated the last of these alternatives. He himself was far from eager for reform, on its own merits ; but he considered that the government were now so deeply committed to it that it had become a point of honour to leave nothing undone that should enable them to carry the Bill. Howbeit, the majority of the Cabinet were but too glad of a plausible excuse for dropping it. The arguments with which Clarendon pressed his views on the Prime Minister might scarcely be thought worth presenting here, were it not for the insight they give into the relations of a hopelessly divided Cabinet.

To Lord Russell.

F.O., 23*rd June* 1866.—I think you are perfectly right in requiring as a condition of the government remaining in, that the H. of Commons should pledge itself to a real measure of reform at the earliest opportunity. How to make this sufficient for the government and acceptable to the House, is the question, as the whole party would be made ridiculous if a vote of confidence was proposed and was not supported by a good majority. I don't myself see much difficulty in the matter ; but Gladstone must show himself rather more conciliatory than he is likely to be while guided by Bright, who, for his own purposes (which are not, or should not be, ours) is bent upon dissolution.

I quite agree with you that you cannot with honour or usefulness lead half the party, and that if the question of dissolution seriously arises, resignation must be the immediate consequence, as the question will not be between Whigs and Radicals, but with your own Cabinet.

I never wish to make myself of any importance. Upon matters of opinion I am quite ready that the majority should bind the minority; but upon a matter which, to me, would be one of conscience, I must act as my conscience dictates, and I could be no party to a dissolution which I believe would do no good to the cause of Reform and would be fatal to the Liberal interest.

On 25th June the Cabinet having decided in favour of resigning,[1] Lord Clarendon renewed his remonstrance.

25th June.—The decision of to-day causes me such distress of mind that I cannot help asking you to consider whether some form of resolution cannot be found that will command a majority and, at the same time, satisfy—I will not say the honour of the government, but the exigencies of Gladstone; and they are distinct things. Neither you nor any of your colleagues, except Gladstone, wishes to humiliate the House of Commons, or is unprepared to make such reasonable concessions as are necessary where compromise and conciliation are honestly desired; but he wants a triumph over them, to which they will not submit, and therefore wants to put words in the resolution beyond what are required for the real interest of reform (with which measure I am the first to admit our honour is linked) and which he knows men as honourable as himself cannot accept. I am as convinced as any one can be of what has not yet happened, that the indignation at our having refused such a resolution of confidence as Craufurd would have moved will be universal *and just*.

I have no *personal* interest in the matter; such as I have is in favour of resignation, for official life is most distasteful to me; but I have very strong party feelings and I cannot bear the thought that an act of ours should be the construction of a party for Derby and Co., and that will be the inevitable consequence of what we are doing.

I have also, if you will permit me to say so, an equally strong

---

[1] For analysis of the voting, see Morley's *Gladstone*, ii. 209.

feeling for your reputation, and I cannot bear that the last act of your official life should be to break up the party by which you have been so long and so faithfully supported. It cannot promote the cause of reasonable reform, and, when the truth comes to be known, it will be fatal to Gladstone, whose services and abilities would fit him to guide the destinies of this country if his arrogant ill temper did not repel the sympathies upon which a leader must rely for support. Until to-day, I was unable to understand the feeling with respect to himself that he has created in the House of Commons.

For the third time Lord Derby undertook the formation of a ministry while in a minority in the House of Commons. Now, in the whole of the Conservative party there was none, not even Disraeli, who so readily roused Clarendon's ire as did Lord Derby ; nor had his distrust of him as a politician been mitigated in the slightest degree by the marriage of his daughter to Lord Derby's son. That being so, and having regard to Clarendon's invariable eagerness to escape from or to avoid accepting office, one cannot affect surprise at the result of the following correspondence, however much it may be regretted that here was a fair occasion lost for that fusion of parties by the voluntary cohesion of the best men on each side, which has been the dream and ideal of so many good thinkers. As a Whig, Clarendon practically differed with Lord Derby only on fiscal policy ; whereas he looked upon John Bright's principles and projects as revolutionary and dangerous to the State ; yet so searching was the shibboleth of party that he chose deliberately to row in the same boat with Bright rather than tread the quarter-deck with Derby.

St. James's Square, 28th June 1866 — 8 p.m. — Dear Clarendon,—I have just returned from Windsor, where, after a long and satisfactory audience of the Queen, I have undertaken the duty of attempting to form an Administration. It is my wish, and was that of a considerable number of my friends whom I met this morning, to construct it on an enlarged basis, including some of the more moderate of the Liberal party. You will see by the enclosed letter how anxious the Queen is (but not more so than I am myself) that the thread of our foreign diplomacy should not be broken, and that you should feel yourself warranted, in the interest of the country, in continuing to hold your present office in the new Administration ; and, should you desire it, I shall be happy to concert with you the means by which you may not come alone. I really think it is a matter of great importance, and I hope you will reflect before you reject it. All my arrangements are at a standstill till I know your decision. No one will be more relieved by your acceptance than your intended successor. I have just shown Constance the direction of the enclosed, and have sent her off to the opera in a fever of excitement.—Ever yours sincerely,

DERBY.

(Enclosure).

WINDSOR CASTLE, 28th June 1866.—The Queen has seen Lord Derby to-day and finds him ready to undertake the formation of a govt. wh. he is, above all, desirous to constitute upon the widest possible basis. In talking over the various arrangements, a principal subject had naturally been as to the conduct of foreign affairs, and the Queen found that Lord Derby entirely concurred with her in wishing that, if possible, any break in the conduct of those affairs should be avoided. The Queen cannot express too strongly her hope and earnest wish that Lord Clarendon may find himself enabled to accede to the proposal, wh. the Queen knows Lord Derby will make to him, of remaining in his present office. Lord Derby showed himself quite aware, in speaking to the Queen on this subject, of the difficulty which Lord Clarendon might feel in joining a new Administration alone, and the Queen has every reason to believe that he wd. be quite prepared to consider any arrangement that might obviate that difficulty.

This seems so important a matter to the Queen that, if Lord Clarendon shd. wish to see her before giving an answer, she wd. be very glad to receive him, and she feels sure that Lord Clarendon will be as anxious as she is herself that the present crisis shd. end in the formation of an administration on Liberal-Conservative principles, that wd. have a chance of lasting.

28th June 1866.—Lord Clarendon presents his humble duty to your Majesty and humbly begs to acknowledge the receipt of your Majesty's letter, which was forwarded to him this evening by Lord Derby, accompanied by the expression of his own desire that Lord Clarendon should retain the seals of the Foreign Office in the Administration which he is about to form.

Lord Clarendon takes the liberty of transmitting a copy of

his answer to Lord Derby, and at the same time begs to express
his unfeigned regret at finding himself unable to obey your
Majesty's gracious command, which, however, as a mark of
your Majesty's confidence he will always hold in grateful remembrance.

To your Majesty's own high sense of honour and excellent
judgment upon all personal, as well as political, questions,
Lord Clarendon ventures to appeal in favour of the decision
which he has been compelled to take.

GROSVENOR CRESCENT, 28*th June* 1866.—DEAR DERBY,—I
assure you with perfect sincerity that I am much gratified by
your wish that I should continue to hold the seals of the Foreign
Office in the Administration which you are about to form.

I am certain that upon questions of foreign policy no important difference would arise between us. I am thankful
to you for the desire you express that I should not be alone in
accepting your offer. I feel bound by every tie of gratitude
and duty, if possible, to obey the commands of the Queen, and
I wish you success in your arduous undertaking. I have therefore strong motives for joining you, although I have no personal
ambition, and official life is distasteful to me, and, if I decline
your offer, I hope you will do me the justice to believe that
my decision is the result of calm reflexion, and that it has been
arrived at in no unfriendly spirit towards yourself or your
government. The grounds upon which this decision is founded
may be stated in few words. I cannot quit my party, because
allegiance to party is the only strong political feeling I have.
I do not hold extreme opinions on reform, but, as a member of
the government which introduced the Reform Bill, I feel myself
equally with my colleagues responsible for it ; and as, since
our resignation, you have condemned that bill in no measured
terms, the country will, of course, expect that upon that important question your policy will be different to ours.

I know, therefore, that I may appeal to a man of high honour
like yourself as to what my position would be with my colleagues
and my party if I abandoned them to join you, and I know also
that, when I say I should feel dishonoured in my own eyes as
well as theirs, and therefore valueless to you, you will consider
that I have not come to a wrong determination.

In the present state of affairs there may be some difficulty, or
rather some trouble, in gathering together the threads of our
foreign diplomacy ; but this will soon be overcome by a man

so able and industrious as Stanley ; [1] and, if he will accept it, he shall have all the assistance that I can give him, with the same frankness and cordiality as if I were his colleague.—Yours,

CLARENDON.

WINDSOR CASTLE, 29*th June* 1866.—The Queen has recd. with concern Lord Clarendon's letter, but she fully appreciates the motives wh. have led him to decline the offer to continue at the Foreign Office.   His loss, however, will be severely felt.

27 CHESHAM PLACE, 29*th June* 1866.—MY DEAR CLARENDON,— I expected (as G. Grey could tell you) that Ld. Derby would make you an offer to continue in the Foreign Office, & I anticipated also your refusal.   Derby could hardly overlook the great advantage he would derive from your remaining in office to guide our foreign affairs, & I think he was justified in making the proposal.

But I entirely approve of your declining to join a new party. In these days suspicion is so rife, that your name would have been confounded with those of men who can never act in a liberal spirit, either in domestic or foreign politicks ; so that I think you have drawn your head out of the affair in a manner highly becoming, and to an effect which is most honourable to you.

I return the letters.   I wish I could have any confidence in Lord Stanley as Foreign Minister ; but he may live to respect the ' elderly statesman ' whom he denounced years ago.—Yours truly,   RUSSELL.

The *Times* having announced Lord Stanley as successor to Lord Clarendon at the Foreign Office, Lord Russell resented this as a fresh offence on the part of that journal.

27*th June.*—I see Lord Stanley is announced as your successor, and that Lord Derby has done that which I would not do, namely, submitted his appointments to Mr. Delane before submitting them to the Queen.   This is a new constitution of itself, and one much to be deprecated.

Clarendon, however, thought that the *Times* had merely given emphasis to what was current rumour.   Russell also differed from Clarendon in feeling more confidence in Lord Derby than in Lord Stanley.

2*nd July.*— . . . I have been reading the character of Stanley in the *Spectator*, which I believe to be pretty correct.   I own I

---

[1] Lord Derby's eldest son, afterwards fifteenth Earl of Derby.

should dread Stanley at the Foreign Office if Derby were not over him to keep up the traditional policy of England. I should dread Stanley as Prime Minister as a fore-runner of the downfall of this country.

During the ministerial crisis, Liberals and Radicals succeeded at last in rousing a considerable number of the populace from their indifference to reform and to indignation at the defeat of the out-going government's attempt to deal with it. A monster meeting was summoned to demonstrate in Hyde Park on 23rd July; the Home Secretary, Mr. Walpole, issued orders prohibiting the use of the park for such a purpose : and the heads of the various processions, arriving at the several park gates, found them closed and guarded by police. The mob had only to lay hold of the rotten old park railings to obtain easy entrance : when the guards arrived on the scene the demonstration was over, at the cost of a few broken heads. Walpole had better have handed matters over to the Office of Works to have the railings repaired and the flower-beds replanted. Instead of that, he invited Mr. Beales and a deputation of the rioters to an interview at the Home Office, where it is said that he was so much impressed with their earnestness as to be moved to tears. It is refreshing to read Emily Eden's view of the episode, taken from the old Whig standpoint.

EDEN LODGE [*July* 1866].— . . . I attempted a drive round the park and am so indignant at the sight that I feel boiling and bloodthirsty. As for Beales, I suppose the meekest of babies would hang that man as soon as look at him, and also I do not see how we are to die peacefully in our beds without having exterminated that wretched coward Bright. I wonder his own people do not see through and despise him. When we are hanging demagogues, would you mind a small inexpensive gibbet for Layard ? Did you like that man when he was your under-secretary ? or did you only put up with him ? About 20 years ago I remember writing to Lord Ellesmere, who was rather *enjoué* with his Niniveh book, that I could forgive Layard for having discovered Niniveh, tho' I was quite satisfied to take it as Jonah left it ; but that I could not forgive Niniveh for having discovered Layard. I thought so then and think so still.[1] Poor dear Walpole! there never was anybody so little up to the *hauteur des circonstances*. How could he *cry* to Beales ? However, it seems to have answered.

'Twas too convincing—dangerously dear—
In Walpole's eye th' unanswerable tear.

Lord Clarendon to Lord Blomfield.[2]

FOREIGN OFFICE, 26*th June* 1866.—A long cabinet and the necessity of going directly to the House of Lords prevent my writing to you, but you will learn by the telegraph, before you receive this, that we have resigned. There were various attempts made at a patch up, but they were considered not to cover the honour of the government, and that the clear and unmistakeable course was to leave it to our successors to deal with Reform as they think best.

27*th*.—I am very sorry that our (to me) most pleasant relations have come to an end, and my regret is not diminished by the conviction that the government might have continued in office with honour ; but in parliamentary, as in private life, it must not be forgotten that men are led by their sympathies, and that an unconciliatory spirit never fails to generate obstacles.

I can tell you nothing of the new government, except that Stanley is to be my successor ; an immeasurably better man he will be than Disraeli, who coveted this office in the exact ratio of his unfitness for it. . . . Pray say something civil for me to Count Mensdorff by way of valediction, and tell him how very cordial and friendly my relations have always been with Apponyi. I wish he had come to Paris, where we might have made acquaintance, and where I possibly might have been of some use to Austria with the Emperor.[3] I regret all the more that he did not make an appearance there, for even if the Conference had made *fiasco*, Austria would have made her case, and, above all, she would legitimately have gained the time for preparation that I fear she wanted then and even now stands in need of.

The anxiety here is great, for everybody wishes her well and fears that she is not ready to meet her very active enemy. . . .

---

[1] (Sir) Austen H. Layard, M.P. (1817-94), excavator of Nineveh, afterwards Chief Commissioner of Works and from 1877 Minister at Constantinople.
[2] British ambassador to Vienna.
[3] The proposal for a conference of the Powers in Paris came to nought, through the refusal of the Austrian government to attend it.

By this time the Seven Weeks' War was half over. Diplomatic relations with Prussia remained undisturbed, as shown by the following note from Clarendon to Lord Augustus Loftus, British ambassador at Berlin ; but it also shows what was the well-nigh unanimous feeling in England in sympathy with Austria, and against Prussia as the aggressor. The world was beginning to realise its Bismarck !

F.O., *9th May* 1866.—Pray offer our hearty congratulations to M. de Bismarck upon his escape.[1] We don't like his policy, and we think him responsible for the awful state of things which now exists in Europe, and we have never, as frank opponents, made any secret of our opinions ; but we don't want him to die, and we rejoice that he has been saved by himself from assassination. I need not tell you that the pluck and courage he displayed on the occasion are thoroughly appreciated in this country, as they will be, no doubt, in his own. In fact, as the assassin failed, the attempt will greatly add to his prestige and power—an inevitable event, but not an agreeable reflexion. . . .

H.R.H. the Duke of Cambridge to Lord Clarendon.

GLOUCESTER HOUSE, *5th July* 1866.— . . . Alas ! the game is, I fear, played out, and might has triumphed over right, thanks to that horrible needle-gun,[2] which has ruined everything. How we could all of us have shut our eyes to this fact I cannot imagine, and I intreat of you, before leaving office, to record your opinion as strongly as possible that our army should at once be armed with a breech-loading rifle, for otherwise we shall be powerless.

As matters stand, I more deeply deplore than words can describe your leaving the Foreign Office. . . . I entreat of you to assist the new government in the difficult task of directing the foreign affairs of the country. Your country will thank you for aiding in so good a work, and our high position in the scale of nations may be kept intact ; but we require immense tact and the greatest *firmness*, and the courage to say we will agree to such and such things, but to no more. If we do not

---

[1] From an attempt to assassinate him.

[2] The Prussian army were armed with breech-loading rifles, against which the Austrians had no chance with their muzzle-loaders.

take a decided line of our own, we shall become nothing more or less than a third-rate power, and then—good-bye to Old England. . . . Even though out of office, I hope you will at times look in upon me and have a chat together on the great events of the day. Our views, I think, don't differ much. Put in a good word for poor Hanover if you can, remembering that our family comes from there.

Lord Clarendon to Lady Salisbury.

5th July 1866.—Events crowd upon each other with tremendous rapidity. The war is as good as over and everything plays into L[ouis] N[apoleon]'s hands—Venetia ceded to him, and his mediation asked for by poor bleeding, prostrate Austria. He wants a great slice of land for himself as the reward for having abetted the quarrel ; but Bismarck will only negotiate about that with a breech-loader in his hand. . . .

b.a. is an odd man, and I can understand why he makes no friends among men.

In declining to join D[erby] I wrote that I would give S[tanley] all the assistance in my power with the same frankness and cordiality as if I was his colleague. Nevertheless he [Stanley] said that was not direct to himself, and *so* he sent Freddy [1] to me to say he would be glad to see me if I had no objection ! I made notes of everything that would be useful to him, and it took 2½ hours to put him just as much *au courant* of affairs as I am myself. If he had been my own brother I could have done no more. He is not *simpático*. . . . Abercorn and Naas [2] for Ireland ! It is all very alarming ; but D[erby] is in uproarious spirits, being quite unconscious of the volcano under him. It *may* go well, but if Bright is not in office before a twelvemonth I shall be most agreeably mistaken.

I hear there are many complaints—none so loud as Henry Lennox's,[3] who, aspiring to the Cabinet, was offered the Treasurership of the Household ! . . .

9th July.— . . . I think you will have been amused at D[erby] saying last night that he had looked everywhere for a leader instead of himself, but that he could not find one or see

---

[1] Colonel the Hon. F. Stanley.

[2] Succeeded his father as sixth Earl of Mayo in 1867 ; assassinated when Governor-General of India, 8th February 1872.

[3] Lord Henry Lennox, M.P. (1821-86), third son of fifth Duke of Richmond.

one or even *hear* of one! He was very friendly in his expressions towards me ; but he annoyed me greatly, for he gave it to be understood that there was no difference of *political* opinion between us ; whereas I said that I did not anticipate any difference between us upon *foreign* policy. Moreover, I laid stress upon my being responsible for the Reform Bill as much as my colleagues, and that I should be dishonoured in my own eyes as well as theirs if I left them to join him, who was probably about to pursue a policy on that question at variance with ours. I was on the point of getting up to set all this right, but those near me whom I consulted advised against it, and I let the moment slip, for which I am now very sorry. . . .

I had a sort of instinct that Bulwer [1] would sniff Cowley's resignation and rise to the surface again . . . in the hope of being shoved to Paris by the Eminent Novelist [2] and the Jew ; but if that intrigue succeeds, it will be the ruin of *b.a.* Lyons would be, on the whole, the best man, but he has the great disadvantage of being unmarried. A wife is as necessary to an ambassador as to a parson. . . . I hate myself for appearing to have a *guignon*, which I haven't, against Bulwer, but I know how bad his appointment to Paris would be for our relations with the Emperor.

Lord Howden to Lord Clarendon.

Paris, *8th August* 1866.— . . . With regard to English politics, here are my speculations. I do not think it possible for Derby to go through next session. I opine that Gladstone has dished himself by his partnership with Bright. I conceive that there are many Liberals who begin to be frightened, and many Conservatives who begin to believe that *something* must now be done ostensibly in the way of reform—*quand même ce ne serait que pour la frime*—and here is my conclusion. You may recollect that I told you honestly my opinion two years ago about a *fusion*, when there was a great talk about it. It was not the time, and it would not have suited you (which was, in fact, the only thing I cared about). It *was* necessary to get rid of J[ohn] R[ussell], and perhaps it *will* be necessary to get rid of Derby individually ; but if he cannot get on, I conceive

---

[1] Sir Henry Bulwer (1801-72), succeeded Lord Stratford de Redcliffe as ambassador at Constantinople, 1856-65 ; created Baron Dalling in 1872.

[2] Sir Edward B. Lytton-Bulwer (1803-73), brother of Sir Henry ; created Baron Lytton in 1866.

the time would *then* be perfectly ripe to make a government
out of the two parties. The Queen, I doubt not, would wish
you to form it, and you might be the Soul of it, if not the Head.
I hoped you would go back to the F.O., and I daresay you would
refuse to go opposite.[1] In that decision I am inclined to think
you would be right, and there would be no humiliation there,
as you might, from your position, actually name your man.
Why not take Lord Hartington ? He has name, personal
respectability and, I am told, application. I assure you that
I consider such a fusion as the only means of a combination able
to carry on the government of the country and to stave off serious
and innumerable inconveniences, if not worse. . . .

PARIS,   [1866].— . . . I recollect telling you many
years ago what I repeat now—that, *nolens volens*, England
will have to come to a conscription (modified perhaps in some
way) *at last*. . . . I don't know what Cromwell's soldiers were,
but I am perfectly sure that what is called a ' citizen soldier '
is, nowadays, no match to the *troupier tout d'une pièce*. . . . I
am really sorry and irritated at this mania for Prussianising our
army, which will be developed and intensified by the eternally
German tendencies of the Court. . . . I feel very convinced
that there is no army in Europe to be compared with the French
army, especially in all its internal regulation. I know that to
take a leaf out of their book will always be a bitter bolus to the
United Service Club, but believe me, *you must do something*.
England has always had severe apprenticeships, and things go
on at too fast a pace to tolerate slow learners.

The castle and lands of Kenilworth, after having suffered
sorely at the hands of Cromwell's officers, who dismantled
the Earl of Leicester's fine palace and demesne, were bestowed by Charles II. upon Lawrence, Viscount Hyde,
second son of Chancellor Clarendon. Hyde was created
Earl of Rochester, and the property descended from him
to Thomas Villiers, first Earl of Clarendon in the second
creation. It appears from the following note to Lady
Salisbury that, like the Laird o' Cockpen's, our Lord
Clarendon's ' mind was ta'en up wi' affairs o' the State,' so
that his own affairs were neglected. So well was it spoken
by one of olden time—*Male agitur cum domino quem villicus*

---

[1] To the Treasury.

docet—it goes ill with the master who leaves everything to his bailiff.

10*th August* 1866.— . . . I am going next week to Kenilworth, where I must stay 4 or 5 days, as my affairs there are in utter confusion.   The agent whom I thought the incarnation of order and regularity is dead, and it turns out that he kept no accounts and never did any repairs, etc. etc.   In short I don't know what my liabilities may be, which is pleasant for a pauper like me ; but I have settled to go and poke it all out for myself—the sort of job which of all others I detest the most.   I can look decently after the affairs of other people, but my own are always repugnant to me, so I have always lived in a scrambling fashion, which is very stupid and very wrong, but it's the nature of the beast. . . .

CHAPTER XXIII

FOREIGN TRAVEL

Vectatio, iterque et mutata regio vigorem dant.
SENECA.[1]

MOST of the late Cabinet spent the autumn and winter of 1866 on the Continent. The Gladstones, the Cardwells, the Duke of Argyll and the Clarendons met in Rome, where Clarendon's training in diplomacy seems to have stood him in good stead, for Abraham Hayward wrote to Lord Halifax,[2] ' Manning reports that the Pope was charmed with Lord Clarendon, disappointed with Gladstone, and bored with the Duke of Argyll.'

This report was confirmed by Gladstone himself, who used to quote what the Pope said—' I like, but do not understand, Mr. Gladstone ; Mr. Cardwell I understand, but do not like ; I both like and understand Lord Clarendon ; the Duke of Argyll I neither understand nor like.' [3]

One gets an amusing glance at Gladstone on his holiday in a letter from Clarendon to Lady Salisbury :

ROME, *24th November*.— . . . Italian art, archæology and literature are Gladstone's sole occupation. Every morning at 8 he lectures his wife and daughters upon Dante and requires them to parse and give the root of every word. He runs about all day to shops, galleries and persons, and only last night told me that he hadn't time for the reading room, and had not seen an English paper for three or four days ! . . . He is a curious man ; but mental and physical restoration has made him very moderate in all his opinions. Of course he may be quite different when he gets home to his old haunts and habits.

[1] Voyage, travel and change of scene brace one up.
[2] Sir Charles Wood, having met with a severe accident out hunting in February 1866, was compelled to give up the India Office and retire from public life. He was then created Viscount Halifax.
[3] Morley's *Gladstone*, ii. 218.

Lord Russell to Lord Clarendon.

FLORENCE, *5th December* 1866.—There is one subject upon which the Pope address'd you which seems to me urgent. You did right to point out to the Pope the loss of voluntary contributions which the Irish Catholic clergy would suffer by accepting State support. It was not necessary to go further into the matter with the Pope. But when I compare Ireland 65 years after the Union with Scotland 65 years after *her* Union, I cannot but perceive the contrast. That contrast does not arise from any difference in the law of landlord and tenant, tho' some improvements may be made in regard to the security of the [Irish] tenant. It does arise, in my opinion, from this glaring fact— that the Scotch got security for their Church, and the Irish have imposed upon them the Church which Charles II. and James II. tried to impose upon Scotland.

I know how difficult, and even desperate, the struggle will be, and how little likely I am to carry the Liberal party with me ; but, in spite of everything, I must declare in parliament that unless Ireland is satisfied by some new distribution of Church revenues, there is no hope of permanent peace in that country or real union with England ! I wish you to speak on this subject to Granville, to G. Grey, and to Roundell Palmer, if you meet them. *Do not write.* Gladstone, I think, is aware generally of my opinion.

The Liberal ranks were in no condition for a campaign at the opening of the session of 1867. Lord Halifax, laid on the shelf, received doleful reports from his old comrades, as a few gleanings from his post-bag will show.

Lord Dalhousie to Lord Halifax.

24th January 1867.— . . . I thought your gathering at Woburn was a political one. I hope wisdom will wait upon your discussions, but where are the dinners ? I see no sign of the leaders spreading their boards. It is a mistake and (you may laugh if you like) a great one. The world will say the chiefs are disunited, and all sorts of evil rumours will get abroad. . . .

Hon. H. Brand, M.P. (Chief Whip), to the same.

29th.— . . . We are as much at sixes and sevens as the government. Grosvenor is whipping the Cave and corrupts them with a dinner on Monday. . . .

31st.— . . . There will be no [Liberal] dinner either for Lords or Commons. The truth is, Gladstone feels a difficulty both about leaving out or taking in Bright. But you must not conclude from this that Gladstone has greater proclivities for Bright. He speaks of him as an 'impracticable demagogue,' which has a healthy sound.

Lord Granville to the same.

31st.— . . . Gladstone is come back, well and exceedingly keen. We all thought he and Russell ought to give parliamentary dinners, but he refuses. He dares not ask Bright and funks omitting him. The latter is a bad symptom, but he calls Bright a demagogue. . . .

Sir David Dundas, M.P., to the same.

2nd February.— . . . There seem to be no leaders, no plan, no union, no sympathy. The government people ask if they need send us a copy of the Speech as usual. Of course Lord John cannot be here in time. Mr. Gladstone, to be sure, has just arrived, but what he thinks or does, or is said to be thinking or doing, nobody seems to know. If such things count, one hears of a Peer's dinner—no Commoners'. To be sure (strange enough) Lord Grosvenor gives a dinner to the Squadrone Volante, but why are not the flags we are to fight under unfurled? No marshalling of our host (if we have any)—no signs of union or sympathy among us. . . .

The compiler of the present narrative is happily exempt from the obligation to review the parliamentary history of 1867. It would, in truth, be no grateful task for him as an old Conservative to trace out the tactics whereby the very men who, a few months before, had overthrown Russell's ministry in its attempt to add less than half a million to the register, cajoled their party into enfranchising nearly a million new voters. So truly did Clarendon remark to Lady Salisbury at the close of Disraeli's administration—'We are a long way from the end of the evils entailed by two years' weak and reckless government.' That staunch, outspoken Tory James Lowther declared that he did not know how he should face his constituents after having refused a moderate measure from a good Christian and accepted an extreme one from a bad Jew ; a sentiment which was shared, not always silently, by many of the party. Lord Derby congratulated himself on having ' dished the Whigs.' He may have done so, but the result of the manœuvre was more searchingly summarised in a letter to the *Times* over the initial of a well-known Liberal,[1] containing the sentence—' It is not a party they have destroyed ; it is a creed they have annihilated.' [2] Be it our lighter office to glean out of Lord Clarendon's correspondence such fragments as may illustrate his views upon the matter ; but first there is a passage to be noted in Lord Halifax's journal of these days :

4th February 1867.— . . . Clarendon and I walked home together. He thought that Lord Russell had shown himself unfit for the chief place, and that Gladstone should be chief. I said I thought it would be better to have himself or Granville at the head. As I expected, he disclaimed the possibility of himself, and we then discussed Granville. Clarendon thinks the responsibility would keep Gladstone more prudent, but admitted his ignorance of the world and of men and his want of tact. It is amusing that at the end of last session, as Granville told me, nothing could exceed Clarendon's depreciation of Gladstone.[3] On Sunday last, he went up to Granville to say how highly he appreciated him and that he was indispensable.

Lord Clarendon to Mrs. Edward Villiers.

Grosvenor Crescent, *8th February* 1867.— . . . I feel five of six years younger than I did last summer. We had a ball at the Grove, which was all the more successful for being an impromptu. Mesdames Essex, Cork and Sandwich, who danced the cotillon, said at 5 A.M. that they had never enjoyed themselves more. . . . The session has come in like a lamb ; whether it will go on like a lion will depend on a certain Hebrew who is master of the situation and who is not thought capable of devising an honest measure of reform. If he did bring in such

---

[1] [Sir] William Vernon Harcourt.   [2] *Times,* 2nd May 1867.

[3] In 1860 Clarendon spoke of Gladstone to Charles Greville as ' an audacious innovator with an insatiable desire of popularity ' and ' a fervent imagination which furnished facts in support ' of what he designed. He pronounced him ' a far more sincere Republican than Bright, for his un-gratified personal vanity makes him wish to subvert the institutions and classes that stand in the way of his ambition ' (*Greville Memoirs,* 3rd Series, ii. 291).

a one, there is every disposition to consider it favourably and to get rid of the question ; but the country is in no mood to be trifled with, and if any dodges for delay are attempted the consequences may be very serious. I sincerely hope the government may remain in, as it will do the Whigs good to remain out in the cold, and the party could not construct a satisfactory government just yet. I may be selfish in this, as I look with unspeakable disgust to a return to office. . . .

The government stumbled heavily at starting, for on the morning of 25th February, the day appointed for the introduction of the bill, three Secretaries of State—Lord Carnarvon, Lord Cranborne,[1] and General Peel—resigned the seals of their departments rather than have any hand in it. Lethal, surely, to any government, especially to one with a minority in the House of Commons. Nay, but they managed to get the bill read a second time without a division, the Opposition being even more deeply divided than the Ministerialists. Early in April forty or fifty Liberals met in the tea-room of the House of Commons to protest against Gladstone's proposal to bind the Committee on the Bill by instructions. ' A nice mess you are in with the Reform Bill,' wrote Lord Dalhousie to Lord Halifax. ' Cave No. 1 was bad enough, but this Tea Cave has riled me more than I thought any political event could have done. It is treason to the Liberal party, and among the traitors are names that make one's hair stand on end.'

Clarendon expressed himself quite as forcibly in writing to Lady Salisbury. He distrusted Disraeli profoundly, and the harshness of the terms he employed in writing about him reminds one of similar language used in later years by Conservatives about Gladstone. In both cases the source of bitterness lay in genuine fear for the consequences of what was being done.

27th May 1867.— . . . The extreme Liberals make no hesitation in saying they prefer Dizzy to Gladstone for leader, because, having neither honestness, earnestness or principle, he is the creature of pressure and can be moulded like wax. I am no more an alarmist than I am a Radical ; but when I know that

---

[1] Succeeded in the following year as third Marquess of Salisbury.

such a Radical as Bright is alarmed at the consequences of giving political power to ' the residuum,' as he politely calls the dregs of society, I cannot but feel uneasy about our future. There may be some exaggeration in Lowe's speech of last night ; but that some of his forebodings will come to pass I have no doubt. . . . *b.a.* seems to look at the whole thing exclusively in a party light and not to care one straw for the general interests of the country ; yet this seems unconceivable when one re- members how last year he predicted ruin and desolation from adding 200,000 to the constituency in one direction, and that he now deems it safe to add at least 500,000, not only in the same direction, but going much lower into the depths of it. . . . Altogether it is a curious result of ten months of Conservative rule ; yet not an unnatural one, when Newmarket practice comes in support of Hebrew thimble-rigging. I had a letter from the Queen of Holland quite delighted by your kindness in going to her. Her life is so solitary and she is such a *femme incomprise* among the Dutch, that the prospect of exchanging ideas with such a woman as *ma très chère cousine* [1] is balm to her soul. . . .

19th June.— . . . I don't meet a single Liberal whose fear does not seem to be genuine about this leap in the dark, and no man can understand how Dizzy has succeeded in such thorough demoralisation of the House of Commons. . . . It is wonderful how his party adopt the *mot d'ordre* and swear that nothing was ever so conservative as the Reform Bill, which Bright in all sincerity calls revolution. . . . I dislike Bright very much ; but I must say that his conduct on the whole has been worthy of all praise this year, and he has lost caste with the extreme party thereby. . . .

' It seems to me,' wrote Lord Cowley from Paris, ' that Gladstone is not the man to conduct an Opposition, much less a Government ; and, if that is so, it is very serious for the Liberal party. As to Dizzy and Co. : they have given a blow to the character of public men which I fear will hurt others as well as themselves.'

' Politics,' wrote Lord Dalhousie to Lord Halifax, ' are disgusting to think of. . . . Derby has set himself to prove that dishonesty is the best policy, and he has succeeded. It makes one moan over the times we live in. The Reform

---

[1] Clarendon always addressed Lady Salisbury as his *très chère cousine.*

Bill may be a leap in the dark to him ; it is none to me. Where we lifted the sluices of democracy an inch, he and Dizzy have raised them a foot. My only hope is that they will be the first to be washed away in the flood.'

Lord Clarendon to Lady Salisbury.

WIESBADEN, 12*th August* 1867.— . . . Pray thank my lord for his message, and tell him that the cognomen of Radical does not apply to me, who brought myself with the utmost difficulty to agree last year to an augmentation of 200,000 to the constituency, and that I opposed his voting papers in the truest conservative sense because I know they must lead to that greatest of abominations—the ballot. . . . He has lived lately among so-called Conservatives and has unconsciously become Radical *malgré lui* ; so the first time I have the pleasure of going to Hatfield, I must be greatly on my guard against so advanced a Christian as he has become. . . .

THE GROVE, 6*th October* 1867.— . . . I have a letter from Howden who is alarmed at the state of things in France and the war proclivities of the Emperor. Notwithstanding his *wish* for peace, he is playing Bismarck's game and cementing German unity more every day. . . . Howden's opinion upon French affairs is always correct, . . . nevertheless I believe in peace, for Prussia will never attack France and the Emperor will not be mad enough to compel Prussia to make a defensive war ; but his policy, or rather his mind, is so wavering, and the consequences are so injurious to credit and commerce, that people in both countries will soon desire war in preference to uncertainty.

There was a large gathering of crowned heads in Paris during the summer of 1867 on the occasion of a great industrial exhibition. The question of the Duchy of Luxembourg was exercising the equanimity of both French and Dutch statesmen, who were apprehensive of Prussian aggression. The possession of Luxembourg had been guaranteed to the King of Holland by a treaty of the great Powers in 1839, but Prussian troops were in occupation thereof in 1867. A conference of the Powers assembled in London in May and agreed to a treaty securing the evacuation of the Duchy by Prussia, the dismantling of the forts and the strict neutralisation of the territory. The Queen of Holland had got into the habit of appealing to Lord Clarendon for advice in her difficulties, and did so in connection with this matter :

HOUSE IN THE WOOD, *7th June* 1867.—I give this letter to Lady Salisbury, whose visit has been to me a source of great enjoyment. Her affection, her admiration, her trust in you were refreshing to listen to. She has the heart of a woman with the mind of a man—an earnestness of purpose, a depth and cultivation of intelligence, which made me blush for my frivolity and ignorance. The *only* thing I did not like was the account she gave of your health. It was the drawback of the enjoyment of this visit. Let me entreat you to be careful. It is nearly a year ago you were taken so ill at Kenilworth : very frequently maladies return about the same period. Pray be prudent! Think of all those to whom your life is so precious.

I have long wished to consult you on a subject which weighs on my mind. During the second week of May, whilst the conference was sitting, France proposed to us a treaty offensive and defensive, *nous garantissant l'intégrité de notre territoire.* As usual, we hesitated. When the conference was concluded—a peaceful result obtained—they returned with this offer, *which to this hour we have not accepted.*

As we are wavering and reluctant, Baudin uses strong and bitter urgings, assuring us that *if* there is to be war, we will be forgotten at every treaty of peace. This proves to me clearly that there will be war—that France would like to use this country to disembark her troops to enter Prussia this way. If we continue to refuse, we will not only have the threatening enmity of Prussia, but lose the assistance of France and remain utterly forsaken. What is to be done ? Pray give me your advice. Having *no* friends is the worst of positions for a small country as we are—it leads to destruction. I need not say this must remain a secret to every one, except dear Lady Clarendon. I know too well how safe you are. It is important and weighs on me ! Pray do not answer this except thro' the messenger of the F.O. I should be frightened about the post. . . . I *feel*, notwithstanding the fêtes and triumph in Paris, the sky is dark and threatening. How I long for your advice, my ever true friend ! God bless and keep you. Remember me to dear Lady Cl.

SOPHIA.

Lord Cowley appears to have complied for a while with Lord Russell's embargo upon his private correspondence with Lord Clarendon ; but he felt free to resume it after the change of government.

Lord Cowley to Lord Clarendon.

PARIS, 12*th June* 1867.— . . . The King of Prussia does us the honour to dine here [1] to-day, and we have endeavoured to justify his condescension by getting together as much of the beauty of Paris as a short notice would allow of. He is very amiable, and has pleased generally, and, strange to say, so has Bismark ; while the Czar, by his hauteur and abrupt speech, has failed altogether. As things have turned out, the *attentat* has been favorable to him,[2] for it produced a reaction or protest on the part of France against all participation in the infamous outrage ; whereas, if it had not occurred, H.M. would have been exposed to daily insults.

I know nothing *positively* of what the Russians have obtained politically, but I suspect *not* much, and that they are not satisfied. I had a conversation with the Czar on announcing the Garter to him, but none with Gortschakoff. There was nothing new in what the Czar said—protestations of disinterestedness in dealing with Turkey—only led on by sentiments of humanity, etc.—in short, the old story. In the meantime, he would forcibly separate Candia from Turkey if he could. . . . I have had a good deal of conversation with Bismark, who certainly is one of the most remarkable men I have met with. He is very dubious as to French intentions. I tell him (as I believe) that if Prussia is prudent, peace will be preserved ; but if she goes too fast with southern Germany I will answer for nothing. He replies that he does not want the southern States and would rather be without them, but that he cannot withstand public opinion if the States themselves ask for annexation. I am quite sure, however, from his language that he will give no encouragement in that direction. They go away on Friday, and I should think the Emperor will be heartily pleased to be rid of them all.

The Princess Royal did not please here ; she was thought stiff. Princess Alice made a better impression.

---

[1] At the British Embassy.
[2] The Emperor Alexander II.'s life had been attempted on 6th June by Berezowski, a Pole. He was assassinated by a bomb in 1881.

You ask whether there is any chance of an appeal for a general disarmament being listened to here. I am quite convinced that there is none ; but there are those who believe that some such scheme has been discussed with Russia, and that a convention will be the consequence. My own opinion is that any convention of the kind would be the best provocation to war from the constant recrimination to which it would be sure to give rise. . . . I open my letter to say that I had a very satisfactory conversation with the King of Prussia and Bismark last night as to the impression made upon them by their visit. Bismark had a long interview yesterday with the Emperor, which appears to have been attended with the best results. Bismark is convinced that, unless some new incident should arise, the maintenance of peace between France and Germany is secured.

Lord and Lady Russell returned in October from prolonged continental travel. He resumes correspondence with Clarendon.

PEMBROKE LODGE, 18*th October* 1867.—I am very glad to have your welcome. Lady Russell's maid reminds me that it is a year to-day since we went abroad. It has been, with some drawbacks, a very happy year, and the task—

    ' e terra alterius magnum spectare laborem '—

is a much easier one than that of having oneself to steer the ship thro' the tempest.

Napoleon III. has, as you say, never had a harder problem to solve. I have a bet of a sovereign with Mme. Jarnac that he dies on the throne ; but I don't care if I lose. Tho' the pot does not boil over, he always keeps it simmering. What should he do ? I say, abstain from a fresh expedition to Rome, but make terms with Victor Emmanuel (who is quite a Papist) to protect the Pope's person with the great Italian army, treating him as a sovereign Prince and respecting his spiritual independence. The folly of the Italians in trying to make Rome their capital is in the way of this plan, but surely the diplomacy of France and Italy might untie the knot.

I shall ask you and about 15 other peers to dine with me on the 18th. A glass of wine and a friendly greeting can do no harm. Gladstone says he cannot keep abreast of me in this respect ; but I think he is wrong. He ought to ask Bright, who, according to Bessborough, must be a member of the Cabinet,

in case of a change of government. B. says the Tories would
expect it and acquiesce in it. Indeed, as Derby's reform bill
is a democratic version of Bright's scheme, Bright ought *now* to
be in office. Education is my hobby, and I am working at it.
I am getting rid of a cold caught at Baron's Court. Abercorn [1]
is doing admirably ; but think of a country divided between
Archbishop Cullen and Lord Roden—both very strong and both
quite rabid. Yours affectionately,   J. R.

From Knowsley Lord Clarendon wrote to Lady Salisbury
on 31st October :

. . . We came here on Monday last on our road to Lathom,
of course not being able to pass Constance. The host looks
ragged and weak—something like a buck at this particular
season ; but is in high good humour and spirits, talking freely
about foreign affairs, of which he seems to know something, and
silent about reform and the operation of the bill, about which
he evidently knows no more than when he was crammed for the
second reading. He congratulated himself on not having to
assist at the banquet at Edinbro', where Dizzy was to be made
all sorts of things ; and he laughed when I asked whether
among them he would be made a Christian ; for altho' there
was abundant evidence of his circumcision, there was none of
his baptism. . . .

Lord Russell to Lord Clarendon.

PEMBROKE LODGE, *2nd November* 1867.—MY DEAR
CLARENDON,—I am always glad to get a letter from you, and
any scrap of news from Knowsley must be interesting.

Dizzy's speech at Edinburgh was calculated to open the
eyes of the most blinded by his talents, and I should not wonder
if Derby were to recover his sight—partially, if not completely.
I agree in what you say of the inclination of Tories and Radicals
to get out of Dizzy—the Tories as many places—the Radicals
as many destructive measures—as they can ; but I am of so
pugnacious a nature that I am determined, while I have a voice,
to fight them both furiously and fiercely.

I admire the *North British*, the *Quarterly* and the *Pall Mall*,
and in some degree the *Edinburgh*, tho' it is shabby and half-

---

[1] James, second Marquess and first Duke, was Lord-Lieutenant of
Ireland at this time.

hearted ; but if all the independent press speaks this way, why should statesmen be silent ?   I shall try and reconcile Gladstone and Lowe, and Lowe and Bright.   We are sure to succeed in the long run ; but how long, no man can say.

I am glad to see the Italian affairs are prosperous.   A foreign garrison in Rome during the Pope's life, with all the Roman territory in Italian occupation during his life, and Rome itself after his death, is my idea of an euthanasia of the temporal power.

. . . I really believe Stanley has done good to Turkey by refusing joint intervention in regard to Crete.   I am quite Prussian, but neither Russian nor Austrian in European politics. I am glad you will dine with me on the 18th.   We can talk of February as well as of November.

Emily Eden is very well, and goes out in her carriage.   I am ashamed of Buccleuch and Dalkeith.   The Scotch sold their king in the 17th century : in the 19th they have sold their country.   Yours truly,   J. R.

The Queen of Holland to the same.

HAGUE, 4*th November*.—I arrived here last night, having staid a day longer at Heidelberg than was intended, as both my sister and my sister-in-law petitioned for it, and the perfect rest and the family circle—the *home* reminiscences—were sweet after the bustle I left !   I hoped to find a letter here—but there was none !   It was a sad feeling—that silence of welcome.   My last letter went to Knowsley.   I sent it the 29th : I hope it reached you.

I had one long, good talk with the Emperor when he came to lunch with me quietly—Alex., he and myself.   He believes—at least he told me—the interior situation to be good.   He was bitter against the Italian government, and not without bitterness against Prussia.   But I sincerely believe he does not intend war.   He assured me Bismarck had asked him to take Belgium. I said—'Ne le faites jamais : cela vous brouillerait avec l'Angleterre.'   'Non : je ne le ferai *jamais*,' was the answer. He does not, or will not, confess the events of last year turned out unfortunately for France ; but pretends—' maintenant elles ne seront plus [*illegible*] contre nous—la Prusse *et* l'Autriche, ce sera toujours l'une ou l'autre.'   On Tuesday, when I came to take leave, he was ill in bed ; but sent word thro' the Empress he wished to see me.   She brought me to his bedside and I took leave. He wanted me to promise to return soon ; but I did *not* promise, and I do not wish it. *She* made some excuses about having seen me so little ; but the fact is she was absorbed by the Austrians and her playing Marie Antoinette—in dress and all. I think, also, she did not like my refusal to go up with her *in a balloon,* which she did at last with the youngest Archduke. *He* [the Emperor] yields to her in all, and I was shocked by her unpopularity, even among the Court people. I like her —her grace, her beauty, her sweetness. *He* often talked of you, wishing your return to office. His admiration for you is deep and sincere.

I am writing a desultory letter, but I am tired and nervous— people coming in and out—nothing settled. My boys are well : the eldest is happy to see me ; but alas ! I hear of new debts. I will write again very soon.

Lord and Lady Clarendon spent the winter of 1867-8 in Italy, where Lady Emily Villiers, their youngest and only unmarried daughter, became engaged to Lord Russell's nephew Odo,[1] who had been retained at the British Embassy at Rome on special service ever since the withdrawal of the mission at Naples in 1860. Clarendon announces the event to Lord Granville and Lord Howden, who, with Emily Eden, were almost the only surviving intimates of his youth.[2]

To Lord Howden.

ROME, *2nd February* 1868.—I cannot let an old friend like yourself hear by common report an event most interesting to us, and which will therefore, I am sure, not be without interest to you. Emily is to marry Odo Russell. It has been an attachment of old standing on his part, and as she has become very certain of its depth and sincerity, they came to an understanding two days ago. His worldly goods are not superabundant, but he is very rich in all the qualities likely to make a woman happy : he is very clever and accomplished, and I speak with a knowledge of him for many years when I say that he is one of the best-tempered and kindest-hearted men I ever was acquainted with. Such a son as he has always been must make a good husband. In short, we are all very happy. . . . There is great expectation at Rome that Italy will break up and that the Holy Father will

---

[1] Created Lord Ampthill in 1881.
[2] Charles Greville had died in 1865.

recover his provinces. Italy, mishandled as she has been by quacks, is doubtless very sick ; but she is still proud of the union, and will fight for it against all comers. . . .

To Lord Granville.

ROME, 4th February 1868.— . . . I have now a special reason for a letter, which is to tell you that Emily is to marry Odo Russell, and I don't think it will be uninteresting to you to know that we are much pleased thereat. He won't endow her with a *super*abundance of worldly goods, but he has qualities both of heart and head just of the kind to make her supremely happy, and that is all we care about, being neither greedy nor ambitious for our children. It has been an attachment of some standing on his part, and it was thoro'ly reciprocated as soon as there was no doubt of its sincerity. It will entail staying here rather longer than we intended, for the marriage can hardly be before May, as those two inconvenient girls Constance and Alice mean to be confined in April, and without their presence nothing would induce Emily to consider herself legally married. I suppose, however, that there will be nothing to do in England except watching the undeserved success of the Tories and the hopeless disunion of the Whigs, which, so far as I am concerned, may be done as well in Rome as in London. You must be a far better judge than myself, but I cannot discover a germ of approximation to Gladstone, or an attempt to discover how he can be done without. There seems a determination to distrust him, and to find fault with whatever he does or does not do. His genius and eloquence enable him to soar high above the heads of his party, who are always suspicious of what he may devise when he gets into higher and unknown latitudes.

From Lord Howden.

BAYONNE, 16th May 1868.—MY DEAR C.,—I saw an account of the wedding in the newspaper while at Arcachon. I felt, as if it had happened to myself, the empty place at breakfast and at dinner—the *one less* flat candlestick on the table at night—all those little (nay, not little) remembrances of what was, and is not ! One pretends not to think of these things, and how keenly one *does* think of them ! . . . My dear friend, if ever Gladstone comes into power with Mr. Bright in the Cabinet, it will not be *couleuvres*, but boas, that he will swallow at his daily repasts, to say nothing of his suppers after the House of Commons. What I think a serious misfortune is a general election on a religious cry. People in England, while despising southern superstition, are wonderfully and wofully bigotted about their own matters of faith, and are more unamiable in manifestation than the Familiars of the Inquisition. . . .

Lord Derby's retirement from public life at the close of 1867 set everybody speculating wildly about his successor. Opinion was divided between Lord Stanley and Disraeli, the first of whom had no personal friends in his own party, and the second had made enemies of such of the Tory remnant as had refused to be educated.

I know nothing (wrote Lord Clarendon from Rome to Lady Salisbury on 26th February 1868) about arrangements, but it seems impossible that the Jew should not be in the first place, for *b.a.*[1] cannot occupy it without going to the H. of Lords, and I suppose he would not like to be buried alive there before his father's death left him no option. He has not the qualifications that the other possesses for leading the H. of Commons, and there is nobody who could take his place at the F.O. The Jew, who is ' the most subtle beast in the field,' has, like Eve's tempter, ingratiated himself with the Missus and made her forget that, in the opinion of the Great and Good, he ' had not one single element of a gentleman in his composition.' He has also got a number of newspapers, whose natural proclivities are towards an adventurer, to write up his fitness. I therefore expect that he is at this moment reigning over us. . . . The Liberal *rouges* would of course prefer a man who has not a principle or a fixed opinion, and who would fall in with their mischievous designs whenever it suited his own purpose. *b.a.* wouldn't stick at trifles, but he has not the elasticity of the other, who looks the political acrobat he is. Altogether, it is a nasty state of things for critical times. . . . Gladstone seems to have been occupied in establishing the true position of Neptune in Phœnicia (at least Reeve tells me that the article on that subject in the *Quarterly* is by him), which is important at the present moment and likely to bring his party back to him !

FLORENCE, *8th March* 1868.— . . . What a curious dinner that was at Lord Cairns's ! and what a curious position was

---

[1] Lord Stanley, who married Lady Salisbury in 1870.

yours at it !—both the host and the Jew [1] aware that no one was so well acquainted as yourself with their real opinions before they were bribed to change them. The game, however, is not yet played out, for the Jew will educate the no-surrender man to go at the Irish Church, and the now rabid Chelmsford will have an earldom or some other sop thrown to him, and before the session is over will entirely agree with his friend on the woolsack.

It is rather good fun to see the Tory magnates scraping off the dirt they have heaped upon Dizzy for the last ten years, eating and affecting to like it. Hardwicke writes to his family at Cannes that the Jew's appointment is the apotheosis of the British Constitution, and Elcho declares it is the grandest event of modern times. With all the Jews for him and all the press, and knowing better than anyone how to manipulate the H. of Commons, and with the Opposition disunited, I see no reason why his success should not be complete and lasting. . . . I have only a telegraphic report of his speech, but I must admit I liked what he said about our foreign policy. Belief in the selfishness that dictates our present system of isolation has reduced our importance, and therefore our influence, on the Continent to zero. Europe now cares no more about England than she does about Holland, and I have suffered many things on that account during the last two months.

PARIS, 18th March.— . . . I have not seen the Emperor yet, but dine at the Tuileries to-night together with Lyons [2]—the first time he has been invited. He has made himself a good position, and is respected as an honorable and straightforward man by all who know him ; but he has some solid disqualifications which are thought serious. He has no wife or substitute for one —he drinks no wine—he doesn't smoke, and he neither rides nor shoots. It seems absurd to attach importance to any of these shortcomings ; but the fact is, they cut him off from a good deal of the intercourse out of which information is extracted. . . .

Lord Salisbury died on 12th April, an event which altered for a time the tone, though it did not interrupt the frequency, of his widow's correspondence with Lord Clarendon. In one of his letters he expresses a wish that her stepson, the new Lord Salisbury (who, with Lord Carnarvon and General

---

[1] Disraeli, who had become Prime Minister on Lord Derby's retirement.
[2] Lord Lyons had been appointed Ambassador at the Emperor's Court in July of the previous year.

Peel had seceded from Lord Derby's Cabinet upon the Reform Bill of 1867) ' would make up his mind to expose the profligacy of his former chief,' and goes on to say that he would like intensely to do it himself, but his hands were tied by the bonds of family; to lead an attack upon the father-in-law of his own daughter would have tended to disturb the harmony of their relations.

Mr. Purcell, in his *Life of Cardinal Manning*, has lifted a corner of the curtain before a charming little comedy of errors, wherein Lord Clarendon is portrayed as a dangerous conspirator against the Holy See. The *Neri* suspected him of a deep design for bringing the Irish priesthood under control of the Whig party, and Cardinal Manning wrote warning Mgr. Talbot to be on his guard :

8 YORK PLACE, 19*th January* 1868.—I write one line—too late I fear—to put you on your guard lest Lord Clarendon should be urging the endowment of the Catholic clergy in Ireland. This is done with the avowed intention of gaining a hold over them. It would absolutely separate them from their flocks. And I fear there is a strong party forming to try and carry it. If any colour or countenance could be extorted or stolen from the Holy See in its favour, we should be paralysed here. We are in a great crisis, but I am hopeful. Always affectionately yours,

H. E. M.[1]

P.S.—I suspect that some expressions of yours have been written home by Lord Clarendon. He is one to whom you may apply your warning *Cavete ab hominibus*.

Mgr. Talbot was fully of Cardinal Manning's opinion :

I agree with your Grace. . . . Regarding Scotland, I see the absolute necessity of creating a hierarchy, notwithstanding the protest of Lord Clarendon, who has somehow got to hear of the project. He had the impertinence to speak against it to the Pope, but I do not think his Holiness is inclined to listen to him.[2]

Very different was Manning's advice to Talbot respecting Mr. Gladstone, who also was in Rome during this year also, and from whom he had, if not assistance, at least neutrality, in regard to the Pope's temporal power.

[1] Purcell's *Life of Manning*, ii. 399.   [2] *Ibid.*, p. 400.

Gladstone is coming to Rome in October. *Show him all the kindness you can.* I am anxious about him. He has been driven and goaded into extremes and may become dangerous, but for a long time he has been *silent about Rome* and the temporal Power. . . . I think he will do nothing hostile. . . . He does not come as an enemy and may be made friendly, or he might become on his return most dangerous. . . .[1]

They were mistaken—these high ecclesiastics. It was Gladstone, not Clarendon, who by his fulminations against ' Vaticanism ' incurred the wrath of the Holy See and sacrificed his friendship with Manning ; and we have it under Manning's own hand that ' Lord Clarendon, better informed by Odo Russell, whose letters I have preserved, always opposed Gladstone and, in the end, was justified.' [2]

The days of the Disraeli government were soon numbered. Early in 1868 Mr Gladstone introduced his resolutions for disestablishing the Church of Ireland, and ministers sustained three severe defeats in resisting them. On 4th May Disraeli informed the Queen that he could no longer carry on the government, but advised that the sense of the country should be taken through a dissolution. Ministers accordingly resumed office ; Gladstone introduced and passed through the Commons a Suspensory Bill arresting all ecclesiastical patronage in Ireland until 1st August. This bill reached the House of Lords in June, where Lord Salisbury led the opposition to it. Lord Carnarvon, however, who had resigned with Salisbury upon the franchise question, announced that he would support the measure, thereby encouraging the Liberals to hope that he would enlist permanently in their party, which was very weak in the upper chamber. Clarendon, resuming correspondence with Lady Salisbury, criticises freely her stepson, still calling him by his old title of Cranborne :

GROSVENOR CRESCENT, *22nd June.*— . . . I never had a thought of moving the Suspensory Bill. I was asked as I came into the House one evening to give notice of the 2nd reading,

---

[1] *Ibid.*, p. 388.　　　　　　　　　　[2] *Ibid.*, p. 490.

which I did *in the absence of Lord Granville*. This cause was not reported, and I am consequently in the newspapers as first fiddle on Thursday next. I don't even mean to speak if I can help it, as so many will want to air their eloquence on a question for and against which everything possible has been said twenty times over. The well-wishers of Cranborne as a man of ability and *avenir* are, I am told, regretting beforehand the great speech he is to make in defence of that which is indefensible. . . .

26th.— . . . Carnarvon's speech last night was really very powerful and will raise him immensely in public estimation. Cranborne's was as able as it was acrid ; but, as was expected, he took his stand upon the oldest Tory doctrines, and I wish him joy of the lot at whose head he put himself. Derby, knowing that Carnarvon would open the debate, took care not to appear till after dinner, when Cranborne had settled to speak ; and his servile *nobbling* of him seemed to have been successful, for C. alluded to his noble friend only once, in order to agree with him, and he carefully abstained from pitching into the government as Carnarvon had done. The latter must have a good store of moral courage, for he not only separates himself from his party and his particular friend, but from his wife also, for she told me last night, in answer to my compliments on his speech, that we were all wrong and that she could not approve of disestablishment. As to Cranborne, I am always sorry when I see an able man, albeit an opponent, make a false move. He is marvellously unwise, *being in the H. of Lords*, to enter the ranks or take the lead of rank old retrograde Tories, who will be left higher and drier than they ever were before when the tide of democracy sets in next year.

—— *June.*— . . . Confidence in Gladstone seems on the increase thro'out the country, tho' it remains feeble and stationary in the H. of C. On the other hand a demoralised nation admires the audacity, the tricks and the success of the Jew, and the fight between the two will be as personal on the hustings as it has been in parliament.

Lady Augusta Stanley, who is an authority on Court matters, told me that Dizzy writes daily letters to the Queen in his best novel style, telling her every scrap of political news dressed up to serve his own purpose, and every scrap of social gossip cooked to amuse her. She declares that she has never had *such* letters in her life, which is probably true, and that she never before knew *everything*! . . .

Freddy S.[1] has this day determined to leave Preston where his chances are doubtful, and to go in for North Lancashire, where he is told they are certain—at an estimated cost of £25,000 ! but the father is willing and desirous.

Parliament, having been prorogued in July, was dissolved in November, and the first fruits of Disraeli's ' leap in the dark ' was the crushing defeat of his party and the return of the Liberals with a sweeping majority of one hundred and fifteen. Protestant Lancashire, indeed, showed Gladstone the door, but he found another seat in Greenwich, and it was for him that the Queen sent when Disraeli resigned on 1st December.

Clarendon's correspondence during the summer and autumn yields a tolerably consecutive record of his movements, moods, and meditations. The most exciting novelty of the London season was the visit of Mlle. Schneider, a daring exponent of Offenbach's *opéra bouffe*. Clarendon, always a devoted playgoer, reports as follows to Lady Clarendon :

19*th July*.— . . . We went to see *La belle Hélène* the other night, which was a regular *fiasco* as far as concerned those indecencies which prudish but prurient British females expected to see and here. They were all clean excised, Bradford [2] having been frightened by the newspapers, tho' he didn't himself understand a tithe of what Schneider said, sang and looked. He has been overwhelmed by letters of remonstrance against her. On the other hand, the Heir Apparent and the Scotch metropolis [3] bully him about interfering with her ways of pleasantness. To my surprise I saw Salisbury sitting in a box by himself, and on coming out he informed me how much he had been disappointed. . . .

WILDBAD, 15*th August*.— . . . I don't envy Gladstone the formation of a Cabinet, with the loud calls there will be for ignorance and inexperience under the name of *new blood* !

The present writer has the best of reasons—that of experience—for knowing that there never was a kinder-hearted

---

[1] Clarendon's son-in-law, the Hon. F. Stanley, afterwards sixteenth Earl of Derby.

[2] Third Earl of Bradford, Lord Chamberlain, 1866-8.

[3] H.R.H. the Duke of Edinburgh.

man than the sixth Duke of Northumberland, but nature had chosen perversely to mask his real qualities under a somewhat grim countenance and chilling manner. When Lady Salisbury was left a widow in 1868 the Duke placed Syon House at her disposal until she could set up house for herself; whereupon Clarendon writes as follows to her ladyship:

29th August.—I have always hitherto felt that, if I was a jug of cream and was looked at by the Duke of Northumberland, I should instantly turn sour; but now I am prepared, if it would do them any good, to invoke blessings on the Duke and Duchess for the comfort that their kindness and consideration appear to be procuring for you. To me, it is quite a new feature in his character, and I shall never again even think that he *looks* peevish, but shall always regard him as a rare exception to that hideous selfishness which wealth generates, and which has always made me content with being poor. If virtue being its own reward was not one of many lying axioms, why should half Northumberland House have been burned down? The Duke is somewhat in the same case as the late Lord Londonderry, who, after dedicating a trumpery volume of Eastern travels to Lady L.—'the partner of my joys, my sorrows and *my bed*'—began his preface thus—'It has pleased Providence to burn down Wynyard, but' (then came a variety of reasons) 'I shall build it up again!' . . .

Lord Russell to Lord Clarendon.

37 CHESHAM PLACE, *20th September* 1868.—Baron Bauch [?] was here the other day and I asked him—

R.—Is France going to make war?

B.—No; but as Bismarck says he cannot give us any assurance that at some time or other he may not feel compelled to advise the King to consent to the union of the South of Germany with the North, we cannot be dependent on Bismarck's pleasure.

R.—But you cannot make war on a hypothesis?

B.—No; but we may be prepared for what may happen. For instance: Maréchal Niel was told last year that Lille, a first-rate fortress, was not armed with modern cannon and science. He asked how long time would be required to place the proper armament in Lille. He was told 25 years. He ordered the change to be made in three years.

R.—So that in two years from the present time we may look for war ?

B.—War—no : but it is the business of the Minister of War to be ready, in case the honour or interests of France make war necessary.

There is not much in this ; and, according to men's temper, either war or peace may be inferred from it. I asked him about the Chassepot rifles. He said some rifles carried further ; others made a more fatal wound ; but on the whole the Chassepot rifle combined more advantages than any other.

Gladstone, I expect, will insist strongly on retrenchment, and the nation will go with him. . . .

P.S.—I do not see how, if all Germany is united in a confederation, France will be justified in making war.

Lord Clarendon to Lady Salisbury.

WILDBAD, 1st *October* 1868.— . . . I am glad to have made the acquaintance of General Moltke here. As Chef d'État-Major he is perhaps the most remarkable man of modern times. The success of the last campaign was entirely owing to his power of organisation and wonderful foresight. He is a modest, silent man—something between a notary and a professor—and looks no more like a soldier than I do. He told me they had been misinformed in 1866, and that if they had known that the French could only bring 140,000 men into the field, they would have *finished off matters at once and for good in a very different fashion.*

WILDBAD, *October* 1868.— . . . Hayward told me that two new vols. by Kinglake would be out on the 10th. They are strategical and not political—hostile to the French and not complimentary to the English. It is now 10 years since Lady Raglan made over to him every letter and paper she possessed for the immediate vindication of her husband. Hitherto he has but damaged Lord R.'s reputation a little ; but he has much pleased the woman he is in love with (Mme. Blaise de Bury) by foul abuse of the Emperor. I found Gladstone yesterday reading the memoirs of Bunsen (by his widow, I believe), which he said interested him more than any other book of the kind he had read for years.

The widow M—— has returned from Paris with jet black hair. She told us she adored Worth, who had made her aware of the good points of her shoulders and their neighbourhood, and there was nothing in the way of dress to prevent our forming an opinion for ourselves of the whole locality. . . .

9th November.—I told Gladstone last July that I had a perfect horror of returning to harness ; since that time I have had no communication with him—direct or indirect. I hope he may have taken me at my word, as it is not my custom to say one thing and mean another.

The same to the Duchess of Manchester.

GROSVENOR CRESCENT, *2nd November* 1868.— . . . I went to Castle Puss [1] on Monday and found him in tearing spirits, caused, I thought, more by the existence of his child than the prospects of his party. However, they are as happy as possible, and that ticket in the lottery of marriage, which might have been *such* a blank, has really drawn a prize. . . . People seem divided in opinion as to whether the Chief Rabbi of the Jews or Soapy Sam [2] will be the new Archbishop of Canterbury. I heard rather a good definition of a Conservative—a man who turns round and round so often that at last he becomes *dizzy*.

Lord Hyde, Clarendon's eldest son, was Liberal candidate for South Warwickshire at the general election of 1868. He was beaten there, but obtained a seat for Brecon in the following year.

The same to Lady Caledon.

GROSVENOR CRESCENT, *10th November* 1868.— . . . We are in a state of anxiety, imaginable but indescribable, about Hyde's election. He has worked like 10 horses for many weeks and has made himself quite a reputation for his tact in canvassing and his power of speaking ; so, if he fails, I shall not grudge paying the money *I haven't got* for so good an apprenticeship in public life. . . .

The same to Lady Salisbury.

November 1868.— . . . Alas, Hyde is beaten. I suppose it is foolish and a sign of old age, but I take his defeat bitterly to heart, and am quite unhappy. Things electoral have gone very ill to-day, but still it is said that the majority will be 100.

[1] Lord Granville's house. He married, secondly, in 1865 Miss Campbell of Islay, and their first-born, Lady Victoria Alberta, came in 1867 and married Mr. Harold Russell in 1896.
[2] Samuel Wilberforce, Bishop of Oxford.

Heaven knows, however, of what materials it will be composed, and one can only feel sure that such a team will require to be driven by a more skilful Jehu than Gladstone. Altogether I don't like the look of our future, and I care a good deal more about that than any party interests.

I don't make out what the little P. Lodge hermit [1] is about, and whether he expects to be sent for by the Queen or to return to the F.O. in a government formed by Gladstone. If you see him again before you leave Syon, do fish a little for his intentions. At present he is rather a dark horse. . . .

Lord Clarendon to Lord Russell.

PEMBROKE LODGE, 14th November 1868.— . . . I fear Gladstone will be worked up by his meetings to a state of excitement which Christmas will hardly cool. I am ready to endorse all his speeches, but *not* Bright's. The free breakfast table, and committees to do the work of First Lord of the Admiralty and War Secretary, are sad heresies. Why does he put these notions forth ? Is it that he wishes to avoid office ? Once in office, I feel sure he would be very practical, and he would not have gone so far as Lord Derby and Lord Stanley in comprehending all householders.

I think there will be nearly 100 members of the House of Commons upon whom no one can depend—a Liberal majority in general, but very fickle and fastidious. It was reserved for Derby to destroy the constitution ; but if he and Dizzy are put aside, it may linger on for some time. . . . I feel confident of Gladstone's return for Greenwich, if not for South Lancashire ; but, as Lord John Manners wisely remarks, we shall know more on Tuesday.

I suppose Disraeli wishes to disestablish the Church of England ; but it will outlive him, and perhaps last till the end of the century. . . .

Lord Clarendon to Lady Salisbury.

November 1868.— . . . Cranborne was in the House this evening, and the *agaceries* of his former chief [2] were more active than ever. The outward and visible signs of cordiality between them are so manifest that whenever, if ever, C. turns upon him, I am sure my lords will be surprised, tho' the great majority of

---

[1] Lord Russell at Pembroke Lodge.   [2] Lord Derby.

them will in their hearts be delighted. He is the only man who could show up the 'Flower of Chivalry' with real *connoissance de cause*. . . .

. . . I wish I could take a rose-colored leaf out of my predecessor's book [1] and look at complications with the same wise *sang froid* that he did; but I was born and shall die *Monsieur Tant-pis*. In some respects I don't regret it, because I am always prepared for the worst that can happen, and then if things stop short of the worst, I put it down to the credit side. The difficulties about the Conference seem smoothing down. . . . I hope our trusty and well-beloved cousin L. N. will run true; but he generally tries to use such gatherings for some purpose of his own. . . .

THE GROVE, 1*st December* 1868.— . . . I hope the Missus [2] will send for the Pembroke Lodger,[3] because it would please him and assuage his pain at getting older as time goes on; but for her own interest she ought to send for the elect of the people,[4] and to give no color to the notion that is rife of his being utterly repugnant to her. When left to himself, there is a large fund of aristocracy in our little man, and his fear of Bright, Forster and other levellers is very genuine; but I believe that all such men—Gladstone included—are far safer when weighted with responsibility and a desire to retain any office they may get into, than if they are left out in the cold, trying to keep themselves warm by intemperate agitation.

As for my part in the Cabinet you and he have formed, I must not do anything that could with justice be considered shabby towards G[ladstone] or the party; but I mean, if possible, to let that cup pass by me. I have no affectation in the matter, but I can't bring myself to believe that I am wanted—*i.e.*, that the fewer old occupants of places return to them, the more agreeable it will be to the *criards* among the Liberals and their press. To do that which is hateful to myself in order to dissatisfy others, seems to me absurd. 'New blood' is the cry, and why should not the cry have its way? . . .

Disraeli's appeal to the country met with an unfavourable answer. In the general election held in autumn, although Gladstone and Lord Hartington were both unseated in Lancashire (Hartington by Clarendon's son-in-law Colonel

[1] Lord Stanley's.
[3] Lord Russell.
[2] The Queen.
[4] Mr. Gladstone.

Stanley) the Liberals were returned by a majority of more than a hundred. The Queen laid her commands on Mr. Gladstone, who, of course, wished to have Lord Clarendon at the Foreign Office, but he met with unexpected objection from the Queen. Something had set her against her former Foreign Secretary; whether it was his tone in reporting his observations at the Frankfort conference in 1863,[1] or whether he had given Her Majesty offence in some other way, does not appear; but that she had taken umbrage is clear from certain entries in Lord Halifax's journal at this time:

25th November.—I told Charles [2] that he should point out to the Queen that Lord Russell had made Clarendon his Foreign Secretary, and that Lord Derby had offered the post to him; so that in the opinion of both leaders he was the best man for the post.

26th.— . . . The essential point of the Queen's message was her objection to Clarendon as Foreign Secretary. She told Charles that he was the only one of her ministers who had ever been impertinent to her, and that she could not submit to him in the position of Foreign Secretary which brought him into such constant communication with her; that he was too intimate with the Queen of Holland and was influenced by her, and that his opinions against the German unity and views of Russia, which she considered so right and necessary, rendered him unfit for that post on public grounds. She did not object to him in another post: would prefer Granville, in which case Clarendon might be President of the Council, and would not object to Kimberley; or it might be well to bring Lyons home, in which case Clarendon might go to Paris. . . . She said that both Clarendon and Lowe were very sarcastic, and she did not like such people in intimate communication with her. . . . Charles thinks that the Queen must have heard of Clarendon having used expressions about herself which she cannot forgive; neither he nor Sir T. Biddulph at all knows what it is. I remember hearing some three or four years ago that she was very angry with him for presuming, as she thought, to give her advice in a manner not very respectful, about the Prince of Wales. Charles says that she is very difficult to speak to or advise in any matter

---

[1] See page 281, *ante*.
[2] General the Hon. Charles Grey (1804-70), the Queen's private secretary.

concerning herself, and that he has lost all influence in such matters.

27th.—Heard from Charles Grey enclosing a memorandum in the Queen's handwriting repeating more strongly than ever her objections to Clarendon in any situation. . . .

28th.—Heard from Gladstone that he could not come to meet me, but would be glad to see me at Hawarden, to which place I went accordingly, arriving about an hour before dinner. I had two long conversations with him, Mrs. Gladstone being present. I told him everything I had heard from Charles, both in his letters and in our conversations, as I thought it only right that he should be in full possession of all the information I could give him. I began by saying that I came for this purpose only, and not to give any opinion at all. I was only the channel through whom the Queen wished to communicate to him her wishes and feelings on certain points, before she could properly communicate with him directly, and also because it might render her communication with him more easy. He was taken aback, as I expected, and spoke very strongly on the injustice of condemning Clarendon, as the Queen had done, on reports of conversations which were not proved, and without allowing him the opportunity of contradicting the report. . . .

2nd December.— . . . The Queen will not object to Lord Clarendon as President of the Council.

9th December.— . . . Gladstone described his government as :

Peelites.	Whigs.	New Men.
Gladstone	Granville	Page Wood
Cardwell	Hartington	Goschen
Argyll	Clarendon	Bright
	De Grey	Childers
	Fortescue	Bruce
		Kimberley
		Lowe.

It does not appear when, how or by whom the Queen's objection was overcome ; but on 9th December Clarendon kissed hands at Osborne as Foreign Secretary.

THE GROVE, 10*th December* 1868.—DEAR LADY SALISBURY,—I meant to have written yesterday, but did not reach F.O. till nearly 4 from Osborne. . . . The Queen was just in her old form, and resumed the usual talk just as if it had not *enjoyed* (so far as I am concerned) a 2½ years interruption. She seemed mightily

pleased at the manner in which we stand respecting the Conference and hoped the Prince of Wales would read my *excellent*
letter to the King of Greece. En voilà du sucré ! I had written
to the Heir Apparent by her desire to say that, under present
circs., he couldn't go to Athens.

Bright seems to have made a very good impression, and she
spoke of his kind and gentle manner. She made no allusion
whatever to the late government ; nor, of course, did I.

. . . On Friday I had a long official talk with S[tanley] who
was most friendly and communicative. I did not detect a shade
of difference of opinion between us. I wish he was *unhand-
cuffed* from the party with which he can have no sympathy.
His father did him no good turn when he prevented him from
accepting Palmerston's offer.

From the Queen of Holland.

HAGUE, *last day of* 1868.—DEAR LORD CLARENDON,—God
bless you and yours 1869 and each following year ! Let me close
the year with these wishes, coming from a devoted heart. Remember that your friendship is among the few earthly treasures
I possess, which I hope to preserve *till I go before you.* I have a
favour to ask. Will you kindly place on your writing-table in
the room downstairs at Grosvenor Crescent the little clock which
this week's messenger takes with him ? It is just à *la hauteur des
yeux* : it is to remind you at night of the proper time to go to
rest—of curtailing your work at late hours. Ask Milady to
remind you to look at it sometimes for that *useful* purpose.
Your health is more important than peace or war.

For the last 48 hours we are without a telegraph, almost
without post. The hurricane smashed everything to pieces. It
is a dreary year's end. But I must not be gloomy. I end with
many a wish for health and happiness to dear Lady Cl., yourself,
and your children.—Faithfully yours now and ever,

SOPHIA.

CHAPTER XXIV

LAST DAYS

Πᾶσι θανεῖν μερόπεσσιν ὀφείλεται, οὐδε τις ἐστὶν
Αὔριον εἰ ζήσει θνητὸς ἐπιστάμενος.

> 'We pass: the path that each man trod
> Is dim, or will be dim, with weeds;
> What fame has left for human deeds
> In endless age? It rests with God.'

THERE is little material forthcoming to enable one to follow
Lord Clarendon's course through the stormy session of 1869.
The ranks of his intimate correspondents were sadly thinned.
Lady Theresa was no more; Emily Eden was nearing her
end;[1] Lord Howden still lived, but feebly, in retirement
at Bayonne. Nor was Lord Clarendon's strength unim-
paired. He was in his seventieth year, afflicted by frequent
returns of gout, and lacked the superfluous energy which in
former years enabled him to remain at his desk till the
sparrows were chirping in the eaves. Yet he neither showed
nor felt any abatement in the zest of life, nor did he ever
incur the penalty of him 'qui de son âge n'a pas l'esprit,
de son âge a tous les malheurs.' He still maintained
constant communication with Lady Salisbury; but there
is little in his letters to her to show how he felt as the colleague of John Bright, whom a few months before he had
held to be a dangerous revolutionary, nor what heart he
had in the chief measure of the session—disestablishment
and disendowment of the Irish Church—an institution for
which he once felt and expressed unflinching loyalty.[2]

Lord Clarendon to Lady Salisbury.

21st January 1869.— . . . *Merrypebble*[3] has not been
hatching the Irish egg alone at Hawarden, but has had Puss[4]
with him and the Irish Attorney-General.[5] He writes in hopes

[1] She died on 5th August 1869.　　[2] See vol. i. p. 298.
[3] Mr. Gladstone.　　[4] Lord Granville.
[5] Sir Edward Sullivan (1822-65), appointed Irish Lord Chancellor in
1883.

of being able to submit a plan of detail—principle being long since agreed upon—to the Cabinet next week. I have not the remotest idea what it will be, and shall be slightly curious to know. . . .

27th.— . . . There was a cabinet yesterday, but I did not sit near Gladstone and had not a word with him, so I have no idea how his visit to the Queen went off and whether he talked Church to her ; I only know that he did not to his colleagues, for he said that the returns to his enquiries were not completed, and that it would be useless to discuss a measure for which the data were wanting. Everybody agreed, just as one agrees to go to the dentist to-morrow instead of to-day.

1st February.— . . . Wm. Harcourt intends to take up and invest himself in the mantle which he believes has fallen for ever from the shoulders of the disgraced Bright ; which being interpreted means that he is furious at not being Solicitor-General, tho' he has never before been in the House of Commons, and his only practice has been before parliamentary committees.

10th.— . . . I don't think it very decent—at least it is somewhat contrary to practice—that a man should be a judge in the morning and a bitter political partisan at night ; but I can't wonder at the party preferring Cairns to Malmesbury. I am sorry that Robert [1] accepts him as his leader. He would have much more influence if he remained independent. . . .

26th April.— . . . Salisbury came out against the government rather in his old partisan fashion the other night ; but, tho' cynical, it was not as ill-natured as his old party would have desired. On the other hand, your brother [2] has taken his seat behind the Treasury Bench and made a very effective speech on army organisation. I shall be most curious to know what Cairns *wants*. I can hardly believe that he suggests himself from gratitude for past favors. He is a most acrimonious and disagreeable party leader, and I don't think his side are satisfied with his special pleading, for it is nothing else. Malmesbury, tho' of course inferior in ability, had more of the *genius loci*.

European politics were unwontedly tranquil at this time —the lull before the tornado of 1870—but the *Alabama* claims remained as a running sore in British relations with the United States. Lord Russell, when Foreign Secretary and also when Prime Minister, had firmly resisted the demand that these claims should be submitted to an inter-

---

[1] Her stepson Lord Salisbury.   [2] Sixth Earl de la Warr.

national court for arbitration. Lord Stanley, succeeding him, had agreed that they should be so submitted, whereupon President Johnson's government insisted that the recognition by Great Britain of the Southern States as belligerents should be included as a charge for indemnity. To admit this was impossible, and negotiations were dropped. There is no saying to what deplorable issue the quarrel might not have led had President Johnson remained in office, but in 1868 he was impeached by the House of Representatives for various high crimes and misdemeanours ; and although the necessary two-thirds majority of the Senate did not vote for his conviction, wherefore he was held to be acquitted,[1] he did not seek re-election in autumn of the same year. General Grant was chosen President, and on 14th January 1869 Lord Clarendon and Mr. Reverdy Johnson, the American ambassador, concluded a treaty for submitting all the disputed claims to arbitration. Everything seemed in train for a settlement, but when the treaty came before the American Senate, Mr. Charles Sumner denounced it on the ground that arbitration, whereon President Johnson's government had insisted, was derogatory to the honour of the United States, and the treaty was rejected almost unanimously. ' The news from America,' wrote Clarendon to Lady Salisbury on 9th May, ' is very bad, and I believe that Grant and Sumner mean war ; or rather that amount of insult and humiliation that must lead to it. The culminating point of the Lord Rector's [2] good luck was escaping from the F.O. at the time he did, and I am rightly served for allowing myself to be talked back to that *galère* again.'

Lord Cairns failed to win Clarendon's approval when chosen to lead the Conservatives in the House of Lords in succession to Lord Derby.

The same to the same.

19*th May* 1869.— . . . Cairns, I am sure, is not liked, even by his own side. He is *nisi prius* all over, and there is a legal

---

[1] The voting was—Guilty 35, Not Guilty 19.
[2] Lord Stanley was Lord Rector of Glasgow University, 1868-71.

combativeness about him that is redolent of a brief and carries
no conviction.   I wish I had leisure to read Lecky's book. . . .

24th.— . . . We intended to give a ball at the F.O. on the
Queen's birthday, but found that the fewest we could ask was
4000 ! so, of course, the idea is abandoned ; but we mean to
give two parties. . . . Salisbury made a sensible and liberal
speech upon life peers this evening.   He is an enigma to me, and
I wish you would tell me *what he really is*.   An old college
friend of his told me that he had no real sympathy with the Tory
party, or indeed with any other ; and that he was cynical because
he only knew the bad side of human nature and didn't believe
in the possibility of good or unselfish motives.   I rather doubt
that being true, because nothing you have ever said to me
indicated that such was your opinion.   He was a good deal
cheered on our side, whereas the grim faces of Derby and Cairns
were worth photographing. . . .

On 5th June it was resolved at a meeting of Conservative
peers, held at the Duke of Marlborough's house, that the
Irish Church Bill should be opposed.

The same to the same.

5th June.— . . . The general belief yesterday was that my
Lords were more afraid of the pressure now brought to bear upon
them than of the irreparable mischief they will do to their House
and their Order by throwing out the bill. . . . I had to say something last night *in re* Alabama, and did justice to my Lord
Rector.[1]   I wonder whether—*mutatis mutandis*—he would have
done the like by me ! . . .

The bill came before the House of Lords on 14th June.
Clarendon spoke in support of it, and, citing his own experience of Ireland, maintained that the measure was both
just and necessary ; but he descended to lower ground when
he declared that both justice and necessity were of less
moment than the effect which the rejection of the bill would
have upon the House of Lords.   The second reading was
carried after four nights' debate by 179 to 146—majority 33.
Lord Salisbury, Lord Carnarvon, and thirty-four other
Conservative peers were in the majority.   In committee,

---

[1] Lord Stanley.

however, the Lords played havoc with the disendowment clauses, and the danger of a collision between the two Houses became serious, whereof Clarendon expressed his apprehension to Lady Salisbury :

26th June.— . ... Heaven only knows what will be the result of the lordly disfigurement of the bill, which is by no means over yet, but the deadlock may be quite as bad as if the second reading had been rejected. Salisbury seems to have repented him of the prudence he at first displayed, and to be rather intoxicated by the manifest preference for him over Cairns ; but it is not wise for a man who aims, and with good right, at the first place to defy and irritate the H. of Commons, which was very well disposed towards him. . . .

17th July.— . . . I have not, for many years, been so generally and particularly ill as this last week ; but I am creeping out of it and am now going to the cabinet, where I expect some indecision as to the course we should take with the utterly disfigured and unrecognisable bill. There was shown such a want of consideration for the Commons in the lordly proceedings that I cannot wonder at the wrath of the former.

22nd.— . . . Salisbury was in the worst form of the worst R. Cecil times, and I can't call to mind any speech of any man that has caused such general *disgust (passez-moi le mot)* in the circs. under which it was delivered. He probably glories in having made it and will do nothing to soften or retract it. Six weeks ago he was on the threshold of a grand position, and might have saved the majority from the influence of Derby and the ill-will of the country ; but that is gone now, at all events for the present, and people agree in Dizzy's dictum that ' S. will always be found a flighty young gentleman.'

When the crisis was most acute and the aspect of affairs most devoid of peaceful symptoms, a way of escape was devised by the Conservative leader in the House of Lords. Lord Cairns was an Ulsterman and an Irish Churchman of the strictest stamp ; he had led the opposition to the bill in the second reading debates as well as through all the long discussions in Committee ; but he now saw nothing to be gained by dogged resistance ; he would resort to negotiation. Without consulting the chief men of his party, he sought private interview with Lord Granville, and arranged terms with him on the question of commutation of livings which the House of Lords, weary of controversy, proved fain to accept.[1]

The Clarendons went to Wiesbaden in August, but the Foreign Secretary has to content himself with change of scene as a restorative, cessation of work being out of the question.

The same to the same.

WIESBADEN, *7th September* 1869.— . . . I have done my Gortchakoff, having met him at Heidelberg as a place equidistant between here and Baden. The conference lasted $3\frac{1}{2}$ hours, and we agreed that it *must* lead to a right good understanding between the Lion and the Bear. Be that as it may, I am glad I went, as we certainly arrived at agreement upon several points. Perhaps, however, the crafty man was only practising upon my youth and innocence. . . .

Returning to England towards the end of September he found Gladstone busily incubating legislation on Irish land. Gladstone had sloughed off his Whig respect for property almost as completely as he had rid himself of his earlier Tory devotion to the principle of Church establishments. Not so Clarendon, who seems to have been startled by the drastic scheme which his chief had conceived.

The same to the same.

THE GROVE, *1st October* 1869.— . . . As I am not, and don't mean to be a spoliator, I thought the opportunity a good one to protest against wild schemes. Merrypebble may think I went too far ; if so, I shall be glad to have it out with him. I have warned him that if he used the Irish landlords roughly, the English ones would assuredly fraternise with them, which would be more injurious to the government than dissatisfying the agitators, who are, one and all, irresponsible, pennyless and dishonest. . . .

7th.— . . . Your conversation with Manning must have been very interesting. . . . It would require the faith that removes mountains in order to swallow the exposition of the Syllabus of

---

[1] The negotiations are described in detail in Morley's *Gladstone,* ii. 274-8.

which he delivered himself the other day. His audience may
have been middle-aged people, but he must have taken them for
people of the middle ages. . . . I am no sceptic now, but believe
in the resurrection of man and his admission to paradise. I
believe, too, in the miracles of old, as mesmeric influences must
have existed then as now, and I am quite prepared to give equal
credit to the modern workers of phenomena. There are waking
dreams that are better than sleep, and of these I had a full
enjoyment last night. . . .

16*th.*— . . . I have been operated upon by Motley,[1] and, as
I had no chloroform, it was not pleasant. He read me a despatch
of 12 sheets on the Alabama mess ; and tho' it was most courteous
in tone, it re-opened the whole case in all its details from the very
beginning, and re-produced all the old disputed facts and answered arguments, as if it was brand new matter. . . . My
impression is that we are further than ever from settlement and
that a heap of trouble is oncoming.

One needs to bear in mind how the principles of property
and freedom of contract have been honeycombed by the
legislature during the last forty years before understanding
how nearly Gladstone's cabinet foundered over his Irish
Land Bill of 1870.   The confiscation of Irish Church
property had already served to exclude from that cabinet
one of the wisest heads in the Liberal ranks ; for Sir Roundell
Palmer [2] had declined the Woolsack—the richest prize in
the Prime Minister's power to bestow—rather than have any
hand in legislation which he could not reconcile with justice.
He denied that any distinction could be drawn between
private and corporate property ; and that had been the
theme of Bishop Magee's famous speech on the second
reading in the House of Lords, when he warned his hearers
against supposing that an attack on corporate property was
not the sure forerunner of infringement upon rights in
private property.

' Clarendon,' wrote Charles Greville, ' had the great
advantage of being plain George Villiers and having to fight
his way in the world,' before he succeeded to the peerage

---

[1] John Lothrop Motley, American ambassador at St. James's.
[2] Lord Chancellor, 1872-4 and 1880-5 ; Baron Selborne 1872, Earl of
Selborne 1882.

in 1838, when Gladstone was the rising star of the Tory
party. Through what phases of change had Gladstone since
then driven a way to the premier place ; how plastic had
proved the principles once so forcibly professed ; how sinewy
the intellect that could convince itself of the rectitude of
what was presented to it as expedient ! Not so nimble was
the movement of Clarendon's mind. The pillars of public
conduct which guided George Villiers at the outset of his
career remained erect for him at its close. There had been
nothing in his long service under Palmerston to shake
them. Whigs, Liberals, and Peelites—none had contemplated removing the ancient landmarks—all had combined
to resist attempts by Radicals to do so.

As early as 29th May 1869, while parliament was in the
throes of debate upon the Irish Church Bill, Gladstone was
preparing the framework of an Irish Land Bill, and Granville,
admitted to some inkling of its scope, warned him that ' this
question may break us up.' Coming to closer quarters
with the measure in the autumn cabinets, Granville told
Gladstone that he had received two letters from Clarendon
indicating that, in his opinion, the government *must* be
broken up.[1]

On 3rd November the note in Gladstone's diary runs :
' Cabinet. Chiefly on Irish land, and stiff.' The opposition
he had to deal with consisted of Argyll, Cardwell, Lowe and
Clarendon. Our concern here is only with the last-named—
how were his objections overcome ? Never, perhaps ; at
any rate, I have found nothing under his own hand to
explain the process. Probably his knowledge of Ireland
enabled him to share the view expressed by Lord Salisbury,
that the bill contained ' points white, grey and black '—
things which he admired exceedingly (the creation of a
peasant proprietary and compensation for improvements),
things whereof he respected the intention but distrusted
the means to effect it, and things, such as interference with
free contract and compensation for eviction in default of
rent, which he condemned with all his heart.

In one respect the Foreign Secretary stands apart from

[1] Morley's *Gladstone*, ii. 290.

other ministers. His mind is concentrated, his energy absorbed, his time consumed, in the contemplation and discharge of matters beyond the sphere of domestic politics. There is strong inducement for him to withdraw attention from what goes on outside the doors of his own department, and, so long as he can remain in accord with the general policy of his colleagues, to leave upon them the responsibility for details of legislation. I have no warrant for offering this as an explanation of Clarendon's surrender on the Irish Land Bill of 1870, but it is one which has been known to make the action of other Foreign Secretaries intelligible. At the same time, it would be blind to leave out of account the contagion of enthusiasm with which Gladstone, having once convinced himself, was able to fuse the wills of others and run them into his own mould. The momentum was strongly centripetal at first ; no statesman of modern times has had such a hold upon the popular fancy as Gladstone then possessed, enabling him to deal with the Irish Church, the land and the franchise as he wished ; not until fifteen years later was the current reversed and cast him derelict on the reefs of Home Rule. At all events, Clarendon had plenty on his hands during the early months of 1870 to leave him little inclination or strength to interfere with the work of other departments of State. The United States government had renewed the negotiations so abruptly broken when they flung aside the Clarendon convention of 1869. Letters and despatches, interminably argumentative, passed and re-passed incessantly between Washington and Downing Street. Although Clarendon had learnt much from Palmerston— almost as much how *not* to do it as how to do it—he never followed him in taking a line in foreign affairs independently of his colleagues or without their knowledge. ' I grieve to trouble you with so much manuscript,' he wrote to Gladstone on 17th March, ' but I don't venture single-handed to conduct a correspondence with the United States. . . . All this correspondence can do nothing but harm, and I have made my answer as short as is consistent with courtesy. I should like to send it on Saturday ; but if you have not

time to look at it, or think it ought to be seen by the Cabinet,
I could make an excuse for the delay to Motley.'

Arising directly out of the *Alabama* embroglio and based
on the report of a royal commission in 1868, was the bill
amending the Foreign Enlistment Act, framed to render impossible the recurrence of international disputes of that kind.

Nearer home, Clarendon was closely engaged during the
early months of 1870 in negotiation with the French government for a simultaneous reduction of armaments, which at
one time seemed not so impracticable as later events of that
year proved it to have been.

But it was not Lord Clarendon's lot to witness the result
of these labours. At midsummer he was confined to his
house, 1 Grosvenor Crescent, by a sharp attack of gout, a
malady with which he had been painfully familiar for more
than half his life. This time the symptoms were severe.
' Clarendon,' wrote Lord Granville to the Duke of Argyll,
' was only saved from gout in the stomach by strong
stimulants to his feet.' This proved a palliative, but no
remedy ; on 27th June he passed away in the presence of
his devoted wife and his eldest son, 'dying,' as Lord
Granville announced that evening in the House of Lords,
' under the weight of affairs, in the very act of trying to
arrange a matter necessary to civilisation in Europe.'

In appraising Lord Clarendon's rank among European
statesmen, one may not neglect the testimony of those
who worked alongside of him. Let that of his latest chief
stand first. Mr. Gladstone has commemorated his ' un-
swerving loyalty, his genial temper, his kindness ever overflowing in acts yet more than in words, his liberal and
indulgent appreciation of others ' ; and in his diary occurs
the brief tribute—' An irreparable colleague, a statesman
of many gifts, a most lovable and genial man.' Twenty
years later Gladstone told Lord Morley that, of the sixty
men or so who had been his colleagues in the Cabinet,
Clarendon was the very easiest and most attractive.[1]

Another contemporary (and it is upon contemporary

[1] Morley's *Gladstone*, ii. 447.

judgment that one has to rely for a clue to Clarendon's peculiar influence over men and women) describes him as 'a hater of platitudes, understanding how to dash off in a few daring, if slightly contemptuous, phrases the main features of a political situation and the leading traits of the European statesmen whom he had known ; yet these conventional indiscretions were always good-natured.' [1] 'His ringing laugh,' wrote Henry Reeve, who knew Clarendon intimately, 'and ready repartee enlivened the formality of courts and gave a charm to the gravest political discussions.' [2] It was these natural qualities which, aided by a perfect fluency in several languages, secured for him an unrivalled reputation among British diplomatists of the period and caused him to rank very high among those who have controlled the foreign relations of his country.

Over the Emperor Napoleon III. Clarendon acquired a singular ascendency, as was proved upon several occasions, already referred to. The two men liked each other, and Clarendon always gave the Emperor credit for honest intentions, though he often doubted his power to carry them into effect. The following striking testimony to this influence comes from a high source. In 1871, after Odo Russell succeeded Lord Augustus Loftus as ambassador at Berlin, he and Lady Emily attended a party where they met Count Bismarck. Lady Emily was sitting beside the great man, when he suddenly said to her—'Never in my life was I more glad to hear of anything than I was to hear of your father's death.' Lady Emily was naturally taken aback by such an extraordinary speech, and showed it ; whereupon Bismarck, patting her hand, said, 'Ach, dear lady, you must not take it like that. What I mean is that, if your father had lived, he would have prevented the war.'

Personal charm, however much it may attract and secure friendship, has little to do with the making of a statesman unless there are sterling qualities behind it. That Clarendon possessed such qualities in no ordinary

[1] Sir E. Russell, *That Reminds Me*, pp. 26, 27.
[2] *Fraser's Magazine*, August 1870.

measure must appear plainly when it is remembered that, being the scion and heir of a Tory house who took for a wife the daughter of another Tory house, he had therefore no claim upon the Whig leaders for their countenance in approaching, or their aid in surmounting, the barriers which then guarded the entrance to that most exclusive of services —diplomacy. It is true that his uncle Lord Morley, like Lord Palmerston, drifted after Canning's death into the Whig ranks, and it may well be that Morley first drew Palmerston's attention to the qualities of the obscure Commissioner of Customs. Clarendon never forgot that it was to Palmerston he owed his release from routine duties and admission to a field where he could put his abilities to a fair test. Once in that field his tireless industry, lucid despatches, and firm consistency in Liberal principles soon proved his capacity for work of a higher order. Returning from Spain at the age of thirty-nine he manifested that trait which is surely rarest among public men—namely, a total absence of personal ambition and supreme indifference to the advantage or emoluments of office. Virgil's aspiration left him unmoved—

> Temptanda via est, qua me quoque possim
> Tollere humo victorque virum volitare per ora.[1]

In the course of the next few years he declined two of the most coveted appointments to which a British subject may aspire—the Governor-Generalship of Canada once, and the Viceroyalty of India twice. When Prince Albert in 1848 expressed to him a strong wish that, if Lord John Russell should carry out his threat of resignation, he —Clarendon—should undertake to form a ministry, he received the assurance that nothing would induce him to take the premiership. Four years later, when the feud between Russell and Palmerston was at its height, it was the wish of many that the difficulty should be got over by calling Clarendon to the head of affairs ; but again he would not hear of it. He had already declined the Foreign

---

[1] New ways I must attempt, my grovelling name
To raise aloft and wing my flight to fame.
                    (*Georgics*, iii. 9.   Dryden's trans.)

Office after Palmerston's dismissal in 1851, fearing lest he should wound the feelings of his old friend or give any appearance of truth to the rumour that he was intriguing against him as a rival.

Through no effort or wish of his own, contrary, indeed, to his private inclination, Clarendon became a member of successive Cabinets simply because he had proved himself indispensable. Fluent beyond the common with his pen, he made no pretension to eloquence either within or without parliament ; what his colleagues valued in him was his consistent yet rational Liberalism, his unwavering loyalty to his chief, and his transparent honesty.

In one respect Clarendon fell short of the highest ideal of statesmanship. An able and fearless administrator, a most accomplished foreign minister, and an untiring champion of freedom and toleration, he allowed his full influence to be crippled by too dutiful an allegiance to party. He appears never to have been able to give a Tory ministry credit for honest purpose or sound policy. It seemed to him as reasonable to expect grapes from thorns or figs from thistles as useful legislation from Derby or Disraeli. When he became convinced that Palmerston's eastern policy in 1840 was driving the country straight into war with France, he would not give effect to his conviction by resigning office, and cared not to conceal his reason for remaining in the Cabinet—namely, lest the government should be broken up and the Tories get into power. Admitting that he was justified in regarding the alternative as one of two evils, surely the greater disaster would have been a war with France ; but *maluit cum Scaligero errare*.

Again in 1866, when Lord Derby invited him to remain at the Foreign Office, and, lest he should feel out of place as a solitary Whig in a Conservative ministry, undertook to give him some colleagues of his own party, Clarendon's modesty cannot have hindered him from perceiving that the interests of the country would best have been served if he had continued in control of its foreign relations at that most critical time. It was obligation to party, as he conceived it, that deterred him from setting so admirable a precedent.

Henry Reeve, who did not make Lord Clarendon's acquaintance before he had reached the *medium filum*—nearer fifty than forty—has left a sketch of his personal appearance.

By the common consent of those who are acquainted with the society of England, Lord Clarendon was regarded as the most finished gentleman, the most charming and genial companion, and the most accomplished Foreign Minister of our times. His person in early life was singularly handsome. He had the air of refinement which Vandyke was wont to give to his portraits, and which seemed as much an inheritance of George Villiers as his name. Even in age, when the hair grew thin and the face blanched with toil, his eye had lost none of its brightness nor his figure any of its unstudied elegance. His manners to men of every degree and of every country had a charm which unbent the most rugged antagonist, and inspired confidence alike to the timid and the suspicious.

It is of little avail to treat of one who has borne an active part in public affairs or to penetrate the motives which lay behind his conduct, unless some insight can be had into his attitude towards the eternal problem of Hereafter. The difficulty of doing so is perhaps greater in the case of an English Protestant than it is in respect of men of other nations and religions, because of the habitual reticence of men of his race and creed upon spiritual matters. Probably the majority of thoughtful men (I do not venture to speak of women, whose nature inclines them to wholehearted surrender of self) when they repeat a creed would encounter some perplexity in defining (1) what they entirely believe ; (2) what they are afraid *not* to believe, and (3) what no effort whereof they are capable enables them to believe. It is easy for a man whose faculties are constantly exercised upon weighty matters exacting severe mental work that must be relieved by intervals of repose and relaxation, to avoid the effort indispensable for arriving at such a definition. Consequently we do not find that Clarendon indulged in much speculation upon the divine mysteries. He continued through his life to conform to the observances and to attend the services of that wing of the Church of England which is denominated Low; but except in a single letter to his sister in early youth there is no trace of evangelical enthusiasm. He felt an unconquerable aversion for religious controversy and for that dogmatic theology which so powerfully attracted the intellect of his great colleague, Gladstone. Clarendon's simple creed seems to have been expressed in words of the prophet Micah : ' What doth the Lord require of thee but to do justly, and to love mercy, and to walk humbly with thy God ? ' Nowhere else can I find more articulate expression of what I conceive to have been his guiding faith, than in the profession of Spinoza the Pantheist :

The only unmistakable tokens of the true Catholic faith and the true fruits of the Holy Spirit are justice and benevolence. Wheresoever these are found, there Christ assuredly is present, and wheresoever they are not found, there Christ is not present ; for it is only by the Spirit of Christ that we can be brought to delight in justice and benevolence.[1]

Of the tenour of Lord Clarendon's private life and the warmth of affection that bound his wife and children to him, enough has been shown in the letters quoted in these pages ; but independent evidence is not wanting from other sources, and space may be found for a few sentences written by a lady who was intimate with the family and well qualified by her own social qualities to be esteemed a capable judge :

In brilliancy and playfulness of wit he surpassed all his contemporaries ; but it was without effort, and there was no self-consciousness. Deeply read, serious when seriousness was in place, he was withal skilled in the profound art of nonsense. Neither did he reserve his bright sallies or his more serious views for the learned and superior, or for such men as Sir George Cornewall Lewis, his brother-in-law, or his brother Charles

---

[1] Justitia et caritas unicum et certissimum verae fidei Catholicae signum est, et veri Spiritus Sancti fructus ; et ubicunque haec reperiuntur, ibi Christus reverâ est ; et ubicunque haec desunt, deest Christus : solo namque Christi Spiritu duci possumus in amorem justitiae et caritatis.

Villiers, although they met him on more equal grounds than the majority of his companions. Lord Clarendon, in fact, did not demand to be tried by his social peers, for in the society of the women who surrounded him—his own wife, his own daughters and nieces—he shone as brightly and took as great a delight in captivating his listeners as he could possibly have done had his audience been one of the largest and most distinguished, as it certainly was one of the most loving, in the world.

A word of explanation seems fitting here. The reader of the foregoing pages may have received the impression that Lord Clarendon wrote more frequently and fully to correspondents—men and women—than he did to his wife. Nothing could be further from the truth. It is the case, indeed, that the present writer has quoted freely from Clarendon's letters to others and made very few extracts from those to Lady Clarendon. This was not from want of material ; there remain boxes full of letters which she received from him, carefully stored and ranged in orderly bundles through all the thirty-one years of their married life. No doubt these contain much information upon passing events, for hardly a day passed in Lord Clarendon's frequent absence on duty that he did not send the chronicle thereof to his wife. But it is equally certain that they contain much more—the sacred annals of the home—hopes and anxieties for children—unreserved confidence of husband to wife ; with such neither author nor public has any concern. These letters, therefore, remain undisturbed by me ; use has been made only of a few which lay scattered among general correspondence.

Such was the man, of a type not unfamiliar, indeed, yet none too common, among British legislators—a single-minded, experienced servant of the State—whose place was suddenly made void by the stroke of fate. One might incline to murmur at the decree which denied that such a useful life should exceed the prescribed span of threescore and ten years. Lord Clarendon had just fulfilled that measure ; yet who shall declare that Clotho dealt more harshly with him than she did with his brother Charles, whose thread she left unsnapped for many later years, during which he perambulated, feebly and ever more feebly, that House wherein he had won his renown before five-sixths of the members around him had left school, registering dumb and docile votes, and creeping home to a solitary fireside to chew the cud of far-off memories ?

Say rather of Clarendon *felix opportunitate mortis*. What man of spirit—of affairs—would not choose to obey a short summons while yet in the full exercise of his faculties ? rather than tarry while

> The wine of life keeps oozing drop by drop,
> The leaves of life keep falling one by one.

THE END

INDEX

373

Printed by T. and A. CONSTABLE, Printers to His Majesty
at the Edinburgh University Press